D1428631

Mr. and Mrs. Larz Anderson aboard the SS *Laconia,* 1927.

LARZ AND ISABEL ANDERSON

Wealth and Celebrity
in the Gilded Age

STEPHEN T. MOSKEY

Architectural Drawings by
Harry I. Martin III
American Institute of Architects

Larz and Isabel Anderson:
Wealth and Celebrity in the Gilded Age

iUniverse books may be ordered through booksellers or by contacting:
iUniverse
1663 Liberty Drive
Bloomington, IN 47403
www.iuniverse.com
1-800-Authors (1-800-288-4677)

Because of the dynamic nature of the Internet, any web addresses or links contained in this book may have changed since publication and may no longer be valid. The views expressed in this work are solely those of the author and do not necessarily reflect the views of the publisher, and the publisher hereby disclaims any responsibility for them.

Cover Illustration:
The Winter Garden of Anderson House
Bruce M. White
Used by kind permission of Mr. White.
Copyright © by Bruce M. White. All rights reserved.

ISBN: 978-1-4917-8874-5 (sc)
ISBN: 978-1-4917-8875-2 (hc)
ISBN: 978-1-4917-8873-8 (e)

Library of Congress Control Number: 2016903623

Print information available on the last page.

iUniverse rev. date: 06/23/2016

Contents

Illustrations

Frontispiece. Mr. and Mrs. Larz Anderson aboard the SS *Laconia*, April 11, 1927. (Montauk Photo Concern, author's collection.)

Figure 1. Nicholas Longworth Anderson house, Washington, DC, November 1883. (Photograph by Marian Hooper Adams. Collection of the Massachusetts Historical Society, Boston.) xvi

Figure 2. Larz Anderson, May 26, 1911. (Bain Photo, author's collection.) 16

Figure 3. Mrs. Larz Anderson at the National Capital Horse Show, Washington, DC, 1920. (National Photo Company, author's collection.) 32

Figure 4. Larz and Isabel on their honeymoon, August 1897. (Photo by J. & J. Williams, Hawaii. Howard Gotlieb Center for Archival Research, Boston University.) 42

Figure 5. Aiglon aerial photograph of the Anderson estate, Brookline, ca. 1925. (Courtesy of Historic New England, General Photographic Collection, Boston.) 60

Figure 6. Charles A. Platt's watercolor of the Anderson Italian Garden, Brookline, 1905. (Frances Benjamin Johnston Collection, Library of Congress, LC-J717-X103-13.) 65

Figure 7. The garden system of Weld. (Drawing by Harry I. Martin III, author's collection.) 71

Figure 8. What Weld might have looked like if Larz had gotten his way: Charles A. Platt's painting *In the Gardens, Villa d'Este*, 1893. (Author's collection.) 72

Figure 9. Ground floor of Weld. (Drawing by Harry I. Martin III, author's collection.) 75

Figure 10. Second floor of Weld. (Drawing by Harry I. Martin III, author's collection.) 75

A Note on the Architectural Drawings

The floor plans presented in chapters 5 and 7 were newly created from copies of the blueprints for Anderson House and Weld by Harry I. Martin III, AIA, using AutoCAD. Sources: Anderson House, Archives of the Society of the Cincinnati, Washington, DC; Weld, Frederick Law Olmsted National Historic Site, Brookline, MA.

Larz Anderson Vignettes

Five of Larz Anderson's pen-and-ink vignettes, which Larz originally published around 1920 in a privately printed booklet, *Larz Anderson USA*, are reproduced on pages 79, 125, 151, 189, and 209. These charming sketches depict some of the people, places, and events described in this book and exemplify Larz's artistic talents. (Author's collection.)

Preface

Tracing the Andersons: A Personal Journey

I likely first saw Anderson House, the 1905 Beaux-Arts mansion in Washington's Dupont Circle neighborhood that was once the winter home of Larz and Isabel Anderson, in the late 1960s. As an adventuresome undergraduate at Georgetown University who felt constrained by the stone walls of the hilltop campus, I made a habit of escaping into the city to look at buildings and landscapes.

In early 2010, recently laid off from a job in nonprofit management, I began again to take urban walks and rediscover buildings I'd enjoyed seeing more than forty years earlier. For the first time I took the tour of Anderson House, headquarters of the Society of the Cincinnati, located only four blocks from my own home on Massachusetts Avenue. A chance encounter with the society's library director and a question to her about how the Andersons entertained their guests led to an invitation to visit the organization's library to read Larz Anderson's typescript journals.

I quickly became immersed in the details of the Andersons' life, and by midsummer the society's staff had invited me to give a lecture on my research. I presented "The Foodways of Larz and Isabel Anderson" at Anderson House in August 2010. Within a few months, and largely with the encouragement of Washington historian James M. Goode, who had attended the lecture, I began the process of planning a book-length study of the life and times of Larz and Isabel Anderson.

As an amateur historian with no formal training in history other than a few college courses in American and European history supplemented by a lifelong program of reading biographies, I naively assumed research for the book would take about a year and the book itself would be written within another. I was not sure there was even enough of a historical record to write more than a slim volume or perhaps just a series of articles. Early on, one longtime resident of the capital asked me, "Given Larz and Isabel's social prominence and the importance of Anderson House in Washington history, don't you think someone would have written a book by now if there was enough material?" The question did not deter me. I guessed (correctly, as it turned out!) that people who lived as large and as long as the Andersons did—people who left behind buildings and land that still bear their name, people who knew presidents, politicians, royalty, and thousands of other people—must have left behind a very large footprint. What I found was not a footprint but more like a mudflat filled with thousands of tracks frozen in time and hidden in plain sight.

My primary goal in writing this book has been to make readers feel as though they know Larz and Isabel personally. I want Larz and Isabel to come alive for modern readers. My other goal has been to help readers understand how Gilded Age society actually functioned. It was an interconnected and relatively small elite global village where everyone knew everyone. Wherever they went in the world, Larz and Isabel knew someone who lived there—or at least they knew someone who knew someone who lived there and brought with them letters of introduction that opened doors and got them invited to dinner and tea. Readers will recognize the names of the people who lived in this "village"—Henry and Clover Adams, Louisa May Alcott, Alice Pike Barney, Alva Vanderbilt Belmont, Elizabeth Sherman Cameron, Katharine Cornell, Maud Howe Elliott, John Hay, Henry James, Isabella Stewart Gardner, Robert Todd Lincoln, Frederick Law Olmsted, General John Pershing, Theodore Roosevelt, Elihu Root, John Singer Sargent, William Howard Taft, George Washington Vanderbilt, Charles Frederick Worth, and many more.

As the book was nearing completion, I came to see that there was another outcome that I had not anticipated: this biography returns Isabel Anderson to her rightful place among great American women of the twentieth century. She was a centennial baby, born in 1876 and raised by parents who had solidly nineteenth-century views of what it meant to be a young, elite American woman: namely, a private education, a chaperoned grand tour of Europe, a high-profile wedding to a man of means, and then a life as a wife who facilitated her husband's career and social standing through her role as the couple's society hostess. Isabel did all those things, but unlike her husband, she had no interest in remaining locked into the expectations, pomp, and protocols the nineteenth century imposed on women like her. Isabel was from her earliest years an independent spirit who saw the possibility of a new and exciting place in American society for women at the dawn of the twentieth century. On social issues, she was ahead of her time, as readers will discover here.

The acknowledgments at the end of this volume thank the many people who have been of enormous assistance over the past several years, but those from four organizations go to the top of the list: the Society of the Cincinnati for magnificent assistance in so many ways; the Town of Brookline for opening its records and files on the Anderson estate, now Larz Anderson Park, and giving me extraordinary access to the park itself; the American Library in Paris, which hosted me for a month as a visiting researcher while I started the first draft of this book, studied Larz's French connection, and explored the parts of Paris he knew and loved; and finally, the Larz Anderson Auto Museum for generously sharing its wonderful collection of Anderson materials. I am most of all indebted to Isabel Anderson's relatives who welcomed me into their homes, shared family stories about Larz and Isabel, and allowed me to experience firsthand some of the places described in this book.

I hope you will enjoy reading this story of an extraordinary Gilded Age couple and learning about a fascinating period of American history. I encourage you to visit Anderson House in Washington, DC; the Larz Anderson Park and Larz Anderson Auto Museum in Brookline; and the many other places Larz and Isabel enjoyed that you are going to read about here.

Stephen T. Moskey
Washington, DC
September 4, 2015

Prologue
From a Patient's Nursing Notes
(October 12–November 3, 1948)[1]

When the end came on November 3, the patient had been in room 716 of the Phillips House wing of the Massachusetts General Hospital for three weeks and a day. She had been admitted to Phillips in the early afternoon of October 12, 1948, after tripping on a rug in her bedroom that morning. Unable to lift herself up off the floor, she had her servants call for a doctor. He used a portable x-ray machine to diagnose a fractured right hip and had her transported to Phillips House. The admitting diagnosis was "Fracture right femoral neck; Arteriosclerosis; Hypertensive vascular disease."

Though she had always been in good health, she was considered a poor risk for anesthesia. Nonetheless, surgeons went ahead with the procedure and wired her fractured hip to try to keep it together and let it heal. She did not rally from the surgery. Indeed, she was in great discomfort in her private room, attended by her own nurse. She was tired yet slept only intermittently. She had difficulty swallowing, and her speech was sometimes slurred, sometimes distinct.

On October 17, she ominously exclaimed to her nurse, "I am turning black!" The nurse observed no dementia or disorientation. The patient was a playwright and poet who understood the power of metaphor: black—the color of death.

A week later the patient asked her nurse, "Why don't I die?" And then she said emphatically, "I want to go home." She did not mean the home she had shared with her husband for forty years. She understood her medical condition. After all, she had been a nurse in war zones and epidemics and had seen enough sickness, suffering, and death to know she was next.

As the end approached, she started sleeping soundly and quietly and for longer periods of time. The more her physical condition deteriorated, the better she slept. Of death she had once written, "It is, after all, the spirit going home to the region whence it came, after a hard day's work, to be at peace and with friends."

The dying patient knew she would soon see her beloved husband and best friend in life, Larz Kilgour Anderson.

Figure 1. Nicholas Longworth Anderson house, Washington, DC, 1883.

I

LARZ KILGOUR ANDERSON

By the time of Larz Anderson's birth in 1866, eight generations of Andersons had lived and prospered in the New World. The first generation arrived in Jamestown from England in the seventeenth century. The generations leading up to Larz's birth were native-born Virginians, Kentuckians, and Ohioans.

Eighteen-year-old Thomas Anderson (b. 1616) was the first of Larz's ancestors to arrive in Jamestown, on January 2, 1634, aboard the merchant ship *Bonaventure*. Thomas's father, Richard (b. 1585), and younger brother Richard Jr. (b. 1618) arrived in Virginia in July the following year, though they sailed on separate ships to reduce the risk that both would be lost at sea. These early Andersons were members of the Church of England, were loyal to the Crown, and came to the Virginia colony seeking opportunity.[1]

The Andersons of Goldmines, Virginia

Richard Jr.'s son Robert Anderson I (1644–1712) belonged to the first generation of Andersons born in the New World. Three generations later, on January 12, 1750, the man who our Larz Anderson called Great-Grandfather Anderson, Richard Clough Anderson (1750–1826), was born on the Goldmines plantation in St. Martin's Parish of Hanover County, Virginia, not far from Richmond. Known to his family as Dick, he witnessed many key events and battles in the American War of Independence.[2] His war adventures and capture by the British inspired generations of Andersons. On December 16, 1773, while in Boston Harbor as the supercargo of a ship from Richmond, Dick witnessed the Boston Tea Party. When he returned to Virginia, he told his friend Patrick Henry about what he had seen at the harbor. Dick thus gave one of the Founding Fathers a firsthand report of the earliest days of the Revolution in Boston.

In 1776, Dick raised a company for the Continental Army and was commissioned a captain of the Fifth Virginia Regiment, Continental Line. He was wounded when a Hessian soldier shot him in the hip at the second battle of Trenton on January 2, 1777. After five months in a Philadelphia hospital,

Dick returned to the fighting and saw battle at Brandywine, Germantown, and Monmouth. He was promoted to the rank of major in the Sixth Virginia Regiment in 1778. He passed through Valley Forge on his way south to serve under Casimir Pulaski at Savannah and was with the Polish nobleman when he died. Within a short time, Dick was taken prisoner in Charleston.[3]

Dick's release from captivity came during an exchange of prisoners. Eventually detailed to the Marquis de Lafayette, Dick served as the Frenchman's aide-de-camp in the Virginia campaign against Cornwallis and was subsequently promoted to lieutenant colonel of the Third Virginia Regiment. In 1783, at war's end, Richard Clough Anderson became an original member of the Society of the Cincinnati, a moment in family history in which Larz took great pride and enshrined in a mural at Anderson House in Washington.

A group of former officers appointed Dick surveyor of the Virginia Military Land District in Kentucky County (then a part of Virginia). He was to oversee the allotment of land given to Continental Army officers in lieu of payment for their service during the war. Dick himself received a choice piece of land near the Falls of Ohio (now the Hurstbourne area of Louisville), where he built a house he called Soldier's Retreat. Over the next four decades, he worked in a small office at the intersection of what is now Third and Main Streets in Louisville issuing land grants, resolving ownership disputes, and setting property boundaries.

In 1787, Dick married Elizabeth Clark (1763-1795), sister of William Clark of the Lewis and Clark expedition. Dick taught both Meriwether Lewis and William Clark the art of surveying and gave them his theodolite, a surveying instrument used to measure angles, for their expedition across the Louisiana Purchase to the Pacific Northwest.[4] In 1797, after Elizabeth had died, Dick married Sarah Marshall (1779-1854), a cousin of John Marshall, the famous US Supreme Court chief justice. From their earliest years in America, the Andersons married many times into families bearing important names in the history of the American Republic.

Sarah gave birth to their first child at Soldier's Retreat. They named him Larz Anderson (1803–1878; hereafter Larz I). This was the first appearance of the name Larz in Anderson family history. It would proliferate and show up in every subsequent generation of Andersons descended from Richard Clough Anderson, even into the twentieth century. In early America, before and after independence, parents gave their children names drawn from biblical stories, historic events, and geography to connect the children with the wider context of world history and geography, as it was then understood. Africa Hamlin (b. 1760), an officer in the Continental Army and an early member of the Society of the Cincinnati, for example, had brothers named Asia, Europe, and America. *Larz* is perhaps a reference to the family's Scandinavian origins hundreds of years earlier. The Andersons arrived in Scotland with Danish or Norse invaders as early as 1350.[5] Naming an Anderson boy *Larz* connected the family not to Britain but to its almost-forgotten roots in Scandinavia.

In his early youth, Larz I had private tutoring to prepare him for Harvard, where he enrolled in 1818 at the age of fifteen. He was the first of many Andersons descended from Richard Clough Anderson to study there. He graduated in 1822 and returned to Louisville where, like many men in the nineteenth century who wanted a career in the law, he studied under a practicing lawyer, Henry Pirtle, a prominent Kentucky lawyer and later judge. Larz I became Pirtle's first law partner, a connection that helped him establish a successful career in law and commerce.[6]

Cincinnati and the Anderson-Longworth Connection

In 1828, firmly established in Kentucky, twenty-five-year-old Larz I married Cynthia Ann Pope. Complications during the birth of their only child, Richard Clough Anderson II (1829–1879), led to Cynthia's death a few months later. For the next five years, Larz I raised his son by himself. In 1834, the thirty-year-old widower moved to Cincinnati to marry nineteen-year-old Catherine Longworth (1815–1893). Catherine's father was the prosperous Cincinnati vintner, merchant, and art patron Nicholas Longworth (1783–1863). For some forty years, Longworth produced a popular sparkling wine made from a hearty, indigenous grape, the American Catawba. He became a wealthy man worth millions.[7] Longworth's patronage supported the work of ten artists, including his most famous protégé, the sculptor Hiram Powers. Larz and Isabel owned a marble bust of Larz's great-grandfather Nicholas Longworth by Powers.[8]

The Longworth family grew in size and wealth over subsequent generations, and its members contributed substantially to the growth of Cincinnati. The family plot in Cincinnati's Spring Grove Cemetery is one of the largest there. Longworth's descendants also left their mark on American history. His great-grandson Nicholas Longworth (1869–1931) became Speaker of the House in the early twentieth century, and the Longworth House Office Building in Washington is named in his honor. His great-granddaughter Countess Clara Longworth de Chambrun was a leader of the expatriate American community in Paris. She helped found the American Library in Paris in 1920, and in 1941, eighteen months after the city fell to Nazi occupation, she became the library's director.

After his marriage to Catherine, Larz I steadily built his law practice in Cincinnati. With the landholdings of the Andersons and the business connections of the Longworths backing him up, he became a prosperous member of Cincinnati society. He was a philanthropist who gave generously to public charities and the arts. His large Greek Revival mansion adjacent to the elegant neoclassical mansion of his father-in-law exuded success and power. (The former Longworth mansion is now the Taft Museum of Art.) In the 1860s he became a director of the Little Miami Railroad, which had among its investors the Kilgour family. The Kilgours prospered by investing heavily in transportation and housing. As his grandson would do a generation later, Larz I participated actively in Republican politics, though in 1860 he declined an invitation to run for Congress, citing ill health.[9] He was much revered by the citizens of Cincinnati for all his good works. His alma mater also recognized his accomplishments and in 1858 awarded him an AM (master of arts) degree.

Larz I and Catherine's son Nicholas Longworth Anderson, our Larz Anderson's father, was born in Cincinnati on April 22, 1838. Like his father, Nick—as he was known all his life—prepared for admission to Harvard College with a private tutor, Harvard alumnus Eben Smith Brooks (1807–1865).[10] In July 1854, at the age of sixteen, Nick traveled to Cambridge to take an oral exam for admission to his father's and his tutor's alma mater. Mr. Brooks prepared Nick well. He successfully passed six entrance exams in Latin and Greek, three in mathematics, and one each in ancient history and ancient geography. When Nick matriculated at Harvard in the fall of 1854, he resolved to apply himself. "I will steadily and manfully bear up," he wrote that September, "spurning the pleasures aside which seek to lure me from the right path."[11] Thirty years later he went head-to-head with his son over exactly those principles.

Nick eagerly explored the intellectual life of Cambridge and Boston. There was no instruction in English or literature when Nick was at Harvard, but he occasionally attended public lectures by the poet James Russell Lowell, who was then in his thirties. The distinguished poet was young enough to be a fun older friend to Harvard underclassmen, and Nick went to parties at his home. Nick's classmates represented Boston's greatest families—Adams, Bradlee, Cabot, Crowninshield, Gardner, Hunnewell, and Sprague. A generation later, the sons of these men would be Harvard classmates and chums as their fathers had been.

When Nick graduated from Harvard in 1858, he traveled first to the Northwest Territory, perhaps inspired by the subject of his commencement oration, "French Missionaries in the West," or perhaps to see the land explored by his ancestor William Clark.[12] He returned to the East Coast by late summer in time to sail for Europe with his classmates Henry Adams, Louis Cabot, Benjamin W. Crowninshield, and Hollis Hunnewell. He stayed in Germany as a student for two years—first a year in Berlin and then a year in Heidelberg, where he studied German.[13]

After returning to Cincinnati in November 1860, Nick began law studies in the firm of James T. Worthington and Thomas Stanley Matthews. While he was still at Harvard, his father, Larz I, advised him to pursue a career in the law. "Father says I should study law whether I practice it or not," he wrote in his college diary in 1857. "Every man should know how to attend to his own private business, and for this end Law is indispensable."[14] Many years later Nick tried unsuccessfully to get his own son to follow this advice.

The Guthrie Greys

The specter of conflict between North and South interrupted Nick's studies. His great-uncle Major Robert Anderson commanded federal troops at Charleston, South Carolina. The Anderson family well knew a civil war loomed ahead. At the end of December 1860, Nick joined Cincinnati's best pro-Union militia, the Guthrie Greys, named after Captain Presley N. Guthrie and the gray uniforms that state militia wore before the Civil War. When war broke out on April 12, 1861, the Greys answered President Lincoln's call for seventy-five thousand volunteers, and the unit mobilized for three months. That October, when the unit remobilized for three years, Larz I outfitted the entire Guthrie Greys with new uniforms of Union blue.

Nick gave what his daughter-in-law Isabel would many years later call "strenuous service" to the Union cause. Wounded three times, he saw "hard fighting" at Cheat's Mountain, Elkwater, Huttonsville, Stone River, and Chickamauga. When the Greys became the Sixth Ohio Volunteers, he was commissioned a colonel. He was twice brevetted on the battlefield, first as brigadier general and then as major general of volunteers. All this happened before his twenty-eighth birthday.[15]

Toward the end of his military service, in early 1864, Nick began corresponding with Elizabeth Coles Kilgour (1843–1917), the daughter of one of Cincinnati's leading men, Scotland-born John Glenny Kilgour (1796–1858). Kilgour's sons, John (1834–1914) and Charles (1833–1906), were among the movers and shakers of late nineteenth-century Cincinnati. Nick's father, Larz I, had been in many successful business ventures with the Kilgours. With no parents to oversee her choice of husband, Elizabeth's brothers stepped in to fill that void. Nick, a handsome cavalry officer from an old and prosperous Cincinnati family that had partnered with the Kilgours in business deals, was an obvious choice.

Though there are no records of Elizabeth's early life, she grew up in affluent circumstances and had an education suitable for a young woman of her class who was destined to marry well. She had elegant, highly stylized penmanship that to the modern eye is almost impossible to decipher. Elizabeth was well read in English and American literature and, like most American elites, spoke French.

Nick and Elizabeth corresponded for close to a year until he mustered out of service along with the rest of his regiment on June 24, 1864. Nick proposed to Elizabeth in early 1865, about a year after their courtship began. In February, Nick went to Boston to visit some of his Harvard classmates, including John "Jack" Lowell Gardner (1837–1898), who introduced Nick to his new wife, Isabella Stewart Gardner (1840–1924). A month later, the Gardners traveled to Cincinnati to attend Nick and Elizabeth's wedding in St. Paul Episcopal Cathedral on March 28.[16]

In late spring, the newlyweds went to Washington, where on May 4 Nick applied for a passport for travel to Europe. A week later, on May 10, President Andrew Johnson called for a Grand Review of the Armies in Washington on May 23 and 24. Johnson wanted to honor the Union troops and uplift the nation's mournful mood following Lincoln's assassination on April 15. Almost certainly, Nick stayed in Washington to participate in this patriotic exercise of such great importance to the postwar nation.

The newlyweds sailed for Europe that summer, but there are few details of their itinerary. They certainly visited Italy and France and likely England, Germany, and Switzerland. Nick knew Germany well from his student days and also had a special fondness for Lucerne. This was his bride's first trip outside the United States, and Nick wanted to show her the world.

In the spring of 1866, instead of returning to the United States after their year abroad, they rented an apartment at 68 (now 38), rue Marbeuf in Paris, just off the Champs-Elysées, in one of the chic new neighborhoods built by Baron George Haussmann.[17] Elizabeth was five months pregnant. Rather than risk a treacherous journey across the Atlantic, they settled in Paris—then as now a city with excellent medical services.

Elizabeth gave birth to Larz Kilgour Anderson in their apartment on August 15, 1866. A month later, Nick went to make a consular report of his son's birth. Nick was no stranger to the staff of the American legation in Paris, and the newlyweds' sojourn in Paris and the birth of their son attracted more than passing attention from two of the legation's most prominent members. When Nick registered his son's birth at the legation on September 20, 1866, John G. Nicolay, a man who had been one of President Abraham Lincoln's most trusted confidants, made it official that Larz Kilgour Anderson, born in the Empire of France, was a US citizen.[18]

In mid-March 1865, a week after his second inauguration, President Lincoln appointed his two private secretaries from the war years, John Nicolay and John Hay, to diplomatic posts in Paris—Nicolay as US consul and Hay as legation secretary. Nicolay left almost immediately for Paris, while Hay stayed behind in Washington to assist the president in transitioning his administration to the nation's new, postwar realities. On the night of Lincoln's assassination, Hay and the president's son, Robert Todd Lincoln (1843–1926), were at the White House. They were together called to the president's bedside and were present when he died the next morning.[19] Nick was a close friend of Robert Lincoln, one of his Harvard classmates, and their ensuing lifelong friendship eventually played a role in the fortunes of Nick's boy.

In early fall, Larz was baptized in the American Protestant Episcopal Church of the Holy Trinity in Paris, then located on rue Bayard, that is now the American Cathedral in Paris, on avenue George-V. The Reverend William O. Lamson, a native of New York City who had been in Paris since 1858, performed the ceremony.[20] Larz Anderson I sponsored his namesake at the baptismal ceremony and was thus both grandfather and godfather to the boy. Although her name does not appear in the cathedral's record of the baptism, Nick and Elizabeth asked Mrs. Ellen Frances Howard Evans to be Larz's godmother.[21]

Mrs. Evans was one of the city's most prominent expatriate American women of her day. She and her husband, Dr. Theodore Sewall Evans, a dentist, had lived in Paris since the early 1860s. Theodore's brother, Dr. Thomas Wiltberger Evans, was the renowned dentist to Emperor Napoleon III and his wife, Empress Eugénie, during their reign from 1852 to 1870.[22] Mrs. Evans, who outlived her husband and brother-in-law, remained a fixture of the Anglo-American community in Paris until her death in 1914.

When Larz was three months old and safely baptized, the young family left France. They sailed from Le Havre to Southampton and then on to New York aboard the Cunard Line's RMS *Persia*, a paddle wheel steamship famous for crossing the Atlantic in under ten days. A French nurse, Josephine Gobat, accompanied them. By the time Nick and Elizabeth returned to the United States, they had been abroad for eighteen months and were no longer honeymooners. Nick was now a family man. Finding a job and making a home were his priorities.

A Childhood at Home and Abroad

The Civil War had interrupted Nick's law studies, so he was insufficiently prepared for admittance to the bar, but there was no time to return to his law studies now. He had a family to support. Shortly after their return to

Cincinnati from France, Nick went to work as a manager in the central office of the Little Miami Railroad, which operated routes linking the Ohio cities of Cincinnati, Columbus, Dayton, and Springfield to Richmond, Indiana.[23] Larz I and his brother-in-law, Charles Kilgour, served on the railroad's board of directors in the early 1860s, and either was an obvious broker for Nick's job.

Nick and Elizabeth settled into a home in the center of Cincinnati, at 120 East Fourth Street, a plain townhouse built in the 1840s.[24] Life was comfortable for them, especially with the help of four live-in Irish servants. Nick traveled for work and was away for days or weeks at a time. He wrote often to his bride and was never shy to express his love. "I did not nearly tell you yesterday in my letter from Louisville how much I loved you, nor do I deem it possible so to do," he wrote in April 1867. "I am often astonished myself at the depth and strength of my affection."[25]

Soon the family grew. In January 1868, Elizabeth gave birth to their second child, Carl Kilgour Anderson. Carl did not survive early infancy. In August that year, while on seaside vacation at Long Branch, New Jersey, eight-month-old Carl died of what his burial record called "convulsions"—likely infantile febrile seizures. The popular treatment of the day was to wrap a convulsive child in blankets and let him or her sweat it out, a cure that probably killed the toddler. Heartbroken, the Andersons traveled back to Cincinnati, where they buried Carl three days later in a grave near the Longworth family plot. The couple waited five years before having another child.

Despite what were likely modest earnings from the railroad job, the Anderson family lived well. The 1870 census recorded Nick and Elizabeth's net worth at $250,000, split equally between real estate and personal property. Their neighbors on either side, the wealthy pork merchants William Davis and Gardner Phipps, were each worth double that. Nick's parents were still alive, and he had not yet received an inheritance from them, so the marital assets had come primarily from Elizabeth's inheritance.

Nick and Elizabeth quickly joined the city's elite social and cultural scene. In 1874, Nick served on the Special Committee on Life-Saving Apparatus commissioned to demonstrate boat rescue equipment imported from England for exhibition at the Fifth Cincinnati Industrial Exposition.[26] He bid on and won a stall for a costume ball at Pike's Music Hall to raise money for charity.[27] When Christ Church in downtown Cincinnati was refurnished in 1877, Elizabeth purchased the new baptismal font, perhaps with Carl in mind.[28]

In 1872, Nick, Elizabeth, and little Larz traveled to Europe with Nick's Harvard classmate Charles Francis Adams Jr. and his family. They spent enough time in Paris during this year abroad for Larz to be tutored in French and achieve some degree of juvenile proficiency in the language. Larz would, however, acknowledge later in life during a diplomatic posting to Belgium, at a time when French was that country's lingua franca, that his knowledge of the language was limited. An Anderson family scrapbook preserves a note from Larz to his father, written in very good French.[29]

> MON.— CHER.—PAPA
> SUIS.—JE HEUREUX EN CE
> MOMENT DE POUVOIR
> AVEC MA PETITE
> MAIN TE DIRE.COMBIEN
> JE.T'AIME
> LARZ
> 1873
> [My dear Papa. I am happy in this moment to be able to tell you with my little hand how much I love you. Larz 1873]

In addition to learning French, Larz also showed true artistic ability at a young age. Many of his childhood drawings were preserved in a family scrapbook kept by Larz's father during his son's childhood and teen years. (The scrapbook is now in the collection of the Society of the Cincinnati.) Larz's parents encouraged this talent. A dog-eared copy of *Warne's Picture Book* published in 1866 was saved along with other Anderson papers after Isabel's death in 1948.[30] Writing on some of its pages resembles known examples of Larz's childhood block letter printing. The styles and subjects of Larz's early drawings are reminiscent of those in Warne's volume, suggesting it may have helped shape his artistic abilities.

In the spring of 1877, the Andersons returned to Europe for another sojourn of more than a year with Larz and his three-year-old sister, Elizabeth Kilgour Anderson (1874–1921), who was known all her life as "Elsie." They spent the summer of 1877 in England and Scotland and then crossed over to the continent in the fall and stopped in Cabourg on the Lower Normandy coast on their way to Paris for the winter. Larz's charming diary recorded a typical day at the beach:

> Friday Aug 17 '77. Good morning. Sit on beach. Come home take Elsie donkey riding[.] Take a donkey cart and go over to Dives. Go to the Hotel of William the Conqueror in which he slept. Crowded. Go around town. Come back and take

breakfast cooked in a cittcen [*sic*] which was built before Columbus discovered America. Take donkey wagon back to Cabourg. Sit on the beach and listen to the music. Go in bathing and learn how to float. Sit around. Good night.[31]

Nick and Elizabeth had no qualms about letting their eleven-year-old drive a donkey cart around town, a mark of both Larz's independence at a young age and his horsemanship.

During their year in Paris, the family lived at 5, rue d'Antin (now avenue Franklin-Roosevelt), a block from the Seine.[32] Larz studied with a private tutor, walked to the little pond in the Tuileries Garden to sail his toy boat, and "returned to the Champs Élysées again and again to view Punch and Judy at their eternal quarrel." On a 1932 trip to Paris, Larz recalled attending Sunday school and going to church services with his godmother, Mrs. Evans, seated with her in her pew in the American Church of the Holy Trinity (now the American Cathedral of the Holy Trinity).[33]

When Larz I became ill in early 1878, Nick left the family behind in Paris and returned to Cincinnati to see his father, but he arrived two days too late. When word of his grandfather's death reached him, Larz wrote immediately to his father:

> Paris, Feb. 28, 1878. My Dear Papa: Yesterday as we came home from a ride out in the Bois and as we came in the house there was a dispatch for us from Uncle Will [William Pope Anderson] saying that dear Grandpa was dead. I was shocked and I could not beleive [*sic*] it true. This morning I got all my lessons mixed up on account of it. And I have been thinking of you and what a disappointment it would be to you to think you were only a few days late. But there is one thing you can comfort yourself: that is the thought that Grandpa has gone to heaven. Give my love to dear Grandma.[34]

Nick returned to Europe after the funeral, and the family remained in Paris until the autumn of 1878. They toured the Loire Valley before returning to Cincinnati late that year. Nick went back to work in the family law office, which he had joined several years earlier, where he managed Anderson and Longworth assets and property. In 1878, now beneficiaries of their father's trust fund, Nick and his brother Larz II (1845–1902) moved their families to upscale East Walnut Hills, overlooking the city. Nick and Elizabeth lived in a house called Kilgour Place on Madison Pike that they bought or rented from one of Elizabeth's brothers. They stayed there until they moved to Washington three years later.

A European in America

Later in life, Larz enjoyed giving the impression, or perhaps truly believed, that he spent most of his youth in France. The record shows, however, that he did not spend much more than a total of three years there during his early childhood years—one of those years as a toddler. In 1931 he noted in his journal, "When my family had returned from Europe, I had been for years off and on in the hands of tutors." Larz said that his father wanted him to have "experience at some real American school" in order to prepare him for "Harvard College education and life."[35] Larz later amended this entry to read "returned from Europe *in 1882*" [emphasis added]. The well-documented timeline of Nick and Elizabeth's life between their marriage in 1865 and their move to Washington in 1881 makes an 1882 repatriation date impossible to reconcile with the facts documented in passenger lists, census records, and Anderson family papers. It is at best Larz's faulty recollection or, worse, manipulating his chronology to give himself a more prominent French pedigree.

Larz thought of himself as European born and bred, his American citizenship almost an accident of history. He was pleased when his Exeter classmates selected him their class marshal for the school's sesquicentennial celebration in 1931. "I was rather a foreigner still in my bringing up, and I valued the fact that I had gained such recognition among these purely American classmates," he said.[36]

Early Life in Washington

In 1880, the *Washington Post* celebrated "Washington's growing pre-eminence as a social center."[37] Washington had become a place for Civil War officers to retire or seek a second career in the expanding federal bureaucracy, especially during the time their former general Ulysses S. Grant was in the White House (1869–1877). When Nick's friend James A. Garfield became president in 1880, he decided to move his family to Washington. The capital offered far more in the way of opportunity for Larz's career and Elsie's marriage prospects than Cincinnati. Most importantly, Nick had a friend in the White House.

Nick could afford to move to Washington and to give his children the life and education that would assure their place in the national social scene. Though only forty-two when they moved, he never worked again. An 1883 letter from Clover Adams (1843–1885), wife of Nick's Harvard classmate and lifelong friend the American historian Henry Adams, suggests that Nick and Elizabeth's annual income was $30,000.[38] Given that interest rates for various types of financial instruments in 1880 ranged from about 3 percent to 6 percent, Nick and Elizabeth's income must have come from combined trust fund principals of between $5 million and $10 million.[39]

The *Washington Evening Star* reported in October 1881 that a group of "wealthy parties from Cincinnati," including Nicholas Anderson, acquired land at the intersection of Sixteenth and K Streets with the intention of "improving" it. Previously, the area had been home to a coal depot and a lumberyard.[40] Sometime that same year, Nick moved the family to Washington, DC, where they settled into a rented house at 8 Lafayette Square (now 712 Jackson Square). Fifteen years earlier, Major Henry Rathbone lived in the house. Rathbone was with President Lincoln at Ford's Theatre on the night of the assassination and was wounded trying to protect the president. Living in Rathbone's house surely gave young Larz a sense of connection to a tragic moment in US history.

Construction of the Nicholas Longworth Anderson house, designed by Nick's friend Henry Hobson Richardson (1838–1886), began in 1881. The house immediately attracted attention as one of the city's new generation of mansions. The *Washington Evening Star* called the house "spacious and elegant," suggesting that reporters examined building permits and plans filed with the district government even before construction started to satisfy their readers' appetite for real estate news.[41] Early sketches for the house show stables on the property, although these were never built. To remedy this inconvenience, Nick purchased a stable lot adjacent to the house shortly after they moved in.[42]

The house had impeccable artistic credentials. Richardson applied his signature Richardsonian Romanesque style as the unifying design concept. One of Henry Adams's friends, the artist John La Farge (1835–1910), designed stained glass windows for the dining room. (The La Farge windows disappeared when the house was demolished in 1925 and have never been found.) Frederick Law Olmsted (1822–1903) oversaw plans for the lawns, plantings, sidewalks, and curbs.[43] Clover Adams photographed its exterior on November 3, 1883, only days after Nick, Elizabeth, Larz, and Elsie took occupancy of it.[44] (See figure 1.) A few days later, Clover described it in a letter to her father: "The Anderson house is a subject of much discussion and very opposite opinions are held about it; it is emphatically a gentleman's house and the lines are very fine; it is very stern and severe as a whole, but H.H. Richardson is satisfied and says windows and grading will give it all it now lacks."[45]

The house indeed became famous, and many of Washington's elites called on the Andersons to see it. Phoebe Apperson Hearst, one of the great doyennes of Washington's Gilded Age, and her son, William Randolph Hearst (later thinly disguised as the title character in Orson Welles's 1941 *film à clef Citizen Kane*), visited in November 1885.[46] In June 1886, the English poet Matthew Arnold and his daughter showed up at the door unannounced, asking to see the house.[47]

A First-Class Education

During the family's first year in Washington (1881–1882), they integrated themselves quickly into Washington society. On New Year's Eve 1882, they attended a formal dinner at the Russian embassy.[48] Nick and Elizabeth's close friends Clover and Henry Adams, and Clara and John M. Hay—whom Larz once called his "second-father"—lived on nearby Lafayette Square.[49] The Anderson, Adams, and Hay couples had much in common: their distinctive Washington homes had all been designed by their friend Henry Hobson Richardson.

Nick enrolled Larz in the Emerson Institute, a prep school specialized in preparing boys for Harvard. Isabel Anderson later wrote that Larz's transition to formal schooling "was not easy, after all the interruptions in his schooling, for the boy to settle down at once." Charles B. Young, the headmaster, wrote to Nick at the end of Larz's year at Emerson:

> Your son Larz made wonderful progress with us last year in all his studies, but his development of character was far more significant and satisfactory. When he entered my school, he was boyish, unimpressible [*sic*], and, at times, almost defiant. Careful handling soon brought out his good points, and in short time he was a leader in the school. I regard Larz as a young man of the highest promise. I predict for him no ordinary career.[50]

Despite this glowing assessment, Larz did not take any prizes for academic achievement at Emerson's June 1882 commencement exercises—not even in French![51]

In August 1882, Larz left Washington to enter Phillips Exeter Academy in New Hampshire for two years of preparation before entering Harvard. His father's first letter to him at Exeter, dated August 15, 1882, exhorted him to achieve great things: "You are at work now on your own future, and every sturdy stroke you apply now brings you nearer to the goal. You bear an honored name, both from your father's and your mother's family. Be true, and with the aid of Providence, you will succeed."[52]

Nick's letters to Larz provided a steady stream of academic guidance and moral encouragement. In February 1884, Nick advised Larz on a suitable subject for a poetry assignment, explaining it is "like an after-dinner speech; it should either be very eloquent and admirable in its diction and thoughts, or it should be bright, witty, and sparkling, to fascinate only for the occasion."[53] Elizabeth's letters to her son set the tone for their voluminous, lifelong correspondence with each other. She wrote to Larz with details of parties she attended, clothes she wore, the daily routine of the Anderson household, and gossipy news about life in the city. One of her favorite subjects was "the Daily Leiter," Elizabeth's nickname for her friend Mrs. Levi Leiter, who was famous for uttering memorable malapropisms and well-intentioned but awkward sentiments.[54] After Mrs. Leiter's friend Emily Beale McLean died in 1912, she sent the widower a nosegay of violets on Emily's birthday, accompanied by a note that said, "Emily's first birthday in Heaven."[55]

The quality of instruction Larz received privately and at Emerson prepared him well for boarding school. He earned good grades and ranked high among his peers at Exeter. His freshman curriculum included Latin, Greek, English, math, and science, and he earned a 92 percent academic average in his first term. By spring 1884, his senior year, he had achieved a 95 percent average, placing him in the top tier of his class.[56] Nick was pleased. "You have satisfied us at home both by your conduct and your rank," he wrote.[57] Larz's peers elected him class poet at graduation, and he later remembered that "some of the young ladies present had wept" as he read his poem at the event. He called this "a doubtful compliment."[58]

Larz enrolled in Harvard College in the fall of 1884. The tone of Nick's and Elizabeth's letters to their son changed almost as soon as he got to Harvard. They wrote him many admonishing letters about his behavior and finances. His mother gave her advice with a very soft touch. "The governor," she wrote in 1885, using her nickname for her husband, "and I rather think you overlook the fact that college is the place to study."[59] Nick took a much-sterner tone. Early in his freshman year, Larz decided he would enjoy a visit to New York in October. "You have had a long vacation. Time, money and study would be lost without reason," Nick said of the trip.[60] A few months later, he again reprimanded Larz for traveling during the term, saying, "When your idea of college life is to pass your time on the railway between Washington and Cambridge, I certainly object." He added, "It is vain for you to tell me that *tempora mutantur* [times change]."[61] The subject of expenses came up again and again in Nick's letters. During Larz's senior year, his father exploded, "Your last letter is redolent of dinners. You are evidently and literally eating up your allowance, and by the law of the land, I am bound to give you nourishment."[62]

Nick also had concerns about his son's academic program. He worried that Larz took too many easy courses and advised him not to "take courses which are simply conducive to ease and a probably high rank. Secure as much information and material for future use in life as is possible."[63] Larz called his father's advice "lectures."[64] The subjects of Larz's daily English themes, a requirement of all Harvard undergraduates, lent credence to Nick's complaints about his son's indifference to academics. Larz wrote on many trivial subjects, including "Soda Lemonade," "Writing a Daily Theme" (several times), "Dog," "Chalk," and "Pen Wiper."[65] Despite his lax attitudes about college, the distraction of clubs and parties, and a penchant for overspending his allowance on food, travel, and clothing, Larz graduated cum laude from Harvard in June 1888.

He was ready to take on the world.

Figure 2. Larz Anderson, 1911.

II

A NATIVE SON ABROAD

arz Anderson spent the early-summer months after graduation planning a yearlong round-the-world voyage with Malcolm Thomas, future brother-in-law of one of Larz's closest Harvard chums, Frederick Josiah Bradlee Sr. (1866–1951), grandfather of the *Washington Post*'s Ben Bradlee (1921–2014). In the nineteenth century, young men from affluent, prominent families went on a grand tour of Europe or the world after attending college. In May, before graduation, Nick sent Larz money for the trip, two passport applications, and assurances that his friend Secretary of State Thomas F. Bayard (1828–1898) would circulate a letter to "all consuls and officials of the United States" so Larz and Malcolm would be "both fixed up in case of need."[1]

Larz, Malcolm, and their friend Robert "Bob" Forbes Perkins (no relation to Isabel's family) left Boston by train on July 21, 1888. They stopped in Chicago, where they visited the Armour meatpacking plant and saw sausage being made—"most amusing, a bit of comedy in this tragic place," Larz said.[2] Bob, who came from a railway family, suggested they take one of his father's trains to Burlington, Iowa, and decamp at the Perkinses' country place, Apple Trees. With no one else there, the three decided to "make a bachelor hall of it." They had such a good time they stayed three days instead of one.[3]

As they crossed the prairies, the beauty and size of the country impressed Larz. This first look at the United States west of the Mississippi inspired many letters home. "The limitless, rolling prairie, the dim blue line of a distant mountain range on the horizon, a few scattered herds of cattle, all bathed in the glorious colors of a setting sun; it was beautiful," he wrote.[4] His artistic eye and elegant prose allowed him to paint word pictures in a way that photography, even if he had had a camera, could not.

They reached Southern California at the end of July and from there traveled north toward San Francisco, with overnights along the way, including Los Angeles. Larz thought California "the most thoroughly American region, not withstanding its mixed population" that he had yet seen. Only forty years earlier it had been part of Mexico, and Larz was proud to see the state had embraced the nation's identity: "America for the Americans is the spirit, and the Stars and Stripes wave grandly over all!"[5]

Larz and Malcolm arrived in San Francisco in early August and arranged passage on the *City of Peking*, a freighter with accommodations for eighteen passengers, to Yokohama. Larz found the ship to be "a comparatively satisfactory conveyance but not fast."[6] The crossing took more than two weeks, and the boys found ways to make the time pass pleasantly. They joined a "cocktail brigade" that paraded twice a day to the cabin of the *Peking*'s former captain for drinks before luncheon and dinner. His other major distraction besides cocktails with the boys was another passenger, a young lady who became "more and more charming and beautiful hour by hour." He recalled what a Boston fortune-teller had predicted: "Being alone of her kind she attains the preciousness and value of monopoly. I am beginning to like and admire her very much; the first night out, when it was so rough, I pitied her and pity, they say, is the first step. For the 'seer' I visited one Sunday night last winter in Boston told me I should meet my Fate this season! Is this my Fate?"[7]

On Wednesday, August 15, Larz celebrated his twenty-second birthday on the high seas of the Pacific. He read in his almanac that he had been born on a Wednesday and so wrote home, "I am subject to all the good and evil which the middle day of the week may exert." With this as a touchstone, he reflected on his life up to that point. "I could put down that so far all the influences have tended for a perfect, happy and fortunate life. The Future will be—revealed!"[8]

A First Look at Japan

Japan charmed Larz even before the ship sailed into Yokohama harbor. The crew included Japanese cabin boys who provided valet and waiter service for the passengers. Larz became enamored of their attentiveness: "Indeed I am falling into oriental views and methods most easily; especially the luxurious side. These Japanese cabin boys are treasures; they brush your clothes, change your studs, fold your suits … everything in order all the time. At table they stand back of your chair and are so attentive and ready that they almost feed you; and it is very easy to give up doing anything when you can have it done for you."[9]

Larz's almost-mystical fascination with Japan and its surprises began before he set foot in the country. The first sign they were nearing Japan was a fishing junk that appeared out of the mists below the bow of the *Peking*. Larz noted in his diary that he always thought the junks portrayed in Japanese paintings were pure fantasy. They were the "weirdest, strangest-looking" objects he had ever seen. But there they were, riding the heavy swell of the ocean.[10]

The *Peking* sailed into Yokohama harbor on August 28, a crossing of seventeen days "and some hours"—a record for the captain and his crew. Larz and Malcolm went up to Tokyo, where they stayed for several weeks with John "Jack" Gardner Coolidge in his Japanese-style house in the Kojimachi district of Tokyo, a short distance from the Imperial Palace. Jack, a fellow Harvard alum and nephew of the Boston socialite couple John and Isabella Stewart Gardner, worked in Tokyo as an English teacher.

Larz immersed himself in Japanese culture. Count Karasumaru, a friend of Jack's, took Larz on a tour of the Koraku-en gardens. The count headed one of the so-called Kuge families, nobles who served as high-level bureaucrats in the Imperial Household Office. Larz was struck by what he saw, and the count's knowledgeable commentary helped him understand the principles of Japanese garden design. "There is a certain wildness about Japanese gardens that is most lovely," he wrote. "All that is artificial blends and sympathizes with Nature, and it isn't 'Art versus nature' as in our landscape gardening."[11] On another occasion, accompanied by two Japanese noblemen, Larz and Malcolm attended a tea ceremony. They also "stomached" a Japanese dinner, "raw fish and all," and managed their "chap sticks [*sic*] most creditably," Larz said.[12] He even attempted to communicate in Japanese and carried a bilingual dictionary with him.

One of the most important connections Larz made in Japan was Ernest Fenollosa (1853–1908), an American art historian in Japan who was an expert on Japanese art. Japanese scholars and artists still revere Fenollosa for helping establish both the Tokyo School of Fine Arts and the Tokyo Imperial Museum and for his dedication to the preservation of Japanese art. When Fenollosa invited Larz to dinner with his family, it was "a touch of home which was most pleasant."[13] Larz's conversations with Fenollosa fostered in him a deep understanding of Japanese art, architecture, and culture.

If in the future Larz found Boston to be a congenial city in which to explore and develop his interest in Japanese art and culture, he could in large measure thank Fenollosa. The professor was directly responsible for Boston becoming one the most important centers for the study and collection of Japanese art outside of Japan. Two years earlier, in 1886, Fenollosa sold his large collection of Japanese and Chinese art to Isabel Anderson's first cousin Charles Goddard Weld (1857–1911), a Boston physician and philanthropist and one of Isabel's three co-inheritors of their grandfather's fortune. When Charles died in 1911, his will bequeathed the 838 works he bought from

Fenollosa to the Boston Museum of Fine Arts, thereby fulfilling the promise he made to the art historian to keep the collection in Boston after his death.[14]

In early December 1888, Larz, Malcolm, and Jack, who decided to travel with them as far as India, sailed for China. As they were leaving Japan, Larz praised the country effusively:

> The best natured race in the World without doubt, a result probably of their being so easy going; good natured and jolly, always laughing. The artistic sense is inborn in them all, is a part of their nature, and they cannot do anything inartistic— but Goodbye, Japan, Wonderland of the World, Goodbye! Japan, the Beautiful, the Indescribably, Pleasant Land! Four perfect months have I passed, passed only too swiftly, within thy coasts; every hour has been full of new surprises, of new delights, of new experiences! The Future will be full of pleasant recollections! Goodbye—Japan—goodbye![15]

Thus began a lifelong fascination with all things Japanese, a fascination that would sometimes blind Larz to the political realities of a country and a people who distrusted the West.

China and India

China contrasted sharply with Japan in Larz's mind. He found Shanghai to be "filthy and horrible and repulsive—but interesting and well worth seeing once."[16] They stopped briefly in Hong Kong, which Larz deemed "a beautiful place" that reminded him of Paris.[17] When they reached Java, Larz marveled at the excellent roads and railways in the Dutch colony. He sampled his first mango there, and it delighted him: "Mango, ah, the Mango! Flattish and oblong, with a yellowish pulp inside that smells and tastes like roses, a tinge of taste like turpentine, delicious!"[18] The reports Larz sent home, however, were far less interesting than those from Japan. The boys rushed through this part of the trip, eager to get to India.

From Java they sailed for Calcutta aboard the *Palitana*, a three-thousand-ton British ship with deck cabins for the few dozen first- and second-class passengers who braved the Indian Ocean on such a small vessel. Tarps were strung up to shelter them from the burning sun. Americans and Europeans were not the only passengers. The ship carried some two thousand Asian laborers in steerage who were traveling to British India to find work. By the time Larz and his pals reached India, they were very glad to leave their cramped quarters behind and venture into the vastness of India.

In Calcutta, their first stop, Larz took note of the city's great Anglo-Indian architecture. He wrote about the "very fine great palaces" he saw there—the government buildings of the British Raj.[19] From Calcutta, the three headed north to Darjeeling to view the far-distant Himalayas from a vantage point within India. They then turned south to Benares, one of India's holiest cities, where they hired a houseboat to take them along the riverbanks to view the old city and its many temples. Continuing their gradual progress westward toward Bombay, they arrived in Delhi and from there visited the Taj Mahal and the Tomb of Akbar in Agra.

Unlike other parts of Larz's diary, there are no internal date references in his writings about India. Indeed, he made few personal observations about what he saw. His journal entries seem inspired at some later date by a guidebook, as this passage suggests:

> The tomb of Akbar is at Secundra some few miles out of Agra. A great gate with Saracenic arch in its quadrilateral façade, of red sandstone inlaid with marbles, leads into a vast enclosure, a rich garden, filled with mangos, orange trees and peepuls [bo trees]. From the four gateways, in the four sides, broad stone paved causeways, divided by great tanks and troughs, lead to the broad central platform where stands the mausoleum. This is square, and rises like a pyramid in five terraces, each with its pillared portico and row of cupolas, all of red sandstone but the top one, and that of marble.[20]

The boys were so busy cavorting across the Indian subcontinent that Larz cannot be faulted for letting his journal entries lapse.

At Agra, Larz and Malcolm parted ways temporarily with Jack and headed north to Lahore.[21] The three met up again in Bombay, where they toured the city and its most famous sites. The cave temples of Elephanta and the Parsi Towers of Silence impressed Larz in particular. At Bombay, Jack took leave of them to return to Japan, and Larz and Malcolm left India headed for the Universal Exposition of 1889 in Paris.

"I Love Paris"

As the two young men traveled through the Suez Canal on their way to the Mediterranean, they stopped in Cairo to visit the pyramids. Larz was at first "disappointed in the Pyramids; they looked a great pile of rubbish," but he eagerly explored the passages inside the Great Pyramid and, with the assistance of two bedouins, reached its summit. From that vantage point he "began to appreciate the size and massiveness of this gem of Gizeh [Giza], the tomb of Cheops, one of the Seven Wonders of the World."[22]

From Egypt, Larz and Malcolm sailed to Greece, where they visited the head of the American legation in Athens, John Walker Fearn. The American minister took them on an evening tour of the Acropolis. Fearn was a Yale man who had served in the Confederacy's diplomatic missions to Europe and Russia during the Civil War.[23] One can only imagine how the visit went. Being a Confederate diplomat might have been excusable, but being a Yale man was not! Larz and Malcolm passed through Constantinople, Bucharest, Belgrade ("a sort of substantial village," Larz said), Hungary, and Austria. They moved quickly through Central Europe to get to Paris, where the Universal Exposition had opened on May 4.

The two travelers arrived in Paris on May 18, 1889, and spent much time visiting the exposition and its attractions. Although Larz thought the exposition an "immense success" and enjoyed seeing the Eiffel Tower and the exposition's profusion of electric lighting (one of the reasons Paris is still known as the City of Light), he wanted to leave for quieter parts of Europe. "I love Paris," he said, "but not in exhibition years."[24]

Larz left the city in early June headed for what he called the Northland, the last phase of his travels before going home. He went first to Germany and then to Denmark, Sweden, Norway, and Russia. In Germany, he was more than pleased he was not recognized as an American. He decided it may have been what he called his "military walk or generally intelligent air," that made people think he was German or maybe French.[25] Norway and Sweden, he said, affected him "similarly [to Japan] with a sympathy and liking for the people," making the beginning and end of the journey "especially pleasant."[26] He sailed into the Arctic Ocean on the SS *Olaf Kyrre*, a Norwegian ship, and marveled at seeing the midnight sun, "hanging low on the horizon, a glowing ball, the sun."[27]

From Russia, which he called Land of Nihil (Land without Morals), Larz wrote home about the political and economic conditions of the country, lamenting the oppression of the Russian people and the illiteracy of the masses. He noted the presence of police and spies everywhere and took pity on "the suffering of the millions" who were not members of the privileged classes.[28]

Larz sailed from Bremerhaven aboard the SS *Saale* on August 7, 1889, and arrived in New York in mid-August. He immediately made his way to Pomfret in western Connecticut to join his family for their annual summer vacation at the then-famous Ben Grosvenor Inn, "where the dearest of families" gave him "the most welcome of welcomes." Larz had not missed his homeland during his yearlong absence. He had immersed himself in every detail and absorbed much about the world and its cultures. He now needed time to adjust to being home again: "America, after the long absence, struck me as strange as any country I had visited," he said.[29]

Finding a Station in Life

Larz did not do much after he returned from his trip around the world. He was not particularly eager to find work or a direction in life. Within a few months, Nick forced the issue and found a job for Larz at W. F. Milton and Company in New York, a shipping brokerage firm near the docks on Manhattan's Lower East Side. The firm's owner, William Frederick Milton, was one of Nick's Harvard classmates and had commanded the Twentieth Massachusetts Volunteer Infantry, the so-called Harvard Regiment, during the Civil War.

This attempt at a business career was short-lived. Larz quit the Milton job in the spring of 1890 after only a few months. In September, he enrolled in Harvard Law School, perhaps at the urging of his father and certainly following the example of his undergraduate classmate and best friend, Charles Francis Adams III (1866–1954), who was already a law student there. In the late nineteenth century, Harvard's law school was the premier institution of its type in the United States. Its teaching methods involved students in discussion and development of their own analysis of appellate court cases.[30] Nick was certainly proud that his son was back at Harvard studying law, as his own father had advised him to do. But Nick's pleasure did not last long. After two semesters, Larz dropped out. He never again talked about his time in law school.

Nick stepped in again to help his son make something of his life. By the time the Harvard academic year ended on June 24, 1891, Nick's search for a diplomatic position for Larz was well under way. On June 28, while on vacation at Watch Hill in Rhode Island, Nick wrote to Sevellon Alden Brown, chief clerk of the State Department, to thank him for his role in Larz's appointment as second secretary of the American legation in London. Larz was to serve under Nick's old friend and college classmate Robert Todd Lincoln, US minister to the Court of St. James's. In his letter to Brown, Nick stressed that neither he nor Larz had any hand in the appointment. Although he wanted to be sure the record showed that Larz's appointment was on merit and not political patronage, Nick called the job in London "the gift of the Administration."[31]

On July 21, President Benjamin Harrison named "Larz Anderson, of Ohio, second secretary of legation at the court of St James."[32] Larz had left

Ohio a decade earlier as a child, but by naming someone who once lived in Ohio and had important family connections to the state, the president fulfilled a patronage obligation to his home state.

Second Secretary, American Legation, London (1891–1894)

Larz arrived in England in early August 1891 and checked into the Burlington Hotel on Cork Street, an old hotel that provided simple, primitive accommodations—"no bells nor lights, only lamps and candles," Larz wrote.[33] He was a public servant now, without an allowance from home, and needed to live within his own means. The allowance that had started in his teen years—and continued for three years after graduation when he'd had no income of his own—had ended.

After a simple breakfast of toast and tea, Larz took a cab to the American legation, where he met Henry White (1850–1927), the legation's first secretary. White showed him around and gave him a message from Lincoln asking the new second secretary to dine with the minister and his family that evening. Larz was overwhelmed by the pace of his first day. "I began to feel somewhat lost in the bigness of things and the multitudes of details I should have to attend to," he wrote home.[34]

The new junior diplomat was a busy young man inside and outside of the legation. Larz's duties included what he called "weird interviewing"—dealing with Americans and would-be Americans who came to request passports, meetings with Lincoln, or audiences with the queen.[35] Travelers from the States often arrived in London expecting someone from the legation to meet their train, arrange hotel accommodations, and take them on tours of the city. One day an elderly woman showed up demanding to see President Lincoln. Larz was unable to convince her that the president had been dead for many years. Then, a younger woman who had run away from home in Concord, Massachusetts, in hope of a stage career in London asked for a ticket back to the United States. Lincoln approved the request. A man came in asking to see the "boss" and insisted on getting letters of introduction admitting him to the great houses of London. He left, satisfied, when Larz gave him a visitor's ticket to the Royal Mews—the stables at Buckingham Palace.

If Larz was busy during the four hours between 11:00 a.m. and 3:00 p.m. when the legation's offices were open on weekdays, he was even busier with both official and unofficial duties outside the office. One of his first duties was to escort President Harrison's daughter and daughter-in-law to the London memorial service for James Russell Lowell, American minister to Britain from 1880 to 1885. Lowell, whom Larz's father knew from his own Harvard days, had died the previous week in Cambridge, Massachusetts.

Larz decided to send a personal message through the Harrison ladies back to Washington: "I was anxious ... that President Harrison might learn how much I appreciate his appointing me to London."[36]

Larz was popular in London and attended teas, dinners, and the theater as the guest of English and American elites. White invited Larz to his country home, Ramslade House, near Bracknell about forty miles west of London, where Larz enjoyed an American take on weekend house parties in the English countryside. His first experience of English hospitality came in early January 1892, when he spent a weekend at Hardwick House in Oxfordshire, the estate of Charles Day Rose (1847–1913), an Anglo-Canadian businessman, racehorse breeder, yachtsman, and Liberal Party politician. Larz was not impressed. "The so-called informality of [English] entertainment borders on an indifference, a sort of 'we have asked you down, do as you please' sort of way," he wrote. His experience at Hardwick House inspired him to set out his own philosophy of entertaining:

> My idea of hospitality has always been that a guest should be looked after by someone else than a valet or a maid, a little attention "forced on" them even; this has seemed to me a necessary element in hospitality, in the relation between an host and a guest. I miss it certainly when I don't have it; it adds a charm and an artistic quality—if nothing more, it is courtesy instead of mere civility; that is the distinction. It adds warmth where otherwise it is cold.[37]

London in the 1890s was an international crossroads for the arts, literature, and music. Henry White knew many of the great personalities of the day, and he made sure his second secretary met them. Larz spent part of one evening at White's London townhouse with Oscar Wilde, whom he deemed "not as bad as I had expected, not so fat and greasy as I had been told, and his discoursive [*sic*] manner was quite amusing."[38] White also wanted Larz to meet the American writer Henry James, but Larz was already busy that weekend. James later gave Larz his private box at London's Opera Comique for the celebratory fiftieth performance of his play *The American*.[39] Larz decided he liked the kind of American portrayed in James's play, "for though he makes him twangy and slangy, he makes him independent and sympathetic and high-minded."[40] Larz spent another weekend at the White estate when the American painter John Singer Sargent was there. Sargent painted a much-celebrated portrait of Mrs. White that now is in the Corcoran

Collection of the National Gallery of Art in Washington. Larz dubbed the party a "Bohemian Sabbath."[41]

Despite the brilliance of Larz's social circles, the most remarkable and curious friendship Larz made in London was with the American writer and historian Henry Adams (1838–1918), who was the great-grandson of John Adams, second president of the United States; the grandson of John Quincy Adams, sixth president of the United States; and one of Nick Anderson's best friends.

The Henry Adams Interlude

Larz's first six weeks in London were a whirlwind, and he wrote that he was "feeling a bit weary."[42] In October, White decided Larz needed a break from his duties and ordered him to Paris for two weeks. Larz dutifully arrived in the French capital on October 11, checked into a tourist-class hotel, and went directly from there to visit Elizabeth "Lizzie" Sherman Cameron (1860–1944), the estranged wife of US senator J. Donald Cameron (1833–1918).[43]

Lizzie and her daughter, Martha, lived in a gracious three-story townhouse—6, square du Bois de Boulogne—in a parklike area of Paris that was then an enclave of American expatriate society.[44] The Camerons had a home on Lafayette Park in Washington (now known as the Benjamin Ogle Tayloe House) where their neighbors included Larz's parents, Henry Adams, John Hay, and William Wilson Corcoran. Larz knew many people in Paris, so calling on Lizzie so directly after his arrival on an overnight boat-train connection from London can mean only that he went there with a purpose. In view of subsequent events, it is almost certain he went to see his father's friend Henry Adams, who was Lizzie's closest friend and confidant.

In 1890 and 1891, Henry took a round-the-world trip with the American artist John La Farge. The two men traveled together at Adams's expense and stayed many months on the islands of Samoa, Tahiti, and Fiji, where La Farge executed a celebrated series of paintings.[45] In early October, after a year of traveling, they reached Marseille and went from there directly to Paris. Henry was eager to see Lizzie and knew Larz would be in Paris.

Even though Adams was already in the city, he had not yet been to see Lizzie when Larz arrived in Paris on October 11.[46] Within a day or two, Larz and Henry renewed their acquaintance in her home. The two men knew each other but from a decade earlier when Adams lived in Washington and Larz was a teenager. Larz was flattered that Adams remembered him. "He spoke very kindly of seeing me here, which was one of the things he had heard of," Larz said.[47] Henry White and Henry Adams were great friends and corresponded regularly with each other, so it was likely through White that Adams knew Larz would be in Paris.

Larz visited with Adams several times at Lizzie's home, noting in a letter to his parents that the historian was there "all the time." Adams told Larz about his travels in the South Pacific and said he thought he might not return to the United States. "He came from the Pacific Ocean yesterday and thinks of going back to the Pacific Ocean tomorrow," Larz said.[48] Adams did not return to the Pacific, nor did he stay in Paris. A few weeks after Larz returned to his post, Adams arrived in London, and the two men again spent time together. Larz's duties included entertaining American dignitaries in London, but the fifty-three-year-old Adams was not just anyone to Larz. Henry was one of his father's best friends and had known both his grandfather Larz Anderson I and his great-uncle Major Robert Anderson. The twenty-five-year-old Larz had more than an official obligation to Adams. He also had a profoundly personal duty to be as hospitable and helpful to his family's famous friend as he could be.

Larz wrote home about many of his engagements with Adams. The first report was their dinner together on Thanksgiving night at the Bristol Hotel. Larz reciprocated by inviting Adams to a private Thanksgiving dinner for two the next evening in his rooms on Clarges Street. Larz wrote excitedly to his parents about both dinners: "Mr. Henry Adams is coming to dine with me. Now I am anticipating this with much pleasure—for last evening Mr. Adams and I had a night of it; he was just as anxious to go to it and have a good time as any young man, and infinitely more amusing and interesting—I dined with him well at the Bristol and it was one o'clock before I got home."[49]

The dinner on Clarges Street was not impromptu. Larz went to great lengths to make the dinner as authentically American as possible. He purchased a "little fat Norfolk turkey" that his landlady, Mrs. Mace, roasted, stuffed with chestnuts, and served with cranberry sauce, along with "some other courses."[50] The Thanksgiving plans had obviously been in play for at least a few days, with enough time for Larz to make arrangements for the special meal.

In early December, Henry Adams underwent surgery in London for the removal of a lump from his shoulder. In those days, even a minor operation was a dangerous proposition. There were no antibiotics to prevent septicemia if an infection took hold. (Robert Todd Lincoln's son, Jack, died of infection after a similar surgery.) Larz visited the hospital over the several days Adams recuperated. Henry talked of returning to Paris after his discharge from the hospital and then going to Spain. He indeed returned to Paris, on December 14, 1891, but not on his way to Spain. After spending Christmas and New Year's in Paris, Adams returned to London on January 10, 1892. This time he did not stay at his club. He took a furnished room in the same small house where Larz lived, 38 Clarges Street, near Hyde Park.

Adams was more than delighted to be rooming with the young diplomat. His letters to Lizzie were filled with effusive expressions of affection for Larz. On his first day back in London, January 11, 1892, he wrote to her, "I am here at last, in Clarges St., and Larz Anderson for companion. After my long solitude I love him like the sun and moon and planets and Sirius on top of all."[51] The footnote for this first appearance of Larz's name in the collected letters of Henry Adams describes him only as "Larz Anderson (1866–1937) married Isabel Weld Perkins."[52]

Henry and Larz quickly developed an easy domesticity that included having breakfast together every day and Henry seeing Larz off to work. One morning Larz directed his landlady to bake American-style cornbread for their breakfast as a special treat for Henry. On January 15, Adams wrote to Lizzie, "Now that breakfast is finished and Larz gone to see how his chief is, I sit down to read your news,"[53] and on January 21, "A lovely dark day, black as night, and full of refined feeling. Larz and I have breakfasted, and he has gone to his diplomatic duties."[54]

From Larz's perspective, the two men were best of friends and Adams's attention dazzled him. On January 18, 1892, a week after Adams moved in, Larz wrote in his journal, "Mr. Henry Adams and I still breakfast toward ten each morning together, though the last few evenings our ways have been divided at dinner time."[55] Indeed, Larz as a teenager had made an impression on Henry. In 1883, Henry wrote Nick to compliment him on Larz, then in his first year at Exeter. Elizabeth Anderson was not impressed by Henry's attention to her son. "Mr. Henry Adams sent a saucy message to your father to the effect that you were like him but without his faults," she wrote to Larz. "Putting aside the sauce in this speech, you can take the compliment for what it is worth."[56]

On January 18, a week after Henry returned to London, Larz wrote that Adams appeared "to be here indefinitely; at least without definite intentions."[57] Larz did not know Adams already planned to return to the United States and had packed and shipped some of his belongings. On January 23, Adams wrote his last letter to Lizzie from London, saying it was "time for closing and sending [his] last letter." He left London two days later for a week in Yorkshire but did not tell Larz of his plans to leave England.

On January 27, Larz wrote in his journal that Lincoln and White abruptly decided he should travel to the south of France for several weeks. The pretext for the trip was vague advice they had received from a doctor that Larz should take a break "if it were possible and convenient." Lincoln and White made sure it was possible and convenient. Larz said that Lincoln "seemed to insist" he take the trip and had made the arrangements for him. Even more oddly, Lincoln had already asked a friend of his, a Mr. Fischer—a forty-seven-year-old Irish-born American who lived in Chicago—to change his travel plans so Larz could travel with him.[58] If Lincoln wanted to discourage Adams from following Larz to France, sending him abroad with an Irish American businessman might have done the trick. There is no record of Larz and Henry ever seeing each other again.

If Adams was infatuated with Larz in London, years later Larz was infuriated with Adams. When *The Education of Henry Adams* was commercially published after Adams's death in 1918, Larz wrote angrily on the flyleaf of his copy (now in the possession of Isabel Anderson's New Hampshire relatives): "The insincerity of the man and his work is proved by the fact that he doesn't mention his wife or his marriage both of which meant much in his life!" Larz almost certainly figured out Henry Adams was in some way in love with him in London in 1891–1892 and could find no way to express his chagrin other than to excoriate Adams for excising his marriage and his wife from his autobiography.

First Secretary, American Legation, Rome (1894–1897)

During the summer of 1892, after spending several months with Larz in London, Nick, Elizabeth, and Elsie crossed over to the continent, but with separate destinations. Elizabeth and Elsie went to Germany, and Nick went to Lucerne seeking medical treatment for chronic heart problems. The great German surgeon Ernst von Bergmann, physician to Emperor Frederick III, came to Switzerland to examine Nick but could offer no treatment. Nick's health declined rapidly, and he died in Lucerne in mid-September.[59] Larz went immediately to Switzerland to accompany his father's remains to Cincinnati for internment in Spring Grove Cemetery, next to the grave of Nick's infant son and Larz's brother, Carl. From Cincinnati, Larz wrote that members of the Sixth Ohio had attended the service and were honorary pallbearers. "Characters like Father's—brave, upright, honest—redeem the world," Larz wrote. "There is not a memory of him that is not an example. I am happy that I had such a father."[60]

Elizabeth and Elsie stayed in Europe and for the next few years spent most of their time in Paris, on the French Riviera, and in Rome and saw Larz when they could. Larz remained in London for another two years. He was hitting his stride as a diplomat in an important diplomatic post. After Democrat Grover Cleveland's inauguration in March 1893, Lincoln, a Republican, resigned and left his post as US minister to the Court of St. James's two months later. Cleveland appointed the secretary of state from his first administration (1885–1889), Thomas F. Bayard, to the post. The president advanced the legation to full embassy status as a courtesy to Bayard and in recognition of the growing importance of Anglo-American relations. Bayard became the first American ambassador to the Court of St James's. Larz remained in London, the only Republican appointee to do so after Cleveland took office.

A year later, on July 25, 1894, Larz wrote to President Cleveland asking for the post of first secretary of the embassy at Rome "in case a vacancy should occur there."[61] The letter was pro forma. The Senate Foreign Relations Committee had approved Larz's nomination to the post two days earlier.[62]

After he arrived in Rome in the fall of 1894, Larz leased an apartment on the Via XX Settembre, near the American embassy on the Piazza San Bernardo, a fashionable area of the city then, as it is now. Larz's landlady was Countess Laurenius, the former Miss Ruth Leonard of Baltimore and the widow of a Swedish nobleman. She was famous for her education, her good looks, and her family's wealth.[63]

Larz's mother and sister joined him in Rome and remained there for the next year. They took an apartment in a Roman villa and quickly assumed a prominent role in society. Because they were in Rome together, Larz and his mother did not correspond by letter, so there is scant documentation of this period of his life, either professionally or socially, in his letters and journals.

Some insight into the Anderson family's social life in Rome comes from the travel diary of John Lowell Gardner, husband of Isabella Stewart Gardner. Gardner recorded many details of the Andersons' life in Rome during the first months of 1895, when he and Isabella spent the season there.[64] On their first day in Rome, January 4, the Gardners called on three members of the expatriate American community: Ambassador Wayne MacVeagh, Mrs. Thomas Waldo Story (wife of the American sculptor), and Mrs. Nicholas Longworth Anderson. Elizabeth Anderson was an old friend of theirs, and Larz had traveled with their nephew Jack Coolidge in Asia in 1888–1889. John Gardner recorded in his diary that he and Isabella went to several receptions at Elizabeth's villa. On January 16 they attended one of her dinner parties. The guests included Princess Poggia Suaza (née Josephine Mary Beers-Curtis); the American businessman Osgood Field and his wife, Katharine; the Dutch aristocrat Chevalier van Citters; a Monsieur Pascal from the French embassy; and a Miss Simpkins, possibly the sister of Larz's friend C. Ritchie Simpkins. Miss Simpkins attended many other Anderson parties noted in Gardner's diary, suggesting she was a houseguest of the Anderson ladies.

As first secretary of the embassy, Larz was also involved in at least one major diplomatic initiative. In 1896, three Italian-born American citizens were lynched by a mob in Hahnville, Louisiana, on the outskirts of New Orleans.[65] "Anderson sought to bolster MacVeagh's effort to maintain good relations with Italy after a spate of lynchings of Italians in the state of Louisiana," wrote the historian Richard Gentile. Larz took part in "delicate negotiations" with Italy that led to payment of an indemnity to the Italian government and a de-escalation of tensions between the two countries.[66] Thirty-five years later, Larz would again be involved in obtaining justice for another Italian immigrant who had been mistreated by the criminal justice system in the United States, Antonio Scali (see epilogue).

During his time in Rome, Larz became especially friendly with one of his mother's friends, the American writer and Newport socialite Maud Howe Elliott (1854–1948), a daughter of Julia Ward Howe. Maud lived in Rome with her husband, the Scottish-born artist John Elliott (1858–1925). Larz made a favorable impression on Maud when they first met at his mother's villa. Years later Maud recalled the moment in glowing terms:

> I first met Larz Anderson in his mother's apartment in Rome. He had already proved himself one of the most efficient and popular of the younger diplomats. His innate sense of the proprieties made him a valuable member of the staff. He was a born diplomat; his gay and charming temperament made him popular with young and old, rich and poor. Thinking back over those happy Roman days in the Gay Nineties I remember Larz as a gracious and tactful young man on whom I could always count to make my modest entertainments go over en train [enthusiastically].[67]

Maud had more than a passing interest in Larz. She would soon play matchmaker for the young American diplomat and had just the right young lady in mind.

Figure 3. Mrs. Larz Anderson, National Capital Horse Show, 1920.

III

ISABEL WELD PERKINS

When Isabel Weld Perkins was born on March 29, 1876, the year of the American centennial, the two families from which she was descended, the Welds and the Perkinses, had been in North America for exactly 244 years. There were two branches of the Weld family in England, distinguished from each other by religion. The Puritan branch arrived in the Massachusetts Bay Colony in 1632 to escape religious persecution. On June 5 of that year, Thomas, a Puritan minister, arrived aboard the *William and Frances*, bringing his wife and children with him.[1] His brother Captain Joseph Weld arrived in the Colony the following year with his family. Thomas eventually returned to England, but Joseph remained and became the progenitor of a great family that prospered from a more-than-two-hundred-year seafaring tradition. The Roman Catholic branch of the Weld family stayed in England and in 1641 acquired Lulworth Castle, which they have owned and occupied since. Larz Anderson eventually claimed these Roman Catholic Welds as part of Isabel's ancestry.

Within a few generations, the American branch of the family that traced its lineage to Joseph Weld became Unitarians. Isabel descended from this branch of the Weld family through her mother, Anna Minot Weld (1835–1924). Isabel valued her Unitarian heritage, writing once, "Unitarian faith appeals to me most. I can worship well in the open. I like the pine forest."[2]

On her father's side, Isabel was descended from a long line of New Hampshire farmers who had been in New England for exactly as long as her Weld ancestors. Remarkably, the first Perkins ancestor to emigrate from England, the Reverend Captain William Perkins (1607–1682), arrived on the same ship as Thomas Weld—the *William and Frances*—on June 5, 1632.[3] William Perkins was educated in Cambridge at Emmanuel College and Christ's College, which granted him an AB degree in 1628. He settled in Boston and was a member of the general court, the colonial assembly of the Massachusetts Bay Colony. His descendants lived in Roxbury, Gloucester, Topsfield, and Middleton until his great-grandson Roger Eliot Perkins moved from Middleton to Contoocook, New Hampshire. Roger was Isabel's great-grandfather.

"I Adored Him."

Isabel's father, George Hamilton Perkins (1835–1899), the oldest of eight children, was born in Contoocook, New Hampshire, to Hamilton Eliot Perkins and Clara Bartlett George. Isabel's grandfather Hamilton was an attorney and local judge who built and operated mills powered by the river that went through the center of town. In 1844, Hamilton moved the family to Boston, where for a time he engaged in mercantile trade with West Africa. After two years in Boston, the Perkinses returned to New Hampshire. There twelve-year-old George attended nearby Hopkinton Academy and then transferred to Gilmanton Academy, thirty-five miles from Contoocook. It was through Gilmanton that George's prospects in life improved.[4]

Around 1850, Charles H. Peaslee, a Gilmanton alumnus, Concord attorney, and member of Congress for the Concord district, offered George an appointment to the Naval Academy at Annapolis. The Perkinses were at first reluctant to send their firstborn son into a lifetime of military service.[5] They eventually relented, and George entered the Naval Academy as a midshipman in 1851 at the age of fifteen. Though not an outstanding student, George was a much-respected "middy" known for his diligence and winning ways, with traits and characteristics he would pass on to his daughter: "His bright, cheery, and genial disposition, and frank, hearty ways, were very winning; and if in his studies he did not take leading rank, he was esteemed a spirited, heartsome lad of good stock and promise, bred to honorable purpose and aspiration."[6]

George graduated from the Naval Academy in 1856 and was assigned to duty on ships in South American and Mediterranean waters. When the Civil War broke out, George served under Admiral David Farragut and fought in many important naval battles. He took part in the 1862 capture of New Orleans and for the next two years fought on the Mississippi River and in the Gulf of Mexico, rising to the rank of lieutenant commander. On August 5, 1864, at the Battle of Mobile Bay, he was in command of the monitor *Chickasaw* when it forced the Confederate ironclad ship the *Tennessee* to surrender. Admiral David Farragut later said of George that he was the "bravest man that ever trod the deck of a ship."[7]

After the war, George continued his navy service at sea and on shore duty at the Boston naval station. He retired from active duty in 1891. In 1896, the navy gave him the honorary rank of commodore in recognition of his Civil War service, in particular at Mobile Bay. He died in Boston in 1899. Between 1910 and 1945, the US Navy named three destroyers in his honor, and Isabel christened each of them.

Isabel's mother, Anna, was the daughter of William Fletcher Weld

(1800–1881) and his first wife, Mary Perez Bryant (1804–1836). Weld was one of Boston's most prominent citizens in the mid-nineteenth century. He operated a fleet of clipper ships that crisscrossed oceans and engaged in commerce that made him a rich man, as the clipper trade had done for his father, William Gordon Weld (1775–1825). When paddle steamships started crossing oceans on scheduled trips in the 1860s, W. F. Weld realized that the days of wind-driven clipper ships were numbered. Anticipating change, he sold off his fleet of fifty-one sailing vessels and ten steamships and invested the proceeds in railroads, insurance, and urban real estate.[8] After a personal property tax dispute with Boston was settled in the city's favor in about 1878, he moved to Philadelphia. He took with him "all his personal property, bonds, &c., which he deposited in his safe."[9] He no longer trusted Boston or banks. After his death in 1881, his second wife, Isabella Melissa Walker Weld (1813–1908; married 1839), returned to Boston and until her death lived at 115 Commonwealth Avenue, a few doors from Isabel and her parents.

Almost nothing is known of Anna's early life and schooling, though presumably she and her three sisters, Mary, Sarah, and Frances, were schooled in basic subjects such as elocution, music, sewing, and perhaps some French and literature. Unlike other Boston girls of her age and social standing, Anna did not travel abroad to finish her education when she turned eighteen, possibly due to poor health. She eventually did go on her grand tour of Europe in 1865 at age thirty (see chapter 15).

George and Anna met in Boston in 1869 and were engaged on Decoration Day (now Memorial Day) 1870 in the William Fletcher Weld residence at 1 Arlington Street in Boston, across from the Boston Public Garden. They married four months later, on September 15, in a ceremony performed by the great Unitarian minister and Harvard professor of theology James Freeman Clarke.

The couple lived the first few years of their married life in Charlestown, Massachusetts, near the Navy Yard. By the time their only child, Isabel, was born six years later, they were living at 284 Marlborough Street, a simple three-story brick house built in 1872 in Boston's Back Bay. Around 1884, the Perkinses moved to a larger and more stylish house at 123 Commonwealth Avenue. Referred to affectionately by Isabel as "123," this was the house she always thought of as her childhood home. Isabel and Larz occupied it regularly as their in-town residence for many years after Anna Perkins died in 1924.

Isabel's childhood included a vigorous outdoor life in New Hampshire at The Box near Concord, her grandfather's former hunting camp that over time became her father's summer home. This part of her childhood, in close proximity to rural New England values and customs, set Isabel apart from other Boston girls. The social inclinations of her parents did so also. George and Anna were socially reclusive. George's good friend the Harvard horticulturist Charles Sprague Sargent (1841–1927) once noted that although George had "wonderful geniality, and could put everybody into good humor," he and his wife limited their social engagements: "He was much sought after, but he went out comparatively little, for both he and Mrs. Perkins preferred the quiet of their own home to a constant round of social gayety. He had almost as much regularity [in Newport] as in Boston."[10]

There are only a few tidbits of information about Isabel's childhood, so a little sketch she once wrote about her early years is of particular interest:

> My recollections of my father are that when I was a child he was very good to me and I adored him. July and August we spent at Newport, the winters in Boston, and the spring and autumn in New Hampshire where the saddle horses were tied in the morning outside the door and when we went anywhere, we went on horseback. He directed the people on the farm at their work, and I often helped with the haying or the apple picking. We rounded up the colts in truly western fashion every autumn, or put out the forest fires. Both were very exciting. Breaking colts, swimming horses in the pond, and an occasional dog fight kept us quite lively.[11]

Years later, townspeople remembered Isabel as a young girl "flying over the hills on her pony," a testament to the horsemanship she learned from her father.[12] Maud Howe Elliott, who knew Isabel as a little girl, had her own memories. She wrote of once seeing Isabel racing in her carriage behind her father as he rode his fast mare Thetis through the streets of Newport.[13]

The Weld Grandchildren's Inheritance

Many myths have emerged since the late nineteenth century about the extent of Isabel's wealth. Even during her lifetime, there were widely divergent estimates of the size of her inheritance. She was wealthy, but not to the extent people, and especially journalists, suspected. When Grandfather Weld died on December 6, 1881, he left an estate worth approximately $20 million.[14] A *New York Times* article published on December 17, 1881, reported that Weld established individual trust funds for each of his four grandchildren, and each fund, according to the *Times*, was worth around $3 million.[15] However, the true value of the trust funds was actually higher. From his estate, Weld made about $2.7 million in bequests to family, friends, and organizations he admired. After subtracting these from the $20 million estate, there remained $17.3 million to be divided equally among the four grandchildren."[16]

The Philadelphia Orphan's Court that probated his will finally distributed his assets. After all the other bequests were deducted, the four grandchildren each received a trust fund worth about $4.3 million. In addition to Isabel Weld Perkins, the other grandchildren who received a trust fund were William "Billy" Fletcher Weld II (1855–1893), Charles Goddard Weld (1857–1911), and Mary "May" Bryant Pratt (1871–1956). When Billy Weld died in 1893, his share of the trust fund was redistributed equally among Isabel, Charles, and May. Each surviving grandchild thus eventually received approximately $5.7 million.

Between the time of her grandfather's death in 1881 and her twenty-fifth birthday in 1901, including the first four years of her marriage to Larz, Isabel received only an allowance that came from interest and dividends on a $12,000 interim trust fund. She could petition the trustees for advances on her inheritance as needs arose, but Grandfather Weld did not want any of his grandchildren controlling their inheritance until they were well established in life as young adults. In an era when women often married in their late teens and men in their early twenties, he clearly wanted his grandchildren to be married before they inherited, perhaps to prevent them from being courted for their money. His handpicked trustees could, through the trust fund's management practices, oversee and direct the course of his grandchildren's lives in a way that prevented them from mismanaging his money. If he sought longevity for his wealth, leaving it to his young grandchildren, who had no bad money habits or greedy spouses, was the way to do it.

A Boston Education
Despite her mother's $20,000 annual income from Grandfather Weld's estate and the early promise of wealth that would one day be hers, Isabel had a simple, unremarkable education in a private Boston day school for girls. Until the age of ten, she attended Miss Hilliard's School. Then, in 1886, her parents enrolled her in the first class of a new school for girls that had been "gathered" by Louise Winsor Brooks, wife of Francis Boott Brooks, a relative of Henry Adams. The two-person faculty the first year consisted of Louise's sister Mary P. Winsor and a French maid named Eugénie Martin. The school admitted only girls who were at least ten years old and already able to read and write. At first, the school was for girls who "came to town" for six months a year. Eventually, the term extended to eight months. In 1887, Mary took over running the school, and it is today the Winsor School of Boston.

During the eight years Isabel was with Miss Winsor, the school moved to Boylston Street and later to Newbury Street, both within walking distance of 123 Commonwealth Avenue. None of Isabel's school records survive, but the curriculum for 1897 shows that in the early years, pupils received instruction in English composition, reading, spelling, poetry, literature, history, art, geography, French, German, Latin, Greek, mathematics, science, and drawing. Not all subjects were taken in all years, but by the end of eight years at Miss Winsor's, each girl had completed a few years of instruction in each. Beyond language classes at school, Isabel had French- and German-speaking governesses at home.[17] In 1897, the school started sending some of its students to take college entrance examinations at Bryn Mawr, Radcliffe, Smith, and Vassar, but that was after Isabel's time. After completing her education with Miss Winsor, Isabel made her entry into society in Newport during the summer of 1895.[18]

The Winsor School alumnae album for 1910 reported that Isabel took courses at Boston University but never earned a degree. Her only college degrees were honorary doctorates from George Washington University and Boston University many years later.

Grand Tour of Europe and the Holy Land (1895–1896)

After Isabel's society debut in Newport, her parents made plans to send her abroad with their friend Maud Howe Elliott. Young women from good families "finished" their education by traveling abroad to learn about the arts, music, languages, and manners of Europe, especially England, France, Germany, and Italy. Accompanied by a chaperone who had impeccable credentials and entrée to the great houses of Europe, a young woman of good social standing could be introduced to young men of good social standing with the means to marry well. It was indeed time to find a husband. Isabel was already nineteen.

Maud lived in Rome with her Scottish-born husband, the artist John Elliott. She traveled to Boston in the summer of 1895 to visit her mother, the abolitionist and author of "The Battle Hymn of the Republic," Julia Ward Howe. The Elliotts' extensive connections with noblemen, aristocrats, and diplomats, not just in Rome but all across the continent, would give Isabel a wonderful experience preparing her for a place in society. George entrusted his daughter to Maud, telling her, "I want my little girl to grow up to be a noble woman."[19] Maud, however, had her doubts about being a paid travel companion. On August 21, 1895, Maud's friend Laura Elizabeth Richards advised her that chaperoning Isabel would be "good honest work."

> I confess to my mind a more important view than any other,
> it may very likely be the saving of a really fine child, whom

her fool parents are doing their best to spoil. Consider the
position of this lamb, I pray you. Natural (I fancy), bright,
and all her days hitherto spent with absolutely unintellectual
people: fortune-hunters swarming around her like bees: no
wise person to guide or guard her.[20]

Maud accepted Laura's challenge and changed Isabel's life forever.

Maud and Isabel, accompanied by Isabel's New Hampshire cousin Roger
Eliot Foster (1867–1900), sailed from New York for Southampton on October
2, 1895. They arrived in Paris, the first major stop on their itinerary, in mid-
October and checked in to the Hotel de France et de Choiseul, a first-class
hotel on rue Saint-Honoré (still a luxury hotel today, the Costes). It is clear
from Maud's letters to her mother that she was not just Isabel's chaperone
but her mentor as well. "Isabel is a dear good affectionate child," she wrote.
"If she learned one quarter of what I am learning in trying to teach her, it
will be well for her."[21]

While they were in Paris, Isabel studied French, attended plays at the
Comédie-Française, and, like any good tourist, went sightseeing. In November,
Maud, Isabel, and Roger applied at the American legation in Paris for passports
permitting them onward travel to "Europe & East."[22] Once in Egypt, they sailed
from Cairo on board the *Rameses III*, a steamship operated by the Thomas Cook
Company, a British travel company founded in 1841 that had started service
within Egypt in 1869. The *Rameses* cruised up the Nile as far as Assouan
(Aswan), a distance of a thousand miles. They reached Aswan by December
21, where Maud wrote to her mother, "Isabel is the sweetest-tempered creature
alive. It's nearly three months since we set sail; in all this time she has never been
anything but sweet and docile. I think this is remarkable."[23]

Maud used their time in Egypt for Bible study, especially Old Testament
passages about Moses "and all the rest of them."[24] In addition to the Egyptian
antiquities they visited along the Nile, Maud became fascinated with
hieroglyphics and wanted to learn how to read them. Isabel was surely
introduced to their mysteries through her chaperone's curiosity.

By New Year's Day 1896, the travelers were in Palestine, a frequent
destination for elite travelers in the nineteenth century, where they spent a
month in further study of the Bible and biblical history. They visited sites
from the Old and New Testaments, including the Garden of Gethsemane.
In Jerusalem they met Howard Sweetser Bliss (1860–1920), who was
excavating archeological sites and unearthing the old walls of the city. The
depth of Isabel's exposure to ancient and biblical history on this portion of
the trip was remarkable.

The merry band arrived in Rome in late January, in time for Isabel to experience some of the city's glittering social season before it ended. The Elliotts lived on the third floor of the Palazzo Rusticucci on the Via della Conciliazione, within view of St. Peter's Square. The apartment where Isabel was to spend the next few months was a magnificent example of a Renaissance interior with sixteenth-century amenities still in place!

> The floors were paved with red, black and white tiles in geometrical designs. The rooms were lofty with ceilings of carved wood. The ample windows where the sun poured in were so arranged that the apartment was warm in winter and cool in summer. The walls were three feet thick, built to keep out both heat and cold. There was a bath tub:—that sounds modern, but if we wanted hot water for our baths the manner of securing it was almost archaic. Large stones were heated red hot over the little charcoal fires in the kitchen; the tub was filled with water drawn from the tap, and the heated stones were plunged in the cold water.[25]

John Elliott had a spare room in their apartment remodeled for Isabel and installed a fireplace there to ward off Rome's winter chill. Maud arranged for Isabel to have her own maid, a young woman named Franceline, who helped Isabel with clothes, hair, accessories, and all that went into a young lady's presentation of herself.[26] Isabel started to learn what it meant to be a society woman, a role she had not previously known as the daughter of parents who lived a quietly comfortable middle-class life withdrawn from society.

From Rome, the travelers went to Germany for May through July and then hopscotched their way through the parts of Europe they had not yet seen. On their way from Bavaria to Holland, they stopped in Bayreuth for the Wagner festival. In mid-August they reached The Hague, where they were the houseguests of John Louden, Dutch ambassador to Rome. From Holland, they crossed over to London and traveled north to Scotland to visit other of the Elliotts' friends. In September, the trio returned to Paris for a last dose of theater and shopping and to say good-bye to friends before they returned to the United States in early October.

The year abroad bonded Maud and Isabel as friends and confidants for life. The older woman was deeply touched by Isabel's youth, and this awoke maternal feelings in her that she otherwise might never have known. Years later, Maud wrote an appreciation of Isabel and their year together. "She was the nearest thing to a daughter I ever had. In that year we were together I learned to understand something of the joys and anxieties parents feel; the delight of sharing whatever knowledge life has brought with a young and ardent spirit, and of forgetting one's own affairs in the vivid interests of youth."[27]

Isabel experienced the best of Europe under Maud's guidance and tutoring. She learned much about French, Italian, and German music and art and developed proficiency in French and German, a mark of sophistication and worldliness among American elites of her era. Isabel experienced the ancient worlds of Egypt and Palestine and learned much through Maud's vast knowledge of antiquity and biblical history. Through Maud and John Elliott, Isabel met many people who were vastly different from the small world she knew growing up in New England. Most importantly, she learned how to move gracefully among European aristocrats, nobles, and diplomats and how to handle herself in the company of elite Americans who lived abroad.

Maud did everything she could to prepare Isabel for a future with the young American diplomat she would meet on the rooftop terrace of the Elliott palazzo that winter in Rome.

Figure 4. Larz and Isabel Anderson, Hawaii, 1897.

IV

ENGAGEMENT, WEDDING, AND FIRST YEARS TOGETHER (1896–1899)

On January 31, 1896, Larz Anderson wrote from Rome that he had dined the night before at the home of Maud and John Elliott with their two guests, a Mrs. Horowitz of Baltimore and a Miss Perkins of Boston. "A most pleasant evening," Larz reported.[1] Maud later recalled that she and John introduced the two young people to each other that evening on the Elliotts' rooftop. Maud once called the terrace the "crown and glory" of her home.[2] Larz later asked John to paint a picture of it for him as a souvenir. This painting, now known as *Terrace Garden, Rome,* was displayed during the Andersons' lifetime in their Brookline mansion.[3]

Larz actually had seen Isabel on two occasions before their meeting on Maud's terrace, one recent and one a long time before. The most recent sighting was when Larz caught a glimpse of Isabel in Rome's Grand Hotel a few weeks earlier. "I was at dinner at a table in the restaurant of the Grand," he recalled years later. "I could pick out the place now where I sat when she passed by with Mrs. Elliott and Roger Foster to sit down toward the other end of the room."[4]

Then Larz remembered another chance meeting with Isabel Perkins. In 1887, during his senior year at Harvard, Larz had attended a coming-out party in Boston. The debutant had been Isabel's first cousin sixteen-year-old Mary Bryant Pratt, known as May.[5] Eleven-year-old Isabel had been at the party too. Larz recalled the moment: "I remembered her as a little girl with pigtails at May Pratt's coming out party, one of the series of two that the Pratts gave on May's coming out, where I had sat at supper with May at her table (for it all comes back to me so vividly) and [Isabel] had come up to the table as we sat at supper."[6]

Larz quickly became infatuated with the nineteen-year-old Isabel he met in Rome that winter. They saw each other often at teas, receptions, dinners, and balls. Everyone thought they were a good match. "Larz would make the Mouse happy," Jack Elliott wrote to Maud, using their pet name for Isabel. "He is a dear sweet fellow, and I care a great deal for him."[7]

After Maud, Isabel, and Roger left Rome in late March to tour other parts of Italy, Larz traveled to see them on weekends. He met them in Sorrento and in Florence. The pursuit was not at all one-sided. Once when Larz needed to be in Venice, the trio visited him there for a few days, and that was where they all had to say good-bye to each other. When they parted, Isabel gave Larz a practical farewell gift that was perhaps symbolic of their future life together: a change purse. Within a year, Isabel would turn her financial affairs over to Larz. He must have been caught off guard because he had nothing to give in return. He later mailed her a pin of the Lion of Saint Mark, the symbol of Venice. Larz was bereft after Isabel left. "Your rooms at the hotel are empty," he wrote. "I looked up at them; there was no light, or anyone leaning from the balcony, and I realized how far away from me you had gone."[8]

Her Lost Love Letters

Larz and Isabel kept up a voluminous correspondence after Isabel left Rome. Though the originals of the letters and telegrams were destroyed after Isabel's death (see chapter 17), their texts have largely been preserved in an epistolary roman à clef that Isabel published in 1922, *Polly the Pagan: Her Lost Love Letters*. Isabel's preface described the novel as the "letters and the journal of a young American girl traveling in Europe." *Polly the Pagan*'s plot line is simple: a young American woman on her grand tour of Europe with her aunt meets a young American diplomat (called A.D. in the novel) in Rome. They flirt, court, fall in love, and marry. The novel includes many parallels between Polly's story and the courtship of Larz and Isabel. Polly and A.D. went on a picnic to Frascati. So did Larz and Isabel. A.D. sent Polly a Lion of Saint Mark pin. So did Larz.

Isabel left many clues about the relationship between *Polly the Pagan* and real-life events. Many passages in *Polly the Pagan* can be found in Larz's letters and journals. Larz's nickname for Isabel during their courtship in Rome and later in life was Dolly, and *Pagan* may have been a private joke referring to Isabel's Unitarianism. The frontispiece is what definitely gives away the book's secret: a full-color portrait of Polly captioned "From an ideal portrait by DeWitt Lockman." Isabel sat for DeWitt McClellan Lockman (1870–1957) several times during her life. In this "ideal portrait," Lockman portrayed Polly wearing Isabel's signature piece of jewelry—the three-emerald broach that also made an appearance in her 1901 full-length portrait by Cecilia Beaux. The endpapers of *Polly the Pagan* provide another visual record. They depict Larz, Isabel, and John on the rooftop terrace of the Elliott residence, the Palazzo Rusticucci.[9]

Isabel herself described how she got the idea to write *Polly the Pagan*: "I found among my notes a good deal of material relating to Italy, and very many letters. These last put an idea into my head. Why not devise a novel made up wholly of correspondence and see if it would carry the narrative that way?"[10]

Polly the Pagan provides delightful insight into what Larz and Isabel's courtship was like. We see Isabel's playful nature when Polly writes to her suitor about having stayed out too late in Venice and its consequences with Aunt.

> What a heavenly night we had in Venice out in that gondola when we stuck on the sand-bar and didn't care at all, we were so happy. It got later and later and the moon went down and not until the tide rose in the early morning did we float away. When we arrived at the hotel, oh, but wasn't Aunt angry? She did not believe one word we said! ... She suddenly declared tickets had been bought for the Wagner operas and that we must start the next day. I never heard of those tickets before![11]

Polly teases A.D. no end. From Leicestershire, England, she writes about two young men who pay her more than casual attention. "One of them gave me his picture and asked if he couldn't have mine for his watch," she taunts. As if that were not enough to keep A.D. guessing, she changes her strategy completely: "I am not going to write you any more sweet letters. It isn't because I have changed one bit in my feeling toward you but because variety is the spice of life, and if you have too many nice things written to you, you won't appreciate them."[12]

Polly the Pagan did not get good reviews when it was published. "As the story in itself is so slight that it might be told in a few hundred words," the *New York Times* said, "the letters and extracts from Polly's journal are liberally padded out with descriptions of scenes and happenings in Rome and elsewhere, most of which have little or no bearing on the plot."[13] Who cares! The novel is delicious and fun, especially when we imagine it really is Isabel (Polly) putting Larz (A.D.) through the paces of Gilded Age courtship. Curiously, the novel includes a foreword by Basil King, a Canadian minister who claimed he could communicate with the dead.[14] King praised *Polly the Pagan*, putting it on par with the novels of Henry James. The *Times* reviewer objected to this, calling it "too high an estimate on a very ordinary piece of work."

By late summer, Larz decided to propose to Isabel in Boston. He suggested this ever so delicately in a letter dated August 15, 1896, his thirtieth birthday: "I am sorry you are homesick, dear, for I know the pain of it. I also know how strange scenes and people, strange places and ways, have kept you excited, until now you feel a-weary. And that is why, Isabel, I wished to come to you at home in your family surroundings, for then you can measure quietly and more truly what you feel."[15]

He arrived in Boston on Halloween 1896, just a few weeks after Isabel returned from Europe.[16] In his hotel room he puzzled over what to wear for his first visit to 123 Commonwealth Avenue, deciding on a navy-blue rather than a gray check suit—to "create the best impression on the parents whom I had never seen." He was anxious that cold, rainy morning: "I walked round to Commonwealth Avenue, my heart (or what Isabel had left of it in me) in my throat."[17] They became engaged later in the day, making it "a happy day after all." The official announcement would not come until five weeks later, on December 5, after Larz was on his way back to Italy—and safely out of reach of State Department officials who might have been curious about his plans. The *Washington Post* carried the engagement notice and estimated Isabel's fortune to be $16 million.[18] If, like the other parts of *Polly the Pagan*, the details of Polly's engagement to A.D. are based on what happened in real life, then Larz planned a special Christmas surprise for his fiancée. Polly's "Xmas stocking" contained a "heavenly diamond engagement-ring."[19]

Anxious Days in Rome

Larz returned to Rome expecting his stay to be brief. He had already booked return passage to New York and was to arrive on May 1, six weeks before the wedding date the newly engaged had picked—June 10.[20] He was so sure of a quick end to his assignment in Rome that he had given up his apartment before going to Boston. With no departure date in sight, he took a small suite of rooms at the Hotel Royal, a first-class hotel that catered to Americans. His English valet, Westcott, continued to attend him there.

Ambassador Wayne MacVeagh, a Democrat, did not immediately submit his resignation in the wake of Grover Cleveland's loss to Republican William McKinley in November 1896. Although Larz was eager and ready to submit his resignation, he held off until MacVeagh did so. MacVeagh formally resigned on February 6, 1897, a month before Inauguration Day. Larz's resignation followed the next day. He asked President Cleveland if his resignation could "take effect at the earliest convenience of the Department of State," explaining that "private matters of an anxious and urgent nature" required him to go home.[21] The State Department, of course, knew the reason was neither "private" (the engagement had been announced in the *Post*) nor "urgent." It was also not convenient to let Larz leave Rome just at that moment. Cleveland wanted to let McKinley fill the important post of American ambassador to Rome. As first secretary and chargé d'affaires, Larz was, for the foreseeable future, America's man in Rome.

Larz began to plead impetuously with the State Department to let him leave. State's response was no response. Larz's impatience and anger erupted in a journal entry dated February 15, 1897, in which he bawled at how department officials were treating him:

> If the Department either loves me much, or hates me much, it will let me off at once. I wouldn't be a bit hurt in my feelings if a cablegram came marked "urgent," stating "Your resignation accepted with pleasure, to take effect at once," and the at once underlined. I'd knock over the tables and chairs, slam the doors, go home so quickly I wouldn't have time to say, "Jack Robinson!" Then I would cry, "Westcott! Pack my things! Throw them in any way, helter-skelter, pell-mell, in a heap, it doesn't matter. Nothing matters, for we are going home! Hip, hip, hurrah!" I'm all excited at the mere thought.[22]

On Inauguration Day, Larz sent another cable to the secretary of state asking to leave his post. Assistant Secretary of State Alvey A. Adee replied, calling Larz's cable a "pathetic appeal."[23] Adee explained they could not replace Larz until McKinley appointed a new ambassador. Larz had brashly suggested that the American consul general take over as chargé d'affaires, but Adee disagreed, saying, "Italy will not recognize the combination of consular and diplomatic functions." After six years in the diplomatic service of the United States, Larz already knew this.

Up to this point, there was no coverage of Larz's attempted resignation in American papers. On March 25, the day after another of Larz's impatient cables to Washington "begging to be relieved," his struggle with the department went public. Someone at State had had enough and leaked Larz's cable to the *New York Times*.[24] "This condition is mortifying to Mr. Anderson," the *Times* mocked. There was even a backhanded swipe impugning Larz's motives for marrying Isabel. "All arrangements had been made for his marriage to a multi-millionaire lady of Boston, Miss Perkins," the *Times* said.

Two days later, the press fired a second salvo. This time, the *Washington Post* picked up the story and put a new twist on it, calling Larz "desperate and anxious."[25] "Although Mr. Anderson is a very youthful and inexperienced person," the *Post* opined, "he is required to hold down the Embassy, protect the rights, and maintain the honor of the American Eagle in the Eternal City." This public repudiation of Larz as youthful and inexperienced by his hometown newspaper was surely meant to sting. Larz took the hint: there is no record of other cables to the State Department, nor was there any further press coverage.

In May, President McKinley appointed General William F. Draper, a Washington neighbor of Larz's mother, as the new ambassador. Twenty-four-year-old Chandler Hale (1873–1951) replaced Larz as first secretary. Like Larz, Hale had his own history with Henry Adams, fifty-seven, who in 1894 had taken Chandler, twenty-one, on a six-month trip to Mexico and the Caribbean.[26] Though Chandler was young and unknown in social circles, his father, Eugene, was an important Republican senator from Maine. Chandler's appointment to Rome was the start of a long and distinguished career as an American diplomat. He eventually married Rachel Cameron, Lizzie Cameron's stepdaughter. It was to Lizzie that Henry Adams had proclaimed his love and affection for Larz Anderson in London.

On May 2, 1897, with Draper and Hale on their way to Rome, Larz received permission to vacate his post. He left immediately and arrived in New York on May 18, less than a month before the wedding.

Preparations for the Wedding

The Anderson and Perkins households were busy during the months that Larz waited in Rome. Isabel and her mother and Larz's mother and sister, Elsie, collaborated on wedding plans. There were frequent visits back and forth between Boston and Washington. In January, Isabel visited the Andersons in Washington, and Elsie returned with her to Boston to continue their sisterly visit.[27] A month later, the Anderson ladies traveled to Boston, their visit memorialized on February 9, 1897, when they signed Isabella Stewart Gardner's guestbook at Fenway Court.[28] In March, Isabel and her father went to New York for a visit with the Anderson ladies at the Holland House, where George treated them all to dinner. Isabel shopped in New York for gowns and bonnets, and Mrs. Anderson went to Tiffany's to pick out a wedding gift for Isabel. She chose a silver centerpiece.[29] The Anderson and Perkins families were delighted with the match.

Larz and Isabel made plans for their wedding party. Isabel wanted Larz's sister, Elsie, to be her maid of honor and picked bridesmaids from among her circle of young friends in Boston. She ordered gowns for herself and her bridesmaids from Paris. For her attendants, she chose white silk trimmed with pink ribbons and Valenciennes lace. For herself, she ordered a bespoke bridal gown of heavy white satin lined with taffeta and decorated with orange blossoms and antique Mechlin lace. The dress came from the salon of Charles Frederick Worth in Paris, famous for its elegant haute couture for the modern woman.[30] The veil, a gift from Isabel's mother, was specially designed and handmade in Venice. It incorporated the bridal couple's initials *ILA* "interwoven in intricate fashion," a monogram they used for the rest of their lives to symbolize their union.

At his end, Larz made arrangements for his groomsmen. He chose lifelong friend and Harvard classmate Charles Francis Adams III as best man. Isabel's cousin Roger Foster and Larz's cousin Nicholas Longworth, a future speaker of the House, were to be ushers, along with several other Harvard men. The groom and his groomsmen wore knee-length frock coats, an old-fashioned choice. Frock coats went out of style in the 1880s. Morning coats (similar to what are now known as tails) were what the modern groom wore to his wedding.

Assembling the guest list for the wedding took much careful thought and coordination. Larz and his mother drew up their own separate lists, and the Perkins family had their list. Elizabeth relied on Larz to decide who from Boston should be invited, including many of his father's Harvard classmates.[31] By the time the three lists came together, there were more than 330 names.

"But to Mr. Anderson"

Larz married Isabel on the morning of June 10, 1897, in Boston's Arlington Street Church (Unitarian) in a lavishly staged ceremony attended mostly by friends and family. There were a few celebrities present: Massachusetts governor Roger Wolcott, Congressman Charles F. Sprague (husband of Isabel's cousin May Sprague), and Boston socialite art collector Isabella Stewart Gardner, an old friend of Larz's parents. Curiously, the *Boston Globe* did not list any Anderson or Kilgour guests from Cincinnati, though many Perkins and Weld relatives were there. The ceremony was followed by a wedding breakfast for twenty. Later in the afternoon, there was a reception in the adjacent Commonwealth Avenue homes of Isabel's parents and her maternal aunt, Sarah Weld Pratt.

Newspapers played up the most spectacular of the wedding gifts. Larz's gift to his bride topped the list: a diamond tiara of his own design that could also be worn as a necklace. Isabel's aunt Caroline Goddard Weld, who lived in Rome, gave her niece a diamond broach shaped like a lover's knot. Larz's godmother, Mrs. Evans, sent four silver candlesticks from Paris.

Boston had a love-hate relationship with the wedding. The *Boston Globe* took the populist view, hyping the marriage of two great fortunes—Isabel's reported $17 million inheritance and Larz's reported multimillions. Both guesses at the wealth of the couple turned out to be wrong. The paper gushed over the flowers in the church, mostly mountain laurel in full bloom. Despite all the opulent arrangements, the *Globe*'s writer concluded, "There was no attempt at an ostentatious display that has accompanied many of the marriages of great American heiresses. It was all simply planned and admirably executed."[32]

On June 17, 1897, *Town Topics*, the society paper published in New York, expressed a different view of the wedding. Its "casual correspondent" in Boston roundly criticized the wedding and everything about it, especially the parents who hosted it. "The Perkins family—or at least *this* Perkins family, for they are in no way connected with *the* Perkinses—have never been associated with smart society in Boston." The parents, and not Isabel, were to blame for "the excessive publicity of the whole affair," the correspondent decided. *Town Topics* reminded its readers that "little Isabel Perkins was trotted out at a ball with a blare of trumpets" somewhat belatedly in Newport during the summer of 1895. The rag held that Isabel's parents, having not gotten the hoped-for results (an engagement ring), called Maud Howe Elliott "into requisition, and the little heiress was hustled abroad under that lady's voluminous chaperonage, with Rome as an objective point."

"Miss Perkins came back to Boston, *fiancée* to be sure, but to Mr. Anderson," sniped the special correspondent in Boston.[33]

An Epic Wedding Journey

In a 1923 diary entry, Larz recalled that on the day of their wedding they left the reception at around three o'clock and headed for New Hampshire in a horse-drawn carriage, stopping first in Concord to see Isabel's grandmother for "early tea."[34] Boston to Concord is a distance of some seventy miles, and even the fastest carriages of the day could cover no more than ten miles an hour. Leaving Boston at three, they could have arrived in Concord no earlier than midnight. They either went to Concord by train or left Boston the next morning by carriage, giving them ample time to reach Concord for early tea. After the visit, they traveled on to The Box for an evening wedding celebration that had been planned by Isabel's relatives. After sunset on June 11, hundreds of friends and family came from surrounding towns, villages, and farms to welcome Larz and Isabel to New Hampshire. A pathway down the gently sloping hill from The Box to the edge of the lake, a distance of about a half mile, was lit with gaily colored Chinese lanterns. There, on the same spot where Isabel later built her beloved cottage The Boxlet, friends and relatives celebrated their union.[35]

After several days of rest, the couple left on a cross-country train to California, passing through Salt Lake City. They set sail on July 9 from San Francisco aboard the SS *Gaelic* bound for Honolulu. Larz's valet Westcott and Isabel's maid Elin Karlson accompanied them. Elin was a much-loved family servant who was buried in the Perkins family plot in Forest Hills Cemetery when she died a year later. The *Gaelic*, a livestock ship leased by the White Star Line, carried thirty-six passengers. It reached Honolulu six days and three hours later, Larz noted in his diary. Travelers in those days kept track of travel in days and hours the way modern travelers keep track of it in hours and minutes. The Hawaiian Islands were a stepping-stone for the Andersons on their long transit from Boston to Japan. They rented a beach cottage, its terrace canopied with a large grass mat that provided shade for long wicker chairs with an ocean view. Larz added his own decorative touches. "I have put up little Chinese lanterns and it looks quite tropical," he said.[36]

In Honolulu, they were busy honeymooners. The American minister to Hawaii, Harold M. Sewall, invited them to use his seaside bathhouse. They donned bathing suits and rode the surf in a catamaran. A wave knocked Isabel into the ocean, but she "bobbed up serenely till another canoe came out and picked [them] up," according to Larz.[37] They visited the Bernice P. Bishop Museum and spent time with its curator, former Harvard biology professor William Tufts Brigham, who gave them a private tour of the museum. Perhaps on the advice of Brigham, who had written about the Kilauea volcano, they took an interisland steamer to Hawaii to see it. The dormant volcano had last erupted in 1894, and Larz decided it was "a fake."[38]

Isabel's "A Book of Memories" scrapbook includes a poem in French that Larz wrote for her, perhaps while they were in Hawaii on their way to Japan. Isabel placed the poem in the scrapbook near other memorabilia of their courtship, wedding, and honeymoon that she'd saved. It is an enchanting peek into their love for each other.[39]

Beauté supreme	Paramount beauty
Crois-moi, je t'aime	Believe me, I love you
D'un amour extreme	With love extreme
Au "Samedi soir"!	On "Saturday night"!
Dans mon désir	In my yearnings
Toujours j'admire	I revere always
Ce doux sourire	This sweet smile
Que j'ai pu voir!	That you revealed to me!

Larz illustrated the poem with a pen-and-ink drawing of an angelic woman floating in air, presaging a figure that appeared years later in a mural in the couple's magnificent home in Washington.

On August 3, the newlyweds and their servants boarded the steamship *Doric* for the eleven-day trans-Pacific crossing to Japan. Also operated by the White Star Line, the *Doric* offered its passengers a variety of entertainments to keep them active (and perhaps distracted) during the long voyage. "There has been a tournament (with very pretty prizes) with egg and spoon, and boot and shoe races, and cock fights and many other contests, and an obstacle race, very funny too," Larz wrote.[40] The crew asked Isabel to distribute the prizes in the ship's main salon after the festivities. In the evening, there were magic lantern shows and pantomimes, some with musical accompaniment from both a Graphophone and a phonograph. Larz was fascinated that the Japanese men in steerage wrestled and boxed each other.

The Spell of Japan

The Andersons arrived in Yokohama on August 14, the day before Larz's thirty-first birthday. Larz's friend Osame Kamori, a young man whom he had met during his first visit to Japan in 1888, greeted them at the wharf. At the time of the wedding, Osame had been living in Boston and working as a salesman there. Larz had asked him to go to Japan ahead of them to make arrangements for their travel within the country and then accompany them as guide and interpreter.[41] Isabel immediately set about planning a birthday dinner in Larz's honor and invited several Americans, including Captain Charles Vernon Gridley. The captain was a Civil War naval officer who, like Isabel's father, had served under Admiral David Farragut at the Battle of Mobile Bay. Coincidentally, Gridley had assumed command of the USS *Olympia*, Admiral George Dewey's flagship, on Larz and Isabel's wedding day. A year later in May, the captain was immortalized when Dewey ordered him to launch the Battle of Manila Bay: "You may fire when you are ready, Gridley."

The newlyweds spent a week in Tokyo seeing the popular sights Larz had visited in 1888. They called at the house in the Kojimachi neighborhood of central Tokyo where Larz and his travel companion Malcolm Thomas had lived with Jack Coolidge. The landlord recognized Larz and gave them a tour of the traditional-style house and its private garden. From Tokyo they traveled north in a private train car. This attracted attention that Larz enjoyed. "The effect of the private car on the diminutive railways officials was magnificent, for they stood in rows and bowed to the ground, with their little caps in their tiny hands, and it made us feel very fine."[42] *It made us feel very fine.*

Throughout his life Larz was always delighted when strangers bowed and curtsied to him for no reason other than his social class.

They toured gardens and saw great scenic landscapes, including the islands and promontories of the Matsushima islands, before turning south toward Kyoto. The temples, shrines, and crowds of pilgrims in the old imperial city fascinated them, and they stayed longer than planned. When the weather turned bad in early October, they chartered a 150-foot steamship in Kobe and continued their travels by boat along the coast, going ashore at ports and harbors for day trips. One evening in the port city of Onomichi, they sat on the deck and "sang to each other in the flooding moonlight."[43]

While anchored off the island of Miyajima, within view of the Sankei temple, Larz arranged a spectacular entertainment for his bride:

> I had made arrangements to have the temple lanterns lighted in the evening, there were almost four hundred of stone and bronze within this temple and along the shore, and as we came out of our tiny cabin after dinner and got into a sampan to be sculled across the still waters to view the beauty of the scene, it was like magic, a Fairyland, for the tide was just right, at its highest, and the temple seemed to float upon the waters while the hundreds of lights were reflected in the glassy tide as we slowly passed beneath the great tori (which are far out in the water at high tide) and landed.[44]

At Nagasaki, they boarded a Shanghai-bound steamer for a brief visit to China, where they had many new culinary experiences. They sampled such delicacies as roast goose, roast pig, and bird's nest and shark fin soups. They marveled at hors d'oeuvres made from duck, ham, kidneys, jellies, snails, and shellfish. And they saw something they recognized from home—the Huxinting Teahouse pictured in a willowware pattern popular in America and England during the nineteenth century.[45] After four days exploring the city, they boarded their old friend the *Gaelic* bound for Hong Kong, where they stayed a few days before returning to Japan. They originally had hoped to rent a house in Tokyo and spend another six weeks there before returning to the States, but when they could not find one they liked, they returned to Boston in time to spend Christmas with Isabel's parents.

For years to come, Larz and Isabel drew on the rich experiences of this first trip. They found many ways to integrate Japan and its culture into their personal aesthetics. Not only did they hold in high regard Japanese furnishings, decorative arts, and garden design, they deeply appreciated the spiritual and philosophical foundations of Asian culture. "All religions are good, including the Mohammedan and Buddhist," Isabel once said. "Some are suited to the people of the East and Far East; others are better for the West."[46] More than a tourist destination for them, Japan was a touchstone of their life together.

Early Married Life

After Christmas, Larz and Isabel went back to Washington for the 1898 winter social season. They rented the large and stylishly decorated Bellamy Storer House at 1640 Rhode Island Avenue.[47] At the time the Andersons rented the house, Storer—married to Larz's cousin Maria Longworth Nichols—was the US minister to Belgium. The *Washington Post* called the mansion "sumptuous," with an art studio, music room, and library that made it "one of the most artistic and lavishly furnished homes in Washington." The pink reception room (Isabel's favorite color) on the *piano nobile* was furnished with gilded Louis XVI–style furniture.[48]

When war with Spain broke out that spring, Larz enlisted with the US Army Volunteers. General Henry Clark Corbin, a Civil War general from Ohio who would one day be their neighbor on Massachusetts Avenue, encouraged him.[49] Corbin originally offered Larz a commission as a major, but Larz instead asked for the lower rank of captain since he had no military training. General George W. Davis of the US Army Volunteers, one of Larz's father's fellow Civil War officers, assigned the new captain to his staff at Camp Alger, the Second Army Corps headquarters near Dunn Loring, twelve miles from Washington. The base was notorious for its unsanitary conditions and shortages of clean drinking water. That summer typhoid raged through the camp, leaving more than one hundred men dead.

Larz worked as an assistant adjutant general for Davis, keeping records and issuing the CO's orders. On his daily rounds, Larz rode his own mount, Soldier Boy, a white horse Isabel had bought for him from Buffalo Bill Cody.[50] In 1906, Mark Twain immortalized Soldier Boy in his novel *A Horse's Tale*, calling him "a wonder of a horse" with "a reputation which is as shining as his own silken hide."[51] Larz's mother sent out food for the officers' mess, including ham, beef, deviled crabs, biscuits, chops, and corn.[52] Isabel herself went to the camp to deliver huckleberry puddings and capons and told Larz's mother the camp was "quite lovely" after one of her visits.[53] Isabel also did her own public service during the brief war by providing in-home care for soldiers' families in Washington.

In early August, Camp Alger shut down because of the unsanitary conditions. The officers rode their mounts and the soldiers marched on foot to Thoroughfare Gap, about forty miles away. On their arrival at the gap, Larz wrote a journal entry in which he expressed his frustration at how the volunteers had been managed. "Oh, we have had a time of it," he wrote about the march on foot. "Sent off by orders at a too short notice, without enough wagons, and forced to march on a hot day with no military incentive. If it were war, it would be all right, but this is on the eve of peace."[54] After bivouacking at the gap for about a month, they started a march to Camp Meade, Pennsylvania, but the war ended before they arrived.

When Larz's duties came to an end, he wrote a note to Isabel romanticizing his brief service:

> What an odd, broken summer! It is over now, and for the best no doubt. I have been in pleasant places, and certain, of all the troops that remained in this country, our Division, with its plucky march through Virginia, has been the finest! If I had gone to "Cuby" or Porto Rico, I might have been dead. Today I am looking on the bright side of things, and glad to be alive. Soon I will put my sword over the mantelpiece in the little library and start the fire, sitting next to you, and be at peace.[55]

"Making Out Our Future Plans"

After the war, Larz decided they needed another trip abroad to give them more time to reflect on their future together. "One of the reasons I wanted to take this trip at this time was to give ourselves a chance of making out our future plans, for we weren't quite decided in our minds," he said.[56] They sailed from the United States in early fall 1898, accompanied by Larz's valet Westcott and Isabel's maid Sophie. Their itinerary took them halfway around the world again, this time to India in the opposite direction, by way of Europe and the Suez Canal.

In London, they stayed in Larz's old rooms on Clarges Street and called on many friends from his days at the American legation. They dined one evening with Larz's old boss Henry White and his wife, Margaret. In addition to a heavy social schedule, Larz and Isabel attended plays and musicals and ordered custom-tailored clothes to take with them to India.

Their stay in Paris was very different from London, even though Larz considered the city a second hometown and knew many people there. "I don't think we'll trouble to look [up] anyone, for Isabel and I can enjoy Paris together very well," he said.[57] Larz knew Paris intimately and was always invigorated by visits there.[58] They took drives through the Bois de Boulogne, went out to lunch and dinner alone, and visited racy Parisian night spots that Isabel wanted to see. "I do not think she will care to revisit [them]," Larz said. They called on a few old friends, including Larz's godmother, Mrs. Evans, and dined with Whitelaw Reid, former American ambassador to France, and his wife.

In early November, they left Paris by train headed for Rome, where Maud and John Elliott met them at the station. The Andersons booked themselves into the Grand Hotel on the Via XX Settembre, where Larz had caught a glimpse of Isabel when she'd first arrived in Rome in 1896 with Maud and Roger. Unlike Paris, they filled their time in Rome with social engagements. Many old friends were eager to see them. One of the highlights was a twenty-minute private audience with Pope Leo XIII. Larz left no record of their conversation, but he and the pontiff likely shared many interests. Leo made the Catholic Church more open to scientific and historical analysis and had a connection to Washington, DC. In 1889 he authorized the establishment of the Catholic University of America.[59]

Though they did not yet have a home of their own, the Andersons went shopping in Italy for art, furniture, and large pieces of architectural decoration. In Florence they bought "glorious" sixteenth-century altar carvings that Larz said were by "Riccio," the sculptor and architect Andrea Briosco (1470–1532). In Rome they purchased a sixteenth-century fireplace "in Greek marble" (Larz said Isabel could easily stand in it) and a "gorgeous" sarcophagus he thought could go in a stable yard someday. He also browsed the jewelry in the Florence shop of Settepasse, his "old jeweler friend." When they finally boarded their ship at Naples bound for Port Said, their baggage included another purchase—a guitar, "which Punk is going to learn to play on the voyage," Larz said, referring to Isabel by one of his pet names for her.[60]

The Andersons reached Ceylon in early December. In Colombo they hired an Indian man named Bhana Rutton to travel with them for the rest of the trip as their guide. Bhana's origins are obscure, though Larz once described him as a Christian convert and a married man with several daughters. There is some evidence Bhana was a Dhedh, a member of one of India's untouchable castes, who with the help of Christian missionaries had become a teacher.[61]

The Andersons enjoyed the lush greenery of Ceylon and for part of the time stayed in a bungalow with an exotic landscape as their vista. They crisscrossed the island and marveled at its varied topography and climates, stopping in the dry lowland heat of Kandy on their way to the cold highlands of Nuwara Eliya, six thousand feet above sea level. From Colombo, they crossed the Palk Strait to Tuticorin (now Thoothukudi) in India. There they boarded a train for the five-day, arduous journey to Madras (Chennai).

Larz loved everything about the south of India and described the long, uncomfortable trip in glowing terms that expressed his enthusiasm for all they saw:

> The places and the people have been deeply interesting, and no one has really seen India who has not seen the South. The great deep temples, reeking and crowded, with the graven images all filthy with oil and water and faded flowers, where great elephants perform the daily duties, and noisy flutes and cymbals and drums are playing, and within which are gorgeous jewels and great cars and chariots and palanquins of gold and silver for the processions. And above all rises the grotesque and rich sculpture of the gopuras and around are the naked, wretched people, and it is all very, very wonderful.[62]

From Madras, they traveled across the subcontinent by train, reaching Bombay in the early morning hours of Christmas Eve 1898, in time to witness the spectacular arrival of the new viceroy and vicereine, Lord and Lady Curzon, on December 30. Larz knew Lady Curzon, the former Mary Leiter of Washington.[63] Her parents, Levi and "Mrs. Malaprop" Leiter, lived in Dupont Circle and were friends of Larz's parents. The Andersons attended the glittering evening reception in honor of the vice regal couple, who stood on a gold rug as they received their 1,400 guests.[64] In January, Larz and Isabel again saw the Curzons in Calcutta and lunched with them at Government House.

As they had in Italy, Larz and Isabel did very high-end shopping in India. They acquired the gemstones that became Isabel's signature piece of jewelry, the three-emerald pendant broach. In a letter written from Bombay in late December 1898, Larz said they had inspected some large emeralds and other jewels for sale in Madras that cost between $30,000 and $60,000 apiece.[65] Writing in 1931 about their first trip to India, Larz confirmed their purchase of gems:

> We also tried to find Tawker and Sons on the Mount Road, where we had our original bargaining for some jewels on the occasion of our first visit [1898], jewels that we were told belonged to some of the Mysore princes. At any rate the bargaining was a long game that lasted all the time that we made our tour of northern India and was only concluded on

arrival in Calcutta on the occasion of the durbars which we had attended in honour of the Curzons when he came as Vice Roy, and Mary Leiter had been very polite to us.[66]

The couple purchased Isabel's enormous emeralds at T. G. Tawker and Sons, a firm that traded in royal jewelry, including emeralds once owned by the Mogul emperor Shah Alum and by Tipu Sultan, the "Tiger of Mysore," in the eighteenth century.[67] Larz himself described the jewels' princely provenance and may have been the instigator of a rumor that Isabel received them as a secret gift from a maharaja who was smitten by her beauty. The emeralds cost between $90,000 and $180,000—several million dollars today.

Three Footholds

In January 1899, Larz wrote from Calcutta that he and Isabel had made decisions about their future. Elizabeth Anderson had already offered them her house at Sixteenth and K Streets as their Washington residence. "Now we may take it, and add to it, as we plan, and make Washington our winter home," Larz wrote, noting that doing so would allow him to "retain [his] residence [domicile] in Washington."[68]

They also decided to establish a double foothold in New England, with homes in Massachusetts and New Hampshire. Larz wrote they would try to get "the old Weld place" in Brookline. "It has a fine house on it, but one we do not like the style of, yet we could live in it and when we got the chance, later on, change it as we please and call it 'Weld Hall' or 'Weld Acres.'" Actually, it was Larz who wanted to change the house "as we please." Isabel always loved the old house and resisted Larz's attempts to replace it. They decided also to try to acquire The Box, her father's former property that her cousin Roger Foster had inherited from his uncle George. Larz called it "a retiring and real rough and ready country place."

The advantage of this plan, Larz calculated, was that he could claim title to three political jurisdictions. He had the choice of two jurisdictions should he wish to run for elected office, say, as a US senator. "If occasion advises I could change my place of residence to either Boston or New Hampshire," he said. Washington, the third jurisdiction, afforded him opportunity for political appointments without the complications of state governors and US senators. In the end, he concluded the three venues gave him and his wife "the very best in the way of comfort and the way of opportunity." As it turned out, he never ran for elected office and kept his domicile in Washington for the rest of his life.[69]

Larz and Isabel sailed from Bombay in early February 1899 bound for

Brindisi and from there onward to London by way of Paris, where their arrival was noted in a local newspaper.[70] Bhana Rutton, to whom they had become deeply attached, accompanied them. He agreed to work for them in America for a year and a half and said he would then return to India to arrange a marriage for his eight-year-old daughter. While he was in the United States, Bhana worked both at Weld and at Elizabeth Anderson's home in Washington. Though devoted to Larz and Isabel, he yearned to return to India. Elizabeth wrote to Larz that Bhana was waiting for "his master" [Larz] to let him leave.[71] Years later, Larz described Bhana as "a picturesque figure in our household, in his blue and gold dress and great turban, standing behind [Isabel's] chair" at dinner.[72]

At Port Said, the Andersons took advantage of a smaller boat that made an express crossing to Brindisi in under three days. They reached Rome at the end of February and were again met by the Elliotts and this time also by Isabel's cousin Roger Foster, who was wintering there. From Rome they went north to Paris and London and spent a few final weeks in each city. They sailed from Southampton at the end of March and reached Washington in time to enjoy the closing weeks of the season. In June, around the time of their second wedding anniversary, the couple went to Newport to spend the summer with Isabel's mother.[73]

It was now time to start a new life together in Washington, New Hampshire, and Massachusetts, according to the plan they had developed in India. Washington would host the public side of their life that Larz would shape, manage, and cultivate as he pleased. New Hampshire would be Isabel's respite from the high life to which Larz aspired. Brookline was to be the commons where they found their most perfect balance as husband and wife.

Figure 5. The Anderson estate, Brookline, ca. 1925.

V

A Country Place of Their Own (Brookline)

Brookline, Massachusetts, was already a fashionable suburb when Larz and Isabel Anderson acquired a summer home there in 1899. For decades, wealthy Bostonians had been building homes there, away from the noise, heat, and grime of the city. Summering in Brookline, just a few miles from Boston Common, made possible quick trips to the city for business or pleasure. Just as important as its proximity to Boston was Brookline's verdant, garden-like appearance: "The whole of this neighborhood of Brookline is a kind of landscape garden, and there is nothing in America of the sort, so inexpressibly charming as the lanes which lead from one cottage, or villa, to another ... there are more hints here for the lover of the picturesque in lanes than we ever saw assembled together in so small a compass."[1]

Brookline was also an important center of American architecture and landscape design. Its residents could hire local talent when they needed something done. The architect Henry Hobson Richardson, the landscape architect Frederick Law Olmsted, and the Harvard horticulturalist and arborist Charles Sprague Sargent were the pillars of this artistic community. Olmsted and Sargent collaborated on the design of the Arnold Arboretum located adjacent to Brookline. Sargent was a close friend of Isabel's parents and best man at their wedding. He served with George Perkins in the battles of New Orleans and Mobile Bay. As a child, Isabel accompanied her father to the Sargent estate every year to get a Christmas tree.[2] Isabella Stewart Gardner, longtime friend of Larz's parents, had a summer home in Brookline on an estate that included a greenhouse, formal gardens, and a collection of Japanese bonsai.

Isabel's three co-inheritor cousins—Mary Bryant Pratt (1871–1956), Charles Goddard Weld (1857–1911), and William "Billy" Fletcher Weld II (1855–1893)—also had homes in Brookline and nearby Jamaica Plain. When Isabel acquired the old Weld estate in Brookline at the request of her trustees, it was a homecoming for her.

In 1882, Billy acquired his grandfather's property in Brookline, then a plot of about twenty acres with a simple clapboard house on it. A hilltop rising some 110 feet at the center of the land inspired Grandfather Weld's name for his home there—Windy Top. Billy soon bought another fifty acres of adjacent land and began to transform the property into a modern country estate. He tore down his grandfather's house and erected a two-and-a-half-story shingle-style house (1887) designed by Edmund M. Wheelwright. The architect installed massive yet elegant semicircular retaining walls of pink Dedham granite on the eastern and western sides of the hilltop to create the large, level expanse of ground needed to build the house. He set the front entrance of the house facing east, giving guests a breathtaking vista of Boston and its harbor in the distance. The interiors were stylish and modern for their day. The ceiling of the white-and-gold drawing room was decorated with panels by Louis Comfort Tiffany.[3]

Billy's new house cost $90,000 to build and included such modern amenities as cast-iron steam radiators and combination gas-electric lighting fixtures. The ground floor comprised a large entry hall with a fireplace; billiard, drawing, and dining rooms; a study; and service areas: a butler's pantry, kitchen, servants' hall, laundry room, and a small, low-ceilinged guest lavatory tucked in under the main staircase.

Billy's expanded acreage included a barn and farmhouse named after the family that built them—the Snow barn and the Snow cottage.[4] The barn provided temporary stabling for Billy's horses and carriages when he first bought the property. (Both structures remained standing until the early 1960s.) As a wealthy and avid horseman, however, he needed more room for more horses. In 1889, at a cost of $40,000, he built a stone carriage house, also designed by Wheelwright, that provided many practical amenities for the estate: stables, work and storage areas, a tack room, and sleeping rooms for male staff. A sportsman, Billy also installed a polo field with a raised spectator area, a small golf course, and a bowling alley in the basement of the carriage house. He purchased several additional acres nearby to set up a dairy and hired the Boston architect Alexander Wadsworth Longfellow to design a cow barn for it.[5]

Billy did not get to enjoy his property for long. He died in 1893 at the age of thirty-five. Two years later, his widow, Ellen Winchester Weld, remarried. Her new husband, Herman B. Duryea Jr., descended from an old patroon family of New York, decided he had no interest in a summer home on the outskirts of Boston and instead wanted a summer home at Old Westbury on Long Island.[6] Ellen had grown up in Taunton and, as Isabel's attorney Roger Amory later said, was "not a proper Bostonian."[7] Herman Duryea did not want the Brookline property but decided the Weld family had been unfair to his wife by "not giving her enough of her late husband's property," according to Amory. Duryea saw the Brookline property as a bargaining chip and filed suits in Philadelphia Orphan's Court, where Grandfather Weld's will had been probated a decade earlier, against Billy's brother, Charles Goddard Weld, and the Weld trust itself.

The court ruled against Duryea, finding that Charles had in fact been too generous toward Ellen under the terms of the trust. The court ordered Duryea to pay restitution to Charles. Bostonians did not like Duryea's lawsuit against the Weld family and treated the Duryeas accordingly. "He was black balled at certain clubs. They were anxious to get him out of town," Amory said. The idea that the Duryeas would continue to own and occupy a Weld property rankled the family. "The feeling [against the Duryeas] was very high."

The trustees decided Isabel should take over the property, but to avoid tipping off Duryea that they wanted it back in Weld hands, they asked the real estate agent William E. Lincoln to buy it from Duryea on behalf of "an unnamed client."[8] At the time of the sale, the property was worth $300,000. Lincoln kept the property without disclosing who the client was. He then sold the property to the trust, which transferred it to Isabel on April 27, 1899, charging the purchase price against her trust fund. The press took notice of the sale. On May 16, 1899, the *Washington Post* carried a short report of the transaction, noting that the Andersons would occupy the house during the coming summer.[9]

Transforming Weld

For Isabel, the Brookline property was a direct link to her maternal grandfather, and so they named it Weld in his honor.[10] Billy had acquired the land when Isabel was six and built the Wheelwright house when she was eleven, so she had some childhood memories of both her grandfather's house on the property, Windy Top, and Billy's house. Indeed, she had a deep emotional attachment to the land and to Billy's house for the rest of her life. After Larz's death in 1937 she vacated the regal-sized bedroom suite Larz had installed for her in the 1914–1916 expansion of Billy's house and moved into the smallest bedroom in the old part of the house. (See figure 10.)

In contrast to Isabel, who liked the property as it was, the new property was a blank canvas for Larz. Here he could execute his vision of a country estate that incorporated European and Japanese aesthetics. He never got the chance to tear down Billy's house and start anew, but he had free rein when it came to landscapes and gardens. He eventually expanded and remodeled the Wheelwright house to something more his style but waited almost fifteen years to do so. In the meantime, there was plenty else to keep him busy. Larz's first priority was creating an exquisite Italian garden to define the aesthetics that would guide future development of the sprawling estate. His vision for the estate was linked intimately to the Italian garden's location, design, and scale. Indeed, the garden became the estate's nexus.

The Italian Garden

Sometime in 1899 or 1900, Larz began working with the landscape architect Charles A. Platt (1861–1933) to design a classically inspired *giardino segreto* (secret garden) for Weld.[11] Construction took about a year and was completed in 1901, the year that Isabel came into her full inheritance. In 1897 Platt had designed a large Italian garden for Isabel's cousin May Sprague at her estate in nearby Jamaica Plain, so the Andersons had firsthand knowledge of his work. The garden Platt designed for Larz and Isabel, however, was on a much-grander scale and of a more complex design than the Sprague garden, and just about everything else Platt ever did. (See figure 6.)

The Andersons chose the spot where Grandfather Weld's house once stood as the site of the new garden. Though sometimes called the first formal Italian garden in America, the Andersons' garden came four years after May Sprague's was completed. Nonetheless, during the Andersons' lifetime the Italian garden at Weld was their most famous project, even more so than Anderson House in Washington. This was due in no small measure to Larz's active and successful promotion of the garden to journalists, writers, and academics as a subject for magazine articles, teaching, and study. In 1929, a typical year for Anderson garden tours, 338 professors, students, and members of professional gardening and landscaping organizations visited the garden. Larz himself took most of these visitors on the tour and interpreted the garden and its features for them.

The Andersons' Italian garden was not a stand-alone installation. It was part of a larger system of adjacent and connected green spaces and architectural elements that formed outdoor "rooms" integral to how the Andersons used the house and gardens for their personal enjoyment and for entertaining guests and the general public. Platt grounded his work in the concept of garden areas that functioned as "rooms," which in turn defined the relationship between indoor and outdoor spaces: "The architect proceeded with the idea that not only was the house to be lived in, but that one still wished to be at home while out-of-doors; so the garden was designed as another apartment, the terraces and groves still others, where one might walk about and find a place suitable to the hour of the day and feeling of the moment, and still be in that sacred portion of the globe dedicated to one's self."[12] His concept of garden spaces as rooms that were connected to each other and to the mansion drove every major landscaping design project at Weld over the next two decades, even when other designers such as Little and Browne or Fox and Gale did the work.

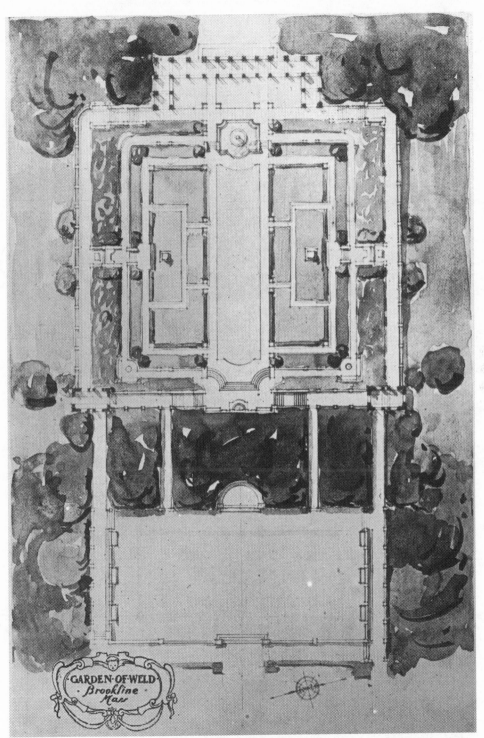

Figure 6. Charles A. Platt's watercolor of the Anderson Italian Garden.

The positioning of the Italian garden relative to the Wheelwright house was a clue to this grander vision: Platt's design was off-center to Billy's house, and its massive size overwhelmed the modest proportions of the house, even though the new garden was placed some distance from it. Larz planned one day to tear down Billy Weld's house and replace it with something much larger that was closer to and on-center with the garden.

The size and placement of two other garden elements anticipated the future new residence. Platt designed a wide expanse of lawn, a *tapis vert* (green carpet) that reflected his vision of formal outdoor spaces as "apartments," and an adjacent bosquet (grove) of pines planted in regimented rows.[13] The Andersons called the *tapis vert* the bowling green. The bosquet produced a verdant wall of trees that hid the Italian garden. The *tapis vert* and the bosquet were further demarcated from each other by an exedra placed between them, much as a sofa would be placed against a wall. Benches were installed on two of the other sides of the bowling green. It was like an outdoor living room with furniture (see figure 6).

Access to the Italian garden itself was along two parallel paths through the bosquet that, like hallways of a house, led from one room (the bowling green) to another (the Italian garden). There was no direct view into the garden from the bowling green. Visitors walked down these shaded gravel paths and then, without warning, stepped into the brilliant, light-infused interior of the Italian garden, filled with a profusion of colors, shapes, sounds, perspectives, and elevations.

The Italian garden was immense. It measured 206 feet by 196 feet—over 40,300 square feet. (By comparison, a football field is 57,600 square feet.) Its main features included a central mall, two fountains, two gazebos, a pergola, and two promenades. The elevated promenades produced ever-changing views for visitors. Walking seven times around the upper promenade was a distance of a little over a mile. A band of trees circled the outside perimeter of the garden, providing additional privacy and a dark-green backdrop for the garden's architectural elements executed in white limestone and marble.

The presentation of the garden was conceived as an almost-theatrical experience for visitors, designed to create anticipation and then amazement. The garden was infused not only with color but also with sound and light. Period photographs of the garden show birdcages placed on top of decorative columns throughout the garden. Songbirds filled the garden with soothing chirps and warbles. Along with the gentle sound of water splashing in the fountain and basins, this produced a soundscape integral to the garden's aesthetics. Isabel's squawking parrot was a summer resident of the garden who greeted visitors with a loud "Halloa!" The pergola was fitted with rows of electric lightbulbs hidden in its skylighted roof, making possible spectacular and well-lit nighttime events. Visually, there was something to catch the eye at every angle: whimsical topiaries shaped like animals, little people, and geometric forms; large, decorative pieces of glazed earthenware pottery; and carved marble urns and benches.

The traditional Italian gardens that influenced landscape architecture in America in the early nineteenth century were planted only with evergreens (for example, boxwood, bay trees, and topiaries) and water plants such as pond lilies. Larz's grandfather Nicholas Longworth had such a formal garden behind his home on Pike Street in Cincinnati. Though Larz's great-grandparents Nicholas and Susana died a few years before he was born, his Anderson grandparents lived next door to the Longworth house for many years. Like a conversation on garden design between Larz and his great-grandfather, the central mall, trellised pergolas, and the evergreen and floral plantings in Nicholas Longworth's nineteenth-century garden in Cincinnati all reappeared in the Andersons' twentieth-century garden in Brookline.

The Brookline firm of Olmsted Brothers designed a traditional arrangement of plantings for the Italian garden. (See figure 12, chapter 6.) The green areas were filled in with lawns and evergreens in formal, symmetrical patterns. Larz soon supplemented or replaced this design with other types of formal plantings. He made two trips to Holland between 1902 and 1905 to purchase bay trees and topiaries. Within a few years, however, the Andersons' Italian garden took on a uniquely different appearance from the Italian examples that had inspired it—perhaps at Isabel's suggestion, for she loved flowers of all types. The Anderson gardeners laid out new planting schemes that produced a colorful profusion of flowers during each of New England's three growing seasons. Some of the plantings included crocuses, daffodils, and tulips in the spring; columbine, foxglove, and roses in midsummer; and Hall's honeysuckle in late summer.[14] In winter months, the greenhouse was the surrogate Italian garden—full of flowers, including lilies, hibiscus, and daffodils that bloomed in the midst of a snowy estate.[15]

While Platt worked on the Italian garden, the Andersons hired the Boston architectural firm of Thomas A. Fox and Edwards J. Gale to plan a horticultural and agricultural complex to supply flowers and food for the estate. Work started in 1901 and was completed in 1902. Fox and Gale designed garden walls, a garden shed, a toolhouse, a bay pit for storing the Dutch bay trees and topiaries in winter, and a year-round residence for the head gardener. The architects chose a foursquare style, derived from the Prairie School of architecture, for the superintendent's cottage. This was the only house the Andersons ever built in an American vernacular style.

The New York City firm of Lord & Burnham worked closely with Fox and Gale to design, manufacture, and install an elaborate greenhouse that included a round atrium and two rectangular wings, a heating system for the greenhouse and adjacent bay pit, and in-ground cold frames.

In 1902, Larz again commissioned Fox and Gale to design additional landscape elements for the estate: an *allée* (two parallel rows of trees creating a walkway between them) with opposing exedras on the lower front lawn, a large basin with a fountain in another area of the front lawn, a tennis court on the western flank of the hilltop, and a rose garden on a gently sloping hill just below the Italian garden. Several years later, in the wooded area above the rose garden, Larz installed what he called his *"Heintzelmenschen* colony,"* painted terra-cotta gnome figurines from Germany, two feet high, posed in amusing pastimes: "smoking, sitting, digging, lounging—such absurd figures as Germans love to have in their gardens," Larz said.[16] Newspapers sometimes called this the "German Garden" or the "Bavarian Garden." Larz loved showing it off to visitors. After Isabel's death, the gnomes were moved to The Box in New Hampshire, where they continued to delight many generations of Isabel's cousins. In recent years, a house fire destroyed the gnomes.[17]

The Gardens of Weld

Although famous primarily for its Italian garden, Weld had other distinctive gardens and landscapes built after the 1900–1903 projects that further contributed to the concept of outdoor spaces as "rooms" on the estate. Around 1907, the Andersons installed a Japanese garden near the bowling green. Their Japanese gardener and interior decorator, Oshige Shinnosuke, oversaw this work. The garden included water elements, stepping-stones that led to a little bridge, and a large collection of stone lanterns, water basins, and statues artfully arranged among small-scale evergreens and decorative plantings. Two large features towered over the garden: a twenty-foot-high replica of Mount Fuji and a spread-winged eagle perched on top of a stone column that imitated a rustic tree trunk. (The eagle is now owned by Boston College, a gift of Isabel's private secretary, Gus Anderson, in 1954.) Visitors entered the garden through large wooden gates that reinforced the sense of walking into another room. In 1909, Isabel published an article in *House and Garden* magazine describing Oshige's work: "Here and there among the greens are bright-colored bowls with grotesque designs, and grey stone lanterns. Above you rises the huge bronze eagle; he is the one high point, the key of the Japanese garden. His piercing eye looks down to frighten you, but, reflected in the smooth surface of a pool near by, sits the calm and smiling Buddha to dispel the fear; and so peace and happiness pervade this little fragment of the far East."[18]

The Andersons offered their guests tea in this delightful and exotic garden, serving "clear green tea" in "tiny porcelain cups," accompanied by bamboo and silver pipes of tobacco and plates of sweetmeats.

There was another prominent Japanese element to the Andersons' landscaped environment—a *gorinto* they bought in Japan in 1913. Based on the architecture of pagodas, a *gorinto* serves as a funeral memorial or grave marker, and each of its five levels has a philosophical concept associated with it. At the top, the jewel-shaped stone represents perfection. Four other symbolic pieces are stacked below the jewel: a crescent for receptivity, a triangle for unification, a sphere for wisdom, and at the bottom a cube representing the four elements (air, fire, water, and earth). The Andersons' *gorinto*, still standing on the property, is a funeral monument to Hachi Ro Zaemon, a member of the Samurai class who died on June 28, 1705.[19]

The Andersons also wanted their estate to reflect English tastes in garden and landscape design. Larz learned about this style during his years in England, where gardens appear to be more haphazard than they really are. A flower garden in the English style achieves its appearance through the gardener's balance of the color, size, and shape of the blooms, and variations in plant height. When the Andersons decided to replace the evergreen plantings Olmsted Brothers had designed for the Italian garden with profusely blooming flowers, they blended English garden influences into the traditional Italian design that dominated the space.

A landscape in the English style artfully arranges trees, shrubbery, and ground cover to create the effect of being undisturbed nature rather than a formal design. The greatest American practitioner of this style in the nineteenth century was Frederick Law Olmsted. In 1910, Little and Browne began designing an English landscape garden for the estate's low-lying area, but Larz halted work during the year and a half they were in Belgium and Japan. Construction resumed after their return, and the English garden was ready in 1916. It was a masterpiece of landscape design and engineering.

One Garden, Four Themes

The centerpiece of the English landscape garden, which the Andersons sometimes called the water garden, was an artificial lagoon created out of an area of the estate already prone to flooding. Gently sloping lawns and hills sent rainwater and melting snow down into the lowest part of the estate, where it gathered in a man-made lagoon that drained excess water off the estate through a spillway. This was an ingenious way to create a large water element for the garden that also prevented flooding and mudflats in low-lying areas.

Three distinctive architectural elements around the lagoon provided visual interest for visitors: a *tempietto* (a domed circular temple) with an adjoining *allée*, and a two-hundred-foot-long trellised garden walkway with a Chinese pagoda towering over it. The presence of a *tempietto* in the English garden was a direct reference to Rome. There the Villa Borghese, which Larz knew well, includes a large English garden with a *tempietto* dedicated to Diana, the goddess of both hunting and childbirth. Local people today believe Larz and Isabel built the *tempietto* in the hope they might have children. In keeping with that legend, the structure—now known popularly as the Temple of Love—provides a setting for engagement and wedding photography.

The *rond point*, a low circular wall with four openings (something like a circus ring), was located near the *tempietto* at the eastern end of the lagoon. Fountains and statues depicting the four seasons identified each opening. The Andersons sometimes called it the Court of the Four Seasons for this reason. It connected to an *allée* of trees that led to a trellised gazebo, where a lion's head spouted water into a basin. The fountain is still there, though hidden in the undergrowth. A hillside of gently sloping lawn above the *rond point* had room for two thousand spectators. The Andersons carefully planned this area of the estate as a venue for outdoor theatrical, musical, and dance performances. It was an early version of the arena theater concept that increased in popularity over the course of the twentieth century. Isabel once called it an "outdoor stage."[20] The *allée* provided an entrance and exit path to the circle for performers. The gazebo at the far end served as a true "green room" where performers could await their cues or change costumes.

The gazebo at the end of the *allée* connected to a chinoiserie trellised walkway, two hundred feet long and some twenty feet wide. This feature was inspired by the royal gardens at Laeken that the couple had visited in 1912 when Larz had served as American minister to Belgium. A tall pagoda tower of latticework halfway between the two ends of the walkway created a striking focal point in the English garden's vista. The far end of the walkway also ended in a gazebo, this one housing a Greek statue rather than a fountain. From this point, another walkway connected to a causeway over the lagoon. The causeway offered a place for strollers to stop and admire a view of the *tempietto* across the water.

Continuing on their way across the causeway, walkers then turned onto a woodland path that made its way along the water's edge back to the *rond point*. Each walkway presented a different landscape architecture concept: *allée*, trellised walkway, causeway, and woodland path. This extended Platt's concept of rooms and passageways from the Italian garden complex on the top of the hill to the four-part English garden below it. (See figure 7.)

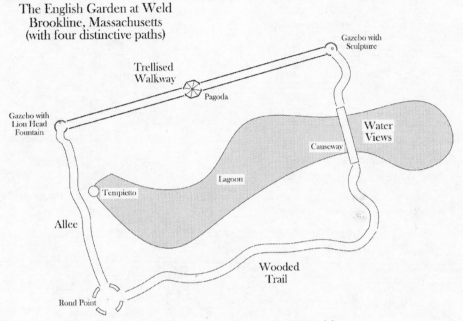

The English Garden at Weld
Brookline, Massachusetts
(with four distinctive paths)

Gazebo with Sculpture

Trellised Walkway

Pagoda

Gazebo with Lion Head Fountain

Water Views

Causeway

Lagoon

Tempietto

Allee

Wooded Trail

Rond Point

Figure 7. The garden system of Weld.

A set of rough drawings in Larz's hand titled "Sketches suggesting terrace and fountain arrangement for hillside above the Rond Pointe [*sic*]" suggest he planned to connect the Italian and English garden systems on the estate.[21] Once he sketched out the plan, Larz commissioned a three-dimensional model of the hillside structure that showed four levels of terraces connected by stairways, a fountain, and a rustic grotto. A photograph of the model survives in a scrapbook housed at the Larz Anderson Auto Museum in Brookline. Almost certainly, the concept came from Platt. His book *Italian Gardens* shows just such a hillside structure at the Villa d'Este in Italy: a massive villa at the top of a hill connected by a long, elegant terraced stairway with fountains and other water elements to a *rond point* at the bottom of the hill.[22] (See figure 8.) Had this outdoor stairway complex ever been built at Weld, a visitor would have been able to pass through Italian and Japanese gardens, proceed down a grand stairway to a *rond point*, stroll through an *allée* to a long walkway inspired by Chinese pagodas, cross a causeway with splendid views of an English garden and Roman *tempietto*, and finish with a walk through a shaded woodland reminiscent of Isabel's beloved New Hampshire. It was a spectacular concept.

Figure 8. What Weld might have looked like if Larz had gotten his way.

Larz and Isabel brought their experience of gardens in many places around the world to their Brookline estate. They had seen many Italian gardens together during their courtship in Italy, Larz knew the parks and gardens of Paris and London, and they had toured gardens in Japan together on their first wedding trip. Like other cosmopolitan collectors and connoisseurs of the Gilded Age, they drew on this eclectic background to produce a unique garden aesthetic of their own.

Expanding the Mansion at Weld

Almost as soon as they bought Billy's house in 1899, they began a yearlong project to update and modernize some of its amenities.[23] The first project was installation of a bathroom in Isabel's bedroom suite, with new tile walls and a $4,200 marble bathtub. They also redecorated the rest of the house, including new electrical lighting fixtures from the firms of J. E. Caldwell & Co. in Philadelphia and Shreve, Crump & Low in Boston. Larz said the new fixtures in the dining room were "horns of plenty out of which lights project."[24] Other rooms got new carpets, wallpaper, wall hangings, table lamps, and furniture. They also bought two pianos, an upright and a mahogany Louis XVI grand piano. They added another modern convenience, a long-distance telephone, although telegrams remained their preferred mode of urgent communication all their lives.[25] They made no further changes to the mansion for the next fifteen years.

In 1914, the year after the Andersons returned from Larz's brief diplomatic service under Taft (see chapters 12 and 13), they at last started the process of expanding and renovating Billy's house. It is not clear why they waited so long or why Larz did not get his wish to tear down the old house and build a new one. Nonetheless, the year and a half abroad gave him many ideas for the project. They had lived in a former royal residence in Brussels, visited great country homes in England and Belgium, and dined with monarchs, royalty, and aristocrats. Now styling himself as Ambassador Anderson, Larz wanted a grand home in Brookline to match his stature.

Though the firm of Arthur Little and Herbert W. C. Browne has generally been credited with the 1914–1916 expansion of the house, Larz himself came up with its architectural concepts. Little and Browne provided refinements, engineering, and construction planning services.[26] To achieve the structural mass and positioning of the mansion required by the size of the Italian garden, Larz conceived a broad facade facing the garden that gave the impression of belonging to a much-larger structure. Behind this, a jumbled and disorienting assemblage of stone and concrete additions, wings, porticos, porches, terraces, steps, parapets, and towers clumsily moved the mass of the house forward stepwise until it was on center with the Italian garden. The additions juxtaposed English medieval, Italian renaissance, and neoclassical elements. Larz applied his knowledge of European architecture to his own sense of place in history to produce a country home that pleased and inspired him.

In an unsuccessful attempt to conceal the major design and engineering defect of the expanded house—attaching a stone-and-concrete addition to what was essentially a wood frame house—the shingled portions of the old mansion and the walls of the new sections were covered with gray stucco on wooden laths. Mica flakes in the stucco added strength and, on sunny days, made the house appear brighter. A fragment of stucco found on the site of the mansion, along with examination of a concrete pergola near the house that was built at the same time as the additions and is still standing, suggests that the stucco had a slightly pinkish hue and thus coordinated with the pink Dedham granite of the retaining walls. The seams between the old and new house were never watertight, and the mansion's roofing needed constant upkeep and repair for the next forty years.[27]

Larz infused the additions with references to Weld and Anderson family history, including his own biography. The largest and most directly visible external reference was to the Weld family's origins in England. Two matching towers anchoring the facade that faced the bowling green replicated those of Lulworth Castle in England, the ancestral home of the Roman Catholic branch of the Weld family, to which Isabel was distantly related. Isabel traced her roots in the New World to immigrant Protestant ancestors on both the Weld and Perkins sides of her family. Even though Larz was a devout Episcopalian who once likened Roman Catholicism to [Hindu] "Heathenism,"[28] there was a castle in Weld family history—albeit owned by the Catholics who stayed behind in England three centuries earlier—and he was determined to claim its architecture as their own. The facade incorporated a garish pixie-statue fountain rescued from the fine arts building of the 1915 San Francisco Exposition, and the logo of Grandfather Weld's Black Horse fleet of clipper ships capped the arch over the fountain. Along the upper tier of the facade, three niches held busts of the American presidents under whom Anderson men had served in the military: George Washington, Abraham Lincoln, and William McKinley. Larz wrote a memorandum summarizing the military service of Anderson men under each of these three presidents, including his own: "McKinley. Larz Anderson. Captain and Assistant Adjutant General of Volunteers; Acting Adjutant of Division in the War with Spain."[29] The facade, surmounted by four immense classical funeral urns several feet high draped in floral garlands, was Gilded Age kitsch at its best.

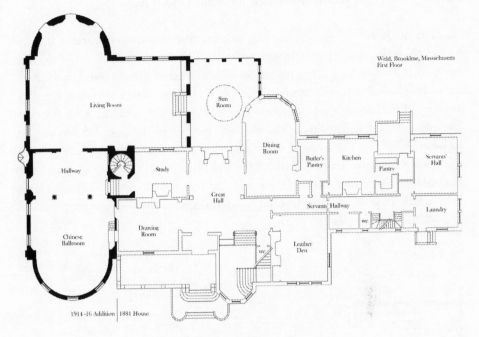

Living Room

Sun Room

Dining Room

Hallway

Study

Butler's Pantry

Kitchen

Pantry

Servants' Hall

Great Hall

Servants' Hallway

Laundry

Chinese Ballroom

Drawing Room

wc

Leather Den

wc

1914-16 Addition | 1881 House

Figure 9. Ground floor of Weld.

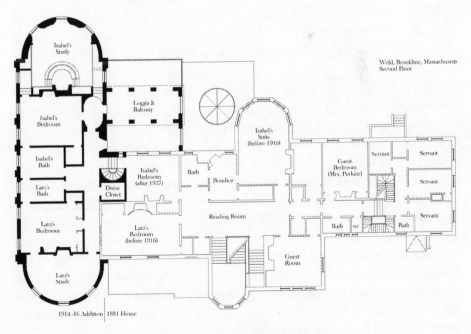

Isabel's Study

Loggia & Balcony

Isabel's Suite (before 1916)

Isabel's Bedroom

Guest Bedroom (Mrs. Perkins)

Servant

Servant

Isabel's Bath

Isabel's Bedroom (after 1937)

Bath

Boudoir

Servant

Larz's Bath

Dress Closet

Larz's Bedroom

Reading Room

Bath

wc

Bath

Servant

Larz's Bedroom (before 1916)

Larz's Study

Guest Room

1914-16 Addition | 1881 House

Figure 10. Second floor of Weld.

The scale of the expanded house was, like the Italian garden it was keyed to, immense. The additions totaled 11,800 square feet. Billy Weld's house originally had 9,200 square feet of space (all of which remained intact after the 1914–1916 renovations). In its new configuration, the mansion was around 21,000 square feet.[30] To create high ceilings on the ground floor of the addition, the elevations of the old and the new portions of the house had to be misaligned. The ground floor of the addition was approximately three feet lower than the ground floor of the old house, and the new second floor was about three feet higher than its counterpart. Together, these offsets created about six feet of additional ceiling height in the new public rooms of the addition.[31] (See figure 11.)

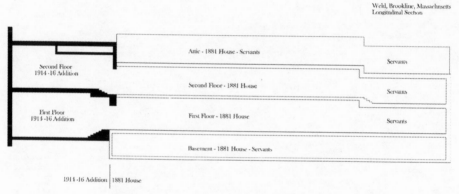

Figure 11. Longitudinal section of Weld.

The new ground floor was very grand. A 1,700-square-foot living room, as the Andersons called it, was modeled after the library of the Palais d'Assche in Brussels, where they had lived when Larz was minister to Belgium.[32] The fireplace, an exact replica of one in the Palais d'Assche, was large enough to stand in. The living room connected to a 750-square-foot conservatory surmounted by a glass dome. Its walls were decorated with murals of the cities where Larz served in the diplomatic corps: London, Rome, Brussels, and Tokyo. The Spanish Steps in Rome and Somerset House in London (built in 1776) represented his service in those cities. During the years Larz was in London in the late nineteenth century, Somerset House was home to the Royal Academy of Arts, the Royal Society, and the Society of Antiquaries. There is no record why Larz chose Somerset House to symbolize his London post. The conservatory was furnished with oversized wicker throne chairs made by prisoners in the Philippines.[33]

On the other side of the house, overlooking Boston, Larz added a

960-square-foot chinoiserie-style ballroom furnished with teak pieces that once belonged to Grandfather Weld. He hung several floor-to-ceiling Chinese paintings depicting birds and trees in the spaces between the windows.[34] A vestibule of 400 square feet that opened directly to the Chinese ballroom resulted in a total area of about 1,400 square feet.

The second floor of the addition contained the most unique set of rooms ever designed for the Andersons: two elaborate bedroom suites joined by a narrow corridor that together made up the entire second floor of the Lulworth Castle–inspired tower addition. Isabel's west-facing suite included a large semicircular study decorated with classical elements of Japanese interior design—sliding *fusama* screens and *ranma* transom panels—and a concave settee sunk into the floor around a fireplace. This was an early take on the conversation pits that became popular in midcentury American interior design. In addition to a bedroom with another fireplace, Isabel's suite also included an oval vestibule, a ten-by-ten-foot walk-in closet with fifty linear feet of clothing racks, and a large bathroom. The vestibule provided Isabel with direct access to her own private loggia and balcony with views that stretched to Mount Wachusett some fifty miles away. On the east side of the addition, with views of downtown Boston, Larz's suite included a smaller semicircular study, a bedroom, an elaborate bathroom with both a tub and a stall shower, and fireplaces in each room. Doors connected the suites to each other.

Public and Private Spaces

In the first eighteen years that Larz and Isabel owned Weld, they spent at least $350,000 on decorating and expanding the mansion's interior spaces and on adding extensive gardening and landscape features.[35] Much of this went to more than doubling the square footage of the mansion, though the expansions were for the Andersons' own private enjoyment, not for entertaining indoors on a large scale. Even if an immense ballroom, vestibule, and living room had been added, there were no commensurate new facilities for entertaining on a larger scale. The additions made no allowance for increased dining capacity, for example. The dining room remained unchanged (450 square feet), as did the kitchen (180 square feet). In comparison, the dining room of the Andersons' Washington mansion is 1,075 square feet and the kitchen, 775 square feet. There also were no new guest lavatories. Before and after the expansion there was only one small restroom under the main staircase in the old part of the house. The new ballroom, large enough for at least two hundred guests, would not be used for a function that large until decades after the expansion was completed.

The additions were clearly intended for Larz's and Isabel's enjoyment. Filled with a lifetime of memories, the mansion's rooms and decorations were an expression of Larz's and Isabel's sense of place in the world—and their relationship with each other. Only the most intimate of friends and family made their way into the mansion's spacious and comfortable interiors.

The couple's use of vast outdoor public spaces in Brookline to entertain strangers and large indoor public spaces at Anderson House to entertain celebrities and friends made for an interesting dichotomy. In Washington, the grand scale of the home's interior spaces was meant to impress the high and mighty of Washington. In Brookline, their landscape and garden aesthetics were meant to impress the world at large. The grounds provided a breathtaking stage for events and entertainments that brought thousands of people to the estate, most of them complete strangers to Larz and Isabel.

Hail, Hail, O Chandler Halo,
my Successor ! ! ! ! ! ! ! ! !

Figure 12. The Italian garden at Weld, ca. 1905.

VI

LIFE AT WELD

Larz was happiest when he was alone with Isabel at Weld, the Andersons' estate in Brookline. This was the emotional and spiritual core of their life together, as Larz once described: "Weld has been a happy home and I would n't wish one single thing changed about it or our life here. For almost thirty years ... it has been the setting of a beautiful Home, beautiful inside and outside, and it has developed its character and charm by embellishment of its gardens outside and our spiritual life inside."[1]

More than a country home, more than a place to entertain, it was the center of their life together. "Our roots are set here and spread in Washington," Larz said in 1928 about their life in Brookline. "I shall be content if I may live out my life in these settings that are so familiar and radiant with happy memories: I have been blessed indeed."[2]

What made the mansion "so familiar and radiant with happy memories" was its vast collection of memorabilia representing every important moment of their lives together. It was a repository for their personal and family papers and their large book collection. In the living room, extensive built-in bookcases with fluted-fabric doors housed hundreds of books inscribed to Larz and Isabel by their authors. The cases also held a series of a hundred or more folios exquisitely bound in red Moroccan leather with gold-leaf lettering. These were the core of Larz's and Isabel's literary output: Larz's own typescript journals, Isabel's bound diaries, and several dozen bound copies of magazines that published articles by Isabel or about the couple.[3] Massive Italian bookcases filled with art and reference books lined the large rectangular landing on the second floor that the Andersons used as a reading room.

Walls and tabletops everywhere displayed hundreds of elegantly framed photographs, certificates, diplomas, letters, and clippings of newspaper photographs and articles about them. The rooms were packed with an eclectic collection of furnishings, *objets d'art*, bric-a-brac, and souvenirs of their trips, including Larz's assemblage of hats and canes from around the world.[4] The walls were hung with commissioned works of art—oils, watercolors, pastels, and pencil drawings—depicting places that were especially meaningful to them, such as a pencil sketch of the Arlington Street Church where they were married or a pastel of an interior of the Palais d'Assche.[5]

Larz and Isabel found many ways to entertain themselves on their estate, indoors and out. They strolled the diverse garden pathways that crisscrossed the estate and visited their greenhouses where lush tropical plants and colorful flowers bloomed year-round. They played tennis on their splendid court and went canoeing on their lagoon. (Their canoe now hangs from the rafters of the Larz Anderson Auto Museum.) They worked separately in their own private studies and came together in the Leather Room, their cozy little den in the old part of the house that had once been Billy Weld's billiard room, for afternoon tea or cocktails. Isabel's upright piano in the White Drawing Room of the old part of the house provided another source of entertainment. They also enjoyed quiet pastimes of playing two-handed card games and listening to the radio together.

Larz installed their first radio in 1923, about two years after commercial broadcasts of news and music started in the United States. He had the antennae strung between the mansion's chimneys and the wires run down into the Leather Room. There they listened to news and musical programs. Larz called the radio an instrument. Early radios looked like pieces of scientific equipment rather than pieces of furniture. Larz loved tuning in to broadcasts from outside the Boston area: Atlanta, Schenectady, New York City, and Philadelphia. He was delighted one year when he found a broadcast of church bells in Montreal ringing in the New Year. They sometimes listened to church services on the radio too, though Larz decided that radio church services were irreverent. During one radio sermon he switched it off. "I … looked about and saw all the people about me in the room smoking and lolling. I quickly shut it off for it seemed to be shocking," he said. "It prevents all reverence."[6]

Weld meant many things to many other people. To Larz and Isabel's inner circle of friends and family, the Anderson summer home and gardens in Brookline were perfect settings for memorable holiday dinners, birthdays, anniversaries, and weekend house parties. To the general public, Weld was a venue for large and spectacular events that included music, theater, dance, fund-raisers, and even dog shows. To the Andersons' twenty-odd live-in servants, the estate was the source of their livelihood and the home where they raised their families.

Entertaining Friends and Family

Larz and Isabel loved to entertain their friends and family at intimate luncheons and dinner parties at Weld. They also enjoyed hosting the occasional celebrity, especially those who wanted to stay out of the limelight during a visit to Boston. The small scale of the mansion's dining room and outdoor terraces was perfectly suited for groups of six or eight couples. The twin gazebos in the Italian garden, each large enough to accommodate tables for up to six couples, provided a delightful outdoor venue for elegant meals.

Entertainment at Weld often marked important milestones of the Andersons' life together, and the couple invited their closest friends and family for these celebrations. In June 1933, on the occasion of their thirty-sixth anniversary, they invited all the original members of their wedding party to dinner. The guests included best man Charles Francis Adams III and his wife, Frances Lovering Adams; usher Frederick Josiah Bradlee Sr. and his wife, Elizabeth Thomas Bradlee (sister of Malcolm Thomas, Larz's round-the-world travel companion in 1888–1889); and two bridesmaids, Eleanor Lyman Gray and her husband, Dr. Henry Dubois Tudor, and Elizabeth Sears Seabury and her husband, Henry Ashbury Christian.

Celebrities sometimes visited Weld at the request of friends of the Andersons. Such visitors enjoyed the same kind of hospitality Larz and Isabel extended to friends and family—on a smaller and more intimate scale than in Washington. These visitors were mostly known for their family connections and are now long forgotten. The Duke of Abruzzi, Prince Luigi Amedeo, a cousin of King Victor Emmanuel III of Italy, visited Weld in 1907. The couple made full use of the Italian garden to entertain the duke at a convivial luncheon:

> The music was quite a success; I put them under the tent to one side and they played sweet soft music that really sounded just far enough off to be magical. Isabel received at the far end of the garden under the pergola, to which we moved the green chairs with their red cushions, so the guests had the whole garden to view, and could sit in the shade of the vine arbor as we gathered—while the fountain played. The tables under the gazebos looked very well, and when tiffin was announced each party passed by its upper terrace to the luncheon, and the luncheon was quite well served.[7]

Prince Fushimi Hiroyasu, a member of the Japanese imperial family, came to Weld in 1910. Alfonso de Orleans y Bourbón, cousin of King Alfonso XIII of Spain, visited the estate in 1928.

On a few occasions, true newsmakers stayed at Weld. In October 1931, Marshal Philippe Pétain, a French World War I hero (later found guilty of treason for collaborating with the Nazis during World War II), was a houseguest at Weld for two nights at the request of Larz's cousin in

Paris, Countess Clara Longworth de Chambrun. The marshal was in the United States as a member of France's delegation to the sesquicentennial celebration of the victory at Yorktown. He wanted to make what Larz called an "incognito" visit to Boston, and Larz was happy to oblige. As part of their entertainment of the French war hero, Larz and Isabel arranged a dinner party at Weld and invited their francophone friends.[8]

The Andersons held very few events that made full use of the mansion's post-1916 capacity. Indeed, the first large indoor event they hosted was a coming-out dance for Isabel's young cousin Polly Gardiner in November 1933. This was the first time they entertained on this scale in the Brookline house. "In Washington it would have been easy with its arrangements and space, but here we had to move furniture and mix things up for several days," Larz said.[9] More than 200 people came to the party: 60 girls, 140 boys, an unknown number of mothers, and the 10-piece Ruby Newman Orchestra. Larz opened his liquor locker generously, serving sixty-two bottles of champagne, "several cases of gin," and an "excellent claret punch."

There were other very large parties, but, with one exception, these were outdoors. Larz hosted five of his Harvard class reunions at Weld between 1903 and 1933. As the 1928 reunion approached, a rumor started that wives could attend. This was not Larz's idea of a class reunion. He thought that only the classmates—men—should attend. When the class secretary prankishly sent out invitations to classmates and wives, Larz had to alter his arrangements. More than 120 people attended, making it the second-largest private party the Andersons gave at Weld. It had been planned as an outdoor event, but when reunion day arrived, it poured rain, and everyone had to move indoors at the last minute. Larz's account of the day provides a rare look into the details of a large Anderson party:

> Yet it all went off beautifully, for all were so glad to get in out of the rain, and find fires and brightly laid tables and excellent music, that they were crowded together and close contact made the meet more general, there was gaiety and singing and a really jolly time. The salon by the entrance door made a splendid bar room, and I can only say that there was some champagne left over. I had tried out mint juleps, thinking some of the class might arrive early ... and they proved a great success.[10]

In the end, Larz was more than pleased by the participation of the wives. He decided "the 'classmated' behaved very nicely so that if I ever had another reunion (which I am determined I shall never have) I might suggest having only the wives and not the classmates!"[11] Larz hosted only one more reunion, the forty-fifth in 1933, and that reverted to stag—no wives allowed.

As a lifelong member of the '95 Sewing Circle, a small women's club started in 1893, Isabel regularly planned club luncheons at the mansion. The circle's members, like Isabel, were women from Boston's best families who had married well. Most were born in the 1870s and made their debut in Boston society in the early to mid-1890s. Only forty-five women could be members at any one time and new members—when vacancies occurred—needed the endorsement of fifteen members in good standing. The club met every Wednesday between December and the end of April, and each week's hostess served luncheon, according to the bylaws, "at one o'clock promptly." When Isabel hosted a meeting in December 1919, she arranged for motor vehicles to pick up members in Back Bay and transport them to Brookline. The circle disbanded in 1961.[12]

Public Events at Weld

From time to time Larz and Isabel opened the estate for large public events that presented great spectacles of music, theater, and modern dance reflecting Isabel's passion for the performing arts. The events benefitted groups in which the Andersons had a particular interest, including cultural societies and war-relief efforts. "Those in which we are interested, are allowed to use the place occasionally," Isabel said.[13]

One particularly elegant event was an outdoor dinner dance in June 1920 to benefit the American Academy in Rome.[14] The program began with a six o'clock concert on the bowling green. Stanislao Gallo's Symphonic Band played pieces by Sousa, Rossini, and Bizet. An outdoor supper (two dollars a person) was served at seven o'clock on the west lawn. At eight o'clock, the soprano Alice Merritt Cochran performed, using the south terrace with its exotic display of Larz's bonsai collection as her stage. The Harvard Glee Club, accompanied by the Gallo band, then presented a program of vocal and orchestral pieces in the Italian garden. The locally popular Braggiotti Sisters, Francesca and Berthe, twirled their way around the garden to the rhythm of the music. The two women operated a dance school on an upper floor of the Brookline fire department. The Braggiottis and their lively siblings were once called "the greatest thing that happened to Boston society since Mrs. Jack Gardner smoked a cigarette in public and built Fenway court."[15] After the concert, guests danced amid a profusion of scented blooms in the softly illuminated Italian garden until ten o'clock.

Some Events on the Anderson Estate 1909–1930

July 1909	Estate open to the public
Dec. 1910	Christmas Party for 150 children with "useful gifts for all"
June 1911	Church of the Advent Sunday school outing
May 1913	Persian Pageant including pantomimes and "oriental dances" in the *rond point* to benefit the Massachusetts Babies' Hospital
May 1915	*The Lure of the Sea*, a "dance-play" presented by the American Drama Society
June 1915	*Strife of Sea Children* and *Tree Children for Earth* presented by the American Drama Society
June 1916	Two outdoor plays, *Strife of Sea Children* and *The Witch of the Woods*, to benefit the Wells College Endowment
June 1919	Ladies' Dog Club Show (five hundred dogs exhibited in tents on the polo field and in the English garden; repeated in 1920)
June 1922	Lest We Forget fund-raiser dance in the Carriage House
June 1926	Boston University College of Practical Arts Class Day
June 1927	The play *A Frolic in the Land of Make-Believe* presented by the Professional Women's Club of Boston
Oct. 1930	American Legion Convention garden reception

The most spectacular event ever held on the estate was the famous Persian Pageant of May 1913, a fund-raiser for the Massachusetts Babies' Hospital in Jamaica Plain.[16] The artist Joseph Lindon Smith (1863–1950) created a ninety-minute pantomime, *A Diversion in Persia*, as the day's main entertainment. Performed in the *rond point* and the English garden, the pantomime called for dozens of actors in the roles of horsemen, servants, huntsmen, ladies of the harem, and relatives of the shah of Persia. The pageant included "Oriental dances." It was a large and colorful gathering of performers. "Groups in gay turbans and huge trousers stopped and posed among the big willows that surround the little pond down by the amphitheater," Isabel later wrote.[17]

The hill above the *rond point* held two thousand spectators seated on folding chairs and straw mats. There was such a large crowd of spectators that many had to park their automobiles in Jamaica Plain and walk over to Brookline. The day's festivities were to include an elephant walk led by Isabella Stewart Gardner, wearing all her famous jewelry and riding on an elephant.[18] When it came time for the parade, Isabella's elephant would not budge. A second elephant was brought alongside to keep him company, but it was to no avail. The *Boston Globe* noted that even though "there were no elephants upon the scene, there was quite enough else to more than compensate for their absence." Tea and refreshments were sold on the bowling green, and all the other gardens were open to the public, even Larz's gnome garden.

Operations at Weld

The Anderson estate was a large, complex, and expensive enterprise that required many technical and mechanical operations and a large staff to keep it running. There were horticultural, agricultural, mechanical, and stable operations. The estate's enormous physical plant consisted of heating, mechanical, and electrical services, a toolhouse, electric-generator shed, and an automotive repair garage.

It took the skills and labor of twenty or more workers to run Weld, even when the Andersons were not in residence there. At least fifteen of these were full-time staff who lived on the estate. Others were hired as day laborers from the surrounding community, as called for by seasonal changes in housekeeping and maintenance. The full-time staff split roughly fifty-fifty between those working inside the mansion and those working on the grounds. About half of the domestic help were women who cooked and cleaned (cook, assistant cook, kitchen helper, parlor maids, laundress, Isabel's personal maid), and half were men (butler, valet, footmen). There were also businessmen who worked full time for the Andersons in the Weld Office in downtown Boston, taking care of banking, legal, financial, real estate, and business matters. Isabel hired secretaries and literary assistants to help with her writing, and some of these worked with her for many years. (See chapter 15.)

Weld provided housing for dozens of employees. Single women had sleeping rooms on the third floor of the mansion, and bachelors were housed in rooms on the second floor of the carriage house. Several of the Andersons' married employees lived in the four residential houses on the estate: the superintendent's house, the coachman's cottage, another staff house known as the Snow Cottage, and what the Andersons called the Washington Cottage (now known as the Widow Harris Cottage). The estate's superintendent and head gardener, Duncan Finlayson, lived with his wife, Christina, and their two children, Douglas and Anna, in the Prairie-style house designed by Fox and Gale. Duncan worked for the Andersons for more than thirty years and, by very strange coincidence, died on the same day as Isabel—November 3, 1948. The Andersons' chauffeur and chief mechanic, Bernie Foy, a longtime, trusted employee, lived in the coachman's cottage with his wife, Annie, and their seven children. The Foys named one of their sons Larz, a sign of the deep bond of loyalty and affection that existed between the Andersons and their staff.

At Christmas, the Andersons hosted large and fun parties for the children of their employees and the employees of Isabel's cousin May Brandegee. The gardeners set up a large Christmas tree in the center of the carriage house, and all the children received presents. A few days after the party at Weld, all the Anderson staff and their families went to the Brandegee estate for a reciprocal party in May's grand ballroom designed by Little and Browne. Isabel herself played Santa Claus at the 1910 party.[19] The 1913 Christmas party at Weld offered what the *Boston Globe* called "a new and interesting feature, a moving-picture entertainment personally given by Mr. Anderson. Views of Belgium and Japan where he represented the United States as Minister and Ambassador, respectively."[20]

Census records show that a cumulative total of more than one hundred people, including spouses and children, lived on the estate between 1900 and 1940. There were many others who worked for the Andersons but did not appear in the census because they lived in town or were not working for the couple when the census was taken. The cumulative number of people who worked for the Andersons over the almost fifty years that they occupied the estate was likely around two hundred. The employees who lived on the estate were for the most part born in Ireland, England, Canada, Scotland, and Massachusetts. Those born in the United States tended to be Irish Americans whose parents were Irish-born. The Andersons preferred to hire butlers born in England. There were occasionally a few employees from other countries— Sweden, France, Japan, and Switzerland—but this was not common. At the time of Isabel's death in 1948, all her household staff were Irish-born.

Detailed records of the Andersons' expenses give us some insight into the cost of operating Weld. Between 1928 and 1937, the year of Larz's death, the Andersons spent an average of about $82,000 a year to run the estate.[21] In today's dollars, that would be roughly $1.5 million a year. There was no return on that investment. It was a gentleman's farm whose residents and staff consumed what was produced, the rest given away to friends and family. Operations at Weld were very much like a series of little businesses that operated on a no-profit or even loss basis.

Weld as Nursery and Florist Shop

The Italian garden, the estate's showpiece, required constant attention through New England's three growing seasons, and it took enormous effort to keep it in top form. This garden more than anything dictated the demands made on the estate's horticultural operations. Seedlings were started in the greenhouse during the winter and then, as spring approached, transferred to the rows of cold frames that covered the grounds of the garden complex. There they were readied for planting in the Italian garden. From spring through fall, the flowerbeds in the Andersons' Italian garden were continuously replanted week by week and month by month at exactly the right time to assure a profusion of blossoms at their peak in all seasons. In the late fall, before the first frost, workers removed the bay trees and topiaries from the Italian garden and put them into the bay house for the winter. The clerestory windows and teak-paneled walls of the bay house assured optimal conditions for their growth and maintenance during the winter months. Trees and shrubs that could not be moved were wrapped in burlap and boxed up on site in the garden to protect them from snow and ice damage.

Other gardens on the estate had their own maintenance routines. The Japanese garden required careful tending to keep it free of debris. Acres of lawns had to be mowed, and the spillway that drained the lagoon needed to be kept clean of leaves and sticks. The rose garden required laborious attention to keep the plants watered, fertilized, groomed, and pest-free. There was even a workshop where Larz's valuable collection of bonsai, bought in Japan in 1913 and later, were nurtured, pruned, and repotted according to exacting Japanese standards.[22]

The heated greenhouses brimmed with flowers year-round, especially orchids and other tropical blooms used to decorate the interiors of the mansion in Brookline and Anderson House in Washington. The Andersons' Japanese servant Oshige San was their Washington florist. He created floral arrangements with azaleas, orchids, lilies, and tulips that were shipped down by overnight train from the greenhouses in Brookline to Anderson House. He wore traditional Japanese dress and stood behind Isabel's chair at dinner in the style of an imperial household usher. Larz called him "one of the most generally useful members of the establishment."[23]

Weld was known everywhere for its extensive horticultural operations. Larz acted as his own publicist and saw to it that dozens of articles about the Weld gardens appeared in popular magazines and professional garden journals.

Weld as a Working Farm

Agricultural operations on the estate provided a bounty of food for the Anderson household and for the staff and families who lived on the estate. Isabel's relatives in New Hampshire and her mother in Back Bay Boston also received a share. During the Andersons' era, fruits and vegetables were an important part of the American diet. Photographs and maps of Weld document the great variety of produce grown there, including tomatoes, green beans, rhubarb, and apple and pear trees. Other popular vegetables of the day included corn, cauliflower, and carrots. The greenhouse, used mostly for flowers, also produced a rare off-season treat that Isabel and Larz loved to share with family and friends: grapes, which were otherwise not to be had for love or money during winter months. Vegetables and fruits not consumed during the growing season were canned for consumption at other times of the year. Homemade pickles made with any kind of vegetable were popular additions to the American diet in the early decades of the twentieth century.

Milk from the Andersons' cows was processed at the estate's creamery into table milk, cream, and butter. The cow barn had nine milking stalls, a large dairy operation for a private home, and a root cellar where turnips, potatoes, and other late-season vegetables were stored.[24] A henhouse supplied eggs and chickens. Though the Andersons never sold the estate's bounty, they sustained commercial-grade operations that produced an abundance of flowers, fruits, vegetables, preserves, milk, butter, eggs, and chickens that any merchant would have been proud to offer customers.

Weld as a Transportation Hub

Despite Larz's early adoption of the automobile, horses remained important to the Andersons over the entire course of their lifetimes. They kept large stables in Brookline and in Washington for their thoroughbred, saddle, driving, and draft horses. Many of Isabel's thoroughbreds were award-winning champions she exhibited at shows in Washington and Boston. The carriage house in Brookline had elaborate stalls separated by marble panels, the occupant of each stall identified by a gold-lettered nameplate. The tack room installed by Billy Weld was a handsome, cozy place with dark paneled walls and a tiled coal fireplace.

Larz's collection of automobiles was more than just a motor pool from which he could select a vehicle to match his whim or his need. It was a carefully curated collection, and there is evidence that at least some of the cars were gifts from Isabel.[25] He prized each of his automobiles and gave them names and mottos in the same way that Isabel named and nicknamed her horses.

Some of Larz Anderson's Favorite Automobiles

1899   Winton Phaeton—Pioneer, "It will go"

1900   Rochet Schneider—Young Eagle, "No steam, no gain"

1901   Winton Bullet—Buckeye, "Catch who catch can"

1905   Electromobile—Port Bonheur (Bringer of Happiness), Ça va sans se dire ("It goes without saying")

1906   Charron-Girodot-Voight—Winnepocket, *Fortix, ferox et celer* ("Strong, ferocious, fast")

1907   Fiat—Il Conquistador (The Conqueror), *No hill me pavet* ("No hill can stop me")

1908   Bailey Electric Phaeton Victoria—La Bonne Fée (The Good Fairy), *Toujours prête et fidèle* ("Always ready and faithful")

1910   Panhard et Levassor—Columbia, *Regarde St. Christophe et va en securité* ("Look to St. Christopher and go in safety")

1911   Renault 40CV Victoria Phaeton—Yankee Doodle, "Null Ice Dam"

1915   Packard Twin Six (twelve-cylinder)—Twelve Apostles, "Bearer of Honor and Trust"

1926   Lincoln Seven Limousine—The Emancipator, *Son courage fait sa force* ("His courage is his might")

Larz's most famous automobile was his Charron-Girodot-Voight, nicknamed "Winnepocket." When he bought the vehicle in Paris in April 1906, the newspaper *Le Journal* published an announcement, noting that its large passenger compartment was to be outfitted with a daybed, a washstand, and a toilet that would make it "the most comfortable and most elegant automobile one could imagine."[26]

Despite his passion for motor vehicles, Larz never gave up his fondness for horse-drawn carriages, and he maintained a working collection of them that was larger than the automobile collection. Some of these belonged to Larz's and Isabel's parents and perhaps even grandparents. One of their favorite winter activities was to take sleigh rides on moonlit nights through the countryside around Brookline. Larz recorded one particularly memorable sleigh ride in 1901:

> Then immediately after lunch the Red Sleigh came up with a
> smart little pair ... looking awfully sweet—and so we tucked
> ourselves in among the deep bear robes and with jingling
> bells we sped off along the slippery roads through the white
> country—all so wintry and clean—with the sun getting lower
> and lower (for it was the shortest day of the year) and the
> fields glinting and a'-sparkling and taking on the roses and
> oranges and deep reds as they reflected the sunset skies and

the beautiful twilight that lasted so long—and still we slipped merrily along till we began to feel the moonlight and saw the silver Queen serene in the deep skies—and still went on—and when we reached Home it was a flooding moonlight night, making all the scene mysterious and too beautiful.[27]

Weld as an Experiment in Housing Development

In the 1920s, Larz and Isabel decided to get in on a housing boom under way in Brookline. The explosive growth of the stock market generated wealth that created great demand for middle- and upper-class housing in the Boston area. Brookline's parklike neighborhoods were a drawing card for city dwellers looking to move to the country. Wealthy Brookline landowners with large tracts of beautifully landscaped land saw an opportunity to cash in on the trend. The Sargent, Williams, and Schlessinger families— Anderson neighbors—subdivided their attractive and famous estates to create building lots.[28]

Larz and Isabel followed the example of their wealthy neighbors, as Larz described it, "in order to keep up with the Joneses." He regretted that the town would require "deadly numbers" as part of the street addresses.[29] Though Larz enthusiastically approved of the housing boom that produced homes for affluent people in Brookline, he railed against the expansion of Washington's housing stock then under way, especially apartment buildings. "Huge tenements (they call them apartment houses) are rising in every direction—cheaply built and ungainly—even in the residential portions of the city," Larz said in 1923.[30] By "residential portions" he meant the parts of the city where he and his friends lived in large mansions, ignoring the fact that an apartment building, especially one in Dupont Circle with elite occupants, was also residential.

The Andersons again hired the firm of Fox and Gale to design three large, elegant homes on Goddard Avenue. The inspiration for the first of these, Blue Top (1925), was a house with a blue tile roof they had seen in Cadiz, Spain. The second, Puddingstone (1927, named for a nearby outcropping of pudding stone on the estate), was modeled after one they had seen in Santa Monica, California. The third house, Stellenbosch (1929), was based on the Cape Dutch Colonial style found in South Africa, which the Andersons had visited the previous year. Each of the houses is still standing and is an architectural gem. Much thought and planning went into their design and construction. "A small house requires almost more study than a large one," Larz said, "and so there was a lot of talk and discussion about this little plan."[31] The Andersons never sold the houses. They used them occasionally as guesthouses for relatives or friends who came for long stays at Weld, especially when Larz and Isabel were elsewhere.

Wherever they went in the world, Larz and Isabel were always happy to come home to Weld. "It was pleasant to be back once more in our cozy home ... and to be greeted with a 'Halloa' by the cross macaw as she spread her beautiful blue and yellow wings," Isabel wrote about one of their homecomings. Their dogs Fluff and Jap "barked at each other and wagged their little white tails for us," giving Larz and Isabel a welcome home unlike any other place they ever lived.[32]

Figure 13. Anderson House, Washington, DC, 1927.

VII

The Genius of Anderson House (Washington)

Isabel Anderson thought of Washington as "the most beautiful of American cities."[1] Along with Cincinnati and Paris, Larz claimed it as one of his three hometowns. He may have considered Brookline the center of their spiritual life together, but Washington defined his public persona and embodied what he sought most in life: celebrity. "We have always been Washingtonians, however great our associations and attachments to Boston," Larz said.[2]

Beyond architectural and landscape beauty and childhood memories, the capital offered Larz advantages for any political career he might wish to pursue, in a way no other American city could. He complained, though, that it took "sacrifice and effort" to achieve such "social opportunities."

> Washington is for us full of opportunities that it would be a shame to miss, where it is so comparatively easy to meet the "good and the great" of the world, and to see and hear so much of interest and value first-hand. We soon found that it was worth the sacrifice and effort, (even if we did n't feel as eager as we used to be) to accept and give, "to give and take", to meet the interesting social opportunities.[3]

When Larz and Isabel started their married life together, Washington had for almost two decades been moving full throttle toward becoming a world-class city. At the dawn of the twentieth century, a new impetus to rethink the architecture and landscape of the nation's capital swept through the city, creating an artistic storm that influenced Larz's thinking about the design of Anderson House. This more than anything else in his life assured Larz a permanent place in the nation's cultural history.

Washington was not always the elegant city Larz knew as a teenager in the early 1880s. The city was so unattractive and provincial after the Civil War that there was talk of moving the government to a larger and more established city with infrastructure and services worthy of a national capital. Civic leaders in midwestern cities hoped the capital would be relocated to a more central part of the country. Washington's business owners and real estate speculators knew the city would not survive if its infrastructure and appearance did not improve dramatically.

In 1871 Alexander Robey "Boss" Shepherd, a Washington native, took over the city's public works department and for a time even served as governor of the federal district. Shepherd changed the face of the city forever. He installed paved streets and sidewalks, a sanitary water supply, and sewers that drained away disease-bearing wastewater. To improve the quality of life, he installed streetlights, streetcars, and public parks. These projects laid the foundation for the Washington we know today.

As Shepherd foresaw, wealthy Americans and foreigners flocked to the much-improved city, buying land and building homes for the city's winter social season. In 1881, Nick and Elizabeth Anderson moved to Washington with their two children in the wake of Shepherd's renewal of the city. People now called it the nation's Winter Newport, a seasonally adjusted reference to the Rhode Island summer playground of old and new money. Just as the wealthy and powerful summered in Newport, so too they wintered in Washington, among their own kind: prominent, accomplished, cultured, well-dressed, gracious, and, most of all, wealthy peers.

Shepherd envisioned parks in grand public spaces created at the crisscrossing of avenues and streets. By the time Larz and Isabel arrived in Washington, these "circles," as they became known, and the tree-lined avenues intersecting them, added beauty and gentility to a city that only a few decades earlier had been very drab. "Like green spokes to a wheel," Isabel once wrote of Washington's garden-like setting, "the streets during the spring stretch out from the bright flowering Circles making cool and shaded aisles with their fine old trees whose boughs meet overhead."[4] One of these "green spokes," named for the cradle of the American Revolution and Isabel's home state, Massachusetts, became the most fashionable thoroughfare in the city.

Washington and the City Beautiful Movement

Shepherd's focus was the city's infrastructure and landscape, even going so far as to level the ups and downs of streets, leaving some houses with front doors several steps above or several steps below the sidewalk. He did little, however, to influence the design of the public and private buildings that were constantly being added to Washington's cityscape. Indeed, the architectural style of government buildings and private homes changed little after Shepherd's work was completed. New construction in the 1880s and into the early 1890s exemplified what the American historian Louis Mumford called the "Brown Decades" of post–Civil War architecture.[5] Despite great stylistic variations, most public buildings and upper-class homes built in the second half of the nineteenth century throughout the United States and in Washington had one common feature—their color. Brownstone, earth-tone brick, and terra-cotta were the main exterior building materials. In Washington, government buildings like the US Pension Bureau (1882–1887) and the Smithsonian's Arts and Industries Building (1879–1881) and private homes like Nicholas Longworth Anderson's house (1881–1883) and Christian Heurich's mansion (1892), now known as the Brewmaster's Castle, were all typical of the Brown Decades.

In 1893, the World's Columbian Exposition held to commemorate the four hundredth anniversary of the arrival of Christopher Columbus in the New World opened in Chicago. A brain trust of America's finest architects and landscape designers gathered to envision, plan, and build a "White City" to celebrate American arts, technology, and industry and to introduce Americans to world cultures. The greatest architects and designers of the day contributed to the plan. Frederick Law Olmsted and Henry Sargent Codman (1864–1893) laid out the exposition's master plan. Augustus Saint-Gaudens (1848–1907) created general guidelines for all sculpture, and the artist Frank Millet (1848–1912) directed interior decoration of the buildings. Daniel Burnham (1846–1912); John Root (1850–1891); the New York firm of McKim, Mead and White; and others followed a set of common design principles for the buildings and public spaces. These included adherence to principles of classical Greek and Roman architecture and its neoclassical revival, a uniform system of measurements and proportions, and the use of one color: white. The wildly popular exposition captured the nation's imagination and stimulated demand for public and residential architecture incorporating the new design principles.

International events also led to a reassessment of Washington's place in the world. In the late 1890s, during the administrations of William McKinley and his successor, Theodore Roosevelt, the United States engaged in a heated dispute with Spain over its colonial territories Cuba and the Philippines. When an American ship, the USS *Maine*, exploded in Havana Harbor on February 15, 1898, American politicians blamed Spain and called for war with the colonial power. Diplomats tried to broker compromises from Spain to prevent conflict. Washington, not Europe, was the venue for these debates. When war did come in April that year, it lasted only a few months. By the time it was over in August, Washington and the nation had been transformed. It "brought many Americans to a new sense of importance in the world, but nowhere more profoundly than in the capital," the American historian William Seale has said of the transformation.[6] Washington's political importance was now on par, if not above par, with London, Paris, and Rome.

In 1901, just as Larz and Isabel started the design process for their

Washington residence, there was change afoot in the artistic vision for what Seale called "ceremonial Washington." In that year, Senator James McMillan convened the Senate Park Commission to review several competing plans for the city's built environment. When the commission released its now-famous plan, it revolutionized how Americans, even laypeople, viewed their capital city. Indeed, one member of the McMillan commission, Chicago architect Daniel Burnham, said he wanted the new plan to "appeal to the ordinary citizen [and] inspire enthusiasm among a broad constituency."[7] Chicago's White City would come to Washington, "reconceived in marble, but its dazzling nighttime character; its landscape setting of space, fountains, and greenery; and its sense of order [would be] continued on an even larger scale," Burnham predicted.[8]

The Andersons and many of their peers looked to these innovative artistic and architectural forms to find inspiration for their Washington homes. Indeed, Larz Anderson not only saw the McMillan Plan when it was published, but he was also close to the McMillan commission itself. His sister, Elsie, married Philip Hamilton McMillan in 1899, and Phil was Senator McMillan's son.

Anderson House

Larz had several options to consider before making a decision about where to live in the city. His mother had offered him her house on K Street. Larz knew that if they took it, extensive renovation and expansion would be required.[9] Built only twenty years earlier, it was a rare example of Henry Hobson Richardson's work in the capital. Despite its illustrious designer and artistic credentials, Larz had no interest in his mother's home. The house was infused with the previous generation's taste in domestic architecture: dark rooms, wood-paneled walls and ceilings, ornate stained glass windows, cozy nooks and crannies—and a brown brick exterior.

Larz briefly considered buying the William Wilson Corcoran house at the corner of H Street and Connecticut Avenue (now the site of the US Chamber of Commerce), which went up for sale after Corcoran's death.[10] In 1848, Corcoran purchased the original Federal-style house on the site from its owner, Massachusetts statesman Daniel Webster. Corcoran hired James Renwick Jr. to redesign the house in an eclectic Renaissance Revival style. Situated next to the homes of John Hay and Henry Adams, and with the White House visible from its front door, the Corcoran residence would have put Larz back in the heart of Old Washington. Larz rejected both of these possibilities. He wanted something more uniquely his own, designed in a modern style consistent with the McMillan commission recommendations, and on a grander scale than either his mother's home or Corcoran's urban villa could provide.

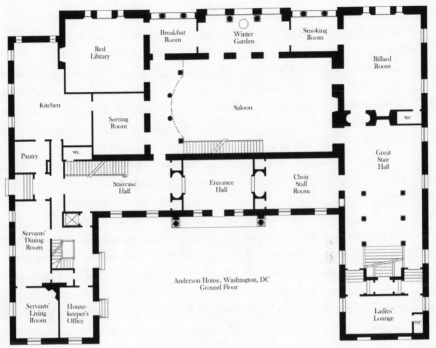

Figure 14. Ground floor of Anderson House.

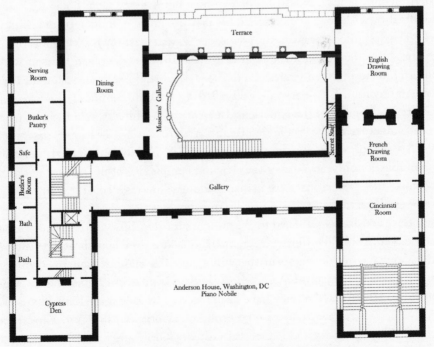

Figure 15. *Piano Nobile* of Anderson House.

On May 23, 1901, two months after Isabel came into full control of her inheritance, the Weld trust purchased one of the last remaining empty plots on Washington's prestigious Massachusetts Avenue near Dupont Circle for an estimated $93,000.[11] The lot was large enough to accommodate a stylish and commodious mansion designed by the Boston firm of Little and Browne. The firm had designed a residence in Jamaica Plain for Isabel's cousin May Sprague in 1894–1896, so Larz and Isabel were well acquainted with the firm's reputation and work.

Larz envisioned more than just a winter home in Washington. In view of his social and political aspirations, he wanted a house that could simultaneously play several roles. "When the house was built many things had been thought out," he said. It was "arranged for official use but it is one of the most homelike houses in the world, a home in every sense of the word, for we live all over it at all times, our beloved Home!"[12] Here he could entertain effortlessly, in rooms perfectly arranged for elegant dinners, luncheons, teas, musicales, and receptions with guest lists of varying length—from a dinner party for a dozen couples to a late-night musicale for hundreds. Such entertainment was the currency of Washington society. In an era when there were no hotels large enough to receive official delegations of such stature, Larz also anticipated offering accommodation to royalty and heads of state at Anderson House. It also needed to be a home away from home for Larz and Isabel, with cozy and comfortable private quarters hidden from visitors.

The design process was already under way, at least in an early conceptual stage, when they bought the land in May 1901. Larz involved himself with his architects and their draftsmen in every detail and likely consulted his first cousin George M. Anderson (1869–1916) in Cincinnati during the process. George, a member of the American Institute of Architects, had been trained in architecture at the École des Beaux-Arts in Paris.[13] The basic design of the house took about six months and was ready by November 1901—a rapid timetable not only because of the size and complexity of the project but also because the Andersons were cruising along American coastal waters on a chartered steam yacht, the *Katoomba,* for much of the time.[14]

Larz and Isabel returned to Washington for the 1902 winter social season and rented Alice Pike Barney's Italianate villa at 1626 Rhode Island Avenue.[15] Larz and the architects spent the winter months making major and minor adjustments to the plans for Anderson House. Original plans called for a two-story winter garden that may have been inspired by Biltmore (1889-1895), the Ashville, North Carolina, country estate of George Washington Vanderbilt (1862-1914) that Larz and Isabel had visited. George and his wife Edith were close friends of the Andersons. The concept for the indoor garden was later scaled back to a single story on the ground floor. Larz also decided on the arrangement of their separate bedroom suites and placed his bedroom between Isabel's boudoir and his own dressing room.[16] The placement of the grand staircase in the house was one of the biggest challenges. The architects originally proposed that the grand staircase be placed in the center of the house, but Larz felt this would disrupt the arrangement and flow of rooms on the ground floor and *piano nobile*.[17] Larz had the architects move the grand staircase to the western side of the house, thus giving them more leeway in arranging the rooms and connecting them to one another. Years later, his best friend, Charles Francis Adams III, marveled at Larz's ability to create "a home, beautiful in conception, perfect in detail"—a reference to Larz's role in planning Anderson House.[18]

In 1902, once plans were final and construction was about to start, the Andersons went away for the summer. They returned to Washington in the fall so Larz could personally supervise the construction of the new house, as the city's society rag, the *Washington Mirror*, reported:

> Mr. and Mrs. Larz Anderson are expected here shortly to supervise the erection of their new house. The Andersons have been abroad for several months, where they collected a number of bibelots and pieces de vertu, with which to adorn what will be one of the finest residences in the National Capital. Rumor has it that they paid the trifling sum of $3,000 duty on their purchases. This is but a bagatelle, of course, to Mrs. Anderson, whose income is that every day.[19]

A Modern House with Many Surprises

With ninety-five rooms spread out over fifty thousand square feet, Anderson House was two and a half times the size of the couple's mansion in Brookline after its 1914–1916 expansion. Only about one-third of the Washington square footage was for the use of the Andersons and their guests. The other two-thirds of the house was for physical plant, service areas, and servant quarters.[20]

There were many modern and old-fashioned amenities at Anderson House. Immense, coal-fired boilers in the basement provided plenty of central heating to all areas of the house. Wood-burning fireplaces in all public rooms and in all guest and Anderson bedrooms supplemented the central heating system, a homey touch reflecting Larz and Isabel's love of a crackling fire at night. The cellar had two coal and two firewood storage rooms. Glass walls enclosed the basement "electrical control machine," as the blueprints called it, allowing it to be safely monitored by a mechanic. Along with other work areas in the basement, there were two bedrooms and a bathroom for the mechanics who attended the boilers and other mechanical systems round the clock. For many years, one of Larz's most trusted employees, Fenton Wilson, an African American, oversaw the building's physical plant. Larz called him "one of those faithful and sober and intelligent colored men that are treasures." Fenton "knew every pipe and plug in the house," and in him the Andersons "had great faith."[21] Born in 1895 in suburban Maryland, Fenton did not live for long periods of time in Washington and worked for the Andersons only when they needed him.

Several elevators facilitated the movement of people and supplies from one floor to another. A passenger elevator operated between the basement and the third floor. The kitchen was outfitted with two dumbwaiters, one connecting to the butler's pantry adjacent to the dining room on the *piano nobile* above and the other to the cellar below where wine, liquor, firewood, and other provisions were stored.

Larz kept a well-stocked wine cellar. At the time of his death in 1937, it held 5,300 bottles of liquor and wine, including 39 cases of Scotch whisky, 39 cases of gin, 51 cases of Italian vermouth, and 107 cases of champagne. The cellar was stocked with hundreds of bottles of French and German sweet white wines—Sauternes, Chablis, white Bordeaux, and Rieslings—that hinted at the Andersons' taste in wine. There was even a case of the very modern-sounding Freezomint, a French liqueur that became popular a half century later in the 1970s.[22] The Andersons opposed Prohibition and were well prepared for it when it happened. "We are bossed and ruled, and laws made and not enforced," Isabel once said. She blamed passage of the Volstead Act on an "untrained electorate, and communities not sufficiently long established to have acquired habits and wisdom to achieve as yet a satisfactory self government."[23] Larz took his opposition to Prohibition a step further: in 1925 he and his friend Eddie Menocal (1873-1942) visited a New York City speakeasy tucked away in a basement beneath a restaurant.[24]

Fire-Prevention Systems

Given the massive heating system and the many flammables in the house—coal, firewood, natural gas, and alcohol—fire prevention loomed large in the Andersons' minds. In early May 1901, during the design phase of Anderson House, a disastrous fire severely damaged the mansion in Brookline. It started in a basement storeroom and propelled itself up the cellar stairway into the central portion of the house. A newspaper account of the fire comically attributed the fire to "rats and matches," but the Brookline fire department's official report concluded it was caused by "careless use of candle." The blaze resulted in $21,000 of damage to the interior, including woodwork, the central staircase, furniture, and draperies. Servants saved artwork and bric-a-brac, but many of Larz's personal papers, family correspondence, and books were lost.[25]

Anderson House was designed with firefighting and fire-safety redundancy in mind. Ten fire hoses—two on each level of the house from basement to attic—put every room within reach of a water supply. There were at least two and in some cases three stairways on each floor that provided emergency escape routes. It has often been said that the hidden stairway connecting Larz's dressing room on the third floor to the gallery on the *piano nobile* offered him a discreet way to disappear from social functions. He may have used it as such, but the secret stairway also housed one of the building's ten fire hoses and was part of the fire-safety plan. Given this concern about fire, it is curious that servant quarters and work areas were illuminated solely by gas fixtures. All public areas, including guest bedrooms and the Andersons' private rooms, had electric lighting.

A Small Hotel

Anderson House functioned as both a small hotel for the Andersons' guests and a large rooming house for their servants. There were forty-seven sleeping rooms scattered throughout the mansion and carriage house. Larz and Isabel each had their own bedroom suite on the third floor at the back of the house. The eight guest rooms, also on the third floor, were mostly on the front side of the house. Isabel's suite was much more elaborate than Larz's, with its own entry vestibule, two walk-in closets, bathroom, boudoir, and a private loggia that gave her a place to step outdoors into the sunshine and fresh air she so loved. This was very similar to the amenities in her bedroom suite in Brookline. The loggia, now closed in by windows but still discernible, is reminiscent of the little porch she had in a corner of her bedroom in New Hampshire—a private retreat away from the hubbub of the house where she could commune with nature.

Anderson House also provided off-season accommodations for the couple. A two-story apartment the Andersons called the Cypress Den for its cypress paneling offered a sitting room with fireplace, a bedroom, a bathroom, and a little balcony with built-in cabinets. Larz and Isabel stayed in this cozy apartment when they were in town off-season or when the full household was not up and running. During the season, they used it as a private retreat away from guests and staff. Larz decorated the walls with an eclectic assortment of framed photographs of people and places, documents, and diplomas he enjoyed viewing and thinking about. The den was furnished for comfort, with overstuffed leather club chairs and throw pillows. Larz's letter-writing desk was here too—complete with a postage scale.[26]

A Carriage House with a Surprise

The carriage house, no longer standing, was perhaps the most unique aspect of Anderson House. Built on a mostly unexcavated foundation, the carriage house consisted of three floors and from the outside looked like an eccentric Italian villa. The building's interior was organized around mode of transportation: the ground floor was for automobiles and the second floor for horses (away from engine exhaust fumes). Living quarters for male staff were located on the second and third floors. The ground floor offered a large parking garage and car wash area, a carriage wash area, a tack room, and a locker room for the grooms where they could change from stable clothes into livery.

To get horses from the ground floor to the second-floor stables, grooms walked the animals up a forty-five-foot-long, gently inclined ramp. The stable had ten stalls, six smaller ones for the draft horses and four roomier ones for show and saddle horses, each with a bell trap that made it easy to hose down the stalls. The second floor also had storage for carriages brought up and down on a lift as needed.

The biggest surprise of all was the private squash club on the third floor. The facility included a locker room with shower, a gallery for spectators, and a squash court paneled in birch. Squash became popular in the United States in private boarding schools during the 1880s, but neither Phillips Exeter nor Harvard had courts at the time Larz attended those schools. He likely learned the sport during his years in London. Until the carriage house was torn down sometime around 1970, a local squash club rented the court for its members. One former member said it was "the most exquisite court" he ever played on.[27]

The construction of Anderson House and its infrastructure was costly. By the time all work on the house was completed (including some alterations in 1909 and 1911), the house, its physical plant, its amenities, and its interior finishing cost $635,000. The carriage house and landscaping added another $103,000.[28] Including the cost of land, Larz spent more than $830,000 on Anderson House, about $20 million in today's dollars, and they had not even begun to furnish or decorate it. This was equivalent to about 15 percent of Isabel's trust fund principal.

The Genius of Anderson House

The most brilliant aspect of the plan developed by Little and Browne in close consultation with their client was the carefully arranged public rooms on the ground floor and *piano nobile*. By the time Anderson House was built, the preference in Washington had shifted from the post–Civil War period's large dinners with thirty or more couples and balls for hundreds to the "modern dinner-party which [had] come to be the favorite form of entertainment ... of especial significance at the capital," wrote etiquette expert Florence Howe Hall, Maud Howe Elliott's sister. Such dinner parties gave "an opportunity for conversation."[29] Isabel took note of this trend, as well as differences between American and European dinner parties: "In America, at a dinner party, one talked with her immediate neighbors, and if one is fortunate enough to sit beside a general or a diplomat or a distinguished statesman, or a minister, he will talk more freely and more interestingly to one person. Now in Europe, the conversation is general, and one person will seize the opportunity for monologue."[30]

The public rooms of Anderson House were designed for these smaller, more-intimate dinner parties that promoted conversation and congeniality. The Cincinnati Room at the top of the grand staircase, where the Andersons met their guests, was an intimate space suitable for several couples at a time, not dozens. The French and English drawing rooms comfortably accommodated a few dozen people who could mix and mingle there before dinner. The drawing rooms were never too crowded or too empty. Like the dining room, they were scaled perfectly to a typical Anderson guest list of no more than thirty people for a sit-down dinner.

The plan of the ground floor and *piano nobile* of Anderson House provided a route along which a dinner party could steadily progress over the course of an evening. Arrival, greeting, cocktailing, dining, and after-dinner entertainment occurred in a series of discrete rooms arranged in sequential order, from arrival to departure. Guests moved continuously through spaces they had not seen previously, each room presenting a new experience of design, perspectives, lighting, and objects. Once the progression started, there was no backtracking. Each phase of a dinner party occurred in a new space or room. This was the genius of Anderson House. (See figures 14 and 15.)

Cocktails at Eight, Dinner at Nine

Dinner invitations to Anderson House were for eight or eight fifteen o'clock. Strict rules of etiquette required guests to be on time, and the only acceptable reason for declining an invitation or not showing up was illness, death, or being called to the White House. On arrival in the Entrance Hall, guests turned to the right, walked through a vestibule the Andersons called the Choir Stall Room, and entered the Great Staircase Hall. After servants took coats and hats, ladies could retire to a lounge tucked under the grand staircase to fix their hair or freshen their makeup. Gentlemen could descend another set of stairs to a lounge under the great hall itself. Both lounges provided lavatory facilities for guests. Couples then ascended the grand staircase—filled with a profusion of azaleas, orchids, lilies, and other out-of-season flowers from the Brookline greenhouses—to the *piano nobile*.

At the top of the stairs, guests entered a reception area the Andersons sometimes called the Cincinnati Room, a reference to the murals depicting both the founding of the Society of the Cincinnati and the early history of the city of Cincinnati.[31] This was the anteroom to the rest of the *piano nobile*. The Andersons also sometimes called it the Key Room, as it is now known—a reference to the meander or Greek key design of the marble floor. The meander represents a labyrinth in linear form and could thus be interpreted as a metaphor for travel, one of Larz's great passions in life.[32] Here the Andersons and their guests of honor greeted couples as they arrived on the *piano nobile*.

After passing through the Cincinnati Room, guests gathered in two adjoining drawing rooms, one in French style and one in English style. Isabel once told the story of a "stiff dinner" they attended at the British embassy: "We entered the big drawing-room to find people standing about in a circle, all dead-silent, and not one familiar face," she said. "After shaking hands with the hostess we joined this impenetrable group and watched the next arrivals go through the ordeal which we had just survived."[33] Stuffy events were not the Andersons' style. They were delightful hosts who mingled with their guests and made sure everyone had a cocktail.

Around nine o'clock, guests assembled in order of social precedence that Larz and Isabel carefully spelled out in "dinner charts" created for each dinner party. Using the chart as his guide, the butler paired each gentleman with a lady for the procession down the long gallery leading to the dining room on the other side of the house. Being paired for the procession into dinner did not mean the couple had arrived together, nor did it suggest they would sit together. Indeed, the procession and seating plan were tools to promote interaction among those present. Even if Larz and Isabel gave modern, smaller dinner parties, they continued to observe the protocols of Old Washington. Certain guests were accorded special precedence based on their social standing, and all other guests were subordinate to them in the procession into dinner and seating at the table.[34] The long gallery, filled chockablock with mementos of Anderson travels, gave silent testimony to the magnificence of the hosts' lives during the formal procession into the french-walnut-paneled dining room.

After dinner, guests exited through large french doors that opened onto the Musicians' Gallery and descended a "floating staircase" to the large room the Andersons called the Saloon, the Anglicized form of the Italian word *salone*. The long, elegant stairway offered guests breathtaking views of the splendid room below, whose proportions replicated the architect Andrea Palladio's famous double cube. The Saloon was usually furnished with cozy groupings of settees, armchairs, coffee tables, and screens that facilitated after-dinner conversation. Isabel once said this was the time when "affairs of state and of international importance may be talked over informally and in that best of humors which comes after a good dinner."[35] (See figure 16.)

The Andersons often treated their dinner guests to musical performances in the Saloon. When they did so, they sometimes invited a hundred or more additional guests to join them for the entertainment. This was a custom that allowed hosts to show off their famous dinner guests to a larger audience than could be seated at the dinner table. Isabel's choice of performers and programs favored European musical traditions. One evening, Mademoiselle Germaine Arnaud, a French-born British pianist and vocalist, accompanied by the Irish pianist, composer, and conductor Sir Hamilton Harty, sang a selection of pieces by Bach, Chopin, and Saint-Saëns. On another evening, Miss Marie Hall, an internationally acclaimed English violinist, performed a program of Polish, French, and Italian music.

The Didactic Element in Anderson House

"In America, the men go off together after dinner; in Europe, they do not," Isabel once said of the American dinner party.[36] Larz's billiard room, adjacent to the Saloon, offered just such a venue where the men could gather for cigars and brandy after dinner. The Winter Garden adjacent to the Saloon offered the ladies their own place to gather away from the men. Isabel could take them through to admire orchids, irises, and other fragrant blooms and the delicate water fountain of which she was very fond. It was one of Isabel's favorite rooms in the house and a place where her beloved parrots could fly free:

> I love to sit in our winter garden, surrounded by palms and blood-red azaleas, pure white cyclamens and sweet-smelling lilacs. A bronze Bacchus peeps at me around a heather bush and a little marble faun looks out of the ivy climbing on the golden lattice … a pair of inquisitive paroquets flutter about my head. Clear water trickles and gurgles invitingly in a fountain; a column of Brescia marble with twin heads supports a huge plate of glorious yellow alabaster, in which lie in the sunshine green orchids with white lips, and, the most beautiful of all, the violet cattleya [orchid]. Rising from the basin on rocks of bronze stands the conquering young Neptune, with his spear lifted, looking proudly down upon the monsters of the deep.[37]

Later in spring, during the time of year in Washington Isabel said was "like fairyland" because of its greenery and blooms, she brought her guests into the Anderson's walled back garden for fresh air and to admire the plantings there: crocuses, violets, pansies, tulips, irises, peonies, and roses.[38]

There was something else to show guests: murals—an important part of Larz's concept for Anderson House. In 1908, he commissioned H. Siddons Mowbray (1858–1928) to decorate three of the public rooms in the house: the Choir Stall Room, Cincinnati Room, and Winter Garden. A year later, he commissioned Oreste Paltrinieri (1873-1966) to decorate the walls of the Great Staircase Hall and at about the same time commissioned Karl Yens (1868-1945) to paint a scene of the Italian Garden in Brookline. These exquisite works of art silently and tactfully emphasized Larz's sense of self and the place he and his family held in American history.

The murals in the Winter Garden were conversation props the Andersons used to engage guests in stories about their life. At one end, Yen's panoramic view of their Italian garden in Brookline wrapped around two walls and gave guests the illusion of standing in the garden at Weld. The mural showed two of Isabel's beloved parrots, one on his perch near the wall fountain and the other appearing to balance himself on a corner of the doorframe. At the other end, Mowbray's two murals gave bird's-eye views of Washington, Virginia, and Maryland. Wall sconces illuminated the map, suggesting they received special attention at evening functions.

On the Virginia map, the Andersons' houseboat, the *Roxana*, and an unidentified white-hulled yacht stand at anchor in the Potomac, just off shore from what is now National Airport. Since the Andersons never owned a yacht, it is something of a mystery why Larz included one in this mural. In 1902, Larz chartered the *Virginia*, owned by the New York City department store magnate Isaac Stern, for a voyage to Bermuda. Over the years, Larz occasionally chartered other yachts for vacation cruises, but he never owned one. When he directed Mowbray to show a yacht flying the signal of the Weld family's Black Horse Line, he may have hoped one day to have one of his own.[39]

The Choir Stall Room on the ground floor, so called because the walls are lined with Renaissance Italian choir stalls made of carved walnut, could just as well be called the "bragging room." Here Larz had Mowbray install colorful frieze and ceiling murals displaying dozens of insignia, crests, seals, and monograms proclaiming Larz's and Isabel's family, patriotic, and alumni affiliations. Most of the devices seem mysterious and exotic to modern visitors, but a hundred years ago they were familiar to Anderson guests. Larz included in the design emblems of his prep school and Harvard student clubs, the insignia of the Society of the Cincinnati and the Military Order of the Loyal

Legion, and decorations he received from Belgian, Japanese, and Italian monarchs. Isabel's insignia represented the Society of Colonial Dames, the Daughters of the American Revolution, and the French War Cross.

Larz had another set of murals installed in the Great Staircase Hall, though these are in monochromatic gray trompe l'oeil and at first glance appear impersonal, especially when compared to the Choir Stall Room and Winter Garden murals. The central mural in the great hall, however, was an understated homage to Larz. The focal point of the decoration in this room is an "ambassador's box" placed front and center in the mural over the fireplace. It is a British tradition to present a newly appointed ambassador with a portable writing desk to mark the new appointee's entry into the highest level of diplomatic service. Larz directed Paltrinieri to work this device into the design and include with it the eagle insignia of the Society of the Cincinnati. Like the yacht he never owned but had included on the Winter Garden map, this mural anticipated a future event. "I had 'cheek' enough to have this box design worked into the fresco work over the fireplace in the great staircase hall of the Washington house," he wrote in November 1912, "to represent my career in Diplomacy ... even before I had a right to do, or even an evident hope."[40] By the time the murals were completed, Larz was still more than three years away from becoming an accredited ambassador.[41]

Larz had the most impressive murals in Anderson House placed in the Cincinnati Room. Painted in a style reminiscent of European tapestries, the murals created a dramatic setting for Larz to receive his guests. He wanted three of the walls to document both the place of Anderson men in the military history of the United States and the patriotic military societies to which they belonged. One wall depicts Richard Clough Anderson in an imagined scene commemorating the founding of the Society of the Cincinnati, identified by the text, "The Society of the Cincinnati Was Instituted in Peace after Revolution." Isabel was Mowbray's model for the winged figure representing peace in this panel.[42] This was her second appearance in a mural by a famous artist. In 1901, she posed for one of the figures in John Elliott's painting *The Triumph of Time*—an allegory of the dawn of the twentieth century—on the ceiling of what was then called the Teachers' Reference Room of the Boston Public Library, where it is still on view.[43]

The mural on the opposite wall portrays the family's role in the Civil War. Larz's father, Colonel Nicholas Longworth Anderson, sits astride his horse, with Fort Sumter in flames in the distance. Sumter is a reference to Larz's great-uncle Major Robert Anderson, who was in command of the fort when it fell to Confederate troops. Robert was a pro-slavery Southerner and former slave owner but absolutely loyal to the Union and thus was considered a good choice to be the fort's commander.[44] The cartouche on this mural reads, "The Order of the Loyal Legion was Born out of Cruel Civil War." An allegorical figure of a woman holds a sword aloft in one hand and a branch of cotton in the other, representing the defeat of slavery by the Union's military might. The woman's face bears a strong resemblance to a photograph of Larz's sister, Elsie.[45]

The third military mural is more obscure, since no Anderson appears in the scene. Instead, the mural portrays a tropical coastline with partisans hiding in the foliage. The inscription reads, "The Order of the Spanish-American War Records a Generous Fight for Freedom." Since Larz, unlike other Anderson men, did not actually see combat and did not go to Puerto Rico or Cuba, he did not have himself appear in the mural. The fourth wall presents a view of nineteenth-century Cincinnati, Ohio, the seat of the Anderson, Longworth, and Kilgour families from which Larz descended.[46]

If the murals did not convey to visitors Larz's sense of self, the Red Library, as the Andersons called it, completed the picture. In Gilded Age mansions, the library was a public room that signaled its owner's knowledge, tastes, and sophistication. The placement of the Andersons' library immediately adjacent to the Saloon, where hundreds of guests could wander in and out over the course of an evening, was no accident. But in the case of the Andersons, their library was more than a showpiece. It was a working library Larz and Isabel used for many types of research and reading. Larz extensively researched the destinations of any trip they took. Months of planning, for example, went into their 1929 cruise from Italy to Turkey by way of Greece (see chapter 10).[47]

The Andersons' library in Washington, like their library in Brookline, contained several hundred books on art, literature, history, and other topics that provided ready access to useful information. Among hundreds of other titles, the library included *Haydn's Dictionary of Dates and Universal Information Relating to All Ages and Nations* (1883), *Literary and Historical Memorials of London* (ca. 1900), and *Chambers' Cyclopædia of English Literature* (1902–1904). There were books to help the couple keep track of friends and acquaintances, including the *Register of the Department of State, American Members of Foreign Orders*, and one of Larz's favorites, the *Catalogue of the Officers and Graduates of Harvard University*. Many volumes reflected the Andersons' special interests: Native American culture (*History of the Indian Tribes of North America*), landscape and garden design (*Beautiful Gardens in America*), and the history of the French monarchy (*The Private Memoires of Louis XV*). Ever the attentive host who loved his cocktails and enjoyed serving them to guests, Larz owned a copy of William Schmidt's *The Flowing Bowl: When and What to Drink*. The three-hundred-page volume provided not only recipes for hundreds of cocktails that led to what the author called "many a happy hour" but also for milk punch, a beverage Isabel served when she entertained "in Southern fashion" on New Year's Day.[48] Schmidt's recipe for it calls for rum, brandy, vanilla liqueur, sugar, and milk to be shaken with ice, then strained into a cocktail glass, and garnished with nutmeg or a lemon peel.

After the Andersons first occupied the mansion in March 1905, their home quickly became one of the most elegant and sought-after addresses on Washington's social circuit. The house, its decoration, its furnishings, and its amenities provided guests with the best Washington society had to offer.

Figure 16. The Saloon as the Andersons furnished it, ca. 1930s.

VIII

LIFE IN WASHINGTON

Three institutions made life go round in Washington during the Gilded Age. The first was the White House. The president and his cabinet were the pinnacle of public life in Washington, and all social standing was measured against them. The second was the US Congress, especially the Senate. With its ever-changing roster of powerful men from across the country who came to Washington accompanied by their elegant wives, Congress infused the city with a new class of power brokers every two years. It also brought industrialists and financiers who followed them to the capital each congressional session seeking to influence what happened in the legislative branch of government. The third and perhaps most important Washington institution was the elite party circuit, where politicians; government officials; businessmen; and leaders in the arts, academia, diplomacy, law and the judiciary, and religion came together. Anderson parties, especially Anderson dinner parties, figured prominently in the city's social landscape.

Over the course of the many seasons they spent in Washington, Larz and Isabel gave hundreds of dinners and luncheons. The Andersons documented some two hundred of these parties in "dinner books" that recorded who they invited and where they were seated at the table. Their first dinner party was on March 29, 1905, Isabel's birthday. Larz's mother, his cousins Ethel and Frances Anderson, and "Mrs. Longworth" (likely Mrs. Nicholas Longworth II) were the guests.[1]

If Anderson dinner and luncheon parties were small compared to those of a generation earlier, with no more than fifteen couples at the table including Larz and Isabel, their frequency made up for the difference. Between January 1 and May 28, 1909, for example, Larz and Isabel entertained 1,925 people at dinners and luncheons, and another 214 people came to an outdoor garden party. In addition to these by-invitation-only events, 90 people a week dropped in for Isabel's Sunday-afternoon "at home" tea parties that year.[2]

Putting on a high-society dinner party required an amazing allocation of time, effort, and money, and Larz and Isabel repeated this laborious process at least a few times a week during Washington's winter season. Isabel, as the official hostess of their parties, was responsible for inviting Washington's most-sought-after guests of honor, though Larz certainly participated in the guest-selection process. Once Isabel and her social secretary confirmed those guests, they filled out the rest of the list with compatible and congenial people. The right mix of people balanced social precedence, celebrity, and professional accomplishment to produce a convivial evening. The Andersons generously included their not-so-famous family and friends at their parties.

The names of several Anderson dinner guests persist in American memory: General John J. Pershing, General Douglas MacArthur, and Colonel Theodore Roosevelt Jr., the war-hero son of President Theodore Roosevelt, all came to dinner. Mr. and Mrs. George Washington Vanderbilt came to dinner many times and often stayed as houseguests. An assortment of European and Japanese princes, barons, and dukes helped fill out Anderson dinner tables even if they were not guests of honor. However, one pair of royals who came to Anderson House was anything but obscure. Prince Andrew of Greece and his wife, Princess Alice Battenberg, came to dinner at Anderson House on March 12, 1923, the only titled guests at the table that evening. This couple is still famous. They were the parents of Prince Philip, the Duke of Edinburgh, consort to Her Majesty the Queen of England, Elizabeth II.[3]

Not all guests were rich and famous. Visitors sometimes brought their children. A longtime Washington resident remembered going with her mother to one of Isabel's weekly at-home tea parties. As the girl and her mother were leaving, Isabel came to say good-bye and handed the child a small notebook with an embroidered cover and a miniature pen attached. "This is for you," Isabel told her. "A lady should never go out in public without a notebook in her purse."[4]

The importance and social diversity of Anderson dinner guests changed over time. Before 1909, foreign ministers, attachés, and visiting European officials made few appearances at Anderson House. Luncheon and dinner guests in the early years were mostly friends, family, and Washingtonians whose names are forgotten to history. Then, starting in 1909, after Taft became president, the makeup of the Anderson dinner table changed rapidly. Larz's friendship and access to the president was no secret in Washington. All of a sudden, European diplomats were frequent dinner guests at Anderson House, including envoys from Russia, Norway, Greece, the Netherlands, the Austro-Hungarian Empire, and Germany. The ambassadors of France and Great Britain did not dine at Anderson House until after the start of World War I in 1914. By that time, Larz was officially a retired US ambassador and one of their peers.

The Andersons gave one of their highest-profile dinner parties for the Prince of Udine in May 1917 during his visit to Washington as the head of an Italian commission seeking military support from the United States. Though forgotten now, the prince was a cousin of Italy's reigning king Victor Emmanuel III and one of the most important foreign visitors in the capital that year. World War I raged in Europe and the presence of an Italian royal at the Andersons' dinner table had both political and social import. The next morning, the *Washington Post* called the Anderson dinner dance "a particularly interesting function" because of Larz's diplomatic past. The brief announcement reminded readers that Larz had married into Boston wealth, been part of the Taft administration, and earlier in life been decorated by the Italian king.[5]

In 1922, the Andersons' dinner parties took an even more interesting turn when the names of US senators started appearing on guest lists. That year, Senators J. S. Frelinghuysen, R. P. Ernst, H. W. Keyes, and Charles Curtis (later vice president under Herbert Hoover) came to dinner. Secretary of the Treasury Andrew W. Mellon, an art connoisseur and one of the most powerful men in America, also dined at Anderson House that season. Larz wanted to be named US ambassador to Italy. On October 13, 1923, he wrote to Secretary of State Charles Evans Hughes asking to be considered for the post, "in case such a vacancy should exist."[6] President Warren Harding died in office on August 2, 1923, and Larz expected his successor, Calvin Coolidge, to appoint his own man to Italy. Larz also asked William Howard Taft, then chief justice of the Supreme Court, to write to Evans on his behalf, which the former president did on October 16.[7] Hughes assured Taft that Larz would receive "proper consideration," but there is no evidence the inquiry went any further. Larz's instinct was correct. In February 1924, Coolidge replaced Harding's ambassador to Italy with his own appointee, the distinguished diplomat Henry P. Fletcher (1873-1959).

Isabel's Social Secretaries

To navigate the intricacies of guest lists and other social minefields, Isabel employed private social secretaries throughout her years in Washington. A 1915 newspaper article highlighted the most important task of social secretaries: avoid "embarrassing situations in smart set hospitalities."[8] Social secretaries were not clerical workers. They were members of society in their own right who often came from distinguished Old Washington families. That social secretaries attended dinner parties as guests and sat at elite dinner tables demonstrated just how valued they were. Two of Isabel's secretaries were Georgiana "Baby" Todd (d. 1939), also known as Georgie, and Edith

Wallace Benham Helm (1874–1962).[9] In 1909, Isabel described a typical morning with Georgie planning social engagements. "In the mornings I sleep late, then comes Sophie to be told how many there will be for luncheon or dinner. Then Miss Todd, while I am eating my breakfast on a tray, to decide on a new dinner to be given, or say that Mrs. B. or Senator C. has given out for a dinner. After that calls and engagements are made."[10]

Edith worked for Isabel in the early 1920s and was a perfect choice for the post, sharing the Andersons' interests in Japan and France. Edith lived in Japan for six years as a child when her father, a US Navy admiral, was stationed there. As a young woman, she lived for two years in France. She was also an author with writing and editorial skills useful to Isabel. In 1913, Edith published a work of naval history for the Society of Sponsors, an organization for women who christened US Navy ships.[11] Isabel became a member of the Society in 1935 when she launched the USS *Perkins* (DD-377), named in honor of her father.

Over the course of her remarkable career as a social secretary, Edith served three US presidents: Woodrow Wilson, Franklin Delano Roosevelt, and Harry S. Truman. In 1954, after her retirement, she published her memoirs, *The Captains and the Kings*. "It has always seemed to me that to be a White House secretary," Edith wrote, "one could paraphrase the inscription over Dante's Hell to read: *All ye who enter here leave friends behind*."[12] Her book mentioned Anderson House briefly as the home of the Society of the Cincinnati but made no reference to her employment as Isabel's social secretary.

Life outside Anderson House

If life inside Anderson House was busy, the couple's life in the city was even busier. Incoming invitations had to be accepted or regretted, and many were turned down. As Larz got older, he increasingly seemed to resent social obligations. "It was a tiresome effort to entertain and meet people, and it was an effort to go away from our homes," he wrote in the summer of 1932. "I was only really happy when alone with Isabel and when inside our own homes."[13] Larz had a similar attitude toward Boston invitations. Writing about the 1928 Christmas season there, he said, they "declined all of many nice invitations to dinners, and to balls and receptions and weddings (for we seemed to be 'on the list' for them all)."[14] Earlier in life, Larz had demonstrated this same indifference to social obligations while serving as minister to Belgium—except when those obligations had involved royalty or aristocrats.

Despite their busy social calendar, Larz and Isabel found time to enjoy the city's recreational pastimes. They rode horses and drove carriages they brought down from Brookline, including the one they called Red Sleigh, which they liked taking out on the capital's snowy streets in winter.[15] They went horseback riding on the trails and bridle paths along nearby Rock Creek, then popular with Washington's elite. Isabel's thoroughbred horses often won trophies and ribbons, and her attendance at horse shows drew the attention of journalists and photographers. (See figure 3.) As they did in Brookline, the couple played tennis on their private court behind Anderson House. Larz and his friends played squash in the court on the third floor of the carriage house.

Isabel was active in many Boston and Washington organizations, but she was especially close to three groups in the capital. Her longest and most active affiliation was with the American Red Cross, which her friend Mabel Thorp Boardman (1860–1946) helped found in 1900. Isabel volunteered to serve as a nurse in Europe from 1917 to 1918 through the Washington chapter of the Red Cross. (See chapter 14.) After her return, she worked again for the Washington chapter during the great influenza epidemic of 1918 and 1919. She volunteered at a dispensary and attended to the sick and dying in their homes around the city. Isabel cared for people regardless of race or social class, including African Americans and Jews. She wrote during a visit to one home: "I took the pulse, temperature and respiration, then proceeded to clean up the two rooms, gathering up all the dirty linen and putting it on the porch, sweeping out the rooms and washing the dishes."[16] Her service was nothing short of heroic in the face of a virulent infection that killed an estimated twenty million to forty million people worldwide. Nursing wounded soldiers in Europe and influenza victims in Washington proved Isabel's utter lack of pretense, her ability to handle hard work, and her sense of duty to those in need. Her practical New England upbringing and Unitarian values inspired her in this work.

Isabel was equally devoted to the Daughters of the American Revolution as a member of the Susan Riviere Hetzel chapter in Washington. When she served from 1923 to 1926 as librarian general of the national society, she took her duties seriously. Her annual reports document the level of professionalism she brought to the position. Isabel traveled to libraries in other parts of the country to study the "latest and best library methods" and brought that knowledge back to Washington, where she oversaw its implementation.[17]

The organization Isabel perhaps prized most was her membership in the National League of American Pen Women. Founded in 1897, the organization brought together women writers, editors, poets, artists, musicians, and performers. As a condition of membership, the league required that its members be paid for their creative work, a principle still upheld by the organization.[18] Isabel's memberships in the DAR and Red Cross reflected her sense of patriotism and duty to her fellow men and women. Her membership in American Pen Women reflected her personal pride in being a published writer. This was a venue where she could be among her peers—women from all walks of life who shared the desire to create something of their own in their own name. Isabel was also a member of the Sulgrave Club, a social club for women founded by her good friend Mabel Thorp Boardman. The club, still located in the former mansion of Mr. and Mrs. Herbert Wadsworth on Massachusetts Avenue, was a venue where Isabel could enjoy the company of her peers away from the hubbub of the city.

Isabel's club and organizational memberships were, with few exceptions, related to causes and principles she believed in. Larz, in contrast, held memberships in private men's clubs that offered him venues where he could relax, socialize with old friends, and make new ones. His obituaries in 1937 noted his New York, London, Paris, and Washington club memberships. In London he belonged to the Bachelors' Club, which he joined in 1891 on the recommendation of Henry Adams, and Ye Sette of Odd Volumes, a dining club that "united once a month to form a Perfect Sette."[19] In Washington, he was a loyal and active member of the Metropolitan Club and the Alibi Club, both located then as now in the vicinity of the White House.

Larz joined the Metropolitan Club as a nonresident member in 1891 during the time he briefly studied law at Harvard. He became a resident member after he and Isabel established their winter home in Washington. He was a devoted and much-respected member of the club. After the original clubhouse was destroyed by fire in 1904, Larz donated $10,000 to help fund the 1907 construction of a new clubhouse. His donation went to the decoration and furnishing of a lounge named in honor of his father.[20] There were only two barbershops in the world where Larz would get haircuts, he once said: one was at the Hôtel de Vendôme in Paris, the other at the Metropolitan Club.[21]

Larz was an equally loyal member of Washington's ultrasecretive Alibi Club. He called it a "unique brotherhood" whose members were "all men of similar sympathies, talking the same language and relaxing as they met together."[22] There were few things in the world that could tempt him to go out without Isabel, but the Alibi was one of them. When Larz died, Isabel donated his collection of more than fifty caricatures of Alibi members by the Washington artist Clary Ray (1865–1916) that had hung for many years in the Billiard Room of Anderson House. When the Alibi was awarded District of Columbia historic landmark status in 1992, the Washington journalist Sarah Booth Conroy made a rare, nonmember visit to its mysterious interior and reported the Ray drawings were still there, hanging in the card room.[23]

Wherever they went, the Andersons attracted attention. Social editors and gossip columnists scrutinized what they wore and how they wore it. Fashion writers described Isabel's clothes down to the smallest details, even mentioning the color of thread used in the embroidered panel of her dress or the color of an ostrich feather in her turban.[24] Larz's attire also drew comment in the press. His stroll up Connecticut Avenue one afternoon in 1914 captured the gushing attention of the *Washington Post*'s society columnist Virginia Tatnall Peacock:

> Mr. Larz Anderson ... has brought from Boston a fashion which promises to become extremely popular among the smartest men in town, the wearing a single large orchid for a boutonniere. Mr. Anderson drew many admiring glances the other afternoon strolling up Connecticut Avenue wearing a superb large yellow orchid in his buttonhole which blended harmoniously with his dark brown clothes. For evening Mr. Anderson wears a white orchid and he also wears either the mauve or green orchid, according to the color of his suit of clothes.[25]

A King and Queen at Anderson House

In early 1931, while on their round-the-world trip, Larz and Isabel received a cable from Secretary of State Henry L. Stimson (1867–1950) asking if they would make Anderson House available for a state visit later that year by King Prajadhipok of Siam (Thailand) and his wife, Queen Rambhai Barni. The king was to travel to the United States for eye surgery at Johns Hopkins Hospital in Baltimore. He also wanted to make a short official visit to Washington before being admitted to the hospital. Larz liked the idea. He felt that Siamese or Japanese guests, in view of "their consideration and neatness," would only add to the distinction of Anderson House.[26] He had always been selective in how he responded to State Department requests and had on previous occasions declined to lend the house. "The thought of Indians in residence there, or Chinese, would be as repugnant as if coloured people had been admitted into its sleeping rooms," Larz said.[27] That the Andersons happened to be in Europe on their way to Siam when the cable arrived also figured into his decision. Granting the department's request would lead to an audience at the palace when they got to Bangkok.

Despite his enthusiasm about having the monarchs as their guests, Larz attached several conditions. His butler and housekeeper were to have "complete charge of the household" because he was wary of the "careless and inconsiderate servants collected by the State Department." He also told State he would cover all the expenses, "except the cost of provisions for unusual entertaining." By paying for the expenses, Larz reasoned, State would have less to say about how the visit was arranged. The department agreed to Larz's conditions.[28]

When the Andersons reached Penang, the Siamese consul met them to extend an invitation on behalf of the monarchs to visit the palace in Bangkok. Though State had already extended the formal invitation by the time the Andersons reached Bangkok, Larz and Isabel were allowed to extend their own pro forma invitation in person during their audience with the monarchs.[29]

As they continued their travel through Asia, Larz consulted by cable with the State Department about the arrangements. He directed his livery-clad footmen to wear white stockings rather than the customary black while the king was in residence, as white "generally indicates the presence of Royalty," he said.[30] He saw to it that "one of the best chefs in Washington" was hired to help Catherine, their longtime cook. The menus the kitchen turned out for the king and queen had a distinctly American character to them, even though they were presented in French: one luncheon offered *jambon de Verginie* (Virginia ham), *épinards au velouté* (creamed spinach), and *pommes de terre Macaire* (twice-baked potatoes). In keeping with protocol, the king's standard flew from the Anderson House flagpole retrofitted with a new finial: a bright red Garuda, the national emblem of Siam. The king's aides took over the Cypress Den as their office. American military and naval liaison officers used the Red Library as theirs, and the Secret Service set up shop in the housekeeper's office, with its own exterior door that opened directly onto the driveway.

Larz and Isabel were immensely pleased that the house accommodated the Siamese monarchs so perfectly. Despite the success of the visit, this was the only time Anderson House ever fulfilled Larz's dream of being hotelier to kings, queens, and heads of state.

The Playhouse

Isabel's avocation as a playwright led to the Andersons' involvement in what is now an obscure chapter in the theatrical history of Washington: the Playhouse at 1814 N Street. Modeled after the Players' Club in New York City, the Playhouse survived only a few years. At the time, however, it was anything but obscure, and the city's newspapers followed every detail of its planning, grand opening, controversies, and demise. Larz and Isabel were prominently associated with the Playhouse until the fall of 1911, when they left for Belgium. Even before the club opened, Isabel announced her intention to write a special children's play to be performed by child actors as one of the first productions. Her play never materialized, and there is no record of the Andersons' involvement with the Playhouse in any of their papers.

It was perhaps the spirit of the times that inspired Washington elites to create their own drama club. In 1908, the New York theatrical producer Heinrich Conried (1843–1909) called for the creation of a new "artistic" theater there, in the continental tradition of the Comédie-Française in Paris or the Burg in Vienna.[31] Conried's proposal led to the founding of the New Theater the following year. With the backing of wealthy elites like J. P. Morgan and Otto Kahn, the incorporators built a theater designed by the celebrated firm of Carrère and Hastings at the corner of Central Park West and Sixty-Second Street.

In 1911, when elite Washingtonians decided they should have their own theater, they cited New York as precedent. "New York has its New Theater, Paris its Comedie Francaise, Berlin, Vienna, and other continental cities their delightful homes of the drama, of music, and terpsichore," the *Washington Post* said, "but it has remained for the exclusive social set of Washington to establish ... The Playhouse, an institution threefold in character—social, artistic, and charitable." It was not just a theater but also a private club planned as "the mecca for exclusive social, official, and diplomatic Washington."[32]

Indeed, the crème de la crème of Washington backed the project financially. A list of its founding members reads like the *Who's Who* of 1911: navy secretary George Von L. Meyer; Gist and Montgomery Blair; Edward McLean; the architect Jules Henri de Sibour; Alice Pike Barney; Clarence Moore; Thomas Coleman du Pont; Senator Stephen Elkins; Robert Roosevelt; Secretary of the Treasury Wayne MacVeagh; Elsie Anderson McMillan's mother-in-law, Mrs. James McMillan; and Larz Anderson were among the incorporators and backers of the project. The *Post* called the roster a list of "men and women whose names mean much to the nation's Capital."[33]

The wealthy theatrical promoter and sometime playwright Preston Gibson (1880–1937) helped set up the new club and served as its first (and only) president. His name appeared everywhere in connection with the project, giving the club its theatrical bona fides, even though he achieved notoriety when he was accused in 1910 of plagiarizing from Oscar Wilde.[34] The Playhouse was to present "plays written by members of the club" performed by "prominent actors," though there is no evidence any prominent actors ever walked its stage.[35] The Playhouse filled a niche no commercial theater in Washington would touch: a stage for amateur theatrical and musical productions that were pet projects of Washington hostesses. The club did not need to compete with the capital's commercial theaters—the Belasco, the Shubert, or Albaugh's Opera House. Playhouse members would compete with one another.

Newspapers carried extensive coverage of plans to remodel the existing structure at 1814 N Street, once the home of Edward C. Halliday, an industrialist who came from a wealthy family of steel manufacturers in England. Halliday's wife, Henrietta, is better known in the architectural history of Washington as the commissioner, in 1908–1909, of what is now the Embassy of Ireland on Sheridan Circle. After the club's incorporators purchased the house in 1910 for $40,000, they hired the Washington architect Ward Brown, also a Playhouse incorporator, to renovate it and install clubhouse and theatrical amenities. Brown's 1911 plan to build a one-hundred-thousand-seat stadium for the capital modeled after the Roman Colosseum drew much attention when he unveiled his designs for it.[36]

Brown renovated the Halliday residence for its new use as a theater club. He designed offices and meeting rooms, an "exquisite" ladies-only "apartment" for card parties and teas, and a gentlemen's "grillroom" in the basement that members entered directly from the street. Brown put the auditorium at the rear of the structure, with seating for two hundred and a three-loge balcony. The seats could be removed to make a dance floor "for the younger set." The stage was "perfect in equipment, even though in miniature" and had dressing rooms underneath it. The theater included a box office to handle ticket sales. The layout accommodated a typical evening of club activities, including fixed-price dinners, shows, and "chafing-dish, after-theater" suppers with dancing. Members could also rent the theater and dining room for private events.[37] After purchasing the building, the incorporators issued a $25,000 bond to fund club operations until it became self-supporting through ticket sales. Most of the incorporators bought bonds for $250 or $500. Isabel bought one for $500. In the end, the Playhouse raised only 60 percent of the funding it needed.[38]

The club opened on February 9, 1911, with a fund-raiser for the Washington Diet Kitchen Association, one of the Playhouse's favorite and frequent charities. The event was deemed a "brilliant success."[39] Dinners, balls, lectures, and drama soon filled the club's playbill. Gibson presented playlets of unknown authorship. Pieces such as *Grabbe and Runne* and *The Elopement* were the first season's highly touted offerings. Dinners and costume parties were popular, and the club offered dancing lessons. The Playhouse functioned more like a private club than a legitimate theater. A lecture by the prominent interior decorator Elsie de Wolfe (1865–1950), who had many famous clients, including the Duke and Duchess of Windsor and Henry

Clay Frick, was perhaps the only culturally significant program in the club's history. De Wolfe is credited with helping shift American tastes in decoration from heavy, dark interiors in the nineteenth century to French-inspired designs in the early twentieth century.

Even during the first season, there were signs the Playhouse was doomed. One of the members, Mrs. Christian D. Hemmick, had a very public fight with the club's management over the production of her play, *The Love of Echo*. In 1911, Mrs. Hemmick, better known as Alice Pike Barney, married twenty-six-year-old Christian D. Hemmick, a State Department employee more than thirty-six years her junior. The official explanation for the dispute was disagreement on how proceeds from the play would be shared with charity.[40] As it turned out, the rift was not about money but about the scandalous theme of the play itself. When the play was finally produced in New York City, Alice and Christian starred in its leading and, for the time, shocking roles. The plot was a thinly disguised vehicle for the couple to flout their unconventional marriage: the female lead, Echo (Alice), lay chained in a cave to be freed only by an "unkissed youth, hitherto unloved and unloving." When Narcissus (Christian) entered the cave, he freed Echo, and they danced together in celebration.[41]

The club suffered a steep decline over the next few years, and the board spent most of 1913 denying a financial crisis. By 1914, the Playhouse offered fewer and fewer theatrical productions and rented out its facilities for more and more private parties. The season opener that year was a playlet called *Is This a Rehearsal?*[42] In 1915, the board decided to recast the Playhouse as a public ballroom. Beaux-Arts architect Jules Henri de Sibour oversaw reconstruction and redecoration of the clubhouse. The *Washington Post* reported it was not "the rage for the fox trot" that had brought about the demolition of the club's theater but rather that "the theatrical ventures have not proved at all satisfactory during the past two winters."[43]

With the Playhouse gone, a new organization quickly filled its place. The Arts Club of Washington was founded in 1916 in the wake of the Playhouse debacle. Though it has had the reputation of appealing to the bohemian side of Washington society, the Arts Club counted (and still counts) among its members professional artists, writers, musicians, and performers who make their living in the arts. Unlike the dilettante Playhouse, the Arts Club survived and now has a century of success behind it.

What It Cost

The Andersons' balance sheets for the decade between 1928 and 1937 show they spent more than $215,000 keeping Anderson House open during that decade ($4 million today).[44] Projected over the thirty-three years they owned the house together, the total cost of operating Anderson House was at least $700,000 ($13 million today). Records of their travel and time spent in Brookline, Washington, and elsewhere show the couple were in Anderson House for a total of approximately sixty-three months over thirty-three years, or an average of less than two months a year. In today's dollars, then, it cost the Andersons about $206,000 to keep the house open for each month they were actually there.

As time progressed, especially after 1925, Larz and Isabel spent less and less time at Anderson House. World War I, the influenza epidemic, and the great influx of middle-class government workers in the years between the wars changed the life of the city forever. It evolved toward a more modern and more egalitarian urban lifestyle. Larz blamed Herbert Hoover for their declining use of the mansion: Washington was "so changed and the Hoover administration seemed socially (as well as officially) so hopeless that we did n't want to open the house in Washington during the 'season.'"[45]

When the Great Depression hit the nation in 1929, it impoverished people the Andersons knew. After the crash of the stock market, no one entertained as they once had, even if they had the money to do so. Nonetheless, Larz maintained Anderson House as he always had and made sure it was ready at a moment's notice to become once again Washington's darling.

DEAR ISABEL !

(AS I SEE HER).

Figure 17. Isabel Anderson on horseback in Colorado, 1920.

IX

A ROUGH-AND-READY PLACE (NEW HAMPSHIRE)

I sabel Anderson was at home in New Hampshire in any season. She spent the springs and autumns of her youth at her father's country place, once a Perkins-family hunting camp, about fifteen miles from Concord. Isabel's grandfather Judge Hamilton Eliot Perkins (1806–1886) bought the property in the mid-nineteenth century when it was still known as the "old Otis Whittier place."[1] Her father, George Hamilton Perkins, spent much of his youth there, hunting and fishing and riding horses.

In 1881, Grandfather Perkins expanded the camp by purchasing an old farmhouse nearby. It was a simple structure—a square of four rooms with fireplaces connected to a central chimney. George named it The Box in honor of its simple geometry and absence of any frills. Over time, he added many rooms to accommodate the friends and family who came to visit for weeks or months at a time. He added a special room with windows on all sides for his wife, Anna, who, because of poor eyesight, needed plenty of daylight for any kind of close work like sewing or reading. There was even a children's dining room—adults not allowed! In keeping with navy tradition, George outfitted some of the bedrooms with hammocks.[2]

During the 1880s, when he still served in the navy, George went up to the farm as often as his duties allowed to help his father manage the property. In 1883, he started buying land of his own and eventually purchased sixteen adjacent or nearby farms until his own holdings totaled 1,800 acres. Even though he was a New Hampshire–born man who did well for himself in the world at large, the locals did not like him at first. "They had a prejudice against him because he had money and spent only a third of the year [at his farm]," wrote his biographer, "and a few thought he was rough and autocratic." Over time, his generosity and kindness won them over, and everyone addressed him as "George," not "Commodore."[3]

George took an increasingly active interest in farming. By the time he retired from the navy in 1891, he was a gentleman farmer with an "absorbing interest in the farm and its operations."[4] He ran the farm with military precision and made it successful. George "delighted in improving any farm which had been allowed to run down ... for his naval training made him abhor anything not shipshape," one local historian noted.[5] His improvements to the farmlands increased their value and provided employment for many men, some of whom George brought up with him from Boston. He started a worker management system based on his navy training that today sounds modern: groups of laborers were "commanded" by one of their own, who was responsible for seeing that the day's work got done.[6]

George Perkins loved going up to The Box after extended stays in Boston or Newport and would exclaim on his arrival, "Oh, isn't it good to breathe this air and think that no one has ever breathed it before!"[7] From the top of the hill where the farmhouse stood, he could see Mount Kearsarge in the distance and, closer by, a meadow that sloped down to a pond. During Isabel's childhood, the Perkins family arrived at The Box around May 1 and stayed until it was time to summer in Newport for July and August in William Fletcher Weld's cottage at 138 Narragansett Avenue. They then returned to The Box at the end of the season and stayed until around November 1, when they went back to Boston for the start of Isabel's school term with Miss Winsor. The regularity of Isabel's childhood visits to New Hampshire established a pattern that changed little for the rest of her life: two visits a year of several weeks each, and rarely more than three months a year in all.

"A Very Picturesque Place"

When George Perkins died in 1899, he left The Box and its farmlands to Isabel's cousin Roger Eliot Foster. George was like "a second father" to Roger, Maud Howe Elliott once said, and Roger was surely the son George never had.[8] Roger had also worked on the farm for years and shared his uncle's vision for it. George feared that if his wife or daughter took over the property, they would stop using it as a farm.[9] He did not leave any real estate to Anna or Isabel, and he left them no money either. He felt they had inherited enough from his father-in-law, as he explained in his will: "To my beloved wife, Anna Weld Perkins, and my beloved daughter, Isabel Weld Perkins, I leave my best love and good will, they both being amply provided for by William F. Weld, deceased."[10]

George was equally hard on Roger and attached conditions to the inheritance, perhaps at the request of his nieces. His will stipulated that the farm should only go to Roger "on condition that he had not in the mean time married some one, who in the opinion of his sisters is not suitable for him."[11] Roger may have already had his doubts about keeping the property and approached Isabel about buying it from him. In 1899, a year before Roger's death, Larz wrote in his journal that he and Isabel would try to acquire The

Box from him.[12] Roger never married and died suddenly in 1900, only a year after inheriting the farm. His family gave the property to Isabel, "without any other consideration than their affection for her."[13] The Fosters may have felt that by right Isabel or her mother should have inherited the property in the first place. For the next six years, Isabel went up to New Hampshire as she always had, in spring and fall, to visit her relatives and her mother, who spent several months a year at The Box. Though she had been reared in Boston, Anna felt more comfortable at The Box and enjoyed the company of her late husband's family.

In 1906, a year after Anderson House opened, Isabel purchased her own lakefront property near The Box. The following year, she bought eighty-five acres of land in Contoocook, including the house where her father was born.[14] She often visited her new lakeside property but stayed with her mother at The Box. Larz sometimes accompanied Isabel on these trips. He once described The Box as "rough, camplike, and uncomfortable" and, perhaps due to the infrequency of his brief visits, did not write about it often in his letters and journals.[15] At other times, he seemed to enjoy his visits thoroughly. At the end of one of his first visits to The Box in August 1899, just before their trip to India, Larz said he would leave "the little Box with a great deal of regret. It is a very picturesque place."[16] After another visit in 1923, he said the "wonderful autumn weather, the sun and the feel of the air were glorious."[17] Despite his own ambivalence about New Hampshire, Larz always took great delight in Isabel's love for the place. He never begrudged her the extended stays that refreshed her spirits and kept her close to her father's family.

After Anna Perkins died in October 1924, Isabel decided she would no longer keep The Box. It was large (twenty-four rooms), and there were many people who were used to staying there for extended periods of time. Four months later, Isabel gave the house and about 230 acres to her New Hampshire cousins. This was a generous gift, but she wanted something simpler and uniquely hers—with no guest rooms.[18]

The Boxlet
Some of Isabel's friends had a lakeside camp in the Adirondacks, and for years she thought it would be fun to have a camp of her own too.[19] (In northern New England, a *camp* is a seasonal vacation hut, cottage, or house in a wooded area or near a lake.) In 1924 or 1925, Isabel asked Milton J. Walker, the farm superintendent her father had hired many years earlier, to build a rustic cabin for her on the shore of the pond. She enjoyed any activity connected with the water—swimming, canoeing, hiking on trails along the water's edge, and picnicking—so putting a cabin of her own there seemed

right. "I.A. had wanted a camp by the lakeside," Larz wrote, "where she could keep house and do her own cooking, and we could be by ourselves."[20] She decided to call her new camp The Boxlet, a smaller and more intimate version of the big house on the hill above.

Isabel had very clear ideas about what she wanted: a cabin for visitors and staff and a separate bedroom cabin for herself, the two connected by a screened "runway" approximately ten yards long. The public side of the cabin, originally a small barn, consisted of a combined living and dining room, two bedrooms, a bathroom, a kitchen and pantry, and a small porch-like room at the back where the servants took their meals.[21] The second floor had three small servant bedrooms tucked in under low ceilings.

Isabel's part of the cabin was plain and functional, consisting of a bedroom, a bathroom, a small dressing area separated from the bedroom by a screen, and a small porch cut into the corner of the room with just enough room for a rocking chair. There Isabel could sit and look out over the water. Her dressing area doubled as a sleeping nook for Larz when he was at the camp. He decorated his corner of the room with framed Valentine's cards and other memorabilia that are still as they were during Isabel's lifetime. Clerestory windows in the sleeping nook provided light and air but no view. Isabel got the view of the pond, trees, and hills. If Larz did not like being in New Hampshire for more than a few days at a time, his sleeping arrangements were one of the reasons. Isabel may have known exactly what she was doing by putting him in a corner of her room behind a screen. He surely would have wanted a suite of his own!

The interiors of The Boxlet were simple but cozy. Isabel directed Milton to keep the interior unpainted and the tongue-and-groove-board walls and ceilings unplastered. The floors were of simple pine in New England fashion, and the mantles were of unglazed red brick. The fireplace in Isabel's bedroom had an old-style warming oven to one side that actually worked. Her cousin Evelyn once said Isabel liked being at The Boxlet when it was cold, so the idea of a bedroom with a warming oven where she could keep a little meal hot without depending on servants appealed to her. Isabel enjoyed cooking for herself when she was at The Boxlet, especially scrambled eggs and a Welsh rarebit cooked over the fire.[22] She often cooked that simple menu for her most important friends and guests, including President Taft and his military aide Major Archibald Willingham Butt (1865–1912) when they stopped in at Anderson House late one evening after the theater.[23]

The Boxlet's furnishings reflected classic colonial New England styles: spindle-back chairs, side tables with spiral-twist legs, a rocking chair with stenciled decorations, and braided rugs. This was perhaps a reflection of the

Colonial Revival period of American architectural and interior design then popular in the United States. Wallace Nutting (1861–1941), an antiquarian and photographer who helped promote popular interest in colonial-era design, was one of Larz's classmates at Exeter and Harvard.[24] Most of these items are still in the camp, exactly as Isabel left them. She bought many of the items herself at local auctions. The overall effect was a comfortable, lived-in country cottage. Isabel draped a selection of exotic fabrics from Africa and Asia over furniture, beds, and walls. She eventually brought up some of the wicker furniture that had once been on the deck of their houseboat, the *Roxana*, along with the boat's plate service bearing the signal of the Black Horse Line and the boat's flatware.[25] If furniture needed refinishing, it was "painted blue by IA herself to match the simplest of blue hangings," Larz wrote.[26] The blue furniture is still in The Boxlet. Isabel brought up from Brookline some family pieces too, including a sideboard from Elizabeth Anderson's cottage at Bar Harbor, "reminding us of other happy days," Larz reminisced.[27]

Unlike Weld in Brookline or Anderson House in Washington, The Boxlet was not chockablock with mementos, collectibles, or art. Isabel selected simple decorations for her walls, especially family photographs she and Larz put into secondhand frames bought at local auctions. In Isabel's room, the arrangement was even more informal, with many photographs and memorabilia simply thumbtacked to the walls, where they remain to this day.[28] The few objects she put out for decoration—colonial-era implements such as candle molds, pewter plates, and cooking utensils—gave the place a homey look. The living room mantelpiece displayed two pairs of white porcelain figurines from Copenhagen, one a set of pelicans and the other of parrots.

One of the curios still at The Boxlet from Isabel's era is a framed text titled "The Legend of Winnepocket." Though not attributed, the passage is the opening section of John Greenleaf Whittier's 1849 poem "The Bridal of Penacook." It is the story of the Indian princess Wetamoo, who married Chief Winnepocket in what is now Concord, New Hampshire, in 1662. Like Larz and Isabel's wedding in 1897, the nuptials of Winnepocket and Wetamoo took place in the chief's village and were followed by a celebration in the bride's village. Isabel printed the legend as a memento for her guests. She also commissioned four stained glass panels to illustrate the legend—two of Native American men and two of Native American women—which are still displayed in The Boxlet's front windows.

Isabel took great pride in all this. Her own simple aesthetics guided the decoration, furnishing, and finishing of The Boxlet's interior. There were no French or Italian influences here. Isabel was very much ahead of her time as a decorator. By today's standards, her decorating style was "shabby chic."

Entertaining at The Boxlet

Despite the small guest capacity of The Boxlet, Isabel eventually started entertaining frequently and over time added another three camp buildings for visitors. One of these, Camp Wetamoo, was a carriage shed Isabel converted to a cottage by having a fireplace and a small kitchen installed. She had the old sap house renovated for use as another guest cabin. Finally, she had a fireplace and shelves installed in an old corncrib on a low hill near The Boxlet, stocked its shelves with eating utensils, and called it The Picnic Box.

When her distant cousin Warren Weld (1908–1964) returned from military service after World War II, Isabel further improved The Picnic Box so he could live there, though there was no kitchen or bathroom. She wanted it to be a place where Warren could rest and recuperate from what would today certainly be called post-traumatic stress disorder. She renamed the cabin The Sentry Box in honor of his military service.[29] Warren was in and out of hospitals for many years and was buried with military honors in the Long Island National Cemetery.

Isabel did not limit her entertaining to friends and family. On Wednesdays and Sundays during the summer season, Isabel opened her end of the pond to the public, allowing local people to use her waterfront. Larz once estimated that as many as three hundred to four hundred people would come to swim and picnic, but given the size of the little beach and the remoteness of the property, he likely exaggerated the turnout.[30] It was not unlike Larz to resent anyone's intrusion into his life with Isabel.

The last major project at The Boxlet during Larz's lifetime was construction of a pavilion, called The Pond House, beside a man-made fishing pool. An inlet with a red Japanese-style footbridge across it connected it to the pond. Isabel had been thinking about such a project for several years and again asked Milton Walker to do the work for her. Larz almost certainly helped design this exotic structure in the New Hampshire woodland and described it as "built in Japanese style, with eaves delicately uptilted at the corners in saucy Oriental manner."[31] A deck jutted out over the water. "Parts of the balustrade of the platform and of the bridge had been painted red, as is customary in Japanese temples," he said.[32]

The interior of the pavilion consisted of one large room with a fireplace and a lavatory. Isabel's workers stocked the pool with fifty brown trout and thirty rainbow trout so visitors were sure to catch something when they fly cast into the pond, even on rainy days when the overhanging roof provided shelter.[33] The inlet, pool, and pavilion (including a mounted blue fin tuna Larz once caught in Florida) are still there, but the miniature bridge is long gone.

The Great New England Hurricane of 1938 damaged the property, leveling lakeside trees and destroying the bridge. The Boxlet escaped destruction.[34]

New Hampshire, in Retrospect

The Boxlet was Isabel's simple counterpoint to the magnificent life Larz pursued for them elsewhere. Even if she could only be there for a few weeks or a month at a time, it gave her breathing space of her own. It returned her to the values and ethics her Perkins family, especially her father, instilled in her. When the authors of an encyclopedia of New Hampshire genealogy lauded the Perkins family for its "energetic industry, attention to details, fidelity to causes they espoused, unflinching courage and preparedness for the issue when the day of trial came," they were also describing Isabel.[35] It is remarkable that these noble traits passed down over many generations of Perkinses, finding what was perhaps their highest expression in a woman born in 1876 in Boston.

By any measure, Isabel's character and emotional footing derived from the simple lifestyle and strong morals of rural New Hampshire. There she had her deepest sense of belonging and feeling connected to things that truly mattered to her: a loving family, pristine nature, inspiring quiet, and, most of all, a sense of control over her own life. She was at home in Brookline and Washington, of course, but not in the way she was at home in New Hampshire.

Isabel loved Larz dearly and for most of the year endeavored to give him the life and the wife he wanted. In return, and to his credit, Larz knew how important New Hampshire was to Isabel and gave her leave to be there with or without him as she wished.

Isabel so loved The Boxlet that Larz once grumbled, "I am almost jealous."[36]

Figure 18. Larz and Isabel Anderson, Allagash River, 1905.

X

At Home in the World

Wherever he went, Larz Anderson was at home in the world. He loved to travel, especially with Isabel, but when she wanted to stay home, he ventured abroad without her. The circumstances of his birth and the family travel to Europe during his youth predisposed him to be an avid and adventurous traveler all his life.

The first trip abroad of which Larz had any memory was his parents' 1872 trip to Europe aboard the Cunard Line's RMS *Russia*. Nick's Harvard classmate Charles Francis Adams Jr. and his wife and child accompanied them, and the two families vacationed on the continent together for several months. The *Russia* was popular with the Andersons, and in 1877 they sailed on it again for another year's sojourn in Europe. Fifty years later Larz relived the thrill of that crossing: "I recalled the days of fifty years ago when we used to sit behind the pilothouse on the stern of the 'Russia' and watch with terror and fascination the 'following wave' which boats of those days used to drag after them and which ever threated to 'poop' [capsize] the ship in case of too sudden a stop."[1]

These early European experiences, especially in Paris, whetted Larz's appetite for world travel when he got older. Larz remembered his childhood visits to the French capital with great affection and nostalgia. Memories of long-ago Paris comforted him, especially as he got older. The city was, he said in 1933, "greatly changed from the old days," but it still made him "recall the days of boyhood and ... forget the changes."[2] He loved travel. Even late in life when his health was failing, he thought about new places to visit. In 1936, a year before his death, he considered going to Arizona or Marrakesh for a winter vacation with Isabel.[3]

Two things made Larz feel at home in the world. The first was his familiarity with the world at large. He had a vast knowledge of geography, history, and world culture that helped him observe and understand what he saw. The other was his social network. He knew people—or knew people who knew people—everywhere. He was part of a vast network of globe-trotting elites who welcomed him into their homes and private clubs and aboard their pleasure craft.

If Larz was born with traveling in his blood, Isabel was not. Until her grand tour to Europe and the Middle East in 1895–1896 with her cousin Roger Foster and Maud Howe Elliott, her childhood travel was limited to the axis that ran between New Hampshire and Rhode Island, with Boston at the midpoint. She enjoyed travel but did not thrive on it as Larz did. Isabel dutifully accompanied her husband on scores of trips but let him go on many others alone.

New Hampshire meant more to Isabel than another trip to Europe. "My darling Isabel loves to re-live her girlhood days at the Boxlet," Larz wrote in 1933 in defense of their arrangement, "so it does me good to re-live my boyhood days in Paris, where I was born and where so many years were spent."[4] When in Paris alone, he became the quintessential Parisian *flâneur*—a gentleman of leisure who strolled the boulevards and sat on café terraces watching the world go by. His arrival in the city, announced in the newspapers, brought "happy invitations" from many friends and acquaintances.[5] He loved going to the Café de la Paix across from the Paris Opera and dining at Voisin's restaurant on rue Saint-Honoré.

During their marriage, the Andersons took some seventy-five trips together. They traveled most frequently in North America (sixteen train and motorcar trips and thirteen cruises on the *Roxana*). Europe was their second-most-frequent destination (fifteen trips together and eleven Larz alone). Isabel's only solo international travel during their marriage was her expedition to France and Belgium in 1917–1918 as a volunteer nurse, an experience vital to Isabel's developing a sense of her own self-worth and identity separate from her husband (see chapter 14). The Andersons made a few long and very complicated trips to distant regions (Asia, Latin America, and Africa), but such travel was not routine for them and mostly occurred later in life.

North American Travel[6]

1901	California and Mexico by the private train car *Imperial*
1904	Southwestern United States via Canada by the private train car *Luciana*; St. Louis Fair by the private train car *Mayflower*
1905	Camping on the Allagash River, Maine; travel to Kentucky and Indiana by train
1907	Adirondacks, Upstate New York
1907	Cruising in southern waters aboard the *Roxana* (thirteen times between 1907 and 1927)
1914	Camping in Ontario, Canada

1915   West Coast, Glacier Park, and the Grand Canyon by the private
        train car *Federal*

1916   Fishing trip to Rangeley Lakes, Maine

1920   Louisville for the Kentucky Derby; camping trip to the Colorado
        Rockies by the private train car *Manhattan*

1923   Trip by automobile to the White Mountains

1924   Fishing trip to Bonaventure, Canada, by the private train car
        Manhattan

1930   Southwestern United States and California by the private train car
        Davy Crockett; fishing and camping trip to Canada by the private
        train car *Henry Stanley*

1932   Montana, Washington state, and the Olympic Games in Los
        Angeles, California, by private train car

1933   The Chicago World's Fair by private train car

1935   Seattle by private train car for the launching of the USS *Perkins*
        (DD-377)

1936   California and Mexico; cruise aboard Norman Woolworth's yacht
        Naparo to Nantucket and Maine

Larz and Isabel were avid and adventurous travelers in North America,
especially the continental United States. Even by today's standards, their
travel to remote desert areas of the Southwest or the north country of New
England was adventurous. In these rural areas, they traveled in chauffeur-
driven cars over dirt roads and slept in tents pitched by their guides. The
drivers did double duty as mechanics to repair the vehicles along the way. Gas
stations and garages were few and far between. Larz and Isabel especially
loved the American Southwest and the southeastern coast (the Carolinas,
Georgia, and Florida). Some of the trips were rough-and-ready camping and
fishing trips. Others were luxury travel by private Pullman car with world's
fairs, expositions, and even the Olympics as their destination.

From their earliest years together, the Andersons traveled to areas of the
country not yet popular or accessible to American tourists. They especially
marveled at the beauty of Native lands, the size of natural wonders like the
Grand Canyon, and the luminous big sky of the West. Larz's journals of
these trips provide fascinating insight into elite Americans' discovery of vast
stretches of the country that were then still federal territories. The Andersons
felt drawn to these lands and their peoples and made the Southwest the focus of
their first domestic adventure together after their first trips to Japan and India.

On Native Lands

In early 1901, Larz and Isabel set off from Boston in the private train car *Imperial* for their first vacation together in North America—to California and Mexico. Their first stop was Mexico. To prepare for the trip, Larz read a new book by the travel writer F. Hopkinson Smith, *A White Umbrella in Mexico* (1900). Smith's narrative made Larz eager to visit the country. The landscapes, buildings, and history of Mexico, indeed everything about it, intrigued him. In Malta, near Oaxaca, they visited pre-Columbian ruins then being excavated by Harvard anthropologist Marshall Howard Saville (1867–1935), to whom Larz and Isabel had a letter of introduction. Saville himself took them out to the site to show them a tomb he had recently uncovered. Larz proudly reported that he and Isabel were among the first to enter it.[7]

In Mexico, despite their distance from home, they celebrated Washington's birthday on February 22 by hanging a portrait of the first president on the wall of their private car and adorning it with flowers. That evening, Larz gave an "appropriate speech" at the dinner table to commemorate the occasion.[8] The Andersons held an annual Washington birthday celebration of some sort almost every year of their lives together, a charming reminder of the importance of George Washington to American identity during the Gilded Age.

From Mexico, the Andersons traveled up the coast of California, making a stop in Los Angeles on their way to San Francisco. There they dined at the famed Poodle Dog Restaurant, known for its French cuisine and fabulous wine cellar. They turned eastward and started home to Boston by way of Salt Lake City. They had been to Salt Lake before on their way to Japan in 1897 but decided to stop again, this time staying on board the *Imperial* rather than in a hotel. After more than a month of travel, their private car was home to them. "The trophies of our trip are hung about, and coats and hats and canes about, with maps of California and Mexico," wrote Larz, "all looking very cozy and comfortable."[9]

In January 1904, they returned to the American Southwest, this time focusing on the interior regions and the territory of New Mexico. Here they acquired their first pieces of Native American arts and crafts, particularly Navajo blankets and Zuni pottery. Interior photographs of Anderson House made by Frances Benjamin Johnston in 1910 show several pieces of Native American pottery on display in the Winter Garden and in Larz's Billiard Room. A photograph of the Cypress Den shows Native American blankets hung like banners from the den's balcony.[10]

Larz and Isabel were overcome by the vast beauty of the West. After a visit to the Grand Canyon, Larz described in poetic terms what he had seen and felt:

Well! It is all so vast and stupendous that it takes time to
take it all in. A great deep cruel wound in Mother Earth's
side it seems to reveal the history of the World from all
time. Its immensity is indescribable—for to say that Mount
Washington could easily be turned upside down in it but
gives a suggestion. And its coloring—which varies with every
light that comes over it—morning—midday—evening (and
moonlight—as we are having it)—is more brilliant that I
had looked for—as brilliant indeed as you may have seen it
painted.[11]

They were also enchanted by Native Americans, especially at the Zuni
and Acoma pueblos. Modern visitors to the Acoma Sky Pueblo, as it is now
called, ride to the top of the mesa by bus. When the Andersons visited it
in 1904, there was no road or shuttle bus service to the top. They climbed
a narrow, steep, and rocky foot trail to reach the pueblo. While visiting
the Zuni people, Larz and Isabel met Matilda Coxe Stevenson (1849–
1915), an ethnologist whose fieldwork was routinely featured in the annual
reports of the Smithsonian Institution.[12] She was renowned for her intimate
knowledge of the language, philosophy, religion, and social life of the Zuni.
Larz and Isabel could have had no better guide than Stevenson, and she
likely inspired and informed much of their appreciation of Native American
culture. Through her they were able to attend a Dance of the Blue Horns in
an underground ceremonial space that Larz called an "estufa." Larz and his
friend Walter Denègre were allowed into the sacred space, but Isabel and
her cousin Kate Peckham had to watch through an opening in the wall from
an adjacent room.[13]

The Incomplete Angler

In contrast to their travel to the arid Southwest, Larz and Isabel made
elaborate fishing expeditions to wild and remote areas of the far Northeast.
They took one particularly interesting and well-documented trip to Quebec's
Bonaventure River in July 1924. Larz made the arrangements through
the Boston office of the Raymond & Whitcomb Company, a travel agency
catering to elites. For the actual salmon fishing, he negotiated directly with
George C. Cutler of Boston, who owned the land, camp, and fishing rights.
Ned Brandegee, husband of Isabel's cousin May Brandegee, had rented the
Cutler camp several times and recommended it to Larz.

Larz had long wanted to go salmon fishing but quickly discovered it
was "about the costliest sport in the World—a few weeks on a river costs

as much as a yachting cruise."[14] The fees for the camp, including fishing rights, came to $2,500 for one week. Supplies ("liquid and otherwise," Cutler said) and services were extra. Larz and Isabel footed the bill for food, mail delivery, boats, camp staff, crates and ice, fishing guides, and gratuities. In the end, they spent more than $10,000 on the two-week trip, the equivalent of some $150,000 today. This included the cost of bringing four guests: Larz's Harvard chums Dr. C. A. "Allie" Porter and Fred Bradlee Sr. and his Exeter classmate Ritchie Simpkins. Allie's wife, Margaret, a close friend of Isabel's, came along to keep her company. Both women went fishing every day with the men. Larz hired Captain Robert H. Stewart, an employee of Raymond & Whitcomb, as their trip manager. Stewart accompanied the Andersons on many of their subsequent trips at home and abroad, and Isabel once called him their "guide, photographer, and friend."[15]

The merry band departed from Boston's North Station aboard the private train car *Manhattan* on July 8 and, after a brief visit to Montreal, reached the Cutler fishing camp two days later. The camp's sleeping cabins accommodated eight guests. Other cabins served as dining room, card room, cookhouse, and quarters for the guides. There was a three-hole golf course "on which large amounts of money have been won and lost in the past," Cutler warned.[16] The camp came with a cook and "cookee" (kitchen helper), river and fishing guides, a postman who brought mail and telegrams every morning, and a carter whose job it was to ice and box up each day's catch and ship it to the anglers' friends and families.

Each day's plan called for morning and afternoon fishing in different spots along the river, with a lunch break in between. Larz did not prove to be a hearty outdoorsman. He limited his fishing to mornings only, in observance of what he called the "Coué method," a reference to the French psychologist Émile Coué, whose advice for daily living was based on the mantra "Every day, in every way, I'm getting better and better."[17] Larz revised Coué's philosophy to "One fish a day and every day." He decided that bringing in a dozen or more fish in one day "was too wholesale," though that was not the reason he avoided fishing. "I am handicapped because I feel too top heavy to stand in the canoe," he wrote. "Never having cast with so heavy a rod before, my wrists and forearms and shoulders tire."[18]

Larz's emotional dependence on Isabel was clear one morning when she, Margaret, and Ritchie set off for two days of fishing at another camp nearby. "I felt terribly lonely without her to take care of me," he whined.[19] Not only was Isabel a hearty angler who outfished her husband, she pitched in around camp in the absence of housekeeping servants. Ever the practical hostess who was not afraid of work, Isabel made up the rooms and beds each day.

The party fished eleven of the fourteen days they were in camp: there was no fishing on arrival and departure days, and, according to camp custom, guides had Sundays off. The Andersons and their guests caught 171 salmon totaling 2,150 pounds. The cooks prepared meals based heavily on each day's bounty, though they had poultry and lamb sent in from local farms for variety. Fish dominated the menus: salmon chowder, fish balls, grilled salmon, and smoked salmon made fresh in camp appeared frequently on the dining cabin's table. What they could not eat themselves was shipped out each day. As the host of the outing, Larz had rights to all the catch, but each angler got to ship some home. Larz arranged for one of his salmon to be shipped to the Metropolitan Club in Washington. It was served at the club's luncheon on July 21, cooked whole and set out on the buffet. "It made a beautiful dish," the club manager later wrote to Larz.[20] It was a Cutler camp tradition that some of the catch went to a hospital. Larz sent two crates of salmon to the Montreal General Hospital, and the chairman of the hospital board, Henry Molson, founder of Molson's Brewery, wrote back to thank Larz for the donation.

On the last night in camp, the anglers celebrated their vacation with a zany dinner. Margaret handed out Japanese paper hats shaped like fish that she'd bought at the Yamanaka Gallery in Boston. Photographs from the party suggest there was much cocktailing.

Travel outside North America

1897	Japan and China by way of Hawaii
1898	India by way of Europe and the Suez Canal
1900	Europe and the Paris Exposition
1902	Europe (Holland, Germany, and Czechoslovakia)
1904	Europe (England, Germany, and Czechoslovakia)
1906	Europe (England, Spain, Paris, and Czechoslovakia)
1907	Larz alone to Czechoslovakia
1908	Larz alone to Czechoslovakia
1909	Europe (France and Czechoslovakia)
1910	Round-the-world trip with Secretary of War Dickinson
1911	Belgium and subsequently Japan (diplomatic posts under Taft)
1913	Larz alone to Czechoslovakia
1916	Panama
1917	Isabel to France and Belgium alone for war work

1921	Larz alone to England
1922	Europe (World War I battlegrounds and Czechoslovakia)
1924	Larz alone to Czechoslovakia
1925	North Africa
1928	Africa via Canary Islands (Senegal, South Africa, East Africa, and Cairo)
1929	Mediterranean cruise (Italy, Greece, and Turkey)
1930	Larz alone to Holland
1931	Round-the-world cruise
1932	Larz alone to Czechoslovakia
1933	Larz alone to Czechoslovakia
1934	South Seas cruise (return by way of Paris and Czechoslovakia)
1935	South America (Panama, Colombia, and Guatemala)

Early in their married life, the Andersons' most frequent foreign travel focused on Europe, especially England, France, Germany, and the Netherlands. Curiously, they made no trips to Italy as a destination of its own, though they did sometimes stop there on their way to or from other places. Starting in the midtwenties, as travel to Europe became more common among middle-class Americans, Larz sought out travel to remote foreign lands. He despised the idea of tourists and the ships and hotels that catered to them. When they sailed to North Africa aboard a Canadian ship in 1925, he described the ship's "tourist" ambiance: "We go to sea and travel to be by ourselves—we know enough people at home without picking up acquaintances—or certainly having them introduced to us by the 'Social Hostesses,' two gaunt persistent Englishwomen, who repeatedly wanted us to join in entertainments and games which our mourning alone would have prevented."[21]

Their trips during the last decade of Larz's life were long voyages of several months, including Africa, the South Seas, and South America. Here Larz was more likely to find people like himself—wealthy, old-fashioned people seeking relief from the lower classes who traveled to Europe.

In Mediterranean Waters

One of the Andersons' most perfectly planned foreign trips was their 1929 cruise in the Eastern Mediterranean. Larz decided they would cruise privately, aboard the massive yacht *Sayonara*, which he chartered from Anthony Drexel Jr. (1864–1934), the Philadelphia millionaire whose father had founded Drexel University. Drexel was a personal friend of King Edward

VII and Kaiser Wilhelm II. This was not the first time the *Sayonara* had been chartered for a unique trip. In December 1914, British Naval intelligence had requisitioned the craft and sailed it under an American flag along the coast of Ireland to spy on Sinn Féin.[22]

The *Sayonara*, manned by a crew of thirty-four Englishmen, was a luxury yacht in every way. It weighed 766 tons and measured 205 feet from bow to stern and 28 feet across. Its draft was 15 feet. Belowdecks, the cabins and staterooms had mechanical ventilation. Guests could run their own hot and cold baths with fresh or ocean water. The galley's ice machine promised cold cocktails and chilled wines even in the hottest weather. There were elegant drawing and dining rooms, and the ship's library was well stocked with reading material. On deck, unobstructed port and starboard promenades ran 120 feet along the entire length of the craft. An outdoor "shelter," as Larz called it, was furnished with built-in upholstered seats that turned into beds. A "finely furnished" smoking room on the deck completed the passenger amenities. Even though the yacht was leased, Drexel installed an open-air saltwater swimming pool on the deck at Larz's request.[23]

Though all their trips were meticulously planned, preparing for this one engaged Larz in an extraordinary way.[24] Traveling on a private yacht meant he could go where he wanted, when he wanted, and see things most travelers and tourists never saw. Though the yacht's captain knew Mediterranean waters well, Larz personally directed him to sail to ports and islands he had never before navigated. Larz coordinated many modes of transportation—ocean liner, train, yacht, and automobile—into a seamless flow that lasted four months, from early May until late August. He specifically planned the trip for summer months, and his reasons for doing so demonstrated his great depth of knowledge about geography:

> The season for this cruise had always been of greatest importance to me: most people cruise in the Mediterranean too early, in winter, in early spring—and the Mediterranean is a wild ocean at such times. My experience in life abroad and travel had taught me that the season to really enjoy southern seas is late spring, early summer, for then not only the waters are at their best but the places visited are at their best—the days are longest—and the daylight means much in cruising through narrow waters and among islands that are little frequented, in many channels where there are not lights at all to guide.[25]

Larz planned the trip to proceed in three phases: first the Dalmatian coast, then Greece, and finally Turkey. He especially focused his preparatory research on Dalmatia, one of the few areas of the world still unfamiliar to him. People "do not care to know anything of such parts [Dalmatia] of this wonderful world," he wrote, "so I determined to miss as little as possible by doing as much as possible."[26] In Greece he was on familiar ground. Thanks to his education in Latin, Greek, and the classical world, he was very literate in the history, philosophy, art, and architecture of the ancient region. Consequently, the Andersons spent more than half their time in Greek waters. They were curious about Turkey, but recent events there, including the Armenian genocide, made them wary of the country, and they did not stay long.

The *Sayonara* sailed from Venice in the late afternoon of May 19 under the colors of the New York Yacht Club, of which Drexel was a member, and Grandfather Weld's Black Horse Line.[27] Longtime friends Fred and Susie Dalton Stone boarded with the Andersons. Susie, a lifelong friend, had been one of Isabel's bridesmaids. Also on board was their trusted aide-de-camp Captain Stewart, a Greek guide, Isabel's maid Agnes, and Larz's valet Skinner.

The next morning, the party reached their first port of call, Zara (then an Italian protectorate, now Zadar, Croatia). For the next several days, they sailed along the Dalmatian coast during daylight hours and laid anchor in a port or harbor during the afternoon. They used the late afternoons and early evenings to explore the port and returned to the yacht for the night. The pattern repeated itself the next day when they set out in the morning bound for a new port of call. They made their way southward along the coast on this leisurely schedule until they reached the port city of Ragusa (Dubrovnik).

At Ragusa, Larz decided he wanted to see the infamous spot where World War I had ignited. Captain Stewart hired motor vehicles and drivers to take them to Sarajevo. After a drive of almost two hundred miles across a landscape dotted with ancient towns, medieval fortifications, and monasteries, they reached Sarajevo as the sun was setting. Their progress that day averaged no more than twenty or twenty-five miles per hour over winding and steep country roads. They checked into the Hotel Europe, an elegant structure built when the city was part of the Austro-Hungarian Empire. In the evening, they dined on the Croatian delicacy *burek*, a spinach-filled pastry, drank what Larz called a "good white wine," and finished off the meal with Turkish coffee.[28] Then they walked out into the city to see the spot where Archduke Francis Ferdinand and his wife had been assassinated on June 28, 1914. Isabel reflected on the enormity of the event. "We stood and reviewed that gruesome act which was to involve nearly the whole world in war and bloodshed," she said.[29]

In the morning, annoyed because the shops were closed due to a national political event, Larz grumbled that they would have to head back to Ragusa without doing any shopping. They reached the *Sayonara* in late afternoon and set sail the next morning on a southward course toward Greece. They stopped briefly at the port of Durazzo (Durrës, Albania), with just enough time to take a "thrilling" automobile drive over the old Roman road to Tirana. "Thrilling, that is, until we began to feel that the road had been little mended … since it was built," Isabel said dryly.[30]

"With Gods and Goddesses"

The Anderson party spent the next three weeks cruising along the Greek coast and zigzagging through the Aegean Sea. This part of the cruise enchanted Isabel. "As a child, I loved Greek mythology and peopled the mountains and vales of Greece—as I saw them in my imagination—with gods and goddesses," she wrote in her book about the trip.[31] When they reached Athens on June 3, her lifetime dream of seeing the city was fulfilled. "I had long wanted to see with my own eyes the most beautiful building in the world—the Parthenon," she said.[32] Indeed, she shaped their itinerary by insisting they spend plenty of time in Athens. She found many ways to enjoy the ancient city. One day, she and Susie decided to go for a swim in the harbor, a novel vantage point for viewing the Acropolis. When they later visited the site, Isabel was overcome with sadness about how the Parthenon had been "mutilated." Over the centuries, its marble and decorative sculpture had been destroyed or looted by invaders from the West and the East. "I went away from that glorious golden ruin with tears in my eyes," she lamented.[33]

At the end of the week, as the Andersons and the Stones were getting ready to leave Athens, John Gardner Coolidge and his wife, Helen, arrived from their villa on Lake Como. Larz had stayed with John during his visit to Tokyo in 1888. From Athens, the expanded party returned to the Peloponnesus and headed north pinball-style among small Greek isles to the port of Volos. Captain Stewart arranged for a private train to take them to the hanging monasteries of Meteora, about ninety miles from the harbor.

Larz was delighted with the day-trip arrangements. Their private train included a "tiny saloon carriage with all the conveniences, even eau de cologne on the washstand," he gushed.[34] The train's composition included a second passenger car, a baggage car, and a "baby engine." By the time they arrived in Kalabaka a few miles from the monasteries, news of their party had reached the town, and many men showed up to greet them. The colorful crowd of "shepherds, monks and men in Turkish costume of fez and full trousers" had heard President Coolidge himself was on the train![35]

In Meteora, they visited the monastery of St. Stephen and the Holy Trinity, the only one open to women. Isabel had heard that in order to see the monastery, visitors were hoisted up the side of the steep rocks in a net. There was, however, only one monk on duty when they arrived, and he could not pull them up alone. Larz was relieved, having "dreaded the risk of breaking ropes and careless monks."[36] They walked the quarter mile to the top along a path that was, as Isabel described it, "hair-raising enough to make up for any disappointment about the hoist."[37] They visited one more religious site before leaving Greek waters: Mount Athos. However, the ladies stayed aboard the *Sayonara*. Then as now, only men were allowed on the peninsula.

The Anderson party reached Turkey on June 21. With the exception of a brief visit to Smyrna (Izmir), they spent all their time in Constantinople. There they stayed at the Pera Palace, a luxury hotel catering to Western travelers arriving from Europe aboard the *Orient Express*. When Larz had last visited the city, in 1889, Ottoman sultans had ruled it. Now he noted the great changes that had taken place in the intervening forty years.

> It had then been the wonderful colourful dramatic city of the Sultan's days—now the Sultans' palaces are public parks and musea and gardens, and we walked through places now that had been death to look at in that long ago; and we saw the treasures which the new Government is keeping (though no one knows how much of it is leaking out)—there is no longer the variety of colour and dress in the streets: it has taken on the drab look of a Republic.[38]

The Andersons seemed wary of traveling outside Constantinople, even of being in Turkey at all. They knew about the persecution and massacre of Armenian Christians and considered the head of the new republic a "dictator-president."[39] Larz wrote very little in his journals about their time there, and when Isabel later published her book about the visit, she supplemented Larz's meager journal offerings with her own recollections and information drawn from other sources.

As they did wherever they traveled, Larz and Isabel called on people they knew in Constantinople, including the British ambassador, Sir George Russell Clerk. They lunched on a terrace overlooking the Bosporus with the American ambassador, Joseph Grew, and his wife, Alice Perry Grew, a cousin of the Andersons' neighbor in Washington, Perry Belmont. At

Constantinople, the Stones left the party to continue their travel in the region by themselves.

The group's only other Turkish port of call after Constantinople was Smyrna. They did not get a hotel in the city that night, preferring instead to sleep on board the *Sayonara*. They may have been fearful of the place. Isabel wrote about the great 1922 fire in Smyrna that killed one hundred thousand people. She devoted several pages of her book about the trip to the plight of Christians in Turkey, reminding her readers of "the atrocities practiced by the Turks upon Christian subjects—Armenian and Greek." She accused the Turkish government of trying to exterminate Armenians and cited the deaths of some eight hundred thousand people to make her point.[40]

After leaving Turkey, the *Sayonara* headed south to Rhodes and set a course for Italy by way of Malta, Sicily, Sardinia, and Corsica. The Gardners disembarked at Palermo to catch a boat to Naples. Larz and Isabel sailed alone into the *Sayonara*'s home port, Leghorn (Livorno). Though their cruise was over, they traveled for another three weeks in Europe, stopping first at Montecatini for cures at the famous thermal baths there. They then wended their way along the Italian and French coasts, reaching Marseille in time to sail back to the United States on August 10.

They arrived in Brookline on August 19, four days after Larz's sixty-third birthday. For all the excitement of their trip, Larz and Isabel were happy to be home again at Weld, "as dear and lovely and full of happiness as ever," wrote Larz. He continued, "We fell into our comforts as if we had never been away."[41] Isabel left immediately for New Hampshire, where she spent the next six weeks. Larz had much to do in Boston, including clearing through customs the many souvenirs of their trip. Even though he was in the seventh decade of his life, Larz continued to augment his collection of souvenirs, never for a moment imagining that one day almost everything he acquired on his travels around the world would disappear.

Coda: Racism and Anti-Semitism in the Travel Journals of Larz Anderson

Racism and anti-Semitism were part of the fabric of life in the Gilded Age. It is sometimes dismissed as a part of the social and political context of an era when "everybody" shared those prejudices.[42] It is exactly because of the social and political context of racism and anti-Semitism in Gilded Age America, however, that it cannot be ignored. It was an integral part of the social and moral fiber of elite Americans in the Gilded Age, including Larz Anderson. He never had much to say about black people or Jews when he was at home in Brookline or Washington. It was when he traveled that he especially felt at liberty to express contempt and ridicule, especially toward Jews, in his letters and journals.

While cruising in Florida aboard the *Roxana* in 1907, Larz decided to ask some black men to come to the boat landing that evening to serenade Isabel. He was outraged when the men failed to show up: "Some darkey singers I had engaged to sing my Isabel to sleep simply failed to materialize (one white citizen who was standing gazing at us, to whom I spoke of my disappointment at their failure, said the only way to get a nigger to do anything was to get the police to 'ask' him to do it)—so I'll ask police aid the next time I want a concert."[43]

On a return trip to Florida the following year, the Andersons wandered into an evening service at a little Baptist church along the Hillsborough River. Larz called the congregants "the blackest darkies in Volusia County." He described the scene with stylistic flourishes that belittled the very people who had welcomed them into their Christian place of worship. Larz mocked the sermon, alleging in his diary that the preacher cried out "how the Lord befo' His deth and suffrage had gone into the garding of Gethseminary." He sneered at the meager offerings on the collection plate. Then he decided Isabel had picked up fleas during their visit: "Isabel ha da seat next a window and so some air, but she was scratching all night long!"[44]

On a visit to Ireland in 1927, Larz ruminated on miscegenation. He saw black people as a sinister threat to the honor of white people. While at Muckross Abbey, Larz fumed over how "colored folk" had corrupted the great names of Irish history:

> McCarthy Mor and his descendants are buried inside the abbey, and O'Sullivans and O'Donoghues, Princes of their time in Erin, also sleep there. Alas, that names held in such esteem in the old country should become a joke in our land, that we fail to realize the splendor of such aristocratic names, of O'Grady, O'Brien, O'Driscoll. It would almost seem as if these great families have suffered as many families in our States have suffered, owing to the assumption by colored folk of great family names.[45]

Larz reserved the worst of his vitriol for Jews. During a visit to Prague in July 1906, he went out for a walk in the old part of the city looking for Jews who fit a certain stereotype. "Today, in wandering about I at last found just a bit of what I had pictured the place must be," he wrote, "narrow, winding, dirty, smelly streets with hooknosed Jews peering out of cellar doors."[46] He abhorred the idea of Jews in public places in the United States. In June 1923, after a visit to the Bronx Zoo in New York, he let loose a vile harangue against Jews and became so obsessed with them that he lost interest in the zoo's exhibits and instead juxtaposed monkeys and Jews in the same breath:

> In certain respects it is a very fine Zoo—it is a bit overdone, the houses too heavy and ornate—but the animals seemed unusually well cared for—even the monkey house—but, again, the people ("the Chosen People" indeed), for they were ALL Jews, and terrible Jews—dreadful looking creatures, greasy men, fat women, nasty children. It was a FREE day— and so of course Jews crowded in, nothing but Jews. There were no particularly interesting things or animals to see.[47]

On a visit to Manhattan in 1925, Larz happened upon a parade. "I was shocked," he said of the event, "at the number of Jewish organizations and how the Jews were daring to parade their importance in our midst."[48]

Larz's hatred of Jews hit home when his beloved Harvard hired a Jew to coach its football team. In his journal for 1931, Larz blamed "the jew Horween" for what he felt was the poor record of Harvard's football team between 1926 and 1930. Larz so despised Coach Arnold Horween that he gave him no credit for his three successive wins against Harvard's archrival, Yale. Larz could not understand how a Jew could coach a winning team and so concluded the team "had risen in its own might and defeated Yale, notwithstanding the poor coaching." He blamed the Jewish coach for Harvard's losses and denied him credit for its victories. Larz praised Horween's successor, the Irish Catholic Eddie Casey, who in his four years at Harvard coached the football team to three losses to Yale.[49]

Larz went to great lengths to preserve his thoughts, words, and deeds for posterity. He wrote the first drafts of his journals with great gusto and verbal dexterity, usually at the time they happened or shortly afterward. They are thus an authentic, contemporaneous record of his thoughts and activities. Once written, they were not then thrown into a box to be forgotten. They were preserved and curated. Larz oversaw a sophisticated editorial process in which secretaries flawlessly retyped the originals. He then had the typescripts gathered in expensive leather-bound folios as his personal archive of what Isabel called "an almost complete account of his life."[50] Larz was proud of this accomplishment. The volumes were displayed prominently in the most important public room of the mansion in Brookline, the living room.

There is no evidence Isabel held such views. Indeed, accounts of her work as a volunteer during the influenza epidemic showed she did not discriminate against people of any race or religion.[51] When Isabel published her 1940 compilation of Larz's letters and journals, she removed all evidence of his attitudes about race and Judaism. She knew it was morally wrong to think, say, and write these things, and that meant Larz knew it too.

MY DEAR BELOVED
PUNK YOU ARE:
AND PUDDING TOO,
AND GUIDING STAR!

AND YOU WILL WITNESS
BY THIS SIGN,
THAT YOU ARE TOO
MY VALENTINE!

Figure 19. The Anderson houseboat, the Roxana, ca. 1910.

XI

ABOARD THE *ROXANA*

When Larz and Isabel Anderson leased a houseboat for the first time in 1907, they were following a trend rather than setting one. The millionaire American tobacco magnate Pierre Lorillard (1833–1901) had already made houseboats fashionable among the nation's elites. Reports of large parties aboard his craft the *Caiman* appeared regularly in society columns. Its destruction by fire in June 1900 made headlines everywhere. Indeed, the vessel's demise was bigger news than its celebrity-infused parties ever were. Lorillard quickly commissioned a replacement, and in March the following year the *New York Times* predicted the new houseboat would be ready by August.[1] Lorillard never took possession of it: he died on July 2. A month later, the *Times* posthumously attributed the popularity of the houseboat directly to Lorillard, concluding this was "in consequence of the luxurious life which the dead millionaire and a party of chosen friends lived in Winter on the houseboat *Caiman* in Southern waters."[2]

Many of Lorillard's wealthy peers had their own luxury houseboats, including the multimillionaire sportsman Alfred Gwynn Vanderbilt's *Venture* and New York businessman Payne Whitney's *Captiva*. Some wealthy Americans leased their houseboats rather than buy them. Levi and Mary Leiter, the Andersons' neighbors in Washington, leased two houseboats in 1915, the *Chaperone* and the *Summer Girl*—one for the Leiters and their guests, the other for the servants.[3] Larz and Isabel, like the Leiters, started their houseboating career by leasing a craft, the *Roxana*.

History of a Houseboat

John Warne "Bet-a-Million" Gates (1855–1911) was a self-made man without much of an education who started out life as a barbed-wire salesman in Texas. He made plenty of money both in his business ventures and at casino tables.[4] When Gates commissioned the *Roxana* from the Racine Boat Manufacturing Company, he wanted something of modest size. The vessel measured 112 feet long and 17 feet across and had a 4.5-foot draft. (In contrast, Lorillard's *Caiman* was 132 feet long and 26 feet across and had a 5.5-foot draft.) Gates named his houseboat for Roxana, the wife of Alexander the Great, a fitting name for the pleasure craft of a king of industry.

On October 16, 1903, Gates launched the *Roxana* on its maiden voyage from Milwaukee to New York City by way of Chicago, the Mississippi River, the Gulf of Mexico, Cuba, and Florida. Another houseboat owner making his way down the Mississippi at the same time noted the houseboat in his diary: "Saturday John W. Gates' palatial yacht, the *Roxana*, passed down while we were at lunch," wrote the observer. "We saw a cook on deck; and two persons, wrapped up well, reclined behind the smokestack."[5]

Twenty-one people were aboard the *Roxana* for its first voyage: Gates and his wife, Dellora; his son, Charles, and daughter-in-law, Florence; a Mrs. Guerney of New York; and the captain and fifteen crewmembers.[6] The party stopped at Port Arthur, Texas, where they spent Christmas, and then sailed around the Gulf of Mexico and over to Cuba. They finally reached the Columbia Yacht Club in New York City on April 11, 1904, a journey of 177 days from Milwaukee. The *New York Times* called the *Roxana* "a finely appointed craft."[7] The next year, Gates stayed on the East Coast, taking the houseboat upstate to the Thousand Islands region for a regatta and then up the New England coast to Nova Scotia.[8]

After that summer, Gates never again cruised aboard the *Roxana* and soon left the United States for the rest of his life. He and his son, who were in business together, dissolved their New York City investment company in 1906, just ahead of the 1907 panic. They moved to Paris in 1907, where the elder Gates died four years later. His obituary noted he had been "adroit" in responding to stock market conditions, citing his decision to withdraw from the New York Stock Exchange at a time when the market was expanding rapidly. The *Times* called him "perhaps the most spectacular figure that this generation of Wall Street has seen."[9]

When Larz first inspected the *Roxana* in 1906, it was boarded up at a marina in New York City. He had not yet made the decision to purchase it, so Gates agreed to lease the vessel to him with an option to buy it later. The boat came with its own captain, Isaac Golden, who had skippered the *Roxana* for Gates during the 1905 summer season. It was a good match: Golden remained with the *Roxana* as its captain for the next twenty years.[10]

Larz immediately began to plan their first houseboat vacation. There was much to do. Working closely with Golden, Larz settled on an itinerary that started in Jacksonville, Florida, took them south to the Florida Keys, and then brought them back north along the coastal waters off the Carolinas, having them arrive in Washington by spring. In early January 1907, the captain and crew set sail from New York and headed south via inland waterways, rivers, and coastal waters. The *Roxana* arrived in Jacksonville nine days later—a record, according to Larz.[11] The crew consisted of Captain Golden, a first mate, a sailor, an engineer, a fireman, an oiler, a chef, and a steward—plus Isabel's maid and Larz's valet. This was a much smaller crew than Gates's fifteen men a few years earlier.[12] Traveling aboard the houseboat in the frigid air and choppy winter waters of the northeastern coast of the United States would have been no fun for Larz and Isabel, so they went to Florida by train, accompanied by their servants Dover and Jennie. They made it from Boston to Jacksonville in a twenty-four-hour nonstop trip that Larz described in one single sentence worthy of Jack Kerouac:

> In twenty four hours travel from Boston, which we had left in zero weather and all snow-bound and wintry, we woke to find ourselves running through the pine woods of the Carolinas, past the long cabins of negroes, the mammies in bandannas and pickaninnies in, well, little bandanninees, all so real, standing out by the kettles in open ramshackle surrounds, where the blue smoke curled up among the green pines, and it was so warm and comfortable that we opened the windows of our drawing room and sat sleepily in the warm soft air, as we sped along into the swamps and bayous, and passed Charleston and Savanna without getting a look at them, till in the afternoon we arrived at Jacksonville.[13]

"Successfully Cozy"

Captain Golden met the Andersons at the Jacksonville train station and took them at once to see the boat. This was Isabel's first look at what became their most private home away from home for the next twenty years. Larz arranged for many supplies and special furnishings, including a small piano, bicycles, fishing gear, and a canoe. Their little piano was late in arriving from Brookline, and this delayed their launch. Larz called it "the most traveled piano in the World."[14] Once the instrument arrived, the crew took it apart to get it into the cabin on the main deck that the Andersons dubbed the saloon, like their name for the largest room of Anderson House.

Larz thought of everything, even bringing along the signal of the Black Horse Line, Grandfather Weld's clipper ship company that had once circled the globe. He proudly hoisted the red Weld pennant with its black flying horse above the *Roxana*'s own signal. The *Roxana* was a colorful craft. Larz said it was "so spick and span, her white hull and mahogany deck houses, her yellow stack, the brightly colored flags, red, white and blue, and black—stiff out in the breeze."[15] The aft engines were open air, but the crew kept them cleaned and polished like pieces of silverware. Larz decided that the part of the engine room visible from above should be decorated with potted palms.

The *Roxana* was spacious and offered attractive, comfortable accommodations.[16] Though there is no known interior photography of the boat, a nearly identical one built at about the same time by the same company, the *Hathor*, has in recent years been restored. Interior photography of the restored *Hathor* shows beautiful woodwork and cabinetry throughout. Isabel had her own stateroom amidships with a large closet, private bathroom, and brass bed. Decorated in what Larz called "pretty chintz," the room also had a lounge bed (something like a sleeper sofa) for Larz, who had his own stateroom and private bath in the forward section of the boat, directly below the pilothouse. In the absence of overnight guests, Dover and Jennie had their own staterooms. When overnight guests came aboard, they moved into two small deck cabins.

The houseboat had gracious entertainment facilities. Larz thought the saloon "quite small," even though its dining table seated eight. He called the main area for living and entertaining "the den"—an open deck furnished with rugs, wicker furniture, and side tables. He eventually installed a fireplace in the outdoor den to make it "successfully cozy."[17]

Once they left Jacksonville, the party headed south along the coastal and intercoastal waterways, taking time to steam up and down Florida's many rivers and inlets. They explored an undeveloped, primitive Florida that has since disappeared. Isabel later said she sometimes felt like Henry Morton Stanley, the explorer of Africa, as they "turned some sudden bend in the sluggish river and looked through the jungle."[18] The *Roxana* called at many ports that are popular with modern travelers, including Daytona, Palm Beach, and Miami. Captain Golden also moored the houseboat alongside docks and landings at many smaller places hidden in the maze of Florida's coastal waterways: Weelaka, Dunn's Creek, and the ominous-sounding Mosquito Inlet.

The *Roxana* frequently steamed into harbors and landings that had great celebrity. In March 1916, while in the Miami area, the party called on the Deerings: Charles Deering, a graduate of the Naval Academy at Annapolis, and his son, James, who was then in the final months of building his bayside villa, Vizcaya. With his characteristic eye for architectural detail, Larz raved about the property:

> This morning we came to the place where Mr. James Deering is building one of the modern wonders of the World, a vast Tuscan Villa with immense garden setting on the shore of Biscayen Bay [*sic*]. The out-houses and walls on the road

are very Italian in spirit, and then the house itself—with its columned porticoes and huge patio and its towers and over-jutting roofs. It is really an amazing undertaking.[19]

Lazy Days

Life aboard the *Roxana* was relaxed and casual. There was a small but well-stocked library that Larz used as his office. He had his typewriter there and one year secretly made valentines for Isabel. One morning he noted in his journal that "Pudding," a pet name for Isabel, was "taking it easy in her cabin, her hair done up in pins and covered with a handkerchief, and reading and writing."[20] Larz and Isabel sometimes used the captain's rifle to shoot at bottles floating in the water and played their ukuleles as the boat drifted along quiet waterways.[21]

They enjoyed everything connected to Florida waters, especially swimming and canoeing. One morning they paddled their little boat around the coral islands near Caesar's Creek in what is now Biscayne National Park. They marveled at the ocean bottom visible through the clear water and went diving for sponges. The couple loved to fish and did so often. Larz was thrilled to catch many varieties—herring, mackerel, red snapper, and grouper—and had their cook, a local whom he'd hired in Miami, prepare them for meals. Isabel said the grouper made good chowder.[22]

They made frequent stops along the way. The couple got back their land legs by walking down country lanes near boat landings, and Larz picked up mail and newspapers sent by prior arrangement to post offices and general stores along the way. At these stops, the crew also provisioned the galley with dry goods and local meats, fruits, and vegetables. The *Roxana* needed a constant supply of coal, and they took on fuel whenever they could. On their first trip, they did not know to order coal in advance, and so they sometimes waited hours for it to be delivered. On future trips, Larz ordered and paid in advance for the hard coal the *Roxana*'s boilers burned most efficiently.[23] When hard coal was not available, the fireman used soft coal that burned hotter but damaged the fire grates. The mechanic learned to bring along replacement grates to repair the damage.[24]

From time to time, Larz and Isabel went ashore for a few nights in a hotel, where hot baths, hairdressers, laundry, and other luxuries were available to them. Being on land for a few nights also gave Larz a chance to have his film developed. He loved sending photographs home to his mother when they traveled. While the Andersons were on shore, the crew serviced the vessel and enjoyed some downtime without the boss on board.[25]

Larz and Isabel enjoyed shopping for souvenirs in Florida, as they did on all their trips. In Daytona, they acquired a particularly exotic remembrance: a talking gray parrot that Larz said he had been "looking for for a long time to take the place of 'Tony.'" He named the bird Tomoka in honor of a nearby river.[26] Despite Isabel's protestations, Larz also bought "a monkey, a wonderful little monkey" that he named Osceola in honor of Florida. The monkey did not last long, however. He went back to the animal show the next day. Larz eventually got another furry pet, a raccoon that was the source of "great amusement" to them and to the crew. "How long he will remain with us, however, is a question," Larz said.[27] On a future trip, Larz went ashore in St. Augustine to buy a few dozen ashtrays for the *Roxana* that "were really much needed," he wrote. There was "a good deal of smoking cigarettes among the owner's company."[28]

The *Roxana* continued on its maiden voyage northward from Florida to Savannah, Charleston, and Norfolk. Larz and Isabel knew many people who wintered along this piece of the southeast coastline and stopped to visit some of them. Just north of Savannah, they heard that Senator J. Donald Cameron and his wife, Elizabeth "Lizzie" Sherman Cameron, were at their winter home, the Coffin Point Plantation on St. Helena's Island, South Carolina, and decided to visit them. The *Roxana* made its way through the maze of marshes and rivulets around the island, at last reaching the Coffin Point landing. Lizzie herself came down from the house to greet them. In Washington, Don and his wife lived on Lafayette Square near the White House. In 1891, Larz had visited Lizzie and her daughter, Martha, at the Cameron apartment in Paris, and it was there that Larz had renewed his acquaintance with Henry Adams. Larz captured the serendipity of the moment in his journal: "It seemed strange to meet her in this remote spot, where there were none but darkies," he wrote. "Yet she seemed as much at home as when I last saw her in her charming apartment in the Avenue du Bois de Boulogne."[29]

The Andersons next sailed into Charleston Harbor, where they viewed Fort Sumter from the houseboat. Larz made arrangements with an old Charleston friend, Colonel George G. Greenough, to visit the fort his great-uncle Major Robert Anderson once commanded. In Charleston, Larz also met with President Theodore Roosevelt's secretary of war, William Howard Taft, whom Roosevelt had anointed as his successor.[30] There is no record of what Larz and Taft talked about, but the idea for a large contribution to Taft's campaign and a correspondingly large ambassadorship for Larz likely came up.

Larz and Isabel reached the nation's capital around April 1 and spent the next two months at Anderson House for the closing weeks of the social season. In early June, they boarded the *Roxana* and headed toward Boston's

North Shore. It was a busy cruise. They stopped in Annapolis to tour the Naval Academy's Memorial Hall and new chapel, which was still under construction. Isabel was hopeful that the academy would honor her father by placing a statue of him in the hall.

Seven years earlier, Isabel had commissioned Daniel Chester French (1850–1931), creator of Abraham Lincoln's statue in the Lincoln Memorial, to sculpt and cast a statue of her father. In 1902, the first casting was installed on the grounds of the New Hampshire State House in Concord, where it still stands. She wanted another casting of the statue to be placed in Memorial Hall, but the Navy Department did not give its approval of her plan. In 1910, after an almost ten-year delay, the Navy Department finally accepted Isabel's offer of a copy of the statue for the Naval Academy's Memorial Hall. She immediately contacted French, who ordered a new casting. The New York foundry Jno. Williams Inc., however, had long before destroyed the original plaster model, thinking their client would never need it. French was forced to make a new cast from the Concord statue.[31] The copy turned out to be too tall to fit the standard statuary niche in Memorial Hall, and the navy refused to alter the size of the niche. French not only had to make a new plaster cast but also had to resize it to fit the niche. The statue is still in Memorial Hall, in a niche on a balcony off the great ceremonial room on the second floor.

Larz and Isabel hosted a luncheon on board the *Roxana* on June 25, 1907. Their cook served a mouthwatering menu that proved the galley's catering standards equal to an Anderson kitchen on terra firma: frothy consommé, ramekin of poached egg with a cheese crust, buttered lobster in wine sauce, veal cutlets, asparagus with cream sauce, punch sorbet, and a cake named after Joan of Arc.[32]

The Andersons' first trip aboard the *Roxana* was a great success and established several precedents for future cruises: great stretches of time on the boat alone without guests; idle and silly moments together fishing, swimming, and strumming their ukuleles; and fresh food that was, in today's terms, "locally sourced." The *Roxana* became known for much elegant entertaining, especially when it was at anchor in Florida waters. The guests who came aboard made the society columns whether they were celebrities like German ambassador Count Johann von Bernstorff or Anderson, Weld, and Perkins family from Cincinnati, Boston, and New Hampshire.

The Andersons, generous hosts in their own right, always took advantage of the hospitality of friends and acquaintances along the *Roxana*'s course. They made several visits to Winterthur, the home of Senator Henry Algernon du Pont (1838–1926) and later of his son, Henry F. du Pont (1880–1969). They knew the du Ponts through Larz's friend and Harvard classmate Fred

Bradlee Sr., whose cousin Frank Crowninshield had married the senator's daughter Louise in 1900.[33] On their first visit to the estate near Wilmington, Delaware, Isabel took note of the splendor of the gardens:

> [The senator's] place seemed to me one of the most beautiful in America. To be sure, it had no view to speak of, but the trees were old and large, and the walks and drives through the estate lovely. The dogwood trees were laden with flowers, pink as well as white, like drifting snow in a sunset. The Italian garden, with its fountain, was small, but exquisitely laid out, and the combination of flowers really unusual.[34]

The Andersons made two other documented visits to Winterthur, in 1920 and 1923. The 1923 visit had an interesting twist to it. Larz phoned from the dock at Wilmington to ask if they and their guests, the Sammy Culbertsons of Kentucky, might visit. Sammy was one of the richest men in Kentucky and later became the president of Churchill Downs. A du Pont butler told Larz the senator was away and his son, Henry Jr., was entertaining a bishop at luncheon and would not be able to see them. Larz asked if they might visit anyway. Through the butler, Henry agreed to let them visit and offered to provide an outdoor tea for them, even though he would not be able to join them. The *Roxana*'s party duly arrived, toured the estate, and ended the visit with tea in what Larz called "a gem of a garden" near the house. During tea, Henry showed up unexpectedly "but was most mysterious about his 'Bishop' who was 'secluded' and back to whom he had to hurry," Larz said.[35]

The *Roxana* Disappears

Larz and Isabel owned the *Roxana* for two decades, though they used it in only thirteen of those years. They did not use it in 1912 when Larz was US minister to Belgium, and they suspended cruising during the years US troops fought in World War I (1917–1918). Despite these breaks, the Andersons' most regular use of the boat occurred before 1920. After 1920, the novelty of the houseboat had worn off, and eventually Larz came to prefer more-exotic itineraries than the *Roxana* could provide.

In 1927, Larz decided they would no longer use the *Roxana*, yet he found it difficult to let go of it. Larz "had a very strong sentiment about selling anything that he had enjoyed," his business manager once said.[36] Larz's first impulse for disposing of the houseboat was "taking her out to sea and sinking her," but Isabel objected.[37] Larz eventually gave the *Roxana* to Captain Golden and kept him on the Anderson payroll for the rest of his life so that he could care for the vessel. The fate of the *Roxana* is unknown.

When Larz later wrote the history of how ownership of the houseboat had passed to Golden, he omitted the part about wanting to sink it.[38]

Figure 20. Larz Anderson in bespoke diplomatic uniform, 1912.

XII

LIFE INTERRUPTED (BRUSSELS 1911–1912)

By August 1911, rumors about Larz Anderson's appointment as ambassador to a European capital had been appearing in newspapers for at least two years. Dozens of articles appeared in major American newspapers speculating about the if, when, where, and even why of such an appointment. Italy, Germany, Russia, the Netherlands, France, and Turkey were mentioned in one context or another.[1] Larz had been waiting for the appointment since at least 1908, the year in which he'd made a $25,000 contribution to Taft's successful presidential election campaign (the equivalent of about $600,000 today). The prior year, in spring 1907, Larz had met Taft privately in Charleston, South Carolina, and there likely discussed the contribution and an ambassadorship.

When rumors of his appointment to Italy appeared in the press on February 13, 1911, Larz curiously distanced himself from the president and denied any interest in seeking office.[2] That same day, someone in Rome released a statement on Larz's behalf reframing his relationship with Taft in two short but contorted paragraphs:

Statement of Larz Anderson, Rome, February 13, 1911

Mr. Anderson and Mr. Taft's families have been intimate for generations and are connected by marriage, and Mr. Anderson has been a great admirer of Mr. Taft all his life. He has done all that he was able to support Mr. Taft's nomination and election by personal effort and contribution to the country and the Republican party, as a candidate so grandly fitted for the great office of President.

Mr. Anderson never has been and is not seeking office; his family and personal ties and his interests of every kind are such that it would be a sacrifice for him to undertake public office again (his appointment to office, originally came unsought); and he could only look forward to such a thing if it came as a continuation of a career to which he had given some of the best years of his life.[3]

The statement carefully avoided confirming or denying any rumors of a diplomatic appointment. Its release in Rome rather than Washington suggests it was intended for American journalists in Italy so that it would be sure to come to the attention of Italian foreign ministry officials. The statement carefully polished Larz's image as a career diplomat who advanced through the ranks on merit rather than patronage. Calling his first posting to London "unsought" was disingenuous, however. His state department file clearly documents that Larz's appointment to London in 1891 was the direct result of his father's intervention with Sevellon Alden Brown and others.[4] More than twenty years later, Larz continued to deny benefitting from political patronage, even though there was nothing dishonorable about it. The statement recast Larz's $25,000 donation as a "personal effort and contribution to the country" rather than the seed funding for the Republican National Committee that it was.[5]

Shuffling the Deck

In late winter 1911, newspapers reported that the unexpected resignation of David Jayne Hill (1850–1932), the popular American ambassador to Berlin, was linked to Taft's decision to appoint Larz to Berlin. The White House never denied these rumors. The uproar over Hill's resignation in the midst of sensitive negotiations with Berlin over potash tariffs drew unwanted attention to the Berlin vacancy.[6] When the German Foreign Office expressed displeasure with the incompetent performance of Mack Henshaw Davis, the State Department functionary sent to Berlin to keep the potash negotiations moving, Larz's hopes of being named ambassador to the court of Emperor Wilhelm II were dashed. The wave of unfavorable public sentiment against anything Taft might do with the Berlin vacancy saw to that. Larz was not a strong enough candidate to overcome the backlash from Hill's resignation.

Taft decided to further groom Larz for high-level diplomacy and arranged for Larz and Isabel, at their own expense, to accompany Secretary of War Jacob McGavock Dickinson (1851–1928) on an official round-the-world trip. The Andersons traveled separately from the official party and avoided anything that suggested the US government paid their way. "The Secretary [Dickinson] doesn't want to take the unofficial members of his party on a transport for fear of comment in Congress," Larz wrote.[7] In the spring of

1911, after their return from the trip, Isabel sent a private note to Dickinson asking if he would make inquiries on Larz's behalf on the progress of the ambassadorial appointment. Dickinson replied that his wife, Martha, had also asked him to intercede on Larz's behalf, and he intended to do so. He promised to speak to Secretary of State Philander C. Knox (1853–1921) and assured Isabel, "You and Mr. Anderson should have a post to your liking."[8]

The president had difficulty finding a prestigious post for Larz, despite support from Dickinson. Belgium, a less contentious post than Berlin or Rome, nonetheless posed political challenges for the president. Charles Page Bryan (1856–1918), then US minister to Belgium, was a popular American diplomat who had begun his foreign service career in 1897 under William McKinley. Taft and his advisors concluded by midsummer that an appointment to Belgium would be the path of least resistance to meeting his obligation to Larz. Elizabeth Anderson wrote to her son on July 11 from her cottage at Bar Harbor to console him about losing Berlin and encourage him about Brussels. "I judge you have at last been approached about Belgium," she wrote. "Many express regret that you do not go to Berlin, but as you never expected that it is no regret."[9] As late as August 2, 1911, a week before Taft finally sent his last package of nominations to Capitol Hill, Senator Shelby Moore Cullom, the powerful Illinois Republican and chairman of the Senate Committee on Foreign Relations, asked Taft not to name Larz to the Brussels post at the expense of Bryan: "He [Bryan] has got fairly fixed up for living, entertaining, etc., and it would be pretty expensive to him to be transferred so soon after being sent to Brussels, and he ought not be, unless he has failed to do his duty, and I do not believe he has."[10]

Clearly, the Republican establishment in Washington feared Taft would remove Bryan from his post so Larz could fill the vacancy. The chairman of the Senate Foreign Relations Committee, a Republican, surely knew this from the secretary of state if not directly from the president himself. Hoping to avoid further delay, Cullom's polite but direct letter to Taft offered a way out of the impasse: if the president put Larz in Brussels and simultaneously promoted Bryan to full ambassador "somewhere in Europe," Cullom would agree to the plan. Though Taft had already decided on Brussels for Larz, Cullom's letter assured Senate approval when the president finally began shuffling his deck of diplomatic cards.

On August 8, Taft sent to the Senate a list of nominations that the *New York Times* called "the long-expected and oft-foretold shake-up in the Diplomatic Service."[11] Bryan moved from Brussels to Tokyo to take up the ambassadorship vacated by Thomas James O'Brien, who had been moved to Italy to take up the ambassadorship vacated there by John G. A.

Leishman, who had been moved to Berlin to fill the vacancy created by Hill's resignation. Leishman was an especially good fit for Berlin. He had made his mark in business as an executive of the Carnegie Steel Company and would be a formidable representative of US interests in the potash tariff negotiations. Larz got Brussels. The storm quieted down for the time being.[12]

"A Post So Delightfully Situated"

Larz and Isabel were aboard the *Roxana* when word of the appointment reached them on the morning of August 8, 1911. They were moored at the Beverly dock, preparing for a lazy afternoon cruise on the coastal waters off Boston's North Shore. Larz later said he had been surprised by the phone call he got from a reporter that morning. The journalist asked how he "liked it" being named minister to Belgium. Then a "lady reporter" showed up on the dock to interview Isabel, and Larz noted in his journal that it was hard to tell which of the two women "was the more frightened when they met."[13] A member of the crew went to get the afternoon papers, which Larz and Isabel read avidly as they cast off for an overnight at sea. "Pictures and articles, rather nice, so far, very cordial editorials in some," Larz said.

Despite the exciting news, or what should have been exciting news, Larz was feeling out of sorts. Life on his own terms as he knew it was about to change dramatically. Just the little bit of press attention at the harbor made Larz want to be "left alone." He said he was "homesick at the thought of going away to leave our life here for so long a time ... separation for much time from Isabel ... and I shall miss her so."[14] After $25,000 and four years of waiting, he'd gotten what he'd wanted—and now he did not want it.[15]

When they returned to port the next day, Larz and Isabel were ready to take their first steps toward Belgium. The quiet hours drifting along the coast at night on their beloved *Roxana* calmed Larz, and he began to formulate a plan. "The more we think about it too the more agreeable it seems to be," Larz said, though he was certain Brussels had no charm of its own. "It is a post so delightfully situated; within striking distance of Paris and London, and we have Holland and Germany so near." And there was something else to like about Belgium besides its geographic proximity to their favorite cities. "The new King and Queen of Belgium look so nice in their pictures," Larz said.[16] He would have access to Royalty, with a capital *R*. There was also family precedent and honor to consider. Larz's distant cousin Maria Longworth Nichols had married Bellamy Storer, who had served as the American minister to Belgium from 1897 to 1899 under William McKinley.

The Andersons disembarked from the *Roxana* and made a beeline to the Taft summer White House in Beverly to express their appreciation to the president for the appointment. Taft was in Washington, and Mrs. Taft was out for the afternoon. They next called at the summer home of Senator Henry Cabot Lodge in Nahant, fifteen miles south of Beverly, but he was on his way to Washington. The senator was a powerful Republican member of the Senate Foreign Relations Committee and crucial to Larz's confirmation. With both Taft and Lodge in Washington, Larz knew he needed to be there too. He decided to take the overnight train to Washington from Boston's South Station to thank the president in person. He also planned to meet with the Republican senators whose votes he needed for confirmation.

A Summer Morning in Washington

Although the White House was packed with visitors when Larz arrived on its doorstep the next morning, he was "smuggled" in to see the president. Taft told Larz he took "much pleasure" in making the appointment and regretted the delay.[17] After meeting with Taft, Larz went directly to the Capitol to meet with Senator Cullom, who told Larz he would "take care of" him in the confirmation proceedings. Barely a month earlier, the senator had objected to Larz's appointment to Brussels if it meant Bryan would lose his job or get anything less than a full ambassadorship to a European country. Now that Bryan was on his way to Tokyo, Cullom fully supported Larz's nomination to Brussels.

Larz met with Republican senators Lodge of Massachusetts, Elihu Root of New York, and Theodore Burton of Ohio. Despite the controversy around Larz's nomination, they all assured him there was "no doubt of confirmation."[18] Armed with these assurances, Larz went over to the State Department to see Secretary Knox, who offered polite and probably sincere congratulations. His own controversial 1909 nomination by Taft to be secretary of state had rocked Washington for three months. Knox surely sympathized with what Larz had gone through. Being at the State Department again was a pleasure for Larz. He enjoyed being greeted by the department's black ushers, who remembered him from the old days. Everyone congratulated him and called him "Mr. Minister."[19]

He dined that evening with a small group of Republican senators—Root, Frank Brandegee of Connecticut, George Oliver of Pennsylvania, and Henry Lippitt of Rhode Island. When Larz got to Anderson House that night after a long, hot summer day in Washington, he wrote he was "getting in touch with many things."[20]

By noon on Saturday, August 12, Larz had made a number of decisions. He planned to sail as soon as possible for Europe, make a stop in Brussels to look for a place to live, and then go on to Marienbad for his annual cure.

Larz had in mind a particular little palace in Brussels that would serve more than admirably as the new American legation. (At that time in US diplomatic history, both the residence and the chancery were often housed under the same roof, and it was a minister's or ambassador's task to find his own building and pay the rent and household costs out of his salary.) Larz wanted to see it for himself and secure it as soon as possible so he could "determine what furniture, etc., we can make use of."[21]

On Sunday, Larz boarded the afternoon *Federal Express* for the twelve-hour overnight ride from Washington's Union Station to Boston's South Station. He arrived in Brookline in time to rest up for a birthday dinner Isabel had planned for him on the eve of his forty-fifth birthday. Isabel's dear friend Maude Howe Elliott, along with two of Larz's Harvard chums, Fred Bradlee Sr. and George Saltonstall Mumford, made up the little party in Larz's honor. This was the only celebration the Andersons held to mark the appointment.

Indeed, Larz wanted no further publicity about the announcement. He wanted to slip away to Europe "without the papers knowing it" and was relieved there had been no controversy about the appointment. He wanted to keep it that way. "There has been no comment that was unfavorable in the papers," he wrote on August 14. "I am from the District of Columbia so that the matter of taxes, etc., cannot be raised."[22] The new minister came to terms with the fact he was going to Brussels, not Berlin or Rome. "Belgium is better than what I had aspired to—whatever the papers may have rumored," he said. He also knew his appointment had been politically perilous for Taft and was glad the president hadn't been "placed in an awkward position."[23]

Larz sailed from New York on August 17 aboard the luxurious French ocean liner *La Lorraine* accompanied by his valet Horton. The press took no notice of his departure. Larz was delighted with the crossing to Le Havre. He lunched, cocktailed, and dined with many friends and new acquaintances. "And so it goes," he cabled home while at sea, "till I seem to know everybody on the shipboard." But he cautioned himself, "Nowadays I have to be nice to them."[24]

Belgian Housing Woes

During the quick visit to Washington, Larz's friend Lawrence "Larry" Townsend, who had served as US minister to Belgium from 1899 to 1905, told him Brussels was "about the best place going."[25] Perhaps Larry reminded him that the former US minister to Belgium, Bellamy Storer, had once rented the Palais d'Assche and suggested how fine a residence it would be for the Andersons. After talking to Townsend, Larz decided "the d'Assche palace is one of the best that can be rented," but he lamented, "the Bruxellois are not given to renting their fine houses any more than we are."[26]

The grand residence, designed by the Belgian architect Alphonse Balat, was built in 1856 for the Marquis of Assche. As principal architect to King Leopold II, Balat also designed many of the royal buildings Larz and Isabel eventually visited during their months in Belgium, including the Royal Palace in Brussels and the Royal Castle and Greenhouses at Laeken. But it got better for Larz. From 1901 to 1909, the Palais d'Assche was the residence of Prince Albert (1875–1934) and Princess Elizabeth (1876–1965), who had ascended to the Belgian throne in 1909. Once Larz set his eyes on the handsome palace, he set his heart on getting it. Its royal pedigree, its exquisite design and size, its French-style interiors, and its stables and garage suited him perfectly. But he feared it would not be available. "The owners are to live in it," he wrote, "as they have a better right to do than even we have, I admit."[27]

None of the other available houses in Brussels would do, Larz decided. He found these buildings had bad smells, no bathrooms, servants' quarters that were like "holes," and cellar kitchens that required servants to carry food up two flights of stairs. He bemoaned the lack of closet space and railed against master bedrooms that were "bare and just all in a row." He wanted a comfortable palace, not an uncomfortable mansion.[28]

By the time Larz left Brussels for his cure at Marienbad in late August, he was resigned to renting Bryan's legation. Located at 44, avenue des Arts, on a busy thoroughfare without a driveway, the building had no artistic or historical appeal to Larz. He complained the house would need another bathroom and a new furnace at his expense. Nonetheless, he found ways to come to terms with the prospect of living in it. From an architectural point of view, Bryan's legation reminded him of the de Renzi villa in Rome that his mother had occupied for a time in the 1890s. "Frankly, I had hoped for a Piombino," he said, referring to a massive and prestigious palace on the Piazza Colonna in Rome.[29] Larz had one good thing to say about Bryan's house: if nothing else, it offered a "sense of continuity" to America's representation in Belgium.[30] However, it was clearly below his standards.

While Larz was in Europe, wrapped up in his fantasies about obtaining a house with royal lineage, Isabel was in Brookline preparing for the move. She went to Washington to pick out furniture and artwork from Anderson House to ship to Brussels. Larz's mother worried that Isabel was working too hard and hoped that when Isabel came to visit her in Bar Harbor she could "make the dear little girl rest."[31] The scale of the Andersons' move was staggering. They shipped clothing, chinaware, glassware, silver, ribbons and cups won at horse and automobile shows, cocktail shakers, motorcars, paintings, drawings, photographs, furniture, books, and "all sorts of little things."[32]

When Larz returned to the United States at the end of September, three of his staff from Brookline—butler and housekeeper Frederick and Sophia Philpott and chauffeur-mechanic Bernie Foy—were on their way to Brussels to receive the pair of automobiles and dozens of heavy crates Isabel had shipped. On the Atlantic crossing back to New York, Larz received a radiogram from the marquis agreeing to give the Andersons a two-year lease on the Palais d'Assche. Larz's mother congratulated him on the coup. "Your getting the Palais d'Assche simplified matters," she wrote.[33]

To Brussels, via Paris

Larz and Isabel embarked for Le Havre from New York at the end of October on the French liner *La Provence*, "a second-rate Pacific ship," Larz called it, referring to the less luxurious passenger ships that sailed between the United States and Asia.[34] He complained about the smells, the noises, and the poor food. "We haven't had such poor comfort in ships in all our married crossings of the Atlantic," he said. He added, "Heretofore we have been able to choose our time and vessel and now we have to travel 'officially' when we must." Already the new American minister chaffed at the requirements of public life.[35]

They arrived in Paris on November 2 and settled into the Hotel Ritz. After three days in Paris to catch his breath and recover from the Atlantic crossing, Larz took a Sunday-afternoon train up to Brussels. Even though the lease had been in place barely a month, he worried that work on the Palais d'Assche was not moving quickly enough. He returned to Paris on Wednesday and wrote a detailed account of the work under way in Brussels:

> The Palais d'Assche is far from ready, and yet all the plumbing is finished and the heating apparatus is installed and working, so the foundations are finished, and now comes the delay in the details of finish, the putting in of woodwork and the painting. The Comte and Comtesse have been busy at the house and, I think, they are going to give us more furniture than I had anticipated. I really never, and in my heart of hearts, expected the place to be nearly ready in time—but when it is finished it will be quite the most up-to-date house in Bruxelles.[36]

He was only in Paris overnight, for he decided that the next day, November 9, would be his official arrival en poste. Isabel remained behind in

Paris. The American legation staff arranged a colorful welcoming ceremony for the new minister's arrival:

> I traveled by the noon train on Thursday in a reserved compartment, with customs privileges at the frontier, and arrived at the Gare du Midi in the late afternoon, where I was met by the Consul General, the Lawyer of the Legation, the Secretary, etc., in top hats who "salued" me "a la gare" [saluted me at the station], and accompanied me out to the electric landaulet with its chauffeur and footman in liveries, with red, white, and blue cockades, where it stood surrounded by a crowd of people who wondered at the automobile, which is the only one that has ever appeared apparently in the Belgian capital.[37]

The Belgian foreign minister was out of town until Monday, so there could be no official welcome at the foreign ministry until after the weekend. After spending Friday at the legation, Larz "ran back to Paris by a late afternoon train on Saturday and rejoined Isabel at eleven in the evening" for a "bit of supper in [their] cozy rooms." He hoped the next time he returned to Belgium, Isabel would accompany him so she could witness "the ceremony of the presentation" at the Belgian Foreign Office.[38]

The Palais d'Assche was not ready when Larz returned to Brussels with Isabel, so they took up residence in their temporary quarters, Bryan's old legation. The new minister's first full week in Brussels was a whirlwind of official duties. He met Foreign Minister Julien Davignon and made the rounds of foreign ministry staff. Larz seemed surprised they spoke so little English. "I hope that my French will come back to me quickly," he wrote, "for while I am still able to speak with a certain correct accent, yet I do not feel fluent, and I am compelled to limit my ideas to the words which I remember rather than being able to clothe my ideas in proper language."[39] The extensive education in France that Larz often boasted about apparently had not been conducted in French.

After Larz and Isabel settled into their temporary digs, he wrote that they were "fairly comfortable" despite feeling "strange and lonely." Their belongings were unpacked and set out in the Bryan house, and this made them "think of home" rather than "feel at home." Larz saw to it that Isabel got the best rooms, which meant the ones with coal fireplaces. He thought these rooms looked "home-like" but lamented that the rest of the house, his rooms included, looked "like a barn."[40] This homesickness and sentimentality for life back home contrasted sharply with Larz's happy-go-lucky travel experiences in his early twenties. It contrasted even more sharply with Isabel, whose nature it was to take any inconvenience in stride. She once wrote in her war diary, without a hint of complaint, "It is so cold I go to bed between the blankets with my clothes on and a hot-water bottle."[41]

Though Larz had many duties to keep him busy, Isabel decided not to make any formal appearance in society until they took occupancy of the Palais d'Assche.[42] She hired a Belgian social secretary, Mademoiselle La Bussière, to help her prepare for the upcoming social season. Isabel's American friend Irene Hare, who lived in Brussels, was like a mentor to her. Irene had married the Viscount de Beughem, grand master of the household of the Countess of Flanders, the king's mother. One of the very few American women in Brussels married to an aristocrat, Irene became a trusted and confidential advisor to Isabel on matters of court protocol. Larz's cousin Caroline Story de Buisseret, married to the former Belgian minister to Washington, Count Conrad de Buisseret, also lived in Brussels and helped Larz and Isabel adjust to the city's social protocols.

Presentation to the King

Larz's big moment came on Saturday, November 18, when he presented his credentials to His Majesty Albert I, King of the Belgians, at the Royal Palace in Brussels. According to protocol, wives did not attend the ceremony, so Isabel stayed home. The day's events started at eleven in the morning. Two state carriages "accompanied by outriders" arrived at the old legation on the avenue des Arts. Larz wore what he described as "military uniform of [his] rank in the war against Spain," explaining in a tortured sentence that "the Belgian Court had indicated its hope that uniform might be worn by American representatives whenever possible."[43] Larz's account of the day sounds like a scene from a Ruritanian romance.

> I was at once escorted to the great coach, which swung on its springs like a channel-crossing steamer; two footmen stood on each side of the steps and assisted me into its luxurious interior. The Aide-de-camp took his seat. The steps were folded up, the door closed, the footmen jumped up behind, and our little procession of prancing horses in gorgeous harness, preceded by two outriders on high steppers, proceeded. My carriage, which was decorated in gold with lamps at the four corners, went first. As we drove through the broad clean streets of the beautiful city to the wide place in front of the

palace, groups of people took off their hats politely and some women even curtsied.[44]

Larz enjoyed seeing strangers bow and curtsy to him as the procession drove through the city, though it did not occur to him they mistook him for the king. He was, after all, riding in the king's carriage, and he and the monarch were close in age and physical stature. When he arrived at the palace, rows of carabineers and buglers stood at attention, and inside many uniformed officers and liveried footmen lined the stairways and halls. Larz described the uniforms of two officers as "gorgeous."[45]

Larz would have dearly loved to wear something fancier for the event. Earlier in the year, he'd ordered a bespoke diplomatic uniform of vague historical precedent from the London firm of Davies & Son, tailors to British royalty. This costume was for his own purpose: to wear in private and for portraiture—not for official use. American public law dating to 1867 prohibited diplomats from wearing any uniform not approved by Congress.[46] The approximate style and cut of Larz's uniform was based loosely on a military dress tailcoat worn by British soldiers from the late eighteenth until the mid-nineteenth century. Larz had a photographer make a formal portrait of him wearing it in the winter garden of the Palais d'Assche (see figure 20). He also had a photograph made of himself wearing his drab US Volunteer Army uniform. When he sent the photographs to his mother, he explained the difference between the two:

> The one in Diplomatic uniform is in the dress of a Minister of the "first-class" (which I am) and is the one which I do not wear (it is about like the one which my predecessor wore and the Ambassadors in Berlin and Petersburg are even a little more gorgeous, I am told). The one in uniform, military dress, is the one I do wear, and which I have a right to wear, as well the decorations on it, a right by Congressional Act.[47]

Larz met Albert in a room so large he was "unprepared for the distance to be crossed to reach the King." Larz beamed when the king acknowledged that the Andersons were to live in the house where all his children had been born. The Americans then went to meet Queen Elizabeth, who also spoke about the nine years she and the king had lived in the Palais d'Assche. She expressed interest in Isabel and said she wished to meet her. The Andersons' family and social connections to Belgian aristocracy were getting them notice!

Now fully accredited, it was time for Larz to announce his arrival. He spent the rest of the day calling on the mayor of Brussels and the papal nuncio and leaving his card at more than two dozen embassies and legations around the city.

After the first rush of arrival in Brussels was over, Isabel returned to Paris. The ground-floor offices of the Palais d'Assche would not be ready until mid-December, and much other work on the *piano nobile* and in their bedrooms remained unfinished. Though she intended to visit Larz now and then, Isabel ended up staying alone in Paris until Christmas.

Two weeks after presenting his credentials to the king, Larz was ready for it all to be over. "I'm sort of tired out," he wrote on November 22. He was also homesick. A visit from an old friend, Walter Denègre, made it worse. Larz was envious when Walter talked about going back to the States. "I am homesick for my simple life at home," he said.[48]

On the Job in Brussels

Despite their separation, Larz and Isabel stayed in close contact through daily phone calls, and Larz made frequent little trips to Paris to see her. He decided he did not need to tell his supervisor in Washington, Third Assistant Secretary of State Chandler Hale, whenever he left his post to be in Paris because "it might hurt his feelings." Though Larz believed that going to Paris was technically "within the regulations," he required prior authorization from the State Department any time he left Belgium. He reasoned that "sometimes others [did] not realize the fact" and decided he could bend the rules simply because he took his work "seriously."[49] Outside his secret trips to Paris, much of Larz's month alone was filled with a busy schedule of teas, concerts, dinners, and official events, including a Te Deum in the thirteenth-century Church of Saint Gudule to celebrate the king's name day. Larz's arrival at the event was captured on a now-lost newsreel he saw several weeks later at a "cinematograph."[50]

After spending Thanksgiving in Paris with Isabel, Larz returned to Brussels to find an invitation waiting for him from Whitelaw Reid, American ambassador in London. Reid invited the Andersons to come for a December weekend at his magnificent estate, Wrest Park, forty-five miles north of London. Larz had met Reid years earlier in Paris when Reid had been American ambassador to France. The invitation was all the more enticing because the British foreign minister, Sir Edward Grey, was expected to be there. Larz cabled the State Department asking for leave, which they granted on December 2. The official reason for the trip, noted in Larz's personnel file, was to meet Grey.[51]

The visit to England did not work out as expected. Grey never showed up, and Larz did not feel like participating in the big event of the weekend, the shoot. Indeed, he abhorred hunting. He was eager to get back to Brussels for other reasons besides not liking the weekend in Wrest Park. With guests coming from America to spend Christmas and New Year's, there were hectic days ahead.[52]

Christmas in Brussels

When the Andersons got back to Brussels, workers were still in the house, and domestic staff were unpacking and arranging things, but the bedrooms were at last ready. Larz selected for himself the room on the ground floor that had been "His Majesty's habitation" during the nine years Albert had lived there. For Isabel, Larz selected the "Queen's Chamber" at the front of the Palais d'Assche, on what he called the State Floor. Larz had the boudoir completely redesigned for her comfort and convenience. The architect installed massive armoires of rich mahogany on three of the walls and built out a bathroom from a corner of the room along the other wall. The bathroom was disguised as an oversize armoire, its door inset with a full-length mirror to distinguish it from the real armoires.[53] Larz also had Isabel's bedroom suite completely redecorated: "[Her rooms are] all in pink brocade, with rich pink curtains, and handsome white carved furniture, all in really exquisite taste. The house, indeed, has been done over, as far as it has been done over, by the French architect Boulanger, with refinement and restraint, and is very pleasing to live in."[54]

With the renovations completed at a reported cost of $200,000 ($5 million today), it was time to unpack their belongings.[55] In addition to mementos, books, photographs, and bibelots, many large things had to be unpacked and arranged. There were antique Japanese lacquered screens that Larz said "will go anywhere."[56] He brought over from Anderson House those of his early seventeenth-century Flemish tapestries that fit the walls of the State Floor. He found it remarkable that one of his Belgian tapestries had "come back home after three hundred years of wandering."[57] Larz directed these installations and arrangements personally. He wanted everything in perfect order and ready by the time their American guests arrived on December 21 for a Christmas visit. On December 19, Larz wrote that the "silver has been taken out and polished, and it is placed around to give an even more homelike look."[58]

On Christmas Eve, the Andersons dined with a group of American friends, including their houseguests Frederick L. Huidekoper (1874–1940), secretary and founder of the Army League, and Lizzie Patterson and Kate

Le Montagne, two of Isabel's Washington friends. After dinner, everyone danced to records played on the Victor phonograph. The party continued until one thirty in the morning, long after the locals had left. At bedtime, Larz and Isabel discovered the Christmas stockings they had left for each other at "our bedside," a rare reference to sharing a bed.[59] Like all people of their class, they had separate bedrooms at home in Washington and Brookline, on the *Roxana*, in hotels, and aboard ocean liners. Isabel's stocking held a shawl of Brussels lace. Larz got fruit in his, "which Isabel proceeded to eat—tho' it was so late," he complained.[60]

As the hostess of the American legation, it was Isabel's duty to plan parties and other public events. She decided to give an open house for the "American Colony" on Christmas Day between three and six in the afternoon. Since sending formal invitations was impossible (there was no list of Americans living in Belgium), she published newspaper ads that she called "intimations."[61] Isabel had no idea who or how many would show up. It was a great success. About eighty people came and were "much better dressed and nicer looking" than Larz expected. The staff placed a lighted Christmas tree in the winter garden, and a live band played "American airs." The American houseguests helped pour tea and serve eggnog. Larz made it a point to write in his journal that Jews with names like "Abrahams and Isaacs" showed up for a Christmas party.[62]

As the end of 1911 approached, Larz reflected on Brussels, the diplomatic life, and the stresses of his post. After a month on the job, Larz found it overwhelming. "The work of the office—the taking up of its detail, and thinking over of its large questions—has really been exhausting," he said, although he admitted he had dealt with "nothing of immediate importance in [US] relations with Belgium." Constant interruptions from people who came in to say hello or ask for something annoyed him. There were "papers to sort out and arrange, every mail bringing in some new question, small or big, that adds to the puzzle."[63] The city, he decided, had "its great qualities and its faults." He was not sure Belgians had any desire to be kind to others, unlike Bostonians. "Isabel insists that Bostonians are more intellectual," he wrote, "but I must add that Belgians are better dressed."[64]

The Brussels social season began on New Year's Day with two royal events: the king's men-only diplomatic reception and the queen's Ladies' Circle for the wives. Isabel had already met privately with Queen Elizabeth on December 17, soon after their return from Ambassador Reid's house party in England. Isabel had worn her furs, a shimmery gray moiré dress, and a "feathery" hat. For the Ladies Circle, however, she amped it up, wearing a gown of gold and white brocade from Worth in Paris and her best jewelry:

emeralds, tiara, pendant earrings, necklace, and a large pendant brooch on her corsage. Larz decided she had never looked so "splendid."[65] The king's reception was canceled due to the monarch's ill health, but Larz still made the rounds of the royal palace, the residence of the Countess of Flanders, and the mansion of the Prince and Princess von Hohenzollern to sign New Year's congratulation books.

The 1912 Season in Brussels

Following New Year's Day and for the next twelve weeks, the Andersons did not just have busy days, they had busy hours. Social and cultural events followed each other in rapid succession. Larz nominated himself for membership in the Cercle Royale du Parc, a prestigious men's club, and joined the American-Belgian Chamber of Commerce and the Anglo-American Club. Freddie Huidekoper helped them buy horses while he was still in town, and they started riding on the city's many equestrian paths. The papal nuncio came to call.

Isabel was a busy legation hostess. She invited children for ice cream and a grab bag. She set Tuesday afternoons as her at-home day when those with whom she had exchanged calling cards could drop in for tea and conversation without an appointment. Larz thought Isabel "very cunning" in how she arranged all this.[66] Friends old and new called at the legation for tea, luncheons, and dinners. Isabel's cousin May Brandegee and her daughter Marion came up from Paris for a court ball. Isabel helped at the flower table of the annual charity event the Fancy Fair. They occasionally even found time to go to church on Sundays.

One of their most important official duties was the continuous and demanding round of dinners with ambassadors, princes and princesses, counts and countesses, baronets and military officers, and Belgian government officials. They attended such a dizzying round of parties that they quickly resented the demands made on them. These were onerous obligations. "We are worrying, day after day, over our dinner parties due in return for the courtesies which we have and haven't received," Larz griped. "These are difficult people to entertain, and so one isn't encouraged to do so."[67]

Other things were not going well either. There were frequent staff problems. Mademoiselle La Bussière did not live up to expectations. Larz called her a "pathetic little mouse, in tears most of the time ... a fool without any ability to help."[68] American and Belgian domestic staff clashed with each other. A Belgian manservant had a nervous breakdown and came close to shooting himself in the garden. Isabel wanted a new chef because she was tired of "Frenchy food" and needed "something more Anglo-Saxon,"

Larz said.[69] In contrast to the household problems he had to contend with, Minister Anderson's office duties weighed ever so lightly on his shoulders. He started work at nine thirty in the morning, broke off when the butler called him for lunch, and then returned to his desk to go through "a basket full of matters ... which I can take up if no immediate demands are made on my time."[70] Larz spent his office hours responding to letters from Americans looking for business opportunities in Belgium and other routine matters. A clerk at the US Supreme Court in Washington wrote asking for a copy of Belgium's civil code in French.[71]

By January 12, the pace caught up with Larz: "I hate to get upski [*sic*] in the morning for there isn't a thing that I look forward to with real pleasure during the day: I tell dear Isabel that I am over here entirely for her sake — and she says she is here entirely for mine — and both are telling the truth, and it is worthwhile for both to be here."[72]

In late January Larz sent for his personal masseur, Mr. Radowitz, to come from Marienbad for a few weeks. "I have been unable to take so little exercise owing to my work indoors, and the inability to get out until after dark," he wrote to justify hiring the masseur. "I think the little bit of rubbing will do me good."[73]

Larz's mood brightened when the final shipment of paintings arrived from Washington. The old English paintings completed the interiors Larz had envisioned, especially the portrait of the Duke of Wellington. Given the proximity to the battlefield at Waterloo, where in 1815 Britain defeated France, America's Revolutionary War ally, Larz thought it especially appropriate to hang a portrait of a British military hero in the American legation.[74]

The American Students Club for Girls

Isabel quickly found a greater purpose for her stay in Brussels. "The life of an American girl studying in any Continental city is always beset with difficulties," she said. "This was no less true in Brussels, the 'Little Paris' of the Low Countries, than anywhere else."[75] In early January, Isabel met with a Mrs. de Fritsch to discuss the formation of a club for American young women in Brussels. She also asked Mrs. Whitelaw Reid in London and Mrs. Robert Bacon in Paris, both wives of American ambassadors, about their experience with similar clubs in their cities. Over the next few weeks, Isabel and Larz went out into the city to inspect rental properties for the new club. Isabel held a working luncheon for women whose support she needed. After lunch, she took the ladies on a tour of the buildings under consideration. The venue Isabel finally chose was on the second floor of 4, rue Bodenbroeck, opposite the picturesque fifteenth-century Church of Our Lady of Sablon.

With a courtyard, driveway, and private ground-floor lobby, the building offered easy and private access to the club rooms on the second floor. The large sitting and music rooms, a smaller general-purpose room, a bathroom, and a restroom provided the amenities Isabel sought.

By the time the club opened on February 1, Isabel had been in Brussels for barely a month. She knew how to get things done. A simple printed card announced the date and encouraged membership.[76]

Notice

The American Students Club for Girls in Brussels opens February 1st, 1912, at 4 rue Bodenbroeck. No dues. Tea served every afternoon free. All Americans Welcome. Members may bring friends of any nationality. Bureau of information.

More than a hundred people came to the opening-day festivities. The world-famous Zoellner Family Quartet of Brooklyn, New York, played classical music. The quartet was a local favorite. It had performed the previous year for the Belgian monarchs, and Queen Elizabeth herself had awarded the Zoellners a gold medal.

The club offered a wide array of amenities and services. Isabel felt that American girls living in Brussels needed a place where they could take baths, which the club offered for fifteen cents. She made sure the writing tables were equipped with pens and stationery imprinted "American Students Club." Larz was proud of Isabel's accomplishment, saying she had "worked so intelligently and hard" to launch a club that was "the result of much consideration."[77] Out of her own pocket, Isabel prepaid the rent through the end of June, "so that if it doesn't seem worth while the undertaking can be given up."[78]

After the club opened, Isabel remained busily involved with it. She served tea to visitors one afternoon a week. By late February, the club expanded its services, offering luncheons that started with cocktails and ended with ice cream for dessert, "in the American manner."[79] The club became so successful that older American women living in Brussels started to use it as their in-town club. These developments discouraged Isabel because she wanted it to serve the needs of young American women, not established society matrons. Larz explained:

There have been people who have taken advantage of [Isabel's] good nature and the Club to make their way, and not as many girls have turned up as Isabel feels necessary for

> its up-keep. The "society" people drop in to "free tea" more
> than the students, so some changes may have to be made, and
> it may die a natural death by the first of July. However, it
> has been a brave effort, and my dearie has given much time
> and good thought to it.[80]

The club did not disband when Isabel left Belgium, though a few years later "the character of the club was somewhat altered," Isabel noted diplomatically. "The membership grew and the treasury swelled, but it became more of an American woman's club, with dances and bridge whist."[81] Though the present-day American Women's Club of Brussels was not founded until 1949, the club that Isabel founded in 1912 surely anticipated it in spirit and purpose.

Things Get Ugly

In late February, Isabel became the victim of malicious gossip that had been gearing up since their arrival. Sometime in February, while she was out in town in one of their automobiles, Isabel was mistaken for the queen. The incident was widely reported in the papers and made its way into society drawing rooms and the bureaus of the foreign ministry.[82] Larz offered an explanation that makes one wonder if he was not at first secretly delighted by the misidentification.

> The story about Isabel being mistaken for the Queen is quite
> true, for our cockades are something like the Royal cockades,
> which are red and yellow and black with a little golden metal
> crown on the tip while ours are red and white and blue with
> a little metal star on the tip—and then the letter "A" on the
> panel (Albert and Anderson) seems to have misled the crowd,
> so that Isabel, who is about the size of the Queen and as
> sympathetic looking, received a very respectful ovation. But
> one funny point is that the whole matter was brought up by
> the correspondent as showing the handsome American cars
> which we had brought over while, as a matter of fact, this
> car happened to be the only one which we had bought here.[83]

Newspapers speculated that Isabel would leave Brussels by Ash Wednesday, that year on February 21. She was leaving, the papers said, so she could "care for her horses in her Two Hundred Thousand Dollar Stable in Washington."[84] It was true that Isabel had decided to leave Belgium at the end of the social season for her own reasons, but Larz said he could not "imagine how that report got started."[85]

The rumors continued and quickly morphed into muckraking that was personal and sordid. Papers started reporting that Isabel was returning to America so she could invite young girls to stay with her at her "magnificent estate" in Brookline. The gossip tied all the pieces together: Isabel's work with the girls club, reports of her early departure, and a perception that Larz and Isabel acted like *they* were the king and queen of Belgium. The subtext of all this was obvious and meant to hurt Isabel's and Larz's reputations among the elite of Brussels.

> [Mrs. Anderson is] going to provide ten days of hospitality at her magnificent estate at Brookline (Massachusetts) to groups of 20 working-class girls at a time. During their sojourn at Mrs. Anderson's château, the girls will enjoy all of the refinements of luxury. Chambermaids will be at their service. They will be able to use the Andersons' automobiles and horses to promenade themselves around the estate and its gardens, as well as take their boats out on the lake. Their meals, prepared by a famous French chef, will be served on the costliest porcelain in the château's great dining room, using napkins of the finest quality. All of the rooms of the immense château will be open to them. In a word, they will be treated and allowed to act as if the estate belonged to them.[86]

Larz and Isabel carried on as best they could. On George Washington's birthday they gave a large and elaborate party. Staff filled the great stairway with azaleas and decorated the legation's bust of Washington with flowers. The Andersons received their guests in the Malachite Room, where some of their tapestries and paintings were on display. The chef prepared a festive buffet with punch, tea, cold roast chicken, and "real American salads." One hundred and fifty guests mingled, danced, and enjoyed themselves, especially the many children who came with their parents.[87]

In late February, Theodore Roosevelt arrived in Brussels just two weeks after announcing his intention to challenge Taft for the Republican Party's nomination in June. Larz was obligated to entertain him at a legation luncheon, even though he despised the former president. "Roosevelt is going down the ages as one of the greatest charlatans of all times," Larz said. He hoped Belgian newspapers would report that Roosevelt had "certainly passed beyond the line" and was "no longer to be respected" for even the high office he had held in the past.[88] Roosevelt was an hour and a half late for the luncheon and was not, according to Larz, suitably dressed. "He is coming out in his true colors," Larz grumbled.

As tired as they were of the routine of diplomatic dinners and social obligations, the Andersons were always up for a royal event. On March 25, Larz and Isabel dined with the king's mother, the Countess of Flanders. The elaborate evening included not only a sit-down dinner but also a late-night buffet of cakes, orangeade, and tea. Larz praised their hostess effusively: "The Countess of Flanders is so gracious and *grande* a dame that her manner makes everything enjoyable and easy, and yet no whit of dignity is lacking."[89]

On April 15, the world was shaken when reports of the loss of the *Titanic* appeared in the morning papers. The Belgian foreign minister came to the legation to express the sympathy of his government. Like everyone, Larz was in disbelief. "I do not believe it to be all as bad as the papers are making out," he wrote. "I do not yet believe any great, if any at all, loss of life has taken place." When details of the tragedy were confirmed several days later, he wrote, "It is slowly coming Home to us that an awful thing has happened."[90]

In early May, perhaps to show their support and help quash the rumors circulating about the Andersons, the king and queen gave a dinner for fifty in Larz and Isabel's honor. The king escorted Isabel in to dinner, and Larz escorted the queen. They sat beside the monarchs at the dinner table. Larz was very pleased. "Few Courts give special dinners like this to Envoys," he boasted.[91]

Disillusion and Denouement

Early in his tenure Larz became disillusioned with the diplomatic life and his distaste for all things Belgian intensified rapidly. On March 2, he described how fed up he was:

> Do not think for a moment that we are being impressed by our experiences and surroundings: we are too used to better things at home (which we miss constantly) and all these things here read better than they are. The longer we remain here the more we are impressed with the dullness of things—and of people in social life, who can talk only of the most personal or trivial things—and some still believe in miracles, belong to another age indeed![92]

Larz's diatribe against all things Belgian continued, "But the fact is that we are spoiled at home by what we have in the intellectual way as well as in the material—and the out-of-date character of this place was the reason I was willing to come here—so we are getting no more medicine than we deserve."[93]

This jumbled thinking may not have been Larz's fault. His journals, especially those entries written during the winter months, made frequent reference to a variety of vague ailments that afflicted him, Isabel, and their staff. These included complaints of nausea, lack of appetite, fatigue, headaches, indigestion, and flu-like symptoms that were not the flu. One of their Belgian staff became distraught and threatened suicide. Larz often wrote he just was not feeling like himself. Isabel sometimes spent the day resting in bed because she did not feel well.[94]

Before they moved in, Larz made two changes in the heating system of the Palais d'Assche. He had a new coal-fired furnace installed in the basement and a coal fireplace installed in Isabel's redecorated boudoir. A coal-fueled appliance not properly sealed or with a back draft could produce a level of carbon monoxide poisoning sufficient to cause both physical and emotional symptoms. Larz's bedroom on the ground floor one level above the cellar might have been especially vulnerable to this. We will never know for certain, but carbon monoxide may have caused the distress of the legation's residents that winter.

The Comedy Is Over

In early March, Isabel decided to spend a few weeks in Paris with her cousin May Brandegee. Isabel needed to escape the increasing nastiness of Brussels and could find comfort and support from May, one of her closest friends and confidants. When Isabel returned to Brussels from Paris, she announced her plan to sail back to the United States in mid-May to spend summer at home. Larz had no say in this. He did not want her to leave, but he understood her desire to do so. The thought of being alone in Brussels made him decide to go with her. On March 26, four months after arriving at his post, Larz asked the State Department for sixty days of leave to return to the United States with Isabel for a summer vacation. The department did not reply for another three months. Isabel booked her passage from Southampton to New York on the SS *Kaiser Wilhelm II*, a luxurious transatlantic steamer whose size and speed made it popular with travelers. Larz loathed the idea of being in Brussels without her. "It will be a perfect Hell for me here without her and I shall hate every moment of it," he wrote. "God knows what I am going to do."[95]

The couple left Brussels on May 13 bound for London. The weather was hot and sunny, and when one of the staff brought Larz a bunch of fresh mint, he decided on the spot to fix mint juleps to mark the occasion of Isabel's departure. All the servants gathered to wish Isabel farewell as she and Larz stepped into the car to be driven to Oostende, a distance of about one hundred miles, for the overnight boat to England. In London, Larz and Isabel checked into Claridge's for their last twenty-four hours together. The next morning, Larz took Isabel to Waterloo station for the boat train and said good-bye to her there. "My heart sank within me," Larz wrote the next day. "I turned to face blank days and went out and felt alone among London's millions." He tried to cheer himself up by having lunch at the railway station's restaurant, something he liked to do when he was sad.[96]

Larz was back in Brussels the next day, but his heart was no longer in it. He moped around the legation, called on people without appointments, and ruminated on how much he hated being there. He turned down invitations and spent his time outside of the office alone. One Sunday evening, he dressed for dinner and ate by himself in the formal dining room, as if presiding over a dinner party, the liveried servants attending the table as they always did. He dined alone in similar fashion on his fifteenth wedding anniversary in June. He pondered how strange and dramatic the year 1912 had been thus far, citing the events weighing on his mind: the *Titanic*'s sinking, the death of King Frederick VIII of Denmark, and Roosevelt making "American people go daft."[97] He brightened when the season officially ended on the last day of the Concurs Hippique, the annual society races. "La Comedia e finite," he wrote. *The farce is over.* "I shall be glad to put away my black hat and top coats and be able to be comfy in my straw hat and short coat and low shoes."[98]

In June, perhaps with an eye to Isabel's return in the fall, Larz hired a publicist to get one of the Paris newspapers to publish a retraction of their previous gossip about her. He hoped that if he could get a retraction in France, Belgian newspapers would follow suit. The Paris *Midi* agreed to publish a retraction, expressing lukewarm "regret" and calling on its colleague papers to do the same.[99] The plan backfired. The *Midi* article inspired another French-language newspaper to publish its "regret," but in a mocking and scornful tone repeating all the lies with great gusto.

> Some newspapers have recently published completely erroneous information about Madame Larz Anderson. It was said that the wife of the distinguished minister of the United States in Brussels was going to offer vacations at her country home in America to groups of young poor girls, working-class women, etc., who would have been able to spend fifteen days out of their existence in the grandest of luxury in order to elevate their minds. All of that is nothing but a fairy tale. Madame Larz Anderson has an interest in

a great number of charitable works in America, performed
with a tact that has always been greatly appreciated. But she
never had such a plan which, in Europe, might appear to be
novel, but if applied in Europe would, without a doubt, have
come to a very bad end.[100]

A Lively Summer

June was a lively month for Larz, despite Isabel's absence. Reports from the
1912 Republican National Convention that month in Chicago both held his
attention and enraged him. "The whole political business makes me so sick
that I cannot think of it," he wrote angrily.[101] Isabel attended the convention
and cabled Larz with daily updates. He sided with Taft and scorned the
challenger Roosevelt, whose progressive ideas, Larz thought, were a threat
to the social and political order of the nation. On the second day of the
convention, Isabel cabled Larz that Elihu Root, a solid Taft man, had been
elected chairman of the convention, but still Larz despaired: "I am looking
for the worst in this unhappy age when everything seems to be bound to the
bow-wows. There is great decency and sense of honor and loyalty and true
quality in our people but it does not seem to be able to compete with the
brazen voice of a demagogue, and it is hard to retain faith and feel that all is
for the best."[102]

When Larz heard that Roosevelt held back the votes of his delegates and
let Taft win the nomination, Larz exclaimed, "The Great Liar has bolted!"[103]

On June 29, 1912, Larz got the news he had been waiting for. The State
Department finally granted him sixty days of home leave, with the caveat
that he would spend the time in the United States. He immediately set to
work preparing for an early-September departure. He let several staff go,
including their footman "Gaston the Elegant" (who went to work for their
Washington neighbor Mary Scott Townsend at her villa in St. Moritz) and
their French chauffeur.[104] Larz took Isabel's jewelry to a bank vault and had
her furs repaired and put into cold storage. Then, he made plans to go to
Marienbad for a cure, even though the department gave him permission only
for travel to the United States.

On the Fourth of July Larz again offered hospitality to Americans in
Brussels. His cook prepared a buffet that included an "especially American"
chicken salad, champagne punch, ice cream, and lemonade.[105] Some guests
appreciated that Larz served lemonade, not the local favorite orangeade.
Lemonade reminded them of home. Each guest received a little American-
flag pin. In the evening, Larz hosted a men-only formal dinner, with toasts
to President Taft and King Albert. After dinner the American staff set off

fireworks in the garden, and an orchestra hired for the evening played the national anthem. The men retired to the smoking room for cigars and drinks after the pyrotechnics.[106]

On July 8, Larz received a cable from London that Gordon Henry Balch, son of Larz's Harvard classmate Frank Balch (an usher at the Andersons' wedding), would soon arrive at the legation. Months earlier, Larz had offered to help Frank's son get started in life by giving him a job as his private secretary.[107] Though Larz would not be in Brussels much longer, he was happy for Gordon's company and took the young man on sightseeing tours throughout Belgium. "He is so very companionable and we get on nicely," Larz wrote. Gordon wanted to explore the world, and Larz fixed him up with a passport for travel to Russia.

"Larz Anderson's Reward"

Larz had been maneuvering unsuccessfully for an appointment somewhere other than Brussels for months. On January 19, 1912, barely two months after his arrival, he had written a personal letter to Taft asking for a promotion out of Brussels to the rank of full ambassador somewhere else.[108]

American Legation, Brussels

Personal

Dear Mr. President-

I have the honor respectfully to ask that my name may be considered in case a movement among the Embassies should provide a suitable occasion. I beg to assure you, Sir, of my sincere appreciation of the opportunity which I now enjoy and of which, I believe, I am taking good advantage. I realize that I am indeed weathering more than my deserts! We have settled here and taken up the work and relations of the mission with real interest and have found a sympathetic reception—but the past months have confirmed two anticipations: one, that my hope and ambition have returned to finish a career, to the extent to which it may be possible, which was begun many years ago as a Second Secretary of Legation, posting to First Secretary and Chargé d'Affaires of Embassy, till now, by your graces, I am a Minister—and the other realization is that of the responsibilities and trusts and realities which have come into my life at home of later years and which I am anxious to bring into accord with my hopes and sense of duty. If I could attain the grade of Ambassador, for such time as the Administration might deem suitable I would feel deeply humbled, and at the end of the time, believe that I had made a real career in our Service. I beg to repeat assurances of my respectful appreciation, Mr. President, and can only hope for such consideration as my experience and circumstances may deserve.

I beg to add my thanks for your photograph, lately received, and for the message conveyed on it, both of which Mrs. Anderson and I greatly value, and I have the honor to be, with sentiments of highest consideration, believe me, Sir,

Yours respectfully, Larz Anderson.

January 19ᵗʰ 1912

Taft received the letter on February 2 and replied on February 8, assuring Larz, "You're in the line of promotion and should the opportunity arise, you may be very certain your proper claim for consideration will not be ignored."[109]

Larz knew Roosevelt's challenge could change the outcome of the election, but still he hoped Taft would offer him a temporary posting to full ambassador status while he was still able to do so. As Larz explained in a letter dated May 2, he did not plan to serve long as an ambassador, but to get the title and then go home:

I should like to be nominated for a few months only to some Embassy, for I am ready to come Home to live at any time—but I don't know how things are going to work out. If Roosevelt were nominated (God forbid!), or elected, I would send in my resignation to Mr. Taft while still President (a custom I should follow in case of the election of a Democrat) for my feeling is strong. I plan, anyhow, to be at Home as much as I can from now on.[110]

A *New York Times* article on August 3, at the height of Taft's reelection campaign, published a major exposé of what it called "Larz Anderson's Reward." Unnamed Washington sources gave reporters the inside story. It was not flattering to Larz or Taft. The *Times* suggested that Taft had not made good on his promise of a $25,000 quid pro quo ambassadorship.[111] It was almost a moot point for Larz. He no longer seemed to care what happened, as long as he left Brussels. If he got his ambassadorship, he would leave Brussels. If he did not get his ambassadorship, he would leave Brussels: "I think I have had my experience of Brussels; whatever happens I do not think we shall remain here again ever for such a length of time. If we do not go somewhere else we shall not stop on [stay] here."[112]

In mid-August, Larz received an encouraging letter from Taft, which he summarized in his journal: "I received a very nice letter from the President in which he practically says he will do all he possibly can for me—and Isabel seems to have found favorable reception on the occasion of her brave little visit when she certainly showed that she was first-rate at the 'game.'"[113] Isabel had gone to the White House that summer after she'd returned from Brussels to talk with the president directly on her husband's behalf. "I delivered a letter from L[arz] and we talked a few minutes," Isabel said of the visit, "after which Mr. Taft invited me to luncheon."[114]

Larz sailed for New York on September 6 and arrived a week later. He and Isabel worked vigorously for Taft's campaign on two fronts, not just against the Democrat Woodrow Wilson but also against Teddy Roosevelt's challenge from the Bull Moose Party. They were very loyal and very busy Taft partisans working on the campaign to reelect the president.[115]

Their reward was coming.

WORKING BEHIND MY PILE OF PAPERS

Figure 21. Ambassador and Mrs. Larz Anderson, Tokyo, 1913.

XIII
DIPLOMATIC FINALE (TOKYO)

lthough Republicans had a majority nationally, William Howard Taft lost the election on November 5, 1912, when Theodore Roosevelt and his Bull Moose Party split the Republican vote and handed Democrat Woodrow Wilson a victory. Larz and Isabel spent election night in New York City with Helen Taft. The next day, with no promotion or new post in sight, they knew they had to return to Brussels.[1] On November 9, they sailed for Europe and arrived in Paris on November 15. They settled into the Ritz, as was their custom. Larz immediately phoned the American legation in Brussels and learned that ciphered cables awaited him in his office. The next morning he took the train to Brussels, alone. In his ground-floor office of the Palais d'Assche, he read the news he had been waiting for:

> The agreement to your apt. having been rec'd from the Japanese Gov. you have to-day been app't'd Amb. to Japan and you may leave for that post at your earliest convenience taking a new oath of office before Secretary of Legation or Consul General the day of your departure from Brussels. Grant-Smith's instructions are not changed and Butler Wright will be Chargé d'Affaires until Mr. Marburg's arrival.[2]

Two days later, on November 18, Larz wrote a long, self-congratulatory journal entry.

> Well, I am at last a real "Excellency", and Isabel is truly dear little Ambassadress, no longer addressed by courtesy only but by right. For wives of "Ambassadors" have the appellation of "Ambassadress" and both can claim to be called "Excellency"!

Years ago I bought an "Ambassador's Box", a silver box with ink well and place for pens and sealing wax, such as was presented to English Ambassadors "on their appointment" in the old days, although it didn't seem then that I should ever be able to make proper use of it:—but here it is now in its proper place: and I had "cheek" enough to have this box design worked into the fresco work over the fireplace in the great staircase hall of the Washington house, to represent my career in Diplomacy (with swords, and "trophies" of my own and my Father's military services, etcetera) even before I had a right to do, or even an evident hope.

And for this end I have been working hard all my life, although it may not seem very apparent: for much has been in a negative way. It was a game that required exhausting patience, for we had to work and wait till a wave [Taft] should come to carry us in, and then we minded no sacrifice, or discomfort. And it looks like "luck" when people are so patient, but it isn't "luck" really. And we get away from Brussels just about in time too—for another season here would have been a trying prospect. The weather is so misty-moisty, depressing, and the highbred society, so dull and tiresome, thinking itself so gay and yet so deadly, would have bored us to death. We have sucked the orange dry here, got all out of it, and we are appreciative, very appreciative, of all the opportunities which we have enjoyed (and of which we have taken advantage, I believe): it has been interesting, very interesting, exhausting, as no other European post could have been.[3]

Larz's successor, the Republican career diplomat Theodore Marburg, was already in Paris. He cabled Larz to ask about subleasing the Palais d'Assche and what furnishings, dishes, and linens he should send from the States. Larz invited Marburg to Brussels for what Larz called "some sage advice," but Marburg was under specific instructions from President-Elect Wilson not to meet with Larz. Larz was livid.

[Marburg] evidently has been "put wise" by that Damn Fool Wilson, who doesn't know anything about Diplomacy and is nothing more than a hard-working clerk with new schemes at how to file away letters (without the least appreciation that most Diplomacy is accomplished without the writing of a word) that he mustn't meet me "in Belgium", as if coming up here officially would hurt him (it would have helped him greatly!) and so he cannot come. So we'll leave him to his own devices and I can't fancy that he'll have time to take much advantage of his post.[4]

Onward to Tokyo

The Andersons made plans for one last bit of entertaining at the Palais d'Assche: a festive Thanksgiving visit from their longtime friends Walter and Bertha Denègre of New Orleans. Larz made several rounds of official farewell calls, including King Albert, the foreign affairs ministry, and foreign diplomatic missions. He said sarcastically that many of the diplomats were "quite as thoughtful and kind in saying good-bye as they were rude and difficult in the beginning."[5]

By December 4, Larz secured train reservations to Korea. After reaching Korea, then under Japanese occupation, he and Isabel would travel on to Tokyo aboard a Japanese train. He obtained visas and customs permits to travel through Russia with their art, furnishings, household effects, and automobiles. The long train trip across Russia and Siberia in the winter with all their belongings was a daunting prospect, but Larz made the best arrangements possible. Unable to get an entire private car on the first leg of the journey, he reserved as much of a public car as was available.

They left Brussels for Paris on December 9 and at Paris transferred to the Express Nord, the train to Moscow. Once on their way to Russia, Larz raved about the train's dining car, noting that one evening Isabel ate caviar and he drank champagne for supper. He wrote, "And so we see we became Russian quickly."[6] He included a picturesque description of the train trip across the western part of the Russian Empire: "We are running across the really lovely wintry snow-white landscape of Russia, and the little collections of farmhouses and of peasants in their yoked sleds moving along the roads, the smoke curling up from the chimneys, and the forests of pine all powdered with snow, reminds us of Tolstoy stories, and makes a lovely panorama as we look out from our comfortable warm car."[7]

Others passengers wandered in and out of their car, annoying Larz. He "sorted out" the situation with a porter but graciously allowed the Russian princesses who were among the intruders to stay and visit with them after the commoners left.

After a few days' rest in Moscow, they boarded a first-class wagon-lit car of the Trans-Siberian Railway to cross the Russian Empire, the longest leg of their journey—nine days. Larz wanted a private Pullman car, but none was available on such short notice. The car he secured for the second leg of the trip was not private either, although he had been able to reserve all of its eight compartments: other passengers walked through the car's public hallway to get to other parts of the train. Larz, Isabel, and their servants—Raymond Clarke, the butler; Horton, the valet; and Caroline, the lady's maid—each got their own compartment. The remaining three compartments served as a library, office, and sitting room. They brought books, games, and other "comforts" with them to help pass the time as they sped across Siberia, Mongolia, and Manchuria, past Samara, Chelyabinsk, Omsk, and Irkutsk. "Our house on wheels is in order," Larz said.[8] The train was scheduled to reach Korea on December 20, and by Larz's calculation, they would be in Tokyo for Christmas.

In Occupied Korea

After going to war with Russia to prevent its incursion into Korea, Japan invaded the Land of the Morning Calm in 1910 and took over the Korean economy and political administration to permanently block Russian influence there. Koreans were seen generally by world powers as unable to govern themselves, although some observers saw the occupation in a longer view. The *Washington Post* opined that the occupation was "abundant proof that Japan sees in the control of Korea the stepping-stone to her future development."[9]

When the Anderson party reached Korea, Japanese occupation officials greeted the train and accorded the new American ambassador every possible courtesy and comfort. Japanese officials transferred them to special compartments in a Pullman car on a train controlled by Japanese forces.[10] Larz was dazzled by the officials' charm offensive and expressed his admiration for them in his journal.

> I believe in the sincerity of the Japanese, and have always found such pleasure in their courtesy and good manners. I think they mean what they do, and so appreciate their kind reception as an indication (of what they repeatedly are saying) of their desire to show their good feeling towards America, for low and behold!—another "Clerk in Charge of Foreign Affairs of the Railway Bureau of the Government-General of Chosen", appeared on the train as we traveled, and brought the first greetings from [Japanese occupation officials in] Seoul.[11]

Larz marveled at the many "investments" Japan was making in Korea.

The Andersons' former Japanese servant Osame met them in Seoul and traveled with them on the train, making cocktails for them along the way. When they arrived in Kyoto on Christmas Day, Larz issued an official statement heaping praise on the Japanese government for their "work" in Korea. Japanese newspapers reported the comments. *Kokumin Shimbun*, a private newspaper widely viewed at the time as a mouthpiece of the Japanese government, published his entire statement in Japanese. "I noticed in Chosen that the administration of the Japanese Government is being satisfactorily carried out and leaves nothing to be desired," Larz said.[12]

He played his Japanese audience to the hilt, pointing out the "good sign" that his first day as ambassador would be Christmas. He reminded his audience that he had met the recently deceased emperor during his visit to Japan in 1910 with Secretary of War Dickinson and planned to "worship the Imperial spirit at the Momoyama cemetery." He described himself as a "constant admirer of Japanese art objects, especially paintings representing bamboo and sparrows, snow on pine trees and such things," and expressed a desire to "spend the remainder of [his] life in Japan."[13]

Despite these auspicious words, Larz knew that his time in Japan would be brief and that they had to start their shopping early, as he wrote on December 26 from Kyoto, "Yesterday morning we took it very easily, but finally got started later in the day, visiting various shops, for Isabel had commissions, and as we may not come to Kyoto again before going Home I was anxious to see what the dealers had, and to revisit the places which I had known years ago."[14]

The Andersons arrived in Tokyo a few days later and settled in at the American embassy, a large white wooden house that looked as if it belonged more in a prosperous midwestern American city than in the heart of Tokyo. Isabel soon hosted her first at-home afternoon tea, but only for members of the embassy staff. Until Larz presented his credentials to the emperor, they could not host official embassy events or even socialize with other diplomats and Japanese officials. For the time being, they were stuck at the embassy with their staff.

Unlike their move into the Palais d'Assche, which was marked by vigorous and animated renovation, decorating, and furnishing, Larz had no interest in any of those things in Tokyo. In a New Year's Day letter, he revealed his lethargy toward living in the embassy and making any changes to it.

We are trying to make things look more homelike by moving the furniture about, but the most successful move seems to be to move most of the stuff entirely away and clear out rather than rearrange. If we were to be here a sufficiently long time of course we could make many changes, but it does not seem worth while for the few months before we shall come home, and although I delight in Japan and the Japanese yet I am already looking forward to next Summer.[15]

Ready to Leave

By January 8, even though he had not yet presented his credentials to the emperor, Larz drafted his resignation letter and sent it to Washington by the next diplomatic pouch. He wanted President-Elect Wilson to "have it on hand" after his inauguration on March 4, almost two months away. In the meantime, Larz decided, they should do all they could to make the short stay "of the best account."[16]

On January 13, the Imperial Household Office notified the embassy that the emperor would receive Larz and Isabel the next day. The emperor and the empress also invited them to a luncheon following the ceremony. Larz, however, was not impressed. "We are really getting tired of lunching with Royalty for this will be twice in a year that we have been so honored," he said. He seemed particularly vexed by the imperial dress code and protocol of a court event. Within hours of receiving the invitation, however, the palace phoned to say the emperor was indisposed and the event postponed.[17] This seems more than coincidental. Could there have been a spy in the embassy who reported to the Imperial Household Office Larz's complaints about having to lunch with the emperor?

Larz waited all of January without word from the foreign office about when he could present his credentials to the emperor. The couple spent the month visiting and entertaining embassy staff and personal friends who lived in Tokyo, but official engagements were still prohibited. They spent a lot of time shopping. One of their most extravagant purchases was a complete dinner service of Imari porcelain encrusted in gold with the American eagle. They never used the service at the embassy in Tokyo. (A few pieces of this set have survived and are in a private collection in Boston.) Larz also decided to buy a new automobile—a Hudson 33—on one of his shopping sprees. His most curious activity during this diplomatic limbo, and a sign of his boredom, was redesigning the embassy's livery. He wanted less red and more blue and a smaller eagle on the cap.[18]

His Excellency the Ambassador, At Last

On February 1, after being in Tokyo for almost five weeks, Larz finally presented his credentials to His Imperial Majesty Taisho, 123rd Emperor of Japan (1879–1926). The Imperial Household Office sent a carriage and detachment from the Imperial Body Guard to transport the Andersons to the palace, where the emperor received them in historic Phoenix Hall. After Larz presented the emperor with his credentials and a letter of recall for Bryan, Larz and Isabel were separately presented to the Empress Sadako Kujo (1884–1951). The imperial couple then hosted the Andersons for a luncheon attended by members of the imperial family and senior ministers of the Imperial Household Office.

Larz was now fully and finally a US ambassador to one of the most important posts of the American diplomatic service. The timing of Larz's appointment could not have been better for American prestige in Japan. British ambassador Sir Claude MacDonald, who had been in Japan since 1900, had resigned and vacated his post before his successor, Sir William Conyngham Greene, arrived in Tokyo. The Imperial Household Office and the Japanese Foreign Office had a long tradition of preferring to deal with ambassadors from English-speaking countries on matters of international importance, and Sir Claude had been a favorite of theirs for more than a decade. With MacDonald's departure, Larz became the most important ambassador in Tokyo's diplomatic hierarchy. Even Larz was aware of this and its implications for the success of American diplomacy in Japan:

> I am an Ambassador in full function now and from the point of view of official advantage, which indeed does not entirely agree with our personal desire to return Home, it is unfortunate that my tenure will not be longer owing to the action of Congress, for it would be a splendid chance for our Embassy here to take a lead. The new British Ambassador will not arrive for some time yet and this would give an opportunity for us to take up certain positions which the British generally assume, as they realize their value. There are many things in which the Japanese prefer to have English-speaking representatives concerned rather than the Continental ones.[19]

It did not matter to Larz that he was in Japan at a unique moment in American diplomatic history: a chance for the American ambassador to become the dean of the diplomatic corps in Tokyo. He decided he could blame Congress for his early resignation on or before March 4, Inauguration Day, even though he had long planned to make his stay in Tokyo as short as possible. He'd precipitously left an important diplomatic post almost two decades earlier and knew he would suffer withering criticism from journalists and State Department bureaucrats if he did so again. He needed to explain his resignation in a way that absolved him of responsibility.

Diplomatic duties and the prestige of the American embassy in Japan were not, however, uppermost in Larz's mind. He became preoccupied with what was going on back at the Palais d'Assche in Brussels. His 1911 lease with the marquis did not allow subletting, but Larz had paid the marquis a "certain lump sum indemnity," as he called it, so Marburg could take over the lease.[20] Larz now worried that Marburg's children might be roller-skating through the palace and that he would be held responsible for damage to the floors. At the same time, Larz gloated over the "amusing news" that Marburg was having problems settling into the residence. As it turned out, Bryan (Larz's predecessor both in Brussels and Tokyo) wanted back the furniture the Andersons had rented from him and which Larz had included in the sublease with Marburg. Larz ridiculed Marburg for "the condition of what little silverware, etc., they had brought over with them."[21] He gleefully reported that Marburg's audience with King Albert was delayed on top of everything else.[22] Marburg, like Larz, was a Republican and a Taft appointee, but in Larz's eyes he was weak because he'd agreed to serve under a Democrat. Wilson clearly viewed Marburg as someone he could trust. Marburg was a Unitarian, a trustee of Johns Hopkins University (where Wilson had earned his doctorate), and an advocate of peace through the rule of law and arbitration.

By Valentine's Day, the Andersons rushed to get in as much entertaining at the embassy as possible, "to fill in till the end of the month," Larz said.[23] He arranged to have the house, the gardens, the grounds, the new automobile and carriage, and the servants photographed. At the same time, an artist sketched the grounds and buildings so Larz could later commission a painting of the embassy.

By turning down many club memberships and chairmanships that an American ambassador to Japan traditionally accepted, Larz signaled his imminent departure, though he made no formal announcement of it. He mentioned in diplomatic and Japanese government circles that he might return to the United States as a result of the change in administration. Taking Larz's statements at face value, some Americans in Japan offered to petition Washington on his behalf.

> Some of the men in Yokohama and in Tokyo have smelled out
> the fact that I might have to go Home and have been most
> kind in offering to cable or write or join together in any way

to keep us here. I much appreciate their good will but have asked them to do nothing and to say as little about the matter as possible, for if I go I prefer to go quietly and without more comment than is possible. I am not so damned anxious to stop on [stay] as to care to turn my hand over. I have worked earnestly and gained what I wanted, and now I shall continue to do my duty but I'm under obligation to no one and do not care to undertake any obligation in the future. Amen![24]

Larz felt no obligation to anyone—not his president, his party, or his country.

Confirmation Complications

One problem complicated Larz's plan to quit his post and go home. The Senate had never confirmed him. This created political problems in Tokyo and Washington. Other of Taft's lame-duck diplomatic appointees remained unconfirmed also, but to resign after a few weeks, before the Senate confirmed him, would forever raise questions about his suitability for the post. Worse, Larz had already presented his credentials to the emperor knowing he had not been confirmed. As the clock ticked closer to Inauguration Day, the Senate seemed to resist acting on the appointment. Larz had barely received the endorsement of Senator Cullom a year earlier for the lower-ranking post of minister to Belgium. Even if the Japanese Foreign Office were in the dark about Larz's plans, Washington was not.

On February 15, two weeks after presenting his credentials to the emperor, Larz cabled Taft's private secretary, Charles D. Hilles, asking for "leave" from the State Department. Larz called it an "automatic termination" to be concurrent with Wilson's inauguration. He told Hilles this was "unusual in diplomatic usage which would certainly be difficult to explain and might be misunderstood by [the] Japanese government." He wanted to submit his resignation directly to President Taft as the "personally preferable method of closing my career in service." In other words, he did not want to deal with the State Department, which had leaked details of his precipitous resignation from Rome in 1897. He ended the cable by calling his current situation as an unconfirmed ambassador who had presented his credentials to a head of state "personally and officially most awkward."[25] Hilles cabled back only that the president expected confirmation and would keep Larz informed.

Taft had already asked Larz to stay on in Tokyo for at least another six months. On February 3, 1913, in a personal letter to Isabel, Taft laid out his expectations: "I do not know how long you are likely to remain there, but

Mr. Wilson is going to have so many appointments to make that I should not wonder if you would find yourselves staying there until next summer or fall."[26]

Some time in late February, still unconfirmed by the Senate and without State's agreement to his resignation, the Japanese Foreign Office and the Imperial Household Office "had come to know 'informally'" that Larz would probably retire "due to the exigencies of the political situation at Home."[27] They could only have heard this from Larz himself. The Imperial Household Office responded to the news by sending gifts on March 1—"expressions of appreciation," Larz called them—even though he had not yet been confirmed, nor had he submitted his resignation.

On March 2 Larz heard through Washington channels that his "retirement" and leave would be approved, even though the Senate had not yet officially voted on his confirmation. He immediately started sending around "p.p.c. cards" (*pour prendre congé*, calling cards announcing home leave), which in Larz's mind seemed "to sufficiently satisfy the needs of the occasion," which he defined as "going on a 'leave' which is permanent."

Larz was now also free to submit his resignation and ask for leave officially. The next day he cabled Hilles at the White House that he had been confirmed and now wanted permission "for leave of absence usual manner."[28] Hilles referred Larz's request to the State Department that day, asking Secretary of State Philander Knox if Larz's request for leave could be "properly granted."[29] The leave was granted, effective March 3 (March 4 in Tokyo). The resignation itself would take effect when the leave of absence expired on May 1. The official reason for his resignation was finally fixed and reported blandly in the Japanese press on March 3 without a hint of the drama behind it: "With the coming into power on the 4th instant of Mr. Wilson, great changes in the diplomatic representatives are expected. Mr. Anderson, American Ambassador to Japan, who is a friend and supporter of President Taft, was the first to send in his resignation; this having been accepted, he is to spend some time in Japan with Mrs. Anderson."[30]

For months, Larz had juggled several versions of a story about why or even if he was leaving Tokyo: he was not leaving; he was leaving in order to retire; he was going on home leave that was permanent; he was leaving because of the change in administration. He spun so many versions of his departure that it is not clear if even Larz Anderson knew why he was leaving Japan.

"The Last of Japan"

On March 4, embassy staff hoisted the American flag in celebration of President Wilson's inauguration. The ceremony was held under Larz's command: he was still officially ambassador to Japan and would keep his title until he was back in the United States.

Part of Larz's calculation of the timing and conditions for his departure from Tokyo was his paycheck. He got the best possible deal from the State Department. If he had resigned, his pay would have stopped. By going on leave, his pay continued until he was back home in Washington.

> By correspondence with the Department I find that, although my functions here cease with the fourth of March, yet compensation to the amount of my salary (17,500.00 a year) shall be continued till my return Home within the maximum time which is allowed for the trip from Tokyo to Washington, forty days. As this seems to maintain my status till my arrival at Home by at least continuing my pay I shall probably not insist on resigning, but shall accept the view of the State Department although I am not so sure that it is the best.[31]

Even though the couple could have left Japan within a few days, Larz decided to wait a few weeks so they could sail on the SS *Manchuria*, a more luxurious ship. When Isabel later edited Larz's journals for publication, she made it sound as though they drove from the American embassy directly to the ship in Yokohama harbor.[32] For the next few weeks, however, they hid out at a mountain resort, the Fujiya, in the little town of Miyanoshita. Then as now, members of the Japanese imperial family and other elite members of Japanese society were frequent guests.[33] Larz arranged for cars to travel back and forth to Tokyo so embassy staff could come visit them at the Fujiya.

On the evening of March 15, Larz and Isabel boarded the *Manchuria* at Yokohama, bound for San Diego. Larz wrote that a bright red moon appeared over "the mysterious cone of 'O Fuji San', Spirited Mountain Top" and interpreted the scene as a "Divine sign that we should sometime come to Japan again." As the ship sailed farther out to sea, "the last of Fuji went with the last of Japan," Larz said poetically.[34] Larz and Isabel would never set foot in Japan again.

The next day, March 16, the *Washington Post* reported that Larz had left his Tokyo post "because the Japanese government had declined to receive him."[35] Though officials in Washington denied this, Larz's "informal" announcement to Japanese officials of his "retirement" before he had been confirmed had apparently backfired. If so, the last-minute gifts from the Imperial Household Office may have been part of an effort to save face and protect the emperor and empress from the embarrassment that would have followed public disclosure that Larz had presented credentials the US Senate had not confirmed.

"Hardly a Diplomat of Consequence"

On March 5, as they were relaxing at the mountain resort, Larz wrote a retrospective summary of the twenty months since Taft had nominated him to Brussels. He reviewed the "anxieties and doubt" about both his appointment to Brussels in 1911 and Taft's defeat in 1912. In thinking about his time in Tokyo, he concluded he had been "on trial." He decided that furnishing the residence had been one of the great challenges of his tenure as American ambassador to Japan. He ended his self-debriefing on a contradictory note. "The past two years have really been very hectic—but very worth while," Larz wrote. "We are quite exhausted but still in the ring and prepared to take it easy for a while now."[36]

When the Harvard scholar of US diplomatic history Richard Leopold wrote a brief review of Isabel's compilation of her husband's papers, *Letters and Journals of a Diplomat*, he deemed Larz Anderson's service in London, Rome, Brussels, and Tokyo "insignificant."

> The student of American diplomacy will find little of value in Anderson's letters and journals. Comments on those vital economic, social, and intellectual forces that shape foreign policy are wholly absent. Anderson seems to have been blissfully unaware of or unconcerned with the factors making for Anglo-American friendship in the early nineties. His diaries shed no new light on Italian-American relations during the same decade. Although he was at Brussels just before the World War and at Tokyo in a critical moment in Far Eastern affairs, Anderson recorded nothing of importance. Instead, his pages are devoted solely to royal receptions, embassy parties, and other trivialities that are merely the trappings of diplomatic life.[37]

After his return from Japan, Larz commissioned two works of art to commemorate his service in the American diplomatic corps: a 1914 portrait by society artist Dewitt M. Lockman for display in Anderson House and a 1916 bronze bust by the Massachusetts sculptor Bruce Wilder Saville (1893–1938) for display at Weld. Both works presented Larz in the fancy-dress uniform he'd designed for himself but never wore in public.[38] In the painting, a bold white-and-red sash accents the uniform, which is decorated with a small constellation of European and Japanese royal orders and insignia placed casually here and there. A double-breasted field marshal's trench coat is cast jauntily over his shoulders. In the background, a single stalk of red gladiolus provides a symbolic point of reference to Larz's biography: the "sword" flower associated both with Larz's birth month, August, and with military valor.

Unlike many diplomats of his era, Larz chose never to publish books or articles about his diplomatic postings.[39] Except for a brief statement in 1915 calling for good relations between Japan and the United States, Larz remained silent about the details of his diplomatic career for the rest of his life.[40]

Figure 22. Isabel Anderson in her Red Cross uniform, 1918.

XIV

IN THE FIGHT FOR FREEDOM (EUROPE 1917–1918)

When the United States entered the Great War, Isabel Anderson responded to a call from the local Red Cross chapter in Washington for fifty women to volunteer as canteen workers in France and Belgium. Though she did not need it, former president William Howard Taft gave her a letter of reference.[1] Like many women of her class, she felt called to serve her country. American women had few opportunities at home to express their patriotism or desire for public service, but the war in Europe gave them a way to change the status quo.

Over the course of the war, from 1914 to 1918, some twenty-five thousand American women, most of them wealthy socialites (or at least able to pay their own way), went to Europe to serve as nurses, ambulance drivers, and canteen workers. There they found the war zone "afforded them scope for independence, for initiative, for entrepreneurship," as one historian noted.[2] Because there was little coordination among volunteer organizations operating in the theaters of war, the women "could move freely among them, and within them could establish their own objectives, adopt their own agenda, devise their own means."[3] Isabel did not have a supervisor or commanding officer in Europe who decided when and where she worked. She learned to be entrepreneurial and self-directed and made her own decisions about where to go and what job to do. If later in life she showed a need for independence and solitude—breathing space from her life as a busy society hostess—this year on her own in a war zone was part of the reason.

In early fall 1917 Isabel sailed to France. She served first in the American Red Cross canteen and hospital at Épernay and then transferred herself to Mrs. Charles Noé Daly's hospital units at Compiègne and Cugny. Mrs. Daly's famous units were attached to the French Army. Isabel's proficiency in French made her an especially valuable member of the hospital's volunteer staff.

After being in France for almost four months, Isabel received a telegram from King Albert of Belgium inviting her to visit him and Queen Elizabeth at La Panne on the Belgian coast, where the monarchs had their wartime headquarters. Isabel accepted the invitation and traveled alone through the battle-scarred countryside of France and Belgium to see them. After her visit with the monarchs and a tour of hospital facilities led by Dr. Antoine Depage, founder of the Belgian Red Cross, Isabel returned to France to continue her nursing duties for Mrs. Daly. Within a few days, Depage cabled Isabel asking her to come work for him at his hospital in Belgium. Isabel scurried around Paris obtaining the necessary travel permits and moved herself to the Ocean Hospital at La Panne, where she worked in the operating room for a few months.[4]

Isabel eventually returned to France and went to work in canteens for the soldiers who were under the command of General John J. Pershing. The general invited her to dinner one night. She arrived too late for a meal with him, but he courteously sat and talked with her as she ate. The harrowing trip by automobile on a dark, rainy night had left her "too cold and shaken to pieces to talk very intelligently," she later said. The only part of the conversation she could remember was Pershing telling her he was "troubled by the lack of ships."[5]

Isabel then decided to go to Paris to work in canteens, just as rumors circulated that the Germans were about to occupy the city. Isabel found everything both "exciting" and "alarming."[6] At times, Isabel and her colleagues had to take shelter in the Paris Métro tunnels for safety.[7] She and her fellow nurses faced danger and showed courage.

> All the dressing-stations behind the trenches had to be evacuated the first day. The regular method of evacuating hospitals was this: first, the nurses were sent ahead in an ambulance lorry; then every patient who could walk had to take the road on foot; the severely wounded were loaded into ambulances and sent off. The hospital staff, left behind, set to work to destroy whatever there was no chance of taking.[8]

Isabel learned to live with little in the way of comfort. The housing for volunteer women consisted of primitive, poorly furnished, and unheated rooms in cheap hotels or abandoned houses. Despite the hardship accommodations, Isabel always looked for something about her room to cheer her up.

> I drew the very worst room engaged by the Red Cross at the hotel. It was in the attic. It was dirty. You could see only the sky and a little piece of a roof. There was one red blanket, and the room was too small even for a chair. Yet I really became

attached to my attic, and began to think the red blanket cheerful. I enjoyed watching the aeroplanes in the sky. At a desk which I made for myself out of my travel bags and by the light of two candles stuck into old bottles, these notes of my life in France as a canteen worker were begun.[9]

Isabel served wherever she was needed, and though she had training as a practical nurse, most of her work was in canteens. These primitive huts and roadhouses were places where soldiers got a brief respite from life and death in the trenches. Isabel served them coffee and sandwiches and did what she could to raise their spirits. As a speaker of fluent French, Isabel especially bonded with the French soldiers, the *poilus*, as they liked to be called. The term, which means "shaggy guys," referred to their unkempt beards. It was an affectionate term like the moniker *doughboys* given to American soldiers.[10]

I cannot say enough in favor of the poilus. They are brave, cheery, polite, and grateful, too. The more I see of them the better I like them, and the finer I think they are. So many have asked me to be their marraine [godmother] that I feel as if I were godmother to the whole French army. They love to write letters. Of course they often sing in the canteen, and here is one of the songs they sing to their marraine:—

Etant en perm' tout dernier'ment, J'suis allé voir ben gentiment, ma marraine! Cel' qui m'envoy' des p'tits paquets, Pour la premier' fois, j'la voyais, Ma marraine!

[Because now I'm in forever, I went to see my godmother, the one who sends me little presents. Now at last, I've met her, My godmother!]

The experience of war left Isabel with a new vision of the modern American woman: "Strong, level-headed women willing to do anything, go anywhere, and obey orders."[11] She knew, though, that women were treated differently, despite great organizational skills that were, in her view, their special strength. Writing of the role of women in the war, she observed that she and her colleagues were "worked hard and kept mostly at the base."[12] This experience led her to question the limited role of women in the military. In this, she sounds very much like a woman of the twenty-first century who seeks to serve her country in uniform: "Women to-day may prefer to be canteeners or nurses rather than fighters, but they do want a chance to work at the front, where they can be of the most service, not coddled in comparative safety at the bases. After all, has n't a woman just as much right to die for her country as a man?"[13]

Despite these progressive views on women in war service, Isabel opposed women's suffrage. Later in life, she wrote that a woman's right to vote would "make but little difference and more trouble. It is all right, but to have so many voting does not achieve any different results, and it makes government—democratic government—even more unwieldy."[14] Isabel was not alone in this view, and opposing suffrage at the time was not universally viewed as unpatriotic or against the interests of women. Many of her wealthy female peers, however, advocated for women's suffrage. One of the most vocal and visible was also one of the richest women in the world, Alva Vanderbilt Belmont, former sister-in-law of the Andersons' friend, George Washington Vanderbilt.

After the war, when Isabel proposed the idea for a book on her experiences in Belgium and France, the publisher asked her, "What new points have you got on the war?" Hundreds of books about the war were already on the market, and a new book by a woman would need to fill a market niche. Isabel readily had an answer: "I can tell you, from a woman's point of view, how it feels to be in the front-line trenches, and what an American woman's experiences are in an auto-chir [ambulance] or triage hospital moving with the French army."[15]

When the publisher then asked what she wanted to call the book, Isabel offered several options, including *Female Feuds at the French Front* and *Female Fools at the Front*. She explained the *Fools* version of the title, saying she had once heard that "an American worker in Paris cabled to headquarters in America: Sending too many intelligent women—send us some fools."[16]

Isabel once said, "Each writer has to work out his own salvation in writing as well as in life."[17] Her choice of the word *salvation*, with its overtones of Christian piety (the sentiment is drawn from Philippians 2:12), is not haphazard. Isabel's war experience was a personal salvation. She was delivered from harm on the battlefield and proved her moral fiber through selfless service to the injured and dying.

POOR PRINT OF
ONE OF THE FAMOUS VIEWS
OF FUJI - BY AN AMERICAN HAKUSAI

REPRESENTING AN HAPPY COUPLE WHO
HAVE REACHED THE TOP OF THE DIVINE
MOUNTAIN TOGETHER AND SEE THE
SUN SET OVER THEIR REALIZED
AMBITIONS·

Figure 23. Isabel Anderson signing books in New Hampshire, 1947.

XV

By Isabel Anderson

There were many influences in Isabel Anderson's life that predisposed her to being a storyteller and a writer. As a girl, she spent much time with her father's family in New Hampshire, a part of the United States with a long tradition of storytelling in which a tale's characters and plots expressed simple truths about life and human nature. Isabel once described how captivated she was by her father's stories of navy voyages around the globe: "the Orient, the Barbary Coast, the Spanish Main, and pirates of the seven seas."[1] She also heard tales of her Weld grandfather's great fleet of schooners—the Black Horse Line—that crisscrossed the oceans and plied the world's harbors: San Francisco, Vancouver, Hong Kong, Manila, Sydney, Yokohama, Shanghai, Calcutta, and many more.[2] To a child whose world was limited to a New Hampshire farm, a Boston brownstone, and a Newport cottage, stories about these faraway places were magical.

When Isabel went abroad with Maud Howe Elliott in 1895 at the age of nineteen, her father encouraged her to start writing about her experiences on the trip. "There's one thing I'll ask you," he said, "and that is that you keep a journal."[3] Although Isabel's journals have not survived except to the extent they were later incorporated into her publications, her interest in writing was deeply rooted in the New England oral tradition, her father's stories, and his advice to her on writing.[4] Also, Maud's renown as an author and biographer certainly inspired Isabel to follow her example. Another famous American woman writer also inspired her, but one from a previous generation—her mother's.

Louisa May Alcott

Although Isabel and Louisa May Alcott (1832–1888) never met, Isabel's mother, Anna, traveled through Europe with Alcott for a year before her marriage to George Perkins. When Isabel was a child, her mother told her about the Alcott episode of her life. It is hard to imagine Isabel reading *Little Women* (1868) or any of Alcott's other popular works without recalling that her mother had traveled with the famous author.

In 1865, Alcott went along with Anna Weld as her paid companion on Anna's delayed grand tour of Europe. Anna's father wanted Alcott to chaperone his thirty-year-old daughter and attend to her health. Left invalid by scarlet fever in childhood, Anna needed a companion who could also nurse her, as Alcott described in her diary: "Mr. W[eld], hearing that I was something of a nurse and wanted to travel, proposed my going with his invalid daughter. I agreed, though I had my doubts. But everyone said, 'Go'; so after a week of worry I did go."[5]

The girls' fathers, William Fletcher Weld and Amos Bronson Alcott (1799–1888), both prominent Unitarians and abolitionists in Massachusetts, agreed to let their daughters travel together at Weld's expense. On July 19, 1865, Anna and Louisa together applied for passports in Boston. Anna's father, a justice of the peace, notarized their applications. Their trip abroad was about to become part of American literary history.

The women sailed from Boston in mid-August, bound for Liverpool. By the time they reached England, Alcott already had second thoughts about the trip. During the crossing, she found she had little in common with Anna, whose physical infirmities did not bode well for travel across the continent.[6] After visiting London, they went to Cologne and sailed down the Rhine to Switzerland, where they took rooms in the home of an English woman in Vevey. Their sojourn in the lakeside town for the next several months took on great importance in Alcott's biography and provided inspiration for one of her most beloved characters.

In Vevey, they met a young Polish patriot, Ladislas Wisniewski, who lived there in exile. They nicknamed him "Laddie." The Pole was the inspiration for the character Laurie in Alcott's most popular book, *Little Women* (1868–1869). Alcott's diaries made no mention of any attraction between Anna and Laddie, even though Isabel later claimed the two were infatuated with each other. A hundred years of Alcott scholarship support Alcott's version of the Vevey sojourn. Alcott and Wisniewski were, as one biographer concluded, "drawn to each other, exchanging lessons not only in English and French, but in the American and Polish rebellions."[7] Alcott's Vevey journals included many dreamy references to the Pole. Her affections for him were genuine.

Louisa and Anna moved to Nice to spend the winter in a more temperate climate, leaving the young Pole in Vevey. Anna continued to annoy Louisa. Anna rested more and did less, and by February Alcott decided to return to the United States. "I'm tired of it, and as she [Anna] is not going to travel," Alcott wrote in her diary, "my time is too valuable to be wasted."[8] In May 1866, Alcott left Anna behind and went on to Paris alone. Anna remained at the hotel and waited for her father to arrive. He accompanied the two women back to the United States that summer aboard the Cunard Line's paddle wheel steamer, the SS *Africa*, the type of transoceanic vessel that had made his clipper fleet obsolete. Anna and Louisa never saw each other again.

An undated essay found among Isabel's papers challenges Louisa May Alcott's version of the story. This is a very different account of the friendship the two women had with the Polish patriot. The essay claims that Laddie was in love with Anna, not Louisa.[9] Isabel wrote the essay but obscured her authorship of it, perhaps in an attempt to increase its legitimacy as a piece of literary scholarship. The essay was written ostensibly by someone who claimed to have "certain relevant information concerning Miss Alcott's European trip in 1865 and concerning the situation involving young Wisniewski." The "certain relevant information" turned out to be a letter from Isabel to the anonymous essayist (actually, Isabel herself). In the letter, Isabel claimed that after Anna Perkins's death in 1924, she'd found love letters between her mother and Laddie. The essayist (Isabel) cited these letters as proof that Laddie had proposed marriage to Anna. Through the anonymous writer, Isabel claimed Anna had turned Laddie down because "he was not well, and he was a foreigner." The divergent interpretations of the Vevey incident would have been easily settled by examining the letters. "Unfortunately I destroyed the letters," Isabel said, "so you have only my word for this."

If the love letters between Anna and Laddie existed, it is hard to understand the circumstances under which Isabel would have destroyed them. After all, she devoted the last ten years of her life to preserving family papers and memorabilia and understood the value letters between her mother and Wisniewski would have to family and literary history. The alternative is even more puzzling: Isabel fabricating the existence of the letters to give her mother some claim to fame of her own. The Anna Weld–Louisa May Alcott encounter is nonetheless of great significance in understanding Isabel's desire to be a writer. Her mother had once been the friend of a very famous woman author. That would be enough to make any little girl dream of seeing her name in print.

Maud Howe Elliott

If the author of *Little Women* was an indirect inspiration for Isabel's desire to be a woman of letters, Maud Howe Elliott was a direct role model and writing mentor for Isabel. Maud was a worldly and wise woman who published four books, including *Art and Handicraft in the Woman's Building at the World's Columbian Exposition, Chicago 1893*, which firmly established her place in American culture. Two decades later, her 1915 biography of her mother, Julia Ward Howe, earned a Pulitzer Prize.

During her year abroad, Isabel learned much from Maud that fostered her adolescent literary ambitions. Most importantly, she learned that women who derive their greatness from the arts and letters are respected and admired—even by reigning monarchs. One day while walking in the woods near Partenkirchen, Germany, Maud and Isabel encountered the Empress Elizabeth of Austria. The empress (assassinated two years later by an anarchist) spontaneously bowed to Maud and her young charge. Maud and the empress had met several times before.[10] The day's lesson was that a woman's celebrity did not have to come from material wealth or political influence but could come from the power of her pen.

A Prolific Output

Between 1909 and 1948, Isabel Anderson published some sixty works across many genres: children's literature, travelogues, short stories, drama and musical theater, historical nonfiction, and poetry. At the same time she was writing books, she published articles, short stories, and poems in local and national magazines and newspapers. Many of these short pieces were derived from her books. Several subjects—for example, Japanese culture and cruises aboard the *Roxana*—appeared over and over again under different titles in different outlets.

Her output was beyond prolific. Book-length works totaled almost ten thousand printed pages. The theatrical pieces she wrote or supervised, including plays, lyrics, and musical scores, added perhaps another thousand pages to her output, and newspaper and periodicals added perhaps a thousand more on top of that. Isabel Anderson's estimated lifetime literary output was thus around twelve thousand printed pages. "Everything I have ever written has appeared either in books or in magazines," Isabel said.[11] She once described how her writing projects got started: "I write at any odd moment, maybe on the train,—and keep a pad next to my bed. I try to put down some interesting experience or description of some new place, ideas, plots for stories. I set aside the morning when I am at home. Interruptions are a great trouble—also a very heavy mail."[12]

By any measure, Isabel worked hard at her writing, but she relied heavily on others to help her achieve her output. Over the course of more than thirty years, at least six literary assistants, each with different writing and editing skills, worked for her: Louise Whitefield Bray, Esther Willard Bates, Eleanor Wilbur Pomeroy, Bertha P. Friend, Katherine K. Crosby, and a "Miss C. Gilman," who may have been Carrie A. Gilman of Honolulu. Isabel often acknowledged the work of these women and occasionally dedicated a book to one of them. Three of these women in particular—Louise, Esther, and

Eleanor—worked for Isabel over many years. Eleanor was the only one who worked full time for more than twenty years.[13] The literary assistants were at times collaborators, coauthors, and coeditors, though never credited as such on the title page. They provided Isabel with access to expertise in such areas as theater, poetry, and literary criticism.

Isabel's literary talent pool helped her experiment with different subjects and literary genres. Louise was a playwright affiliated with the 47 Workshop at Harvard and, like Isabel, had served as a volunteer in France during the war. Esther, once a professor of English at Boston University and the Rhode Island School of Design, wrote a book on theater, *Pageants and Pageantry* (1912). She was an accomplished literary historian who specialized in the manuscripts and bibliography of the American poet Edwin Arlington Robinson. Bertha, a resident of nearby Jamaica Plain who had only an eighth-grade education, provided general editorial assistance. Isabel credited Bertha for her work on *A Yacht in Mediterranean Seas*. Katherine, a 1909 graduate of Boston University, wrote professionally for magazines and had successfully sold some thirty articles and stories by the time she was in her late twenties. She once described her own writing talents as "a decorative sort of style and an inquiring mind."[14]

Eleanor Wilbur Pomeroy

Eleanor Wilbur Pomeroy (1886–1968) was Isabel's closest and most trusted literary assistant and editor for two decades.[15] A 1911 graduate of Emerson College, she worked as a magazine writer and night-school teacher before going to work full time for Isabel in 1929. Eleanor and Isabel had an especially close working relationship, though they never became familiar with each other. They always addressed each other as "Mrs. Anderson" and "Miss Pomeroy." At the time of her death in 1948, Isabel owned the mortgage on Eleanor's house at 34 Concord Square in Boston's South End. After Isabel died, Eleanor continued working on her literary papers, organizing them for the Weld Office and helping gather information for the estate tax arbitration between New Hampshire and Massachusetts. (See chapter 16.) That any of Isabel's papers survived and ended up at Boston University may well have been due to Eleanor's diligence in seeing that they were cared for after her employer died.

Eleanor's testimony during the arbitration provided much insight into Isabel's writing and editing methods and how the two women worked together. There was no routine or predictability in the work she did for Isabel. "One day would never be like another day," Eleanor said.[16] Sometimes Eleanor worked from her own home, but mostly she worked in the mansion in

Brookline. Often enough, Isabel arrived unannounced at Eleanor's Concord Square house to work there, whether the work required Eleanor's assistance or not. On days Eleanor worked at the mansion, she arrived at nine thirty in the morning and went first to the Leather Room, the small den on the ground floor, where Isabel left the day's assignments written out on slips of paper. Isabel came downstairs within an hour of Eleanor's arrival, and the two women worked together for the rest of the morning. Their work session ended after lunch or continued into the afternoon, depending on Isabel's schedule. Once a year during the summer, Eleanor traveled to The Boxlet to spend a working vacation there.

Eleanor Pomeroy said her duties were those of an "under-editor" who focused primarily on proofreading. Given the almost two decades Eleanor worked for Isabel on a wide range of projects, she vastly and perhaps intentionally oversimplified how she characterized her assignments. It was true she proofread, but elsewhere in her testimony Eleanor described the great range of tasks she performed, including working with Isabel on a book of poems, collating and editing Isabel's volumes of Anderson family papers, and attending rehearsals of Isabel's productions at Boston-area theaters as a deputy authorized to approve production details. In 1934, Eleanor even appeared as "the figure of Freedom" in one of Isabel's plays performed at the Boston Civic Theater.[17]

Isabel acknowledged Eleanor's contributions to her books, although not always publicly. When the manuscript for *General Nicholas Longworth Anderson: Letters and Journals* was completed in 1938, Isabel sent Eleanor a handwritten note saying, "Dear Miss Pomeroy: thanks so much for the beautifully done book of Gen. A[nderson]'s [correspondence]."[18] Isabel did not publicly acknowledge Eleanor's contribution to the book, although she did thank Esther Bates and Louise Bray for theirs. Eleanor was closely involved in the production of Isabel's books of poetry. She helped select the poems in the collection *I Hear a Call*. Eleanor, a shy person who never sought any recognition for herself, clearly underplayed her importance to Isabel when she gave testimony in 1949. She wanted to raise no doubts about the authorship of her employer's books and articles.

Children's Literature

Isabel started her career as an author with the publication in 1909 of *The Great Sea Horse*, a large and complex project that took several years to complete. The twenty-five short stories in *The Great Sea Horse* are populated with mermaids and "merboys," seashells, fairies, flowers, gnomes, and humanlike creatures called "brownies and pinkies." The stories are amusing and inventive. If the book were again available in print, it would surely captivate young readers. The *New York Times* reviewer Hildegarde Hawthorne (granddaughter of Nathaniel Hawthorne) called *The Great Sea Horse* stories "most delightful."[19] First published in a deluxe edition of three hundred numbered and signed copies and later in a cloth-bound commercial edition, the volume was lavishly decorated with black-and-white drawings by the Boston artist Frank Downey and color pastels by John Elliott. (Larz accused John of being "careless" in his work and causing delays in the book's publication.[20]) Elliott's work was indispensable to the success of the publication: he designed the cover and created the twenty-five full-color illustrations.

Elliott's association with the book also heightened its profile. When the *International Studio* carried a notice for *The Great Sea Horse*, it did so in the category "Holiday Art Books" rather than children's literature, and indeed the book was a work of art.[21] Elliott's pieces were of such high quality that New York City's venerable art dealer M. Knoedler & Company handled the sale of the originals in 1910. This sale received more notice in the *Washington Post* than did the book itself a year earlier.[22] Isabel bought nine of the original illustrations, which hung for many years in a guest room at Weld.[23] The whereabouts of these pieces is unknown.

In 1910–1911, Isabel published in rapid succession a series of seven more children's books, all illustrated with black-and-white drawings by the Boston artist Horace Boylston Dummer (1878-1945). The stories are about a central character, Captain Ginger, whom Isabel describes in the first volume, *Captain Ginger's Fairy*, as a sickly four-year-old boy named Jimmy. Textual clues suggest that Captain Ginger suffers from tuberculosis. The character was in real life Isabel's godson, James Calvin Cooley, the son of Susie Dalton Cooley, one of her bridesmaids. (Susie and her second husband, Fred Stone, traveled with the Andersons to Greece and Turkey in 1929. See chapter 10.) Isabel wrote the series to give James encouragement at a time when his father, Judge Alford Cooley, was dying of tuberculosis. During World War II, James worked in the Office of Strategic Services, the predecessor to the Central Intelligence Agency, and retired from the CIA in 1972. He died in Washington, DC, in 1997.

In 1920, Isabel wrote one last children's book, an odd little volume titled *Topsy Turvy and the Gold Star* to help raise money for a children's hospital. She sold the book herself in the lobby of Boston's Copley Plaza Hotel and raised $300 in one day.[24] *Topsy Turvy and the Gold Star* tells the saga of an Italian immigrant family beset with bad health and injuries. The book vividly describes sick children. One hospital room is populated by pediatric patients with terrible afflictions: a boy in a plaster body cast, one with infantile paralysis, another with incurable heart disease, and a child with clubfeet.[25] The book's only illustration is a lurid photograph of a Pierrot-esque clown and two sickly girls, one on crutches and the other with an odd bandage around her head—scary enough to make any child afraid of hospitals and doctors.

Isabel stopped writing children's books around the time Maud Howe Elliott wrote her Pulitzer Prize–winning biography of her mother. In the wake of Maud's Pulitzer Prize, Isabel may have been self-conscious about her choice of genre and subject, though Maud took great pride in all Isabel's literary accomplishments. Nonetheless, *The Great Sea Horse* and the Captain Ginger series had gotten Isabel off to a good start as an author. Her sweet disposition, unaffected manner, and experience dealing with many different kinds of people are evident in these children's books.

Travelogues

After 1914, Isabel turned her attention to writing fiction and nonfiction for adults. She drew heavily from Larz's letters and journals in putting these books together. The thirty-eight surviving volumes of Larz's typescript journals show hundreds of pencil markings and notations that gave Isabel's literary assistants and typists direction on how material was to be excerpted and organized into the books she derived from them. Occasionally, Larz himself wrote editorial notes in the margins, suggesting he also helped organize his wife's books. Isabel and her literary team transcribed, excerpted, reworked, and annotated Larz's texts and supplemented them with additional material from other sources—including Isabel's own diaries and notes—to create book-length publications. After publication in book format, Isabel repurposed the content as magazine and newspaper articles. The books and articles were edited skillfully and written in a chatty and personable style.

Isabel's first travel books, written after their return from Larz's brief diplomatic service under President Taft, were *The Spell of Japan* (1914) and *The Spell of Belgium* (1915). Part of the Spell Series published by the Page Company in Boston, these books followed a format prescribed by the publisher. These first two titles established a template for all of Isabel's subsequent travel books: a few chapters about the Andersons' experiences, followed by a few dozen chapters with a potpourri of just about anything related to the country or region at hand. These chapters summarized historical, cultural, geographic, economic, and political information and supplemented the sections about the Andersons' travel. Most of the volumes included bibliographies, but as was the custom of many writers in Isabel's era, there were few attributions for the material in the main body of the book.

Other volumes followed in rapid succession over the next decade: Hawaii, the Philippines, Northern Africa, Sub-Saharan Africa, South America, Greece and Turkey, India and Southeast Asia, and the South Sea Islands. Isabel's personal celebrity and her firsthand experience of the places she wrote about, together with the public's demand for books about the world then expanding around them, made these books popular with readers.

Short Stories

In the mid-1920s, Isabel published three collections of short stories that, like her children's books a decade earlier, showed promise. *Polly the Pagan* (1922, discussed in chapter 4), *The Kiss and the Queue* (1925), and *The Wall Paper Code* (1926) were inventive, entertaining, and, perhaps most importantly, not influenced by Larz's journals or other sources. In her forewords to *The Kiss and the Queue* and *The Wall Paper Code*, Isabel set out her conceit for this pair of volumes, whose relationship to each other was reinforced by identical cover designs. Each collection of short stories is structured around fourteen tales she and her fellow Red Cross canteen volunteers told on Sunday evenings during their service in northern France. Isabel explained this conceit in the preface to *The Kiss and the Queue*: "There was such an atmosphere of unreality all about us that we got to telling stories, and we sometimes introduced episodes from our own lives into the tales that we pretended to invent—episodes which never would have been divulged under ordinary circumstances."[26]

Isabel described the stories as being in "the manner of Boccaccio, of Longfellow's Tales of a Wayside Inn, and Chaucer's Canterbury Tales" and named each story in that fashion, such as "The Infirmière's Tale," "The Tale of an Attaché's Wife," "The School Teacher's Narrative," and "The Crystal Gazer's Tale."[27] Each reflected the storytelling tradition of rural New England. Indeed, Isabel's own contribution to the collection, "Francois' Bill," was drawn directly from a place in New England she knew well: The Box.

In the prologue to her story about New Hampshire, Isabel complains that, unlike the other women, she has "no past to divulge" and is reluctant to admit that she is "a prim puritan without any imagination."[28] At the very moment in the story that the other nurses finally prevail on Isabel to tell her tale, a French Canadian soldier named Francois appears on the scene. In the buildup to the story within a story, Isabel recognizes Francois as someone who once worked for her at The Box and begs him to tell the nurses a story. Francois refuses. One of the nurses then calls out to "Andy," Isabel's wartime nickname, to go ahead and tell the story, and Andy finally consents.

"Francois' Bill" is the story of marital problems between a New

Hampshire woodsman and his wife, Gabrielle. "She want her own way all ze time, and she scol'—oh, how zat woman scol'," Francois explains in Isabel's account of the story. He decides to end the marriage with a "bill of divorce," a legal document that under Jewish law allows a man to divorce his wife, even against her will. In the story, Francois asks "Mis' Anderson" to oversee the division of their belongings because he wants to be fair to his soon-to-be ex-wife. Mis' Anderson, however, advises Francois not to divorce immediately but instead to send his wife home to her father for six months. The trial separation is successful, and Francois has a change of heart. In the end, Gabrielle gives birth to a baby boy, and the couple return to their home, the little Sugar House on Isabel's property. Isabel portrays Gabrielle sympathetically and perhaps thought of herself when she described Gabrielle as "so young, so high-spirited—and perhaps lonely when her man is away at work all day." Like Isabel, Gabrielle is "fond of flowers—generous too."

Isabel wrote her short stories from her own imagination and her own experience of the world. These volumes of short stories, and the epistolary novel *Polly the Pagan* (see chapter 4), assert the simple truths Isabel expresses in her most genuine writing: there are good and bad people in the world, adversity tests one's mettle, and love conquers all. Almost certainly Isabel's literary assistants helped shape these stories, but simple storytelling was a genre Isabel knew well. The uncomplicated plot lines and well-defined characters surely came from Isabel, not her assistants—and definitely not from Larz's journals. In this regard, they are among her most original and important creations.

The Kiss and the Queue did not fare well with critics. The *Saturday Review* found "no single item of the lot seeming to rise above the level of general mediocrity maintained throughout the book."[29] The review acknowledged that the great variety of geographic settings in the stories provided "minor assistance" but called each of the stories a "dull yarn." Modern readers would probably not agree with this assessment, because *The Kiss and the Queue* and its companion volume make for fascinating reading about Isabel's time in Europe during the war. "Francois' Bill" may also tell us something about the Andersons themselves.

The Sale of Anderson House (1907)

"Francois' Bill" may have been a disguised version of something that happened in the Andersons' marriage. Isabel described the collection of war stories as "episodes which never would have been divulged under ordinary circumstances." Some aspects of the tale came from her own life: she set the story at The Box in New Hampshire; Francois and Gabrielle lived in the

Sugar House, a real building Isabel owned; and Isabel believed divorce was sometimes the right option for a couple. "I believe that if people are very unhappy in their married life, they should have another chance," she said.[30] Because so many of Isabel's books were based on her life with Larz, the story "Francois' Bill" leaves readers wondering if there was any event in the Andersons' early married life that might have inspired a story about marital discord, separation, the threat of divorce, and eventual reconciliation. Even the name of the main character might have been a clue: the words *François* and *France* share the same Latin root *francus* (meaning "free man"). Larz was born in France and often claimed the country as his own. The phonetic similarity between *Gabrielle* and *Isabel* may be another clue.

If there was marital discord between the Andersons or, as "Francois' Bill" perhaps implied, the possibility of divorce, it might have occurred around the time of their tenth wedding anniversary. On March 7, 1907, two years after Larz and Isabel first moved into Anderson House, Washington was taken by surprise when Larz told a *New York Times* reporter that the house would soon be the new German embassy.[31] Two days earlier, on March 5, Isabel had purchased in her own name a small plot of undeveloped land at 2200 Massachusetts Avenue, now the site of the Luxembourg ambassador's residence. (A year later, she sold the property *et vir*, meaning she and an "unidentified husband" were the sellers.)

Though Larz was in frequent, almost-daily correspondence with his mother in the days before and after the *Times* article, there is no mention of the sale of Anderson House in the manuscript of *Letters of Mrs. Nicholas Longworth Anderson to Her Son Larz Anderson*. Isabel included her mother-in-law's letters for March 1, 3, 9, 11, and 13, but there are no letters for March 5 or 7, the dates of Isabel's land purchase and the *Times* article, respectively.[32] Elizabeth Anderson might not have written to her son on those dates, but it is just as likely Isabel destroyed the letters or chose not to publish them. Either of those possibilities increases the chance there was an element of truth to "Francois' Bill."

Drama and Musicals

Between 1914 and the late 1930s, Isabel wrote twenty-six plays and musicals that were perhaps her most ambitious creative efforts.[33] Her children's morality plays *Everyboy* (1914), *Little Madcap's Journey* (1919), and *The Witch in the Woods* (1925) were performed several times. *Little Madcap's Journey* was produced at least five times, in 1919 and 1933, and as a national radio broadcast on Christmas night 1934. *The Witch in the Woods* was produced at the Andersons' estate in 1916 and 1925. A scrapbook for the 1916 production, staged in the Italian garden of Weld, shows that the play successfully integrated dance into the action and dialogue. Isabel once explained that she took the themes and characters of her children's plays from *The Great Sea Horse* and the Captain Ginger series.[34]

During the Depression, Isabel shifted most of her literary output to lavish musicals produced in collaboration with Boston-area directors, composers, and lyricists. Isabel drew on her travels with Larz for her creative inspiration. The musicals blended exotic lands with adventure, morality, and Eastern religion and packaged them in colorful sets and costumes accompanied by lively music. Isabel understood the impact of the Depression on Boston's theatrical community, and her complex productions with large casts, scenery, costumes, lighting, and live music employed hundreds of out-of-work actors, musicians, and stagehands. Three works in particular were enormously popular with Boston audiences: *Marina* in 1930, 1932, and 1934; *Dick Whittington* in 1931, 1932, and 1933; and *The Red Flame* in 1939.

A Wardrobe Malfunction

The musical fantasy *Marina* was a particularly elaborate production. Originally written as a children's story, Isabel and her friend Grace Warner Gulesian (1884–1984) collaborated on reworking the play in 1932 for "adult consumption."[35] It was rumored to have cost $50,000 to produce (almost $1 million today). Isabel, Grace, and three unnamed Boston socialites were credited with underwriting the cost of the production. Populated by fantastical sea creatures, mermaids, royalty, foreign envoys, a "lotus land" dancer, and a high priest, *Marina* tells the story of the water-bound mermaid princess who ventures onto land seeking a prince as her lover. The effects of a witch's spell on the princess create opportunities for dancing, singing, and other theatrical merriment.

The costumes were glittery and, by today's standards, campy and fun, but they also were shocking in the context of their time and place.[36] John M. Casey, Boston's city censor, threatened to close down the production before it opened due to the "abbreviated costumes" worn by the society debutantes who volunteered as singers and dancers in the production. Casey claimed the wardrobe was "entirely too scanty." The chorus girls wore what today would be called spaghetti-strap bikini tops. The rest of the costume consisted of a hula skirt of artificial seaweed and a glittery silver turban. Boston's legendary mayor James Michael Curley (1874–1958) stepped in to save the day—and the show. Curley attended the opening performance on January 12, and the next day Isabel announced that no costumes would be replaced. Ever the shrewd politician who understood what was important to his constituents, especially during bad economic times, Mayor Curley commended Isabel and her cofounders for giving work to so many Bostonians. Casey did not attend the next performance, and the show went on![37] The producer, Wendell Phillips Dodge (1883–1976), admitted the costumes "may have slipped" a bit—an early example of what modern readers recognize as a wardrobe malfunction.[38]

Hollywood and Beyond

Isabel long wanted recognition for her work outside of Boston and tried for almost twenty years to have her work produced nationally. She donated one of her scripts, *Sir Frog Goes A-Travelling* (1935), to the western division of the Federal Theater Project of the Works Progress Administration. The FTP produced the play a few times in western states. Other than *Sir Frog Goes A-Travelling*, few of her plays were produced outside Massachusetts. The National League of American Pen Women presented *Everyboy* in two performances at the Willard Hotel in Washington in April 1921 during the league's annual book fair.[39] The Charlotte Lund Opera Company produced another of Isabel's children's musicals, *Renny the Fox King*, to good notice at the Town Hall, New York City's venerable auditorium founded by suffragettes in 1921. The *New York Times* called the production "attractively staged."[40]

In 1929, Isabel invited her musical collaborator Grace Gulesian and Grace's husband, Moses, to visit her and Larz at Anderson House. Over dinner, Isabel asked the couple to take three of her plays to Hollywood and sell them to a movie producer. Isabel was convinced the plays would fetch anywhere from $25,000 to $100,000 each and told the Gulesians that if they were successful in selling any of the plays to a producer, they could keep the money for themselves. Isabel wanted a movie deal and did not care about the money. Moses, a successful industrialist with many business connections, agreed to take the scripts to California but said he needed $1,100 to cover the expense of driving out to Hollywood and back. Isabel counteroffered $300 and explained how a "Mrs. Brown" had made the trip the previous year and kept her travel costs low by staying in "night camps." Such camps—primitive rest areas where travelers could stop for the night—were the precursors of the modern motel. Moses protested, "Mrs. Anderson, I can't take my wife in these night cabins. We have got to stay in some hotel every so often and take a bath and rest a little and then get up and drive again." Isabel would not agree to his terms. The next morning, Isabel cut short their visit, telling the Gulesians she needed to return to Brookline urgently because of the death of an employee.[41]

In 1946, Isabel again tried to get national distribution for her plays. She asked a Boston area real estate agent, Harriet Owen, a friend of the great dramatic actress and theatrical producer Katharine Cornell (1893–1974) and her husband, Guthrie McClintic (1893–1961), to show the couple some of her plays. Isabel offered to compensate Harriet through a commission on the sale of her dairy farm. The real estate agent was reluctant to bother her famous friends. "I did not talk much about it. She asked me a good many times," Harriet said of Isabel's persistence. "I did not like to hurt her feelings."[42] Harriet eventually talked to McClintic, but he had no interest in Isabel's work. Isabel immediately stopped the sale of the dairy, and Harriet was out both her honorarium and her commission.[43]

Newspaper and Magazine Articles

Along with her book and theater projects, Isabel continuously published hundreds of fiction and nonfiction pieces in newspapers and magazines, especially those based in Massachusetts, such as the *Bostonian*, *Boston Breeze*, and *National Magazine* (motto: "Mostly about people"). The subject matter reflected the themes of Isabel's book projects. The articles, however, often lacked structure or coherence. Isabel's article "Sports and Enterprises," for example, appeared in the February 1931 issue of *Boston Breeze*, even though the editor was painfully aware of its shortcomings and did his best to anticipate his readers' reactions:

> In this issue Mrs. Anderson describes some of the tennis matches, trotting meets, football games and golf tournaments which she has attended, as well as some of the bazaars and patriotic assemblies in which she has taken part. She also recalls very vividly the centennial of Lafayette's visit to Boston and includes for good measure a long extract from her husband's journal, wherein he records his feelings when attending the fortieth reunion of the Exeter class of '84.[44]

"For good measure," the article also described how Larz and Isabel spent Christmas one year, their luncheon with friends at a restaurant in Portsmouth years earlier, Larz's trip to Europe to attend a cousin's wedding, and finally a review of some "very lively" birthday dinners for Larz. Although published in 1931, the chaotic article retold events of the early to mid-1920s. When the *National Magazine* published Isabel's article "Tales from a Canteen, III: Her Strange Wanderings," the editor called it "another one of Isabel Anderson's vivid narratives."[45]

Historical Nonfiction

In 1918, after she returned from her war service in Belgium and France, Isabel started writing in a new genre: historical nonfiction. The war had given her a new perspective on the world. She had been part of a great but tragic moment in history—a senseless world war. This experience grounded her with a sense of place and purpose in a larger historical order. Maud Howe Elliott's 1915 biography of her mother, Julia Ward Howe, and other of Maud's volumes of personal and family memoir may also have inspired Isabel to write historical nonfiction. Isabel wanted to document her own personal history and that of the Weld, Perkins, and Anderson families. She approached this new challenge journalistically, integrating her own experience and observation with original source documents to produce factual and lively accounts of family history. Late in life, Isabel said she liked hard work and if she could have one job in the world, it would be as a "newspaper woman."[46] Her books of memoir and family history came closest to fulfilling that aspiration.

Isabel's debut work of historical nonfiction was *Zigzagging* (1918), a first-person account of her year behind the lines in France and Belgium (see chapter 14). Reviewers liked the book. The *New York Tribune* found it to be "not portentous, nor pretentious ... but it was serious, and all the more so because her sense of humor was by no means lacking." The reviewer deemed the book an "informing and veracious ... record of a very important branch of service."[47] *Zigzagging* is without doubt the best of all Isabel's books. A century after its publication, it remains a stirring and inspirational reading experience and is widely available in digital and reprint editions. Most of all, it rings true. Even if literary assistants helped her ready the book for publication, the subject matter, voice, and point of view are entirely hers. This is the story of Isabel's own search for self-identity and adventure. She tested her own mettle in the name of American patriotism, "one of the finest qualities a person can possess," she said.[48] *Zigzagging* compares very favorably with other books of its genre; for example, *Fighting France, From Dunkerque to Belfort*, published in 1919 by Edith Wharton.

Two years after the publication of *Zigzagging*, Isabel issued *Presidents and Pies* (1920), a series of essays and reminiscences of Larz's and Isabel's participation in American society and politics between 1897 and 1919. Populated by a cavalcade of early twentieth-century social and political celebrities, *Presidents and Pies* presents an eyewitness account of the life of a Washington society hostess in the late Gilded Age. William Howard Taft, George Washington Vanderbilt, Senator Henry Algernon du Pont (see chapter 11), and even the showman Buffalo Bill Cody turn up in its pages. Isabel also used the book as a bully pulpit to speak out on an issue that concerned her greatly: the poor treatment of women in jails and prisons.[49] (See epilogue.)

In 1926, Isabel published *Under the Black Horse Flag*, which is, like Maud Howe Elliott's *Three Generations* (1923), an eclectic, tightly knit series of essays about family history. *Under the Black Horse Flag* includes appreciative tributes to William Fletcher Weld, George Hamilton Perkins, Richard Clough Anderson, Robert Anderson, and Nicholas Longworth Anderson, along with synopses of Weld, Perkins, and Anderson family history. Isabel skillfully weaves extensive citations from rare historical documents into the narrative, making the style of the book authentic, personal, and readable. In the volume's last two essays, she summarizes the Andersons' travels in the Bahamas aboard the chartered yacht *The Virginia*—an attempt perhaps to link their waterborne vacations to the seafaring traditions of Weld and Perkins men. The two appendices provide valuable primary historical documents: a list of all the ships owned by the Weld Company and transcriptions of correspondence to and from Admiral David Farragut about George Perkins's Civil War service.

After the publication of *Under the Black Horse Flag*, Isabel set aside historical nonfiction and did not return to it until after Larz's death in 1937, when she launched a series of three volumes commemorating Anderson family history and her life with Larz. These are comprehensive and well-edited anthologies of the letters, journals, and diaries of Larz and his parents. Like Isabel's earlier volumes of memoir and family history, these anthologies remain an important contribution to modern understanding of the Gilded Age. Each volume reproduces original textual materials that Isabel supplements with explanatory essays and detailed footnotes identifying people, places, and contexts that would be otherwise obscure, even to audiences in the 1940s.

The first of these, *Larz Anderson: Letters and Journals of a Diplomat*, appeared in 1940. Isabel originally titled it *Larz Anderson: Journals in Mosaic* but changed the title just before the book went into production.[50] It is a wide-ranging and mostly verbatim anthology of Larz's letters, diaries, and essays beginning with his childhood and early years and ending in 1936, the year before his death. Isabel helpfully fills gaps in the record with her own recollections and observations. The foreword by Larz's best friend, Charles Francis Adams III, provides a rare opportunity to see Larz as his friends saw him. Adams does not memorialize Larz for his political or diplomatic skills. "His greatest talent was for friendship," Adams says of Larz sympathetically. "He was a master of the generosities, the ceremonies, the consideration of the pleasure of others, that mark the perfect host."[51]

Larz originally wrote the material included in *Letters and Journals of a*

Diplomat for private consumption. Over many years, secretaries in the Weld Office transcribed his handwritten and typed originals into a compilation of his life's written output.[52] (Larz and Isabel started using Corona portable typewriters in 1901, and each had a machine.[53]) The transcriptions were bound in red Moroccan leather with hand-tooled gold-leaf decoration, producing what Isabel called "an almost complete account of his life."[54] Everything was preserved in the transcriptions, even material that in its day would have been embarrassing or in poor taste if made public. When Isabel published the journals, she redacted passages that did not reflect well on her husband (see the coda to chapter 10).

Isabel subsequently prepared two companion volumes bringing together the papers of Larz's parents, each with excellent critical notes and commentary. *General Nicholas Longworth Anderson: Letters and Journals (Harvard, Civil War, Washington, 1854–1892)*, published in 1942, reproduces transcripts of Nick's letters to his parents while he was at Harvard, his Civil War diaries, and some of his letters to Elizabeth during their courtship and the early years of their marriage. The volume includes a nearly complete collection of Nick's letters to Larz at Exeter and Harvard. The third volume, *Letters of Mrs. Nicholas Longworth Anderson to Her Son Larz Anderson (1882–1916)*, was completed by the early 1940s, but the war prevented its publication. It remained in typescript at the time of Isabel's death. Elizabeth's letters to her son were chatty and gossipy, and they provide great insight, as Isabel says in her foreword, to "the social and political life in Washington in the 80s and 90s of the last century."[55] Elizabeth was a woman of great cultural refinement who often wrote to her son about the books she was reading and the theatrical and musical performances she attended. She also regularly reported gossip from around town, especially if it came from or had anything to do with "The Daily Leiter"—Mrs. Levi Leiter of Dupont Circle. In this, Elizabeth's letters are still delicious and amusing reminders of Gilded Age society in Washington.

The importance of Isabel undertaking these three collections of letters, journals, and diaries cannot be overestimated. The volumes preserve rare historical materials, the originals of which have been lost or destroyed. Her work has left us invaluable documentation of the customs and people that defined America's Gilded Age.

Poetry as Memoir

It has often been said that American poetry of the first half of the twentieth century was influenced either by Walt Whitman (1819–1892) or Emily Dickinson (1830–1886). Whitman's late nineteenth-century poetry captures the majesty of America, its spirit, and its history. Dickinson's poetry of the same period reflects women's expanding experience of the world, nature, and love. Isabel, a woman born in the late nineteenth century who came of age in the twentieth, wrote poetry that reflected each of these trends. Although she was never close to being a Whitman or a Dickinson, she approached poetry as seriously as she did all her writing projects. Her poetry is an honest and genuine expression of herself, although most of it lacks a foundation in the sophisticated mechanics of the genre.

If Isabel's four volumes of family history were an effort to establish the Weld, Perkins, and Anderson legacies, the three small books of poetry that she published late in life were an effort to establish her own. Most of these pieces appeared in poetry reviews, magazines, and newspapers before Isabel collected them into thematic volumes. Thankfully, she brought the works out of the obscurity of now-forgotten poetry magazines and made them part of the historical record of her life.

The first collection, *I Hear a Call* (1938), might best be described as a collection of ditties. One poem opened with the following stanza:

> Twas past the forts, at dead of night,
> Upon the turret, without light,
> He led the fleet into the fight.

Isabel organized the poems around Perkins, Weld, and Anderson men; the city of Boston and its environs; and her travels with Larz. She was driven more by a search for rhymes than for poetic elegance. Esther Willard Bates and Eleanor Pomeroy worked with Isabel on this collection and are acknowledged in the preface.

The Whole World Over: War Verses (1944), Isabel's second book of poetry, was, despite its title, not a book of war poetry. "Many of these lyrics were written concerning places where fighting is now going on, and which I visited in the past," Isabel explains in the foreword. "They are here presented with the hope that some new understanding may be given concerning other countries and their way of life." The poems are of generally poor quality as, for example, the piece called "Meditation of Tojo (On the Destruction of Japan)" shows.

> No cities are there,
> That I can swear,
> For I stood on a rock to look;
> No shrines saw I,
> I can testify,
> For long, long look I took.[56]

Isabel's last slim volume of poetry, *Near and Far*, despite its 1947 copyright date, came off the press in late 1948. By any measure, *Near and Far* is Isabel's best poetic work. The poems project short, charming images of places and moments in her life with Larz. Here, she at last frees herself from her earlier slavish and unsuccessful obligation to rhyme, meter, and alliteration that make much of her poetry sound forced and amateurish. She called the poems "sketches in free verse." They still have a pleasant, modern feel to them. The last poem in the volume, "The Sun Goes Down (At Weld)," was inspired by one of the final entries in Larz's journal.

> Together in a perfect winter's sunset
> We walked in our enchanted garden.
> A silver moon rose behind a maze of trees.
> A deep red glow lighted up the west.
> Together we had always watched the sun set,
> We let it go down on our happiness;
> It seemed to make our happiness more secure.[57]

There could be no more perfect coda to her life with Larz than this final poem in her final book published in the last days of her life.

Gus Anderson, her private secretary, brought a copy to her in the hospital just days before she died.[58]

Figure 24. Funeral shrine to Larz Anderson at Weld, 1948.

XVI

LIFE WITHOUT LARZ (1937–1948)

I sabel Anderson began life without her husband on Tuesday, April 13, 1937, two months short of their fortieth wedding anniversary. Larz died far from home, but when the end came, she was at his side.

In early January, seventy-year-old Larz traveled to White Sulfur Springs, West Virginia, where he checked in at the Greenbrier Hotel and put himself under the care of Dr. Guy Hinsdale, the hotel's medical director. Hinsdale specialized in the treatment of nervous disorders and tuberculosis. By early April, Larz's condition had worsened. Isabel arrived from Brookline in time to be with him when he died.

His death certificate gave myocarditis (inflammation of the heart) as the primary cause of death. Nephritis (inflammation of the kidneys) and hypostatic pneumonia, common in bedridden patients, were secondary causes. Larz had not been well for many years, a fact noted in his obituaries. A sedentary lifestyle, along with his smoking and drinking habits and a constant struggle with his weight, contributed to a steady decline in his health over many years. Despite their areas of medical specialization, for years his physicians offered no cure for his ailments. His Boston doctor, Roger Irving Lee, specialized in blood disorders, and his Marienbad doctor, Max Porges, in obesity, cardiovascular disease, gout, and edema.[1]

Larz's body was returned to Washington by train the next day, accompanied by W. F. Elliott, the general manager of the Greater Chambers Company, the capital's largest undertaker. Chambers promoted its services in the Washington area by advertising that the father of one of its morticians attended to the body of Abraham Lincoln.

Larz's death provided five days' worth of copy for Washington newspapers. His passing made the front page of the Washington *Evening Star* on the day he died. The next day the *Star* reported that the Anderson homes in Washington and Brookline were in mourning and that there would be a service in Washington's National Cathedral at noon on Friday. On Thursday, the *Star* chronicled Larz's passing in its "Deaths" column and on Friday published a report of the funeral, the only detailed account of the private service.[2]

From Boston came lifelong friends, including Larz's best friend, Charles Francis Adams III, who had served under President Herbert Hoover as secretary of the navy. Alice Roosevelt Longworth, daughter of former president Teddy Roosevelt and widow of Larz's cousin Speaker of the House Nicholas Longworth, sat next to Isabel. Larz's sword and the plumed bicorn hat from his bespoke diplomatic uniform rested atop the coffin.[3] Bishop James Edward Freeman's eulogy from the pulpit of the St. Mary Chapel included the revelation that it was the Andersons' gift of $500,000 to the cathedral's building fund in 1927 that had paid for the chapel where Larz's remains were to be interred.

Larz himself chose this moment for the announcement of his magnificence. "He imposed upon me absolute silence," the bishop intoned from the pulpit, "and it is only now that I am permitted to acknowledge his great benefaction." The bishop quoted extensively from a letter Larz had written to him at the time of the gift, revealing that Larz had long wanted to establish a memorial in Washington "to the glory of God and in gratitude for the many benefits vouchsafed us by Him."[4] It was also a memorial to Larz and Isabel and their final resting place.

Larz had been intimately involved with all aspects of the chapel's design and had communicated directly with the architects, Frohman, Robb & Little, about his wishes.[5] Following medieval tradition, the designers had included images of the chapel's benefactors kneeling in profile in the bottom corners of the altarpiece. The female figure on the right in a nun's habit could be anyone, but the caped, middle-aged man with receding brown hair on the left is unmistakably Larz.

After the funeral service, Larz's body was removed to a crematorium. His ashes were later returned to the cathedral and interred in the northern wall of the St. Mary Chapel behind a Gothic marble reredos in a private ceremony. Isabel wrote the epitaph:

Larz Anderson
Patriot
Diplomat Soldier
Loyal Friend
August 15 1866 April 13 1937
May He Rest In Peace

Isabel remained in Washington for the next few months. Her cousin Anna Spalding Weld came from Boston to be with her at the funeral and afterward. Anna later said she helped Isabel "with the preparation of her mourning."[6] Eleanor Pomeroy, Isabel's literary assistant and secretary, also came to Washington. She stayed in a room across the hallway from Isabel's bedroom suite on the third floor of Anderson House. One morning Eleanor found Isabel "weeping bitterly." When Eleanor tried to comfort her, Isabel replied, "Yes, I grieve, but my grief has outlet in the morning. I take up the work of the day and go on."[7]

In mid-May, Isabel returned to Brookline and spent the summer going back and forth between New Hampshire and Massachusetts. She grieved for her husband, but she also had to take over the management of their assets and make decisions for her future.[8] She was entering a completely new phase of her life and not just because her husband had died. She faced many new realities—maneuvering a modern world soon to be at war, living alone, and managing her own money.

Facing Life's Realities

Before Larz's death, Isabel had no involvement in the couple's financial affairs. Larz was only slightly more involved, to the extent it was he, not Isabel, who delegated everything blindly to their attorney and business advisor, Roger Amory (1887–1960). Larz never wanted details. He often went in to see Amory at his office, but these visits were part of a daily routine and did not include any substantive involvement in the couple's business affairs. As their absolute power of attorney in all matters, Amory paid their bills, signed financial documents, and made investment decisions. Amory knew his clients wished to remain oblivious to such matters as account balances, property values, or taxes. When asked after Isabel's death about the extent of Larz's personal attention to the couple's financial affairs, Amory answered, "None." Management of the Andersons' finances was at Amory's sole discretion.[9]

In the summer of 1937, the country plunged into recession. This more than anything spurred Isabel to look into the financial details Larz had kept from her (and from himself). What she found shocked her. "She had never seen such big figures before," Amory said. "She had never kept the stubs of a checkbook. She had [never] seen such big figures and she had no idea what such a place would cost to run, and it staggered her."[10] That fall, Isabel started reducing her expenses. Even after doing so successfully, she remained worried about money for the rest of her life.

The target of her first wave of retrenchment and cost cutting was real estate she no longer wanted, needed, or could afford. The first to go were the three architecturally distinctive houses on nearby Goddard Avenue that she and Larz had built in the 1920s (see chapter 6). In October, Isabel offered the houses and land to Boston University for use as the Brookline campus of the university's women's division, the College of Practical Arts and Letters. On October 11, 1937, Boston University president Daniel Marsh wrote to Isabel that the board of trustees accepted her offer. The properties were to form the core of a Larz Anderson Memorial Centre that would become "an educational, recreational, and social centre for the faculty, students, alumnae, and other friends of the Boston University College of Practical Arts and Letters."[11] Isabel had known the college's dean, T. Lawrence Davis, since his childhood in New Hampshire. Davis and his parents had attended Larz and Isabel's wedding reception at The Box in 1897.[12] Isabel had long encouraged Davis in his mission to expand educational opportunities for women. She had received a 1930 honorary doctorate from Boston University for her accomplishments as an author and advocate for women's access to higher education. Her other honorary degree had been bestowed by the George Washington University in 1918.

In accepting the gift of land and buildings, Marsh noted that the memorial would be "of permanent and inestimable value to the College in developing its work." One of the houses was to serve as a student residence and another as a social center and study hall for students and alumnae. The third house was planned as storage for "cultural possessions" and would eventually become a museum for the Andersons' vast collection of memorabilia and artifacts, though the plan was never realized. Shortly, and with Isabel's concurrence, university officials rented out one of the houses, Blue Top, to Davis as his official residence.

The 1937 transaction went so smoothly that in 1941 Isabel tried to give the university other property adjacent to the estate—her Barn Theatre. A few years earlier, she had converted Billy Weld's dairy barn on Avon Street into a rent-free theater for community groups. Marsh was blunt and indiscreet when he told Isabel that without an endowment to maintain and develop the theater, the trustees would decline it. The university, which had taken the Goddard Avenue houses without any endowment, now had second thoughts about accepting other property without cash too. "It would be inexpedient to accept the property unless it might be accompanied by money to maintain and develop it," Marsh wrote to Isabel.[13] What Marsh did not know was that Isabel already had made provisions in her will for a $50,000 gift to the university.[14] That bequest was subsequently withdrawn, and none of her money ever went to Boston University. If they did not want her Barn Theatre, they would not have her money either.

Disposing of Anderson House
By spring of 1938, Isabel planned her greatest expense reduction: disposing of Anderson House. She had no use for it. For a decade, the Depression

had taken its toll on Washington society, and those who had managed to hold on to their homes in the city no longer entertained as they had. Phoebe Apperson Hearst's immense, art-filled mansion on New Hampshire Avenue had become a rooming house after she'd died during the flu epidemic in 1919. The Kentucky distiller Edson Bradley had long before retreated from Washington's declining social scene, moving his great mansion on Dupont Circle brick by brick to Newport. Perry Belmont's fabulous mansion on New Hampshire Avenue had been sold to the Order of the Eastern Star in 1935 for use as its national headquarters. The landscape of the city had changed also. The elite Washington Riding Academy on P Street had been demolished in 1936 for a gas station in neoclassical Beaux-Arts style (still standing) that fueled the city's growing population of motor vehicles. Times had so changed that Larz and Isabel, lifelong Republicans, had even voted for Democrat Franklin Delano Roosevelt in 1932 and had gone to his inaugural ball.[15]

By the time of Larz's death, Anderson House had been unoccupied, or visited only briefly, for years. But just as he could not bring himself to sell their houseboat, the *Roxana*, when he no longer had any use for it, Larz could not bring himself to sell the ninety-five-room mansion. After the death of her husband, Isabel had even less use for it, yet in the midst of the Depression, there was no market for houses of its size. Donating it to the Society of the Cincinnati, which had no national headquarters of its own, was about her only option.

When work on Anderson House began in 1902, Larz directed his designers to use two insignia to mark the house as theirs. One of these celebrated the couple's union: the interwoven *ILA* monogram that had first appeared in the Italian lace veil Isabel's mother had given Isabel as a wedding gift. The other device was both historic and personal to Larz: the eagle insignia of the Society of the Cincinnati. He'd had this motif installed in several places throughout Anderson House—in the pediment high above the front door, in the ceiling of the Saloon, in murals of the Great Staircase Hall and the Cincinnati Room, and in the decoration of a custom-designed mantle clock inscribed with Larz's own tribute to Anderson men: "This tablet is inscribed to remember the making of this set of ornaments in commemoration of an inheritance from some who served their country in the Revolution, and the Civil War, and of a share in the War with Spain."[16]

Larz was very certain it was his right to use the emblem of the Society of the Cincinnati as his personal crest. "I have always felt that in America we had no right to coats of arms," he wrote, "but did to emblems of patriotic orders."[17] There is no better proof of Larz's appropriation of the society's emblem as his personal crest than in the pediment of Anderson House.

There the eagle designed by Pierre L'Enfant clutches a pennant inscribed "ANDERSON." The eagle is set against a mantling of war symbols: spears, battle-axes, fasces with axes, and Roman military ensigns mounted by eagles. If Larz wanted to imply that he, like his ancestors, saw battle in defense of the Republic, this hawkish pediment certainly did so.

A passage from Larz's journal has been cited to support a theory he built the house with the intention of giving it to the Society of the Cincinnati.[18] It is true Larz once called Anderson House "an especially suitable place for a gathering of the Cincinnati."

> I felt that Anderson House might be an especially suitable place for a gathering of the Cincinnati, because so many features commemorating the Society had been introduced into the architecture. The Eagle appears in the pediment over the main portico entrance (as well as the Cross of the Loyal Legion and the Spanish War). I have always felt that in America we had no right to coats of arms, but did to emblems of patriotic order. The Eagle also appears in the fresco above the fireplace of the hall at the foot of the great staircase and in the ceiling of the saloon. In the room at the top of the staircase the Society has been commemorated in unusual scenes in the Mowbray wall paintings.[19]

However, when Isabel published this passage in *Letters and Journals of a Diplomat*, she omitted the next two sentences of Larz's original, which made it clear he was talking about how suitable the house was for a luncheon he was planning at the time.

> ... in the Mowbray wall paintings. So I felt the house was ready to receive the fellow members of the Society, no matter how many came. This large luncheon also gave us a chance to make use of an arrangement which we had made when we built the house, for we had placed a large pantry next to the saloon so that the saloon could be served in case we wished to set tables in it. [20]

Isabel gave away Anderson House because she worried about money and expenses. Like the three Brookline houses she gave to Boston University, she had no use for the enormous mansion in Washington. She was practical and frugal by nature, and it was not difficult to make the decision. When the state of New Hampshire presented its case to the estate tax arbitration panel in 1949, it concluded, "Mrs. Anderson had no taste of her own for the opulent surroundings that pleased her husband."[21] Disposing of Anderson House did not bother Isabel. Indeed, it was a relief to be rid of it. "The less property I have, the better I feel," she said about giving Anderson House away.[22]

Ownership of Anderson House was formally conveyed to the Society of the Cincinnati on April 20, 1939.[23] The Society of the Cincinnati inducted Isabel as an honorary member in gratitude for her magnificent gift. The house now serves as the international headquarters for the organization. Anderson House is open to the public as both a museum of the Gilded Age, with programs on art, history, and music, and as a world-class research library on eighteenth-century military and naval history and art.

Changes to the Trust Fund

At about the same time Isabel gave away Anderson House, she decided to divest herself of the commercial real estate investments that formed the core of her trust fund. Years before, her trustees had converted most of her inheritance into four commercial buildings in Manhattan and four in Boston. These properties were cash cows, even during the worst of the Depression.[24] Between 1928 and 1937, the years for which there are Anderson financial records, the commercial properties produced rental income of $250,000 or more a year, supplemented by another $150,000 to $200,000 in dividend and interest income from other investments.[25] The Andersons spent every dollar of this income on travel, entertaining, households, servants, automobiles, gardens, clothing, jewelry, publication of Isabel's books, and more. Isabel's cousin Anna Spalding Weld once said tactfully that after Larz's death Isabel became aware that "they had spent a great deal while her husband was alive."[26]

After 1937, finally aware of the cost of the lifestyle Larz had pursued, Isabel worried about owning commercial properties and possible financial liabilities, including rising taxes and maintenance costs and unstable rents and property values. She decided to trust cash more than real estate. She told Roger Amory to sell the investment properties because "even at a loss it is better to have cash."[27] On October 17, 1938, Amory directed Isabel's lawyers to establish a holding company, the Roxana Corporation, with one thousand shares of stock, all to be owned by Isabel.[28] Over the next ten years, Amory gradually liquidated Isabel's commercial properties in New York City but kept the Boston properties. Amory put the proceeds from the property sales in New York into US and municipal bonds and a select portfolio of blue-chip stocks. At the time of Isabel's death, the Roxana Corporation held almost

$5.4 million in stocks, bonds, and corporate notes. Her trust fund principal had remained essentially intact over the course of her lifetime.[29]

With this restructuring of her affairs, Isabel's annual income fell from an average of $434,000 during the last ten years of Larz's life to an average of $175,000 until her death in 1947. The investments did not produce as much income as the commercial properties had. Her income and expenses were certainly more stable, and unlike some of the years when Larz had been alive, she lived within the budget dictated by her income. For three years, from 1930 to 1933, they had dipped into the trust fund to remain solvent, despite robust real estate income during those years. In other years they had come close to being in the red. Larz kept all this from Isabel, as Roger Amory testified: "I never furnished [financial statements] to her. He wouldn't let her see them. I submitted them to Mr. Anderson and he gave them back to me, and I said, 'Aren't you going to show them to Mrs. Anderson?' and he said, 'The size of the expenditures would just worry her to death.'"[30]

Amory's assessment echoed Nick Anderson's admonition to his son in the 1880s. Larz's father often reprimanded him for the enormous sums of money he spent while an undergraduate at Harvard, and on one occasion Nick reminded Larz that "a large balance in the bank does not authorize you to spend more than you can afford."[31]

Living Smaller

With real estate decisions behind her, Isabel turned her attention to reducing her personal expenses. In the nine years before Larz's death (1928–1936), the Andersons' annual budget for personal and living expenses in Brookline had averaged $220,000 (about $3.8 million today). After 1937, Isabel's cost of living in Brookline dropped by more than half to about $104,000 a year, but during the war and immediately after it (1941–1946), she reduced this further to an average of $77,000 a year. She downsized all operations at Weld to achieve these economies, primarily by cutting back on the upkeep of the grounds, gardens, and greenhouses. In 1938, she gave to the Boston Parks Department the two dozen bay trees Larz had purchased in Holland in 1902.[32] The bay house Larz had kept heated during winter months could then be closed down. She discontinued the dairy's operation and converted the cow barn to a theater. In 1942, she further reduced costs by closing the greenhouses for everything except a few ferns, greens, and orchids for the mansion.[33] The gardening and greenhouse operations took the biggest hit. Home movies of the greenhouses taken in the winter of 1937 recorded the lush collection of tropical and domestic flowering plants the Andersons had kept blooming all winter when Larz had been alive.[34] These were now gone.

No heated greenhouse also meant there were no homegrown grapes in the middle of winter, once a hallmark of the Anderson table.

Isabel also economized inside the mansion. Soon after Larz's death, to save on heating fuel and electricity, she closed off the part of the house he'd added in 1914–1916 and moved into the smallest bedroom in the old part of the house. She never again hired staff. When servants or workers died or quit, she did not replace them. Even with her newfound awareness of costs, Isabel delegated management of the household to others. She gave the bills to her cook Jane Regan to approve, and Jane passed them on to the Weld Office for payment.[35] "Mrs. Anderson never ran anything," Roger Amory said. She "didn't run the house when he was alive, and she didn't run the place [after 1937], and everything sort of ran itself from then on."[36]

Isabel often asked friends to do work for her to keep her expenses low. Her cousin Evelyn Hastings once came down from New Hampshire and brought along a neighbor, Marion Jones, who put up new wallpaper for Isabel.[37] In earlier years, Marion and her husband, Paul, had done outdoor and handyman work in New Hampshire for Isabel. Even Eleanor Pomeroy pitched in, repointing stonework on the mansion, in the Japanese garden, and on the hilltop's retaining walls. Eleanor considered herself a "good mason" but was afraid a union worker would see her and cause problems for Isabel. The attorney who cross-examined Eleanor at the estate tax arbitration commented, in reference to British prime minister Winston Churchill, "You combined masonry with your literary activities the way Mr. Churchill combines laying brick with painting."[38]

Roger Amory witnessed the effect these economies had on the once-pristine Anderson estate. "Less money was spent," he said, and the estate "ran down."[39]

A Simpler Life in New England

In addition to drastic retrenchment in living expenses, Isabel drew back in many other ways from the life she had once known. By 1941, she'd reduced her club memberships from thirty to about half that number. In Washington she resigned from many organizations, including the Sulgrave Club and the local chapters of American Pen Women and the Daughters of the American Revolution. In Boston, she let go of the Women's Republican Club, the Manuscript Club, the Society for the Preservation of New England Antiquities, and the Winsor School Club. She kept memberships that were important to her self-identity, including the Boston Athenaeum (of which she was a shareholder), the Boston chapter of the DAR, the American Red Cross, the National League of American Pen Women, the Women's Press

Association, and the New Hampshire Colonial Dames.[40] Withdrawal from her busy club schedule rippled through the rest of her life, not just simplifying it but also allowing her to focus on those things that meant most to her: her writing projects and spending time with friends and family in Massachusetts and New Hampshire. "She enjoyed simple things, and she didn't enjoy entertaining," her cousin Evelyn Hastings said. "She was tired of it."[41]

When Isabel did entertain at home, she did so on a very small scale, inviting no more than a few close friends or family members at a time. She often treated people to meals at the Chilton Club on Commonwealth Avenue, across the street from the house where she'd grown up. She eschewed the trappings of the life she'd had when Larz had been alive and dressed more simply. Her cousin Evelyn said Isabel "didn't like clothes the way some women do" and limited her jewelry to a simple string of pearls, her engagement ring, and a pin her mother had given her. Isabel wore this jewelry even if she was "out tossing hay or picking apples," wearing the pieces "for sentiment" rather than as a fashion statement, Evelyn recalled.[42]

As had been her custom all her life, Isabel continued to stay in New Hampshire for part of June and July and then again in September and October. In addition to these regular visits, from time to time she made shorter visits to New Hampshire and stayed with her cousin Evelyn at The Box in a room known as "Cousin Isabel's Room."[43]

A Shrine to Larz

After Larz's death, Weld became the repository of Isabel's most-precious memories of her husband and their life together. Weld housed all their papers, Larz's letters and journals bound in red leather, inscribed copies of books written by their friends, and hundreds if not thousands of mementos of their life together. Isabel's boudoir especially held some of the most cherished of these relics. Its walls were hung with her dearest reminders of him, including a portrait sketch of Isabel that Larz had presented to her in 1903 with the inscription "Precious Isabel on our Sixth Anniversary, A Promissory Note To Pay For Another Year Of Perfect Happiness." Another wall displayed a framed poem Isabel had written when Larz had died. "Clouds are weeping for a soul that is gone," it began. The Bible Larz had given Isabel in 1906, inscribed "Yes, I have loved thee with an everlasting love, Larz Anderson," was near her bed. A packet of valentines that Larz and Isabel had sent to each other over the years was tucked away in a drawer. A tin box contained a single small shoe with an attached note that read, "Baby Isabel shoe, fifteen months old." The room held dozens of framed and unframed photographs. Many of these were of Larz, and as a whole they presented a panoramic view of the course of his life: pictures of him as a child of five or six, as a student at Harvard, at his diplomatic posts, and on the grounds of the estate.[44] One especially poignant memento was a photograph of Isabel taken about 1922 that she'd inscribed to her husband, "Twenty-five years after. Even if I am not as good looking I love you more than ever. Punk."[45]

Weld was the epicenter of Isabel's grief. She erected a funeral shrine to Larz's memory in the front hall. The massive 1916 bronze bust of Larz by Bruce Wilder Saville dominated the shrine. Isabel set out Buddhist, Shinto, and Christian religious artifacts around it, including an icon of Saint George— Roman soldier, Christian martyr, and patron saint of England. (See figure 24.)

Travel with a Purpose

Isabel traveled after Larz's death but not as she had when he'd been alive. She traveled with a purpose, most often to visit friends and relatives, but never left the United States. She went with some regularity to New York City to attend the theater and see movies. She and friends saw the film *Jane Eyre* starring Orson Welles when it played in New York City in 1943. In February 1944, on the train to New York City, Isabel ran into Harriet Owen, whom she knew casually from Boston.[46] She invited Harriet to share a picnic lunch she'd brought from home—a habit from the war years, she said. The next day, Isabel phoned Harriet from her hotel, the Barclay, and invited her to lunch, saying, "Here I am over here and nothing much to do." Harriet took her to a performance of Dodie Smith's *Lovers and Friends* starring Katharine Cornell. (Smith is best remembered as the author of *The Hundred and One Dalmatians*.) Harriet knew Cornell and took Isabel backstage to meet the famous actress after the performance. Isabel and Harriet later had a falling out over real estate and scripts (see chapter 15).

Not all of Isabel's trips to New York were so pleasant. In 1945, she was almost killed when she stepped into the path of a bus hurtling toward her. She tripped as she tried to get out of way, fell onto the sidewalk, and broke her arm. The bus narrowly missed running over her legs. Isabel's cousin Anna Weld later said, "The fright that she got from that bus nearly running over her affected her rather badly." Isabel was never herself again.[47]

Isabel spent time with her many friends in Washington from the old days. She sometimes stayed with Larz's cousins Nelson and Rebecca Perin in their elegant townhouse at 1824 R Street near Dupont Circle. She was especially close to Cornelia Knox Kean (1875–1954), wife of General Jefferson Randolph Kean (1860–1950), a distinguished army medical officer who had served in France during World War I. When Isabel died, she left Cornelia a bequest of $2,000, a sign of their long friendship.

Every year or two, Isabel went to Santa Barbara—often by airplane—to visit her cousin Peggy Perkins Greenough. She brought a personal maid with her on these trips but sent the servant to California and back on the train to keep expenses low. In December 1944, Isabel flew to Texas to christen a destroyer named for her father, the USS *Perkins* (DD-877). Her trusted chauffeur Edmund Mettetal, whom Larz had once called "such a perfect Frenchman and chauffeur, clever and friendly but still civil and polite," drove ahead to Texas to meet her when she arrived so she could have her own car and driver for the event.[48]

Anxious War Years

After Pearl Harbor, Isabel's anxiety about money returned, despite the many economies she had made in the years immediately following Larz's death. On July 14, 1942, she wrote to Roger Amory about maintenance and staffing costs in Brookline. "I don't know why I should trouble you or write you about these small things but haven't anyone else to write to, and you keep track of my expenses and advise me as far as possible please."[49]

In the fall of 1942, Isabel worried that her mansion or the carriage house, which had many sleeping rooms and several bathrooms, might be requisitioned by the government for the war effort.[50] Larz's cousin William Pope Anderson II visited Isabel that year and told her one of his houses in Cincinnati had been taken by the government, causing him great financial loss. "To dismantle the house would be quite a job and the house would be ruined," she wrote to Roger. "Would it help, as every house in Boston crowded, if I took in for the winter say two people. I don't want to especially, but maybe Anna Gage and Agnes Howlett [cousins] could stay here, and they could do war work." Isabel's worries were not unfounded. Early in the war, an Army Medical Corps officer notified Roger Amory that the army wished to take a look at the Anderson estate "as one of the few [places] around here that came up to military requirements." Two colonels did in fact inspect the property, but nothing came of it.[51]

Isabel eventually invited a young married couple to live with her during the war. They occupied the two luxurious bedroom suites that Larz added in 1914–1916. After the war, perhaps to alleviate loneliness, she again invited a war veteran and his wife and their baby to live rent-free in the mansion with her. Harold and Joan Whitestone moved in on December 6, 1947, and lived in Larz's and Isabel's former bedroom suites until Isabel's death. Harold later said they only saw Isabel a few times during the year they were there, usually for tea and brief conversations.[52]

Isabel found ways to contribute to the war effort. She offered her estate on several occasions as a training site for the Massachusetts Women's Defense Corps.[53] Established in 1941, the corps served as a statewide force under the jurisdiction of the Massachusetts Committee on Public Safety, the agency that coordinated civil defense during the war. The corps trained eighteen thousand women for volunteer jobs in civil defense agencies that would otherwise have been staffed by men: air raid wardens, drivers, communications staff, canteen workers, medics, chemical detection personnel, and emergency firefighters. As she had done in World War I, she again volunteered as a practical nurse, this time at Massachusetts General Hospital and the Eye and Ear Infirmary.

After Isabel's death, her hospital coworkers recognized her from photographs that appeared with her obituaries. They had known her only as "Isabel," a cheerful and hardworking colleague. She had kept her identity from her coworkers. She did not want hospital staff and her patients to know that she was *the* Mrs. Anderson, widow of an ambassador and granddaughter of one of Boston's wealthiest scions.

She liked being just Isabel.

Figure 25. Removing the wall fountain in the Italian Garden, 1965.

XVII

REDEMPTION OF A CULTURAL LEGACY

I sabel Anderson died on November 3, 1948, in the Phillips House wing of Boston's Massachusetts General Hospital, of complications from a broken hip. Five years earlier, she had written out detailed instructions for her memorial service.

October 16, 1943

Some suggestions to go with my will to be carried out more or less if possible.

Funeral at "Weld" in house or garden if seems best in summer and I die here. If not, very small service at Chapel in Washington if more convenient, or if funeral at "Weld" and my ashes in Chapel with minister and some member of family or office. Minister doesn't matter. If at "Weld", suggest the minister from Arlington church, or if at Washington, some Episcopal minister from the Cathedral. I would like my wedding ring left on. The silver urn already is at Cathedral for ashes.[1]

Within days if not hours of Isabel's death, her trusted private secretary, Gus Anderson, went into her boudoir and found the vellum folder marked "To be destroyed." The folder constituted a lifetime of Larz's and Isabel's love letters to each other, including two bound volumes of letters. Years later, Gus's son, Paul, told the story of his father burning the letters in a bonfire in the middle of Larz and Isabel's elegant neoclassical tennis court, within sight of the mansion.[2]

Isabel's memorial service was held in the mansion at Weld on Friday, November 5. The officiant was the Reverend Dana McLean Greeley, pastor of the Arlington Street Church, where the Andersons had been married fifty-one years before. Friends, relatives, and employees attended the private service, which included a reading of Isabel's will and its long list of bequests large and small. The largest gift went to the Town of Brookline itself, which had no prior knowledge Isabel would leave her estate to the town. The will also provided lifetime incomes for all employees who were working for her at the time of her death, the amount determined by their years of service.

Isabel's remains were cremated later that day at Forest Hills Cemetery, where her parents were buried, and prepared for transfer to Washington. Her ashes were interred in the St. Mary Chapel of Washington National Cathedral. Although Isabel had written her own epitaph, much of it paying homage to her father, Roger Amory penned a more succinct inscription for Isabel, with the words "compassionate benefactress" drawn from the citation that had accompanied her honorary degree from the George Washington University thirty years earlier.[3]

> Isabel Anderson
> Compassionate
> Benefactress
> March 29 1876 November 3 1948
> May She Rest In Peace

Isabel did not rest in peace for at least another two years. Every detail of her life and her private affairs became more public than she ever could have imagined or wanted. For more than a year, her finances, travels, friendships, and possessions were opened to continuous and conspicuous inspection by teams of lawyers and public officials. Nothing was sacred. Even her medical charts were included in the record, with every detail of her physical deterioration open to inspection by attorneys and state officials. Isabel would have been horrified to even imagine that her decision to declare a meaningless legal domicile in New Hampshire, for purely emotional reasons, would one day lead to a total invasion of her privacy.

The Domicile Problem

On November 10, 1948, a week after Isabel's death, Roger Amory and Mary Weld Pingree filed Isabel's will in the probate court of Merrimack County in Concord, New Hampshire. Within hours, journalists picked up the story, and the Boston papers published the details of Isabel's bequests.[4] On May 6, 1949, the probate court for Norfolk County in Massachusetts also admitted Isabel's will and named Roger and Mary the executors for her Massachusetts property. Officials in both states soon learned that each claimed tax jurisdiction over the estate, and they agreed to arbitrate the impasse. Massachusetts designated New York City attorney Thomas Witter Chrystie as its arbitrator. New Hampshire appointed Robert W. Upton of Concord, who later served as a US senator. Both jurisdictions agreed on George Maurice Morris (1889–1954), a prominent Washington lawyer who was a national expert in probate and estate law, as the chairman. The panel convened on June 27 and quickly began its work.[5]

The source of the dispute was that Isabel's domicile in Washington had ended when Larz died. He had always claimed Washington as his domicile for sentimental, political, and tax reasons, and, as his wife, Isabel had been domiciled there also. Now, Isabel needed to select a new domicile of her own. She declared this should be New Hampshire, her father's home state and a place to which she had a deep emotional attachment. The arbitration panel never received any testimony to suggest Isabel's advisors had encouraged her to declare a New Hampshire domicile for tax purposes. Her attorneys had advised her, however, that she should pay taxes, vote, and participate in the civic life of New Hampshire, even if she spent most of her time in Massachusetts.

Each state pursued a different legal strategy. New Hampshire claimed in its brief that because Isabel had declared their state as her domicile, it *was* her domicile. Their legal brief claimed that "if a person has sincerely and honestly, with no 'ulterior' motives, formally announced his selection of one of his homes as his domicile," then that was a sufficient basis for establishing domicile.[6] Massachusetts based its claims on a more rigorous definition of domicile. If a person had two homes, there could only be "one jurisdiction which will determine a man's legal rights and obligations." The domicile was thus "his principal home, his chief residence, his principal residence, his pre-eminent headquarters."[7] Massachusetts set out to prove Brookline had been Isabel's principal residence.

The panel continued its work over the summer and into the early fall of 1949.[8] It subpoenaed hundreds of pages of Anderson real estate, tax, and financial records. Staff scoured thousands of pages of Larz's and Isabel's published and unpublished writings for insight into their relationship, their use of the word *home* and what it meant to them, and what kinds of things they did in Brookline, Washington, New Hampshire, and elsewhere. Histories of the Perkins, Weld, and Anderson families and the properties and houses they had owned were dissected for clues to Larz's and Isabel's attitudes about where they lived. The panel called as witnesses dozens of staff, friends, and family and questioned them under oath about their connection to Isabel, her habits, and her relationship with Larz. This testimony produced more than a thousand pages of transcripts detailing the Andersons' life. Isabel was an intensely private person, and her friends, staff, and family must have found it appalling to be compelled to give this kind of testimony. The panel's staff assembled a master chronology of the Andersons' life supplemented by a statistical analysis of Isabel's whereabouts after 1937.[9]

The arbitration panel made site visits to Isabel's homes, guided in Brookline by her private secretary, Gus Anderson, and in New Hampshire by her cousin Evelyn Hastings. A stenographer produced a verbatim transcript of the tour of each home. A photographer documented the interiors.[10] The panel members and their staff opened drawers, looked in closets, leafed through books, and asked many questions. Newspapers followed all this closely and published detailed accounts of the proceedings. One newspaper article referred to Isabel as "an alert old lady."[11]

In October 1949, lawyers for each state presented their final case to the panel. Robert Lamere, a young staff attorney at the time, recalled that right up to the end, the panel's chairman, Morris, kept an open mind about the outcome. In the end, he and Chrystie voted in favor of Massachusetts and wrote the majority opinion: "Isabel Anderson's predominant and principal home at the time of her death was 'Weld' in Brookline, Massachusetts, and that this home was her pre-eminent headquarters and principal establishment at that time."[12] The panel ruled that all the facts of Isabel's life supported this conclusion and cited such factors as the size and permanence of her Brookline staff; her Boston-based literary, publishing, and theatrical activities; and the amount of time she'd spent in Brookline. Each state accepted the panel's decision, and New Hampshire relinquished its claim.

Loss of a Cultural Treasure

During and after the arbitration, the Anderson estate became a subject of ridicule and scorn in Brookline. Townspeople called it a gift horse and a white elephant.[13] Taxpayers feared it was already a burden to the budget. In early 1949, in anticipation of the transfer, the board of selectmen began a seven-month study of the property and its possible use under the terms of the bequest. They held a special town meeting in June to hear opinions and ideas directly from taxpayers, who voted 129 to 64 in favor of accepting it. With this nonbinding referendum behind them, the board formally voted in September to accept the gift, although as the *Boston Sunday Herald* reported, they did so "reluctantly."[14]

In August 1949, the board of selectmen decided to divest itself of the Andersons' automobile-and-carriage collection. It reached an agreement with the Veteran Motor Car Club of America for that group to take over the preservation and display of sixteen antique motor vehicles and many horse-drawn carriages. Under the plan, the club also moved its national headquarters to the carriage house.[15] The collection was renamed the Antique Auto Museum Larz Anderson Collection and had its grand public opening in October that year. In 1953, the Massachusetts Museum of Transportation took over the collection and renamed it the Larz Anderson Auto Museum.

The Town of Brookline formally took ownership of the property in 1950 and tried to sell it almost immediately. The US Navy sent a team of engineers to inspect the mansion and determine its suitability for use as offices. The engineers found it would take much work to convert the mansion's floor space into "Navy type offices," including plumbing, electrical, communications, and fire protection. The navy did not purchase the property, and there were no other known prospective buyers.[16]

By 1953, the town was still undecided about the future of the estate. The parks department had started using the property and some of its infrastructure. It converted the bay pit and the Snow Barn, one of the oldest structures on the estate, into storage areas. The henhouse became a carpenter shop. Town officials and private citizens disagreed about the benefits and costs of maintaining the property. By one calculation, the town saved $4,000 a year by growing its own seedlings and plantings in the Anderson greenhouse rather than buying them commercially. The Larz Anderson Estate Committee, appointed to advise the board of selectmen, was unable to come to any consensus. It was clear, however, that the mansion itself would have to go. No one could come up with a use for it that met the terms of the will. It had to be used for charitable, educational, or patriotic purposes.[17]

In 1955, in one last attempt to come to terms with the property, the Town of Brookline hired the Brookline-based landscape architecture firm Olmsted Brothers to develop a master land-use plan for the estate. As part of its work, Olmsted prepared topographical maps showing the location and size of all buildings on the estate at the time of Isabel's death. These maps thus preserve details of architecture, landscaping and gardens, and horticultural and agricultural operations on the estate long ago destroyed. Olmsted drew new floor plans for the 1885 part of the mansion and located the Little and Browne blueprints for the 1914–1916 additions. With these materials, the firm's architects documented the interior layout of the house at the time of Isabel's death.[18] Olmsted suggested that the town convert the mansion to a museum, construct an ice rink on the large field in front of the carriage house, and install playing fields and picnic areas elsewhere on the property. The town rejected the idea of a museum but liked the idea of an ice rink and other recreation facilities.

In 1955, the town installed a simple open-air ice rink, not in the front field where Olmsted had recommended, but in the center of Charles A. Platt's masterpiece, the Italian garden at Weld. The fountain, garden ornamentation, architectural elements, and walkways were razed to make room for the rink. All that remained of the once-world-famous *giardino segreto* were a terrace, the upper-tier promenades, and a few balustrades.

The Anderson mansion was torn down at about the same time the ice rink was built. There is no clear account of what happened to the Andersons' furniture, collections, books, and papers. Some items like photograph albums and scrapbooks, leather-bound copies of magazines that published Isabel's articles, and a few odd pieces of furniture were moved to the carriage house, where they remain in storage. Other items went to family members, and there was an estate sale of some sort.

Fortunately, the mansion's terrace, a pergola near the site where the mansion formerly stood, the bowling green, and the bosquet were left in place. In recent years, the Town of Brookline has restored these features of the estate's landscape. The pink granite retaining walls Billy Weld had installed in the 1880s remain intact and help modern visitors envision the scale of the house that was once there. A parking lot with fabulous vistas of Boston in the distance, the same view the Andersons once saw from their front door, now occupies the site of the house.

In 1957, the town parks department built a new service building in what had been the kitchen garden. The greenhouses were put back in service and remained in operation until some time in the early 1960s, when they were torn down. With the exception of the Snow Cottage, all the Anderson-era staff houses survived, more or less as they were at the time of Isabel's death. They are now rental residential properties.

The last defacement of the Italian garden occurred in 1965, when workers jackhammered into oblivion the fountain basin on the northern wall of the garden. It was not in the way of any part of the ice-rink operation, and there is no record of why it was removed. It is still heartrending to read the inscription above the gaping hole left in the wall where the fountain once was: "THIS GARDEN WAS MADE IN 1901 AND NAMED WELD." (See figure 25.)

Restoration of a Cultural Legacy

In the early 1980s, the Town of Brookline came to understand what had been lost and began to make amends for what earlier generations had done. In 1985, the town received state and national historic-site status for what had become Larz Anderson Park. In 1988, a Massachusetts Self-Help Grant funded restoration of many Anderson elements in the park: the estate's perimeter walls with intricate wrought iron detailing, the bowling green, the lagoon, the *tempietto*, and one of the Italian garden's gazebos. Completed in 1993, the restoration received awards from the Massachusetts Historical Commission and the Boston Society of Landscape Architects. In 1995, the town replaced the ice rink's 1950s-era warming hut with a new pavilion and incorporated columns from the garden's original pergola. Visitors now get a better sense of the general appearance of the garden during the Anderson era.

In 2013, the Brookline Department of Parks and Open Space engaged the author to prepare a new historical and cultural interpretation of Larz Anderson Park. Working with town officials, park rangers, and local historians, the author developed a walking tour and wrote a docent manual to train park rangers in the history of the park. "The Andersons left their mark on the estate," wrote Erin Chute Gallentine, Brookline's director of Parks and Open Space, in her introduction to the docent manual, "though in the absence of research and interpretation, much of it has remained hidden in plain sight."[19]

There is great hope that one day the Italian garden will be restored and that visitors from around the world will once again flock to Brookline to see Platt's masterpiece, restored and in full bloom.

The garden at Weld has been thrown open to the public and
they tell us that a thousand people swarmed out over the place
a few days ago, and no damage seems to have been done. I
hoped the garden would prove to be a source of pleasure.

—Larz Anderson, July 15, 1907

Epilogue

THE STORY OF ANTONIO SCALI (1931), BY LARZ ANDERSON[1]

Out of the radio on one afternoon came a mechanical voice that aroused very different emotions in us, although it too brought a shock with its sudden news. For I.A. [Isabel] and I had been working in our dens when at four o'clock I called out to come down to the Leather Room for a cup of tea and to hear the afternoon news bulletins over WEEI. So my beloved I.A. joined me downstairs as the strange, even words of the "Town Crie-er of the Boston Daily Record" began to sound out of the box in the corner of our room. Almost his first news was that Governor Ely had pardoned two prisoners who were in Charlestown Prison for life, and that so-and-so Cummings, who had been in for thirty years, etcetera, was to be released. It was Thanksgiving Eve, and it was customary for the Governor to grant pardons on that Day, but we had not thought about it, we had rather given up hope that the pardon we had particularly desired might even be granted. Till, suddenly, the voice next announced that "Antonio Scali" was the other prisoner,—we did n't wait to hear the rest we jumped up and danced about, and there were tears in my eyes I must admit, for I knew how my I.A. had felt and worked in this case. It was a terribly exciting moment!

Some years ago a prisoner in Charlestown goal, a well known thief, had written I.A. to tell her that he had composed some stories, and asked her how to dispose of them. I.A. gave him some advices and named some magazines, and later he had answered that he had sold one of his tales for $35.00. I mention this man because he had at one time asked I.A. if she would care to see some pictures by a friend of his, a "lifer" in the prison, named Scali. I.A. had gone to see the pictures, to see Scali, and on several occasions had visited the goal, had become quite a friend of the Warden Hogsett and the Chaplain of the Prison, had studied the prison quite apart from any interest in Scali.

But the pictures proved to be quite good, considering the man and the place, and afterwards he had painted many little miniature copies of photographs which I.A. had sent him, which we used as Christmas cards. His story showed such a sterling character, notwithstanding any crime he might have commited, that I.A. looked up Scali's record and determined that, if there ever had been a prisoner who deserved the benefit of the machinery which was set up by the State for helping deserving convicts, he was the one, and so she went to work to free him.

As an Italian immigrant of nineteen, lately arrived in the country, unable to speak a word of English, he had been an ignorant laborer on railway construction near Pittsfield, when, one day, he was joined by a friend and had gone to a movie, had several drinks, and then they had been joined by a third man, whom Scali had never seen before. The three started to walk along the railway tracks to go to another place for drinks, when a train suddenly came at them; the third man was drunk enough to refuse to get out of the way, so the other two threw him to one side and saved his life.

But after the train had passed the third man showed resentment and attacked the others with a knife. (I believe their clothes showed were he had cut at them.) There was a tumble, drunken fight, Scali and his friend drew pistols in self defense, and the third man was shot dead. Scali has always maintained that his pistol had jammed. However, then realizing their plight, the two friends took the dead man's money, to aid in an escape—but were soon arrested. It was then that the police, taking advantage of the ignorance by the prisoners of English and of our law and procedure, "persuaded" them, by some shinannigan, no doubt by some third degree methods, to sign papers of confession—and so they were both sent up for life, mitigating circumstances such as Italian temperament and possible innocence of one or the other in the jamming of a gun and the plea of self defense being apparently disregarded, the country "hick" police claimed a record of efficiency.

At any rate they were up for life within prison walls. And now came the proving of the man Scali, for he went in an ignorant laborer, unable to speak a word of English, and although those blank walls stared him in the face and there was no promise of anything else in the future, he started in to take advantage of the opportunities that the prison life afforded, he learned to speak and write English as well as most high school graduates (far better than the High School graduates that we have had working for us). He learned stenography, so that he qualified for a diploma, and the typewriter—and he taught himself painting so that he proved a real talent in the art. In addition Scali's behavior record was perfect, and the Warden and Chaplain were both in favor of clemency for him. A Mr. McMullin, who was deeply interested in prison work and represented a prisoner's aid association, had picked out Scali as the one man whom he had hoped to save.

So I.A. took up his case, and associated with herself the Italian Consul, Margotti and "Judge" Leveroni, who was a leader among the Italian people of Boston. Both of these were most important allies, for the Consul brought the Italian Government into the matter and Leveroni brought an immense experience in handling such cases and understanding the Italian temperament. The Italian Ambassador in Washington became interested in the case because of I.A. She sincerely believed that Scali was deserving.

At any rate, an unusual element was introduced when the Italian Government expressed its willingness to have Scali return to Italy if released. I.A. took advantage of this to point out in her appeal that, especially in these days of depression and retrenchment, it seemed an opportunity to relieve the State of the cost of such a prisoner for years to come, when he could be deported at once and never return. It may be added that it required some managing to maintain the interest of these men, Margotti and Leveroni, who had so many other affairs to take up their time, but little social attentions, such as invitations to lunch and entertaining the Italo-American Historical Society twice at "Weld," seemed to carry them on and over, so that they were wonderfully nice and efficient, in pursing the matter.

It seems that "lifers" are generally fit for consideration for parole after serving twenty years, so that in 1930 the case of Scali was brought to the attention of the Board of Parole at the State House, and I.A. and the Consul and Judge all appeared and made their appeal. But while one member, Stone, was favorable, the Chairman Brooks and the negro on the board showed no sympathy, and did not recommend release to the Governor, so that although I.A. and the others also saw the then Governor Allen, he took no action.

Accordingly in this year of grace 1931, they determined to appeal directly to the new Governor, His Excellency Ely, disregarding the board, which had meanwhile paroled several prisoners in cases so flagrantly flavoured with political suspicions that the newspapers carried editorials about them. Ely, himself an experienced lawyer, one time Prosecuting Attorney, who had probably himself had experience of the Parole Board in similar cases, had expressed pronounced views about clemency in general. So they were received by the Governor and presented their cases and appeal and came away, uncertain but hopeful. And now, suddenly out of the blue, came this answer on Thanksgiving Eve!

We were discussing what to do after Scali should be released when the telephone rang and Chairman Brooks said that Scali was in his office, what should he do with him. Scali within the hour was already free. I.A. wasn't unprepared, and quickly answered that she would be in the State House in twenty minutes to take care of Scali. Brooks could be heard over the telephone giving an embarrassed laugh, finding it hopeless to catch I.A. off her guard.

So off we went to town, I.A. to "123" [123 Commonwealth Avenue] to see that a room might be arranged for Scali (for it was Thanksgiving Eve and difficult to make other arrangements that night or get Scali certain papers that would be necessary for the completion of his release and departure for Italy until after the holiday) while I went on to the State house to find Mr. Brooks waiting with Scali in the Parole Board rooms. I took Scali in charge, out to the automobile, down to Leveroni's offices where the "Judge" was waiting to have a word of congratulations and greeting and advices. Then we all went up to "123" where I.A. had arranged for a room and supper for Scali.

It was one of the most extraordinary experiences of my life to take in charge this man and realize that, in so many ways, he had to be cared for like a baby. For twenty one years he had been inside a prison, while the whole world outside had changed as it has never changed before in such a score of years. And he knew nothing of it, he had only at best heard of it all, and yet here he was suddenly let loose into its swirling life. He would have to be watched and guided for a time before he could find his way about: he was an innocent child suddenly pitched into the world.

He was in appearance an Italian type, and he had not forgotten his Italian manners, which were quite perfect for one who was undergoing such an exciting hour. His eyes were wide with looking about him, seeing so much that was changed and new since he had last been out in the life of the world. He said it was all that he could do to hold on to himself, but he did; he constantly said, "its a mechanical age; its a miracle." I was apparently more excited than he was, for he controlled himself better than I did. I tried to watch and study his reactions but it was all so sudden that I had n't had time to adjust myself to the opportunity. Think of it, at three o'clock this man was within prison walls with nothing to look forward to, nothing but blank walls about him, that had shut him off from an amazing world for the best years of his life—at four o'clock he was practically a free man, with all the movement and excitement of modern life swirling about him.

This sudden change of everything in life is a terrible risk to a man's nerves and reactions. I hope that our taking Scali in hand at once may have carried him over the most difficult moments of his daze, for it must be remembered that when he went to prison he practically knew nothing of American ways, and yet here he was suddenly pitched into the maelstrom of modern American life. And he had no family or other friends to meet him. At "123" he was put into a small hall bedroom, where with his "cell habit" he seemed to prefer to sit at first, and just look out of the window at the passing show in the street. Into the larger rooms of the house he did n't seem to care to go at first, except to study the paintings and few works of art that appealed to him. We kept him as quiet as possible over the holiday—newspaper reporters came out to "Weld," but could n't find him at "123."

On Friday McMullin took him away, to take care of him for the few days before it could be arranged by the Consul for him to sail for Italy—to go to his old Mother whom, from the first, he had said, was his one desire in life to see; he had corresponded with her regularly through the dreadful years—she was waiting for him over at his old home in Italy. With his knowledge of English, his ability to take dictation and typewrite, his general intelligence, he should be able to find a niche in some foreign trading firm in Italy—and it is rather wonderful that he had saved almost one thousand dollars during his life in jail!

Within an hour I sent off the following cablegram (which he had written himself) to his mother—and surely I.A. may be content with another kind deed done.

SIGNORA TERESA CAMSO TAURIA NOVA SAN MARTINO ITALY

SONO APPUNTO SORTITO SCRIVERO DOMANI ANTONIO SCALI

[*Just released will write tomorrow*]

He wished very much to see and say good bye to his brother who was the only member of his family in America and who lived in New York State, so he was allowed to go there for two days, but he came back faithfully and was met by Mr. McMullin, his passage paid for and his papers provided by the Royal Italian Consulate, little extras provided for his trip, his savings having been sent over to some safe deposit place in Italy, and he sailed away within the week from Boston on an Italian Ship, a free man from the moment he came under the Italian flag, feeling, as Mr. McMullin telephoned us, "like a million dollars."

Author's Note: In October 2015, as this book was being readied for publication, I located the descendants of Antonio Scali in Italy, who were overjoyed to learn that Antonio's story was to appear here. Antonio returned to his family in Italy in 1931 and lived a happy life in Italy and Australia. He married Giuseppina De Marco in 1932, and together they had four children: three sons, Dominic, Frank, and Angelo, and a daughter, Isabella, named after Isabel Anderson. Antonio found work as a private school English teacher. In 1959, he and his family immigrated to Australia, where they lived for many years. When Antonio died in 1977, his remains were returned to

Italy, and he was buried in the little cemetery of Tauria Nova, Calabria. He has many grandchildren and great-grandchildren who continue to revere the woman they call "Principessa Isabella." Antonio painted a portrait of Isabel, which still hangs in the family home in Calabria, where it will rightfully be revered for generations to come. Antonio's great-grandson, the Italian novelist Felice Diego Licopoli, has written a novelized account of his great-grandfather's time in America, *Strisce di luna* (Reggio Calabria: Città del Sole Edizione, 2013).

Acknowledgements & Thanks

Aberdeen (Scotland): University of Aberdeen, Library & Special Collections: Michelle Gait.

Brookline: Town of Brookline: Erin Chute Gallentine and Brandon Schmitt, Parks and Open Space; Greer Hardwicke and Anne McIver, Planning Office; James C. Flaherty, Librarian. Larz Anderson Auto Museum: Sheldon Steele. Brookline Historical Society: Linda Leary. Frederick Law Olmsted National Historic Site: Anthony Reed.

Brussels: Conseil d'État (Palais d'Assche): Monsieur le Président Roger Stevens; Michel Fauconier, Historian. US Embassy: Margaret White and Brian Dick.

Boston: Boston Children's Museum: Rachel Farkas. Boston University Gotlieb Center for Archival Research: Adam Dixon and Sarah Elizabeth Pratt. Isabella Stewart Gardner Museum: JoAnn Robinson. Carol R. Johnson Associates: John Amodeo. Winsor School: Jane Otte.

Cincinnati. Cincinnati History Library and Archives: Anne Shepherd.

New York: Frick Collection and Archives, Art Reference Library: Julie Ludwig.

New Hampshire: Phillips Exeter Academy Archives: Edouard L. Desrochers. Webster Free Public Library: Cathryn Clark-Dawe.

Paris: American Battle Monuments Commission: Joe Barnes. The American Cathedral in Paris (Archives Committee): Nancy Webster and Kate Thweatt. American Library in Paris: Charles Trueheart and Grant Rosenberg.

Washington: National Archives and Records Administration: William Davis. National League of American Pen Women: Sheila M. Byrnes, Candace

Long, and Sandra Seaton Michel. National Society of the Daughters of the American Revolution: Amanda Fulcher. Metropolitan Club: Michael Higgins and Eleanor Lynch. Society of the Cincinnati: Ellen McAllister Clark, Elizabeth Frengel, Rachel Jirka, Emily Schulz Parsons, Caren Pauley, and Valerie Sallis.

Special Thanks: Father Andrew J. Barnas, OSB; Marilyn L. Barth; Eugénie Berchon; Isabel Brintnall; William Busker; Jim Cassell; Hannah Cox; Dennis De Witt; Jim Dykes; Duncan Finlayson; Rolf Fuessler and Norman Goulet; Jana Fuhrmann; Daniel Giosta; James M. Goode; Kevin E. Hamilton; Thomas Head, Mike Cavanaugh, and the Wednesday Night Dinner Group; Reverend Charles H. Harper; Caroline Mesrobian Hickman; Jim Higdon; Andrew Holleran; Marion L. Jones✝; Reverend Canon Ted Karpf; Aiko Kitaya; Hiroko Kitaya; Masahiko Kitaya; Maryjane Kennedy; Robert K. Lamere, Esq.; Antonela Leiva; Warren Little; Boyd Lugenbehl; Harry I. Martin III; Jim O'Shea; Julie Parent; Peter Penczer; Mark Phillips; John Nick Pull; Tom Regan; Robert Sacheli; Carole Sargent; William Seale; Sam Sherman; B. J. Stiles; Isabel L. Taube; Steven Troxel✝; Betsy Tunis; Joel Urbina; John M. Walton Jr.; Bruce M. White; and Robert L. Wiser.

Appendix

Essay on Louisa May Alcott and Anna Minot Weld, by Isabel Anderson (ca. 1938)[1]

One of the chief points of interest in Louisa May Alcott's life was the way in which it joined other lives of similar interest. She belonged to a period overwhelmingly stocked with impressive personalities. In spite of her unsociable habits, she touched many of them, giving and receiving historic influences. She reflected the effects of these contacts for years. Her early biographers and critics did not take account of this rich aura of her existence. Her panegyrists pictured her as a lone towering pine, self-starting from her own roots and those within her family and growing without further assistance to her phenomenal height. Persons obviously important to her life were given only sufficient space in those early records for their initials; and these were not always the correct ones. The omissions were partly due to a naïve idea of the inborn and unique nature of genius, which made all such associations seem unimportant, and partly to the squeamish politeness which dictated the writing of memoirs in those days.

In the accounts of Miss Alcott's first journey to Europe, for instance, a journey which lasted for a year, there was never any mention of the lady with whom she travelled and who made the journey financially possible for her. It might seem to some readers that the name of Miss Alcott's companion should find a place in the records as one of the most important items in her history. One might think that the early biographers would have put it in if for no other reason than thoroughness and accuracy. But they withheld it. A modern biographer would find it almost impossible to follow Miss Alcott in her long pilgrimage through

2

Europe without ever once mentioning the name of her companion. A long and tedious search for the lost lady, however, revealed nothing; until at last when despair and hopelessness were about to shut off all further effort the fact was accidentally discovered. In quite another connection altogether but in such a one that the process of putting two and two together to make four work it out, the name of Miss Anna Weld was arrived at. Though nothing more was to be learned for the time being, one knew at least that Miss Alcott lived in close association with Miss Anna Weld of Boston for the better part of a year.

The second personal influence of the European trip was the young Pole whom Miss Alcott met in Switzerland and afterwards saw in Paris. This young man found his place in the memoirs because he figured as the life-model for that popular hero, "Laurie" in "Little Women," and comparing with it the other portrait incorporated in "My Boys," the biographer came to the conclusion that Miss Alcott was in love with young Wisniewski. The idea seemed to require no great argument. Anyone who takes a good thorough look at "Little Women" and "Rose in Bloom" and who knows anything at all about women,—and men,—would naturally conclude that the author of these books at some time would have been in love and that, as Ladislas Wisniewski was the only person whom she ever gave the least hint of caring for,

3

he was in all-probability the charmer. And so the chapter which described Miss Alcott's journey through Europe with Miss Weld as her fellow-traveler was named for what seemed to be the dominating influence in its course; "Love."

Now we come to the aftermath. The biography was tolerably finished. It was duly issued and spread around by the publisher. The usual sort of advertising copy was sent out to the newspapers. Promptly one of them, the "New York Times," sent the advertising copy back. It would only be accepted, said the accompanying message, if the word "love" in the summary of contents which it contained were deleted and the word "romance" put in its place. The guardian spirit of the "New York Times" resented the mere suggestion of sex in connection with the idea of Miss Alcott, even the most sublimated and refined sort of sex such as a renounced love-affair. To that aunt-like and Victorian spirit, any suggestion that Miss Alcott was capable of normal emotions was an attack not to be tolerated. This horrified protest, had the present writer then foreseen it, was but the prelude to a chorus of outraged cries on the part of literary reviewers who subsequently considered that the mention of Miss Alcott as subject to love was an offense against public decorum and a blow at the body politic.

The moral revolt of the "Times" came like a bolt from the blue. In haste a conference of the parties concerned was assembled but at first all rational action seemed impossible. In a state of daze author and publisher contemplated the ultimatum as if it were some strange animal. Gradually, very gradually, those present revived; and finally, as there seemed

4

no reason, in the world why the word "romance" should not be substituted for the word "love" in a mere ad, the momentous change was made. All that appeared to remain now was to return to blessed normalcy and forget the bizarre episode.

But the subject was destined to be opened again later; this time in a more worthily serious manner. The biography went its rounds presumably among people who cared for Louisa May Alcott and our early American backgrounds and who preferred realistic writing in this field, and eventually found its way into the hands of an interested reader. Mrs. Larz Anderson, the author of many charming children's stories and plays and many books of travel, the public-spirited wife of the former United Sates minister to Belgium and ambassador to Japan, was this reader. Mrs. Anderson happened to have in her possession certain relevant information concerning Miss Alcott's European trip in 1865 and concerning the situation involving young Wisniewski. This information, which she put in a letter, throws a new light on events which developed in Vevey and Nice. It suggests that the two cultivated young ladies from Boston were at bottom human and that in that fact lay a part of the reason for their difficulties in Nice and for the somewhat mysterious account of their difficulties given in the "Life, Letters, and Journals."[2] The letter is here quoted in its entirety, not only for its interesting matter and sincere and easy style but also for its gentle touching on emotions once so poignant to one so close to the writer. It said: ---

"I read with much interest the chapter, 'Love,' in your biography of Louisa May Alcott, in which you mention Miss

5

Anna Weld as travelling with Miss Alcott. It happens that Miss Weld later married, and was my mother. I was more amused than anything else, because evidently you did not know, and perhaps Miss Alcott may not have known herself, the entire situation in regard to the young Pole mentioned.

"My mother said little to me about this trip during her life-time; she perhaps may have mentioned that Miss Alcott was a bit difficult. I can not remember her exact words. She did mention that they met a Pole who was very charming. My mother, if I do say so, and anyone who knew her can tell you, was very pretty (her photographs also show this); and later, as an older woman, she was also very good-looking, far better-looking, I judge, than Miss Alcott. And she was much younger than Miss Alcott--- more the Pole's age. Not only pretty, my mother was very bright and attractive. She was not very strong, however, at the time of this trip—because she had been very ill of scarlet fever that she had had when a young girl.

"It was after her death (she lived to be quite old) that I found among her things some letters written to her by Ladislas Wisniewski. They were love letters, and he asked her to marry him. Unfortunately I destroyed the letters, so you have only my word for this; but it is the truth. I saw no reason to keep them at the time. Because I thought this might be of interest to you, I write this letter.

"I judge the Pole may have accounted somewhat for Miss Alcott's and my mother's difficulties, as you suggest that Miss Alcott was much interested in him.

"I suppose my mother did not care to marry the Pole, as he was not well, and he was a foreigner. I may have heard

6

her say that, but it is all so long ago, and frankly I was not especially interested; and I cannot remember much except the letters which I found. As I also write books, I naturally was interested in your book; and also — because of my mother."

And so by this incident of courageous candor, for which the lovers of the real Louisa May Alcott should be grateful, our knowledge of the human background of "Little Women" becomes considerably enlarged. We have gained a definitely vital comment on Louisa May Alcott's life and works. The situation outlined in the letter indicates that a far more complex problem grew out of Miss Alcott's meeting with the Pole than any biographer had suspected. The circumstances are capable of several interpretations. The one that springs first to mind is that the charming original of "Laurie" was a flirt. One hesitates to suggest this, however, for "Laurie" is in the sub-conscious of every American woman and entrenched there in perfection. Another element in the situation in Nice is here illuminated. Miss Weld's illness there, which broke off the journey to Rome to Miss Alcott's undying disappointment, has remained a good deal of a puzzle. Miss Alcott thought that by making a little unselfish effort she might have gone on; but the letter suggests that the matter was not so simple. Another point made by the letter is valuable. It seems extremely probable that Miss Weld kept her secret for the creator of "Laurie" seemed always to have only the happiest memories of his original. She introduced him in her memoirs always as "her" boy. The one thing that seems certain is that the whole affair was not for Miss Alcott the casual and polite encounter which the American tradition cultivated for young girls assumes it to have been. It was a crisis in which deep emotions were stirred. Yet both of the la-

7

dies behaved admirably. The one retained the satisfaction of knowing that she had acted honorably in a difficult situation and the other preserved an ideal which inspired a delightful book. As for the young Pole, let it be sufficient to say that he remained a charming and unblemished memory in the lives of both.

[verso of page 7, in Isabel Anderson's handwriting]

For Mrs. Anna Wiley [illegible] I.A.

References

Archival Materials

Adams, Marian Hooper. Photographs. Massachusetts Historical Society, Boston.

Anderson Collection. Larz Anderson Auto Museum, Brookline, MA.

Anderson Collection. Society of the Cincinnati, Washington, DC.

Anderson Estate Garden Photographs. Archives of American Gardens. Smithsonian Institution, Washington, DC.

Anderson Estate Photographs. General photographic collection. Historic New England, Boston, MA.

Anderson Collection. Acquisition registry (May 1948). Boston Children's Museum.

Anderson and Longworth families. Wills and estate papers. Hamilton County (OH) Probate Court Records. Archives and Rare Books Library, University of Cincinnati.

Anderson, Larz, and Isabel Anderson. Books and Periodicals from the Library of Larz and Isabel Anderson. Boston Athenaeum.

———. Larz and Isabel Anderson Collection (1895–1948). Howard Gotlieb Archival Research Center, Boston University.

Anderson, Isabel. Isabel Anderson Papers (1895–1949). Manuscript Division, Library of Congress.

Anderson, Larz. Baptismal record (1866). The American Pro-Cathedral Church of the Holy Trinity, Paris.

———. Diplomatic Personnel File (London). Applications and Recommendations for Public Office, 1797–1901. Cleveland, box 2. Record Group 59. National Archives and Records Administration, College Park, MD.

———. Diplomatic Personnel File (Rome). Applications and Recommendations for Public Office, 1797–1901. Cleveland and Harrison, box 3. Record Group 59. National Archives and Records Administration, College Park, MD.

———. Diplomatic Personnel File (Brussels and Tokyo). Applications and Recommendations for Appointment to Consular and Diplomatic Services, 1901–1924. Taft, box 5. Record Group 59. National Archives and Records Administration, College Park, MD.

———. English themes (1885–1887). HUC 8885.324. Harvard University Archives.

————. *Some Scraps.* [Journals, 1888–1936.] 38 vols. Anderson Collection. Society of the Cincinnati.

Vol. 1, *A Post Graduate Course around the World* [1888–1889].

Vol. 2, *Arcs in a Circle around the World: Something of India, the North Cape and Russia* [1889].

Vol. 3, *Days in & out of London* [1891–1892].

Vol. 4, *Our Wedding Journey and Our Trip to India* [1897–1899].

Vol. 5, *More Scraps. A Bit of Mexico in 1901. Kentucky—The Saint Louis Exposition. An Autumn in Brookline* [1901–1904].

Vol. 6, *Yachting on Land & on Sea. Canada—New Orleans—Southwest. South of England—London—North Cape* [1904].

Vol. 7, *Very Scrappy. Leaves of Absence—Presidential Campaigns. Visits—Camps—and Cures* [1905–1916].

Vol. 8, *Abroad in 1906. Morocco—Spain—Royal Wedding—Festivities and After* [1906].

Vol. 9, *Bit by Bit. L. A. a'Hunting in Leicestershire. Holy Week at Seville. Incidents of the Spring and Autumn of 1909* [1906–1907, 1909].

Vol. 10, *Some Inside Ways on "Roxana" & a Royal Visit* [1907].

Vol. 11, *Odds and Ends. Of Cruises of Houseboat Roxana—Charleston in 1907—Hudson River in 1913. Cruising Northward in 1914* [1907, 1913–1914].

Vol. 12, *Afloat and Ashore. From Florida to Alaska—Houseboat "Roxana" and Southern Waters—Republican Convention and the Fjords of Alaska—Private Car "Republic" and Camping in Canadian Rockies* [1908].

Vol. 13, *Some Things in 1910. Imperial Visitors—On Board "Roxana" Again. Southern Plantations and Charleston Gardens* [1910].

Vol. 14, *Some Experiences on a Trip around the World with the Secretary of War* [1910].

Vol. 15, *A Mission to Belgium. Legation in the Palais d'Assche—Volume 1. Courts and Customs and Contretemps in Brussels* [1911–1912].

Vol. 16, *A Mission to Belgium. Legation in the Palais d'Assche—Volume 2. Courts and Customs and Contretemps in Brussels* [1912].

Vol. 17, *An Embassy to Japan. Across Siberia and through Korea to Happy Days and Associations in Tokyo* [1912–1913].

Vol. 18, *Private Car "Federal." Glacier Park—The Pacific—Panama Exposition—Sequoia Giant National Park in the High Sierras—Catalina Island—San Diego Exposition—Grand Canyon and Pueblo of Acoma Again* [1915].

Vol. 19, *Some Side Steps. On Board Roxana in Florida in 1916. Mobile. New Orleans. Panama* [1916].

Vol. 20, *In 1920. Kentucky Derby—"Roxana" to Devon Horse Show. Chicago Convention—Commencement Time. America Cup Race—Foot Ball—Elections. Et cetera* [1920].

Vol. 21, *Travels of the Tribe of Manhattan into the Rocky Mountains of Colorado* [1920].

Vol. 22, *A Drift-Log of a Cruise on Houseboat "Roxana"* [1920].

Vol. 23, *Roxana Rediviva. The Bermudas—D.A.R. Elects Librarian General. Races at New London and Poughkeepsie. Summer Cruises* [1923].

Vol. 24, *Frayed Ends in 1924. Early Winter at "Weld"—Presidential Dinner. Visit to Nassau—Hectic Winter in Washington. Reunions—Short Trip to Europe. In Deepest Mourning* [1924].

Vol. 25, *A Story of the Knights and Dames of the Good Adventure Being a Tale of Salmon Fishing on the Bonaventure River* [1924].

Vol. 26, *In the Year of the Hejiri 1343. A Southern Crossing—White Cities on the Sea. A Caravan through North Africa—Algeria—Morocco. Tunisia—A Stay on the Riviera. Home Again. June Reunions—Roxana in New Waters. Dedication of Memorial in Cincinnati—Autumn in Brookline. Start for Cuba and Stop Off in Florida. Wild Land Speculation There— House Boat through Keys* [1925].

Vol. 27, *Why Not Ireland! Visit to Ireland—Queenstown—Glengarriff. Killarney—Dublin—Cork* [1927].

Vol. 28, *A Joy Ride. Into the Southwest Again—Motor Car Caravan Camping Trips—Into the Mesa Verde and Zion Canyon Country—Los Angeles— Around Santa Fe to Taos Pueblo* [1927].

Vol. 29, *Africa Rediscovered by North Americans—First Part. Cruise down West Coast—Senegal, Sierra Leone, St. Helena to Cape Town—Special Train Trek to Kimberley, Bulawayo, Victoria Falls, Johannesburg, Pretoria to Durban* [1928].

Vol. 30, *Africa Rediscovered by North Americans—Second Part. Cruise up East Coast—Mozambique, Madagascar, Zanzibar, Mombasa—Special Train Trek to Nairobi from Port Sudan to Khartoum, Omdurman, Wady Halfa—Down Nile to Cairo* [1928].

Vol. 31, *Hop, Skip and Jump—First Part. Italy Again—Naples—Rome—Hill Towns—Florence—Italian Lakes* [1928].

Vol. 32, *Hop, Skip and Jump—Second Part. Through Switzerland into Czecho-Slovakia. Fortieth Anniversary Reunion of Harvard Class of 1888— Summer and Autumn at "Boxlet" and "Weld." Penguin Parties— General Activities—Another Royal Dinner. Lists of Conductors, Couriers, Ciceroni. Private Car Trips* [1928].

Vol. 33, *In This Year of Grace 1929—First Part. Winter in Boston and Washington. Trip Abroad and Cruise on Steam Yacht "Sayonara"* [1929].

Vol. 34, *In This Year of Grace 1929—Second Part. Montecatini—Italian Riviera—Autumn at Home Again. Lists of Personal Diaries. Personal Records—Et cetera* [1929].

Vol. 35, *Tours and Detours in 1930. A Private Car Trip into the Southwest— Apache Trail—Agua Caliente—Santa Barbara—Death Valley— Hopiland—Carlsbad Caverns—Winter in Washington and Spring in Brookline—I.A. Receives Degree of L.L.D.—Private Car Trip into*

    Northern Canada—Muscaliunge [sic] *Fishing Jasper Park—Voyage to
    Holland—The Boxlet—Autumn at Weld—Visit to Washington—Vice
    President's Dinner to President—White House Reception—Return to
    Boston Town House* [1930].

Vol. 36, *A Year of Shreds and Patches. Again around the World—Southern India.
    Insulinde and the Golden Chersonese. Home Again—A King and Queen
    in Anderson House. St. Paul's School and Exeter Reunions. Guests of
    Royalty—Scali Pardoned—Visit of Marshal Petain. End of 1931* [1931].

Vol. 37, *More Shreds and Patches. Production of "Marina"—Visit Boca Raton.
    Washington Winter and Activities—Return to Brookline. Coral
    Wedding—Private Car Trip to Black Hills. Glacier Park—Mount
    Rainier—10ᵗʰ Olympiad. L.A. Alone to Marienbad—Autumn in
    Brookline and Washington. Presidential Campaign. End of 1932* [1932].

Vol. 38, *Journals, 1933–1936* [1933–1936].

———. Membership Record. Metropolitan Club, Washington, DC.

———. Archives of Phillips Exeter Academy, Exeter, NH.

———. Last Will and Testament (1937). Wills and Probate Records (1801–
    1999). Archives of the District of Columbia, Washington, DC.

Anderson, Nicholas Longworth. "French Missionaries in the West." Manuscript
    of the Oration Read at the Harvard College Commencement Exercises,
    21 July 1858. Alumni files. Harvard University Archives.

Barney, Alice Pike. Papers (1861–1965). Smithsonian Institution Archives,
    Washington, DC.

Brookline Room. Vertical files. Town of Brookline Public Library.

Frick, Henry Clay. Eagle Rock Papers. Frick Collection and Archives, New York.

Gardner, Isabella Stewart, and John Lowell Gardner. Papers. Isabella Stewart
    Gardner Museum and Archives, Boston.

Johnson, Francis Benjamin. Photographs of Anderson House (1910). Society of
    the Cincinnati, Washington, DC.

Jones, Leslie. Photographs (1934–1956). Boston Public Library.

Laws, Amelia Nyasa. Papers related to Mrs. Ellen Frances Evans. Library &
    Special Collections, University of Aberdeen, Scotland.

Marsh, Daniel L. Papers. Howard Gotlieb Archival Research Center, Boston
    University.

National Periodical Collection. Bibliothèque nationale de France, Paris.

Olmsted Associates. Drawings for Project 1314, Anderson Estate Land Use
    Study, Brookline. Frederick Law Olmsted National Historic Site
    Archives, Brookline, MA.

Olmsted Brothers. Photographs of Project 300, Anderson Italian Garden,
    Brookline. Frederick Law Olmsted National Historic Site Archives,
    Brookline, MA.

Olmsted, Frederick Law. Drawings for Project 676, N. L. Anderson House,
    Washington, DC. Frederick Law Olmsted National Historic Site
    Archives, Brookline, MA.

Paris map collection. Bibliothèque historique de la Ville de Paris.

Perkins, George Hamilton. Papers (Navy League Collection). Manuscript Division, Library of Congress.

Records of Foreign Service Posts. Letterbooks. Vol. 61, Brussels (1912); vol. 59, Tokyo (1913). Record Group 84. National Archives and Records Administration, College Park, MD.

Records of Naval Districts and Shore Establishments, 1784–2000. Real Estate Files (1940–1954). Record Group 181, identifier 4489662. National Archives and Records Administration, Waltham, MA.

Taft, William Howard. Autograph letters. Manuscript File Collection. Howard Gotlieb Archival Research Center, Boston University.

———. Presidential Papers. Manuscript Division, Library of Congress.

Winsor School. Archives and memorabilia. Boston, MA.

Archival Film

VanDyk MacBride Color Home Movies of the Larz Anderson Estate, Brookline, Massachusetts, ca. 1937. (Courtesy of Duncan Finlayson.)

Interviews

Brintnall, Isabel (Perkins family), interview by the author at The Boxlet, 25 September 2011.

Hamilton, Edward (played squash on the Anderson court in the 1960s and 1970s), in conversation with the author in Washington, DC, 7 May 2015.

Harper, Reverend Charles H. (met Eleanor Wilbur Pomeroy, Isabel Anderson's literary assistant, in 1966), telephone interview by the author, 5 January 2016.

Jones, Mrs. Marion† (worker at The Box and The Boxlet during Isabel Anderson's lifetime), telephone interview by the author, 15 December 2010.

Kennedy, Maryjane (met Isabel Anderson as a child), interview by the author at the Arts Club of Washington, 24 April 2011.

Lamere, Robert K. (staff attorney in the Office of the Massachusetts Attorney General 1948–1949), telephone interview by the author, 1 November 2014.

Phillips, Mark (Perkins family), interview by the author at The Box, 15 August 2011.

Steele, Sheldon (executive director of the Larz Anderson Auto Museum), in conversation with the author in Brookline, MA, 13 March 2013.

Works Cited

Adams, Henry. 1893. "Nicholas Longworth Anderson [Obituary]." *Register of Members of the Society of Sons of the Revolution in the District of Columbia.* Washington, DC: Gibson Bros.

———. 1930. *Letters of Henry Adams (1858–1891).* Edited by Worthington Chauncey Ford. Boston: Houghton Mifflin.

———. 1938. *Letters of Henry Adams (1892–1918).* Edited by Worthington Chauncey Ford. Boston: Houghton Mifflin.

———. 1982. *The Letters of Henry Adams.* Edited by J. C. Levenson, Ernest Samuels, Charles Vandersee, and Viola Hopkins Winner. Vol. 3, *1886–1892.* Cambridge, MA: Harvard University Press.

Adams, Marian Hooper. 1936. *The Letters of Mrs. Henry Adams 1865–1883.* Edited by Ward Thoron. Boston: Little, Brown.

Alden, Carroll Storrs. 1914. *George Hamilton Perkins, Commodore, U.S.N.: His Life and Letters.* Boston: Houghton Mifflin.

Allen, Cameron. 2012. *The History of the American Pro-Cathedral, Church of the Holy Trinity, Paris (1815–1980).* Bloomington, IN: iUniverse. Kindle edition.

American Mercury. 1937. Notice of Isabel Anderson, *Zigzagging in the South Seas.* Check List. May, xi.

Anderson, Elizabeth Coles Kilgour. [1943?]. *Letters of Mrs. Nicholas Longworth Anderson to Her Son Larz Anderson.* Edited by Isabel Anderson. Bound carbon copy typescript. Anderson Collection. Society of the Cincinnati.

Anderson, Isabel. 1909a. "A Japanese Garden in America." *House and Garden* 16 (3): 90–91.

———. 1909b. "Home Journal, 1909." Box 11. Larz and Isabel Anderson Collection. Howard Gotlieb Archival Research Center, Boston University.

———. 1909c. *The Great Sea Horse.* Boston: Little, Brown.

———. 1910–1911. *Captain Ginger aboard the Geez Whiz; Captain Ginger Goes Traveling; Captain Ginger's Eater of Dreams; Captain Ginger's Fairy; Captain Ginger's Playmates;* and *Captain Ginger's Sun Boy.* Boston: C. M. Clark.

———. 1914a. *Everyboy, and Other Plays for Children.* New York: Shakespeare Press.

———. 1914b. *The Spell of Japan.* Boston: Page.

———. 1917a. *Odd Corners.* New York: Dodd, Mead.

———. 1917b. *The Spell of Belgium.* Boston: Page.

———. 1918. *Zigzagging.* Boston: Houghton Mifflin.

———. 1920a. *Presidents and Pies: Life in Washington, 1897–1919.* Boston: Houghton Mifflin.

———. 1920b. *Topsy Turvy and the Gold Star.* Boston: privately printed.

———. 1922. *Polly the Pagan: Her Lost Love Letters.* Boston: Page.

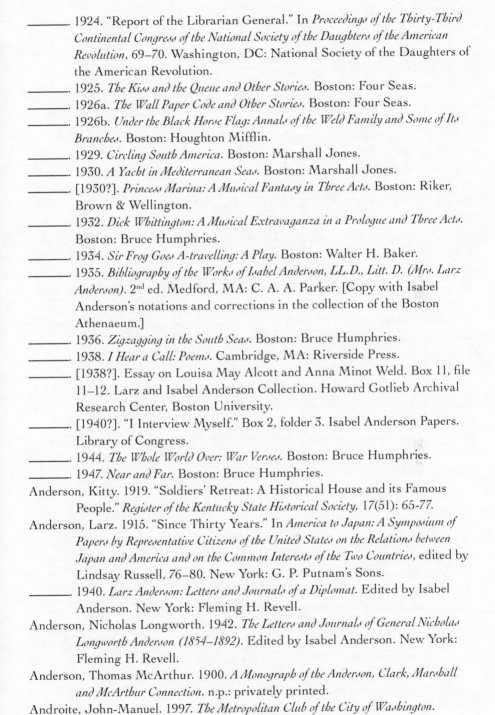

———. 1924. "Report of the Librarian General." In *Proceedings of the Thirty-Third Continental Congress of the National Society of the Daughters of the American Revolution*, 69–70. Washington, DC: National Society of the Daughters of the American Revolution.

———. 1925. *The Kiss and the Queue and Other Stories*. Boston: Four Seas.

———. 1926a. *The Wall Paper Code and Other Stories*. Boston: Four Seas.

———. 1926b. *Under the Black Horse Flag: Annals of the Weld Family and Some of Its Branches*. Boston: Houghton Mifflin.

———. 1929. *Circling South America*. Boston: Marshall Jones.

———. 1930. *A Yacht in Mediterranean Seas*. Boston: Marshall Jones.

———. [1930?]. *Princess Marina: A Musical Fantasy in Three Acts*. Boston: Riker, Brown & Wellington.

———. 1932. *Dick Whittington: A Musical Extravaganza in a Prologue and Three Acts*. Boston: Bruce Humphries.

———. 1934. *Sir Frog Goes A-travelling: A Play*. Boston: Walter H. Baker.

———. 1935. *Bibliography of the Works of Isabel Anderson, LL.D., Litt. D. (Mrs. Larz Anderson)*. 2nd ed. Medford, MA: C. A. A. Parker. [Copy with Isabel Anderson's notations and corrections in the collection of the Boston Athenaeum.]

———. 1936. *Zigzagging in the South Seas*. Boston: Bruce Humphries.

———. 1938. *I Hear a Call: Poems*. Cambridge, MA: Riverside Press.

———. [1938?]. Essay on Louisa May Alcott and Anna Minot Weld. Box 11, file 11–12. Larz and Isabel Anderson Collection. Howard Gotlieb Archival Research Center, Boston University.

———. [1940?]. "I Interview Myself." Box 2, folder 3. Isabel Anderson Papers. Library of Congress.

———. 1944. *The Whole World Over: War Verses*. Boston: Bruce Humphries.

———. 1947. *Near and Far*. Boston: Bruce Humphries.

Anderson, Kitty. 1919. "Soldiers' Retreat: A Historical House and its Famous People." *Register of the Kentucky State Historical Society*, 17(51): 65-77.

Anderson, Larz. 1915. "Since Thirty Years." In *America to Japan: A Symposium of Papers by Representative Citizens of the United States on the Relations between Japan and America and on the Common Interests of the Two Countries*, edited by Lindsay Russell, 76–80. New York: G. P. Putnam's Sons.

———. 1940. *Larz Anderson: Letters and Journals of a Diplomat*. Edited by Isabel Anderson. New York: Fleming H. Revell.

Anderson, Nicholas Longworth. 1942. *The Letters and Journals of General Nicholas Longworth Anderson (1854–1892)*. Edited by Isabel Anderson. New York: Fleming H. Revell.

Anderson, Thomas McArthur. 1900. *A Monograph of the Anderson, Clark, Marshall and McArthur Connection*. n.p.: privately printed.

Androite, John-Manuel. 1997. *The Metropolitan Club of the City of Washington*. Washington, DC: Metropolitan Club.

Banks, Charles Edward. (1930) 1979. *The Planters of the Commonwealth: A Study of the Emigrants and Emigration in Colonial Times (1620–1640)*. Reprint, Baltimore: Genealogical Publishing.

Bates, Esther Willard. 1912. *Pageants and Pageantry*. New York: Ginn.

Beebe, Lucius. 1966. *The Big Spenders: The Epic Story of the Rich Rich, the Grandees of America and the Magnificoes, and How They Spent Their Fortunes*. Edinburg, VA: Axios.

Belknap, George E. 1901. *Letters of Capt. Geo. Hamilton Perkins, U.S.N., Also, A Sketch of His Life*. 2nd ed. Concord, NH: Rumford Press.

Benham, Edith. 1913. *Ships of the United States Navy and Their Sponsors, 1797–1913*. Norwood, MA: Plimpton Press (privately printed).

Benton, Nicholas. 2004. *The Seven Weld Brothers: 1800–2000*. New York: iUniverse.

Betts, Kathleen. 1995. "Ambassador Larz Anderson: The Patriotic Collector." *The 40th Annual Washington Antiques Show Catalogue*. Washington, DC.

Bottin. 1851. *Correspondance entre les numéros nouveaux et les anciens (y compris les rues prolongées et reunites)*. Paris: L'almanach-Bottin du commerce de Paris.

Buxton, Willis G. 1933. *History, Boscawen-Webster, Fifty Years: 1883–1933*. Penacook, NH: W. B. Ranny.

Carson, Gerald. 1983. *The Dentist and the Empress: The Adventures of Dr. Tom Evans in Gas-Lit Paris*. Boston: Houghton Mifflin. Cheney, Ednah, ed. (1889) 1995. *Louisa May Alcott: Life, Letters, and Journals*. Boston: Roberts Brothers. Reprint, New York: Gramercy Books.

Cochran, Joseph Wilson. 1931. *Friendly Adventures: A Chronicle of the American Church of Paris (1857–1931)*. Paris: Brentano's.

Commission of Fine Arts. 1973. *Massachusetts Avenue Architecture*. Vol. 1, *Northwest Washington, District of Columbia*. Washington, DC: Government Printing Office.

Coolidge, John Gardner. 1924. *Random Letters from Many Countries*. Boston: Marshall Jones.

Coué, Émile. 1922. *Self Mastery through Conscious Autosuggestion*. New York: Malkan.

Crosby, Katherine K. 1917. "Contemporary Writers and Their Work: A Series of Autobiographical Letters. Katherine K. Crosby." *Editor* 15 (1): 352–53.

Dahlgren, Madeleine Vinton. 1873. *Etiquette of Social Life in Washington*. Lancaster, PA: Inquirer Printing and Publishing.

Del Tredici, Peter. 2006. "From Temple to Terrace: The Remarkable Journey of the Oldest Bonsai in America." *Arnoldia* 64 (2–3): 2–30.

Downing, Andrew Jackson. 1856. *A Treatise on the Theory and Practice of Landscape Gardening*. 4th ed. New York: C. M. Saxton.

Eliot, Samuel Atkins, ed. 1913. *Biographical History of Massachusetts*. Vol. 2. Boston: Massachusetts Biographical Society.

Elliott, Maud Howe. 1909. *Roma Beata: Letters from the Eternal City*. Boston: Little, Brown.

———. 1923. *Three Generations*. Boston: Little, Brown.

_____. 1930. *John Elliott: The Story of an Artist*. Boston: Houghton Mifflin.

_____. 1944. *This Was My Newport*. Cambridge, MA: Marshall Jones.

Feree, Barr. 1904. *American Estates and Gardens*. New York: Munn.

Fire Commissioner. 1902. *Report of the Fire Commissioner of Brookline, Massachusetts, for the Year Ending January 31, 1902*. Brookline, MA: Riverdale Press.

First Naval District. 1951. "Report on Condition and Estimate of Costs for Conversion of Larz Anderson Property, Brookline, Massachusetts for Use as Office Space for Supervising Inspector of Naval Materials, First Naval District." Records of Naval Districts and Shore Establishments, 1784–2000. Real Estate Files (1940–1954). Record Group 181, identifier 4489662. National Archives and Records Administration, Waltham, MA.

Gentile, Richard H. 1999. "Larz Anderson (15 Aug. 1866–13 Apr. 1937)." In *American National Biography*, vol. 1, 463–64. New York: Oxford University Press.

Gibson, Hugh. 1917. *A Journal from Our Legation in Belgium*. New York: Grosset & Dunlap.

Gilmour, David. 2003. *Curzon: Imperial Statesman*. New York: Farrar, Strauss and Giroux.

Gooder, Jean. 1995. "A Brief Chronology of Henry Adams' Life." In *The Education of Henry Adams*, edited by Jean Gooder. New York: Penguin.

Gopnik, Adam. 2008. "The Back of the World: The Troubling Genius of G. K. Chesterton." *New Yorker Magazine*, July 7. Accessed 3 May 2015 on newyorker.com.

Green, William S., Dudley W. Orr, and Robert H. Reno. 1949. *Proceedings to Determine the Domicile of Isabel Perkins Anderson at the Time of Her Death Solely for Death Tax Purposes*. Concord, NH. Box 3, file 2, Proceedings 1949 (2 of 2). Isabel Anderson Papers. Library of Congress.

Grinnell, Nancy Whipple. 2014. *Carrying the Torch: Maud Howe Elliott and the American Renaissance*. Hanover, NH: University Press of New England.

Gutheim, Frederick, and Antoinette J. Lee. 2006. *Worthy of the Nation: Washington, D.C., from L'Enfant to the National Capital Planning Commission*. 2nd ed. Baltimore: Johns Hopkins University Press.

Hall, Florence Howe. 1906. *Social Usages at Washington*. New York: Harper & Brothers.

Hatch, Alden. 1973. *The Lodges of Massachusetts*. New York: Hawthorn Books.

Helm, Edith Benham. 1954. *The Captains and the Kings*. New York: G. P. Putnam's Sons.

Hill, David Jayne. 1918. *Impressions of the Kaiser*. New York: Harper & Brothers.

Hillairet, Jacques. 1985. *Dictionnaire historique des rues de Paris*. 9th ed. 2 vols. Paris: Les Éditions de Minuit.

Hodermarsky, Elisabeth. 2010. "A Second Paradise: John La Farge's Search for the Sublime in the Twilight of the American Landscape Movement." In *John La Farge's Second Paradise: Voyages in the South Seas, 1890–1891*, edited by Elisabeth Hodermarsky. New Haven: Yale University Press.

Hopkins, Alfred. 1902. "Farm Barns." *Architectural Review* 9 (9): 237–48.

Hughes, Nathaniel Cheairs, Jr. 2008. *Yale's Confederates.* Knoxville: University of Kentucky Press.

Hume, Edgar Erskine. 1938. *Captain Larz Anderson.* Richmond, VA: The Society of the Cincinnati in the State of Virginia.

Hunter, Robert. 1873. *History of the Missions of the Free Church of Scotland in India and Africa.* London: T. Nelson and Sons.

Kenworthy, Richard G. 1991. "Bringing the World to Brookline: The Gardens of Larz and Isabel Anderson." *Journal of Garden History* 11 (4): 224–41.

Kerényi, Karl. 1976. *Dionysos: Archetypal Image of Indestructible Life.* Princeton, NJ: Princeton University Press.

King, Basil. 1919. *The Abolishing of Death.* New York: Cosmopolitan.

Knoedler. 1910. *John Elliott: Exhibition and Private Sale of His Original Pastel Drawings for the Illustrations of* The Great Sea Horse, *by Isabel Anderson.* New York: M. Knoedler & Co.

Landon-Lane, John, and Hugh Rockoff. 2004. "Monetary Policy and Regional Interest Rates in the United States, 1880–2002." Working paper no. 10924. Cambridge, MA: National Bureau of Economic Research.

Lazare, Félix, and Louis Lazare. 1855. *Dictionnaire administratif et historique de Paris et monuments de Paris.* 2nd ed. Paris: Bureau de la Revue Municipale.

Lee, Roger I. 1956. *The Happy Life of a Doctor.* Boston: Little, Brown.

Leopold, Richard W. 1940. "Review of Larz Anderson: Letters and Journals of a Diplomat, by Isabel Anderson." *New England Quarterly* 13 (4): 731–33.

Levin, H. 1897. *The Lawyers and Lawmakers of Kentucky.* Chicago: Lewis.

Lewis, Arnold. 1982. *American Country Houses of the Gilded Age: Sheldon's "Artistic Country-Seats."* New York: Dover.

Lewis, Arnold, James Turner, and Steven McQuillin, eds. 1987. *The Opulent Interiors of the Gilded Age: All 203 Photographs from "Artistic Houses."* New York: Dover.

Lewis, Colin. 2006. "Rejuvenating and Reshaping the Larz Anderson Chabo-hibas." *Arnoldia* 64 (2–3): 56–64.

Licopoli, Felice Diego. 2013. *Strisce di luna.* Reggio, Calabria: Città del Sole Edizioni.

Maxwell, Henry. 1905. "Flowers from Frost to Frost." *Country Life in America,* March, 553–56.

Miller, Wilhelm. 1905. "An 'Italian Garden' That Is Full of Flowers." *Country Life in America,* March, 485–92.

Morris, George Maurice, et al. [1949]. *Arbitration Proceedings to Determine the Domicil of Isabel Anderson for Death Tax Purposes.* Box 3, file 2, Proceedings 1949 (2 of 2). Isabel Anderson Papers. Library of Congress.

Moskey, Skip [Stephen T. Moskey]. 2013. *Reinterpreting Larz Anderson Park: A Docent Manual and Historical Resource Guide.* Brookline, MA: Town of Brookline Department of Parks and Open Space.

Mowry, George E. 1941. "Review of Larz Anderson: Letters and Journals of a Diplomat." *Mississippi Valley Historical Review* 28 (1): 116–17.

Mumford, Louis. 1971. *The Brown Decades: A Study of the Arts in America, 1865–1895*. 2nd ed. New York: Dover.

NEHGS (New England Historic Genealogical Society). 1891. "William Fletcher Weld." In *New England Historical and Genealogical Register*, vol. 45, 115–17. Boston: NEHGS.

Nutting, Wallace. 1936. *Wallace Nutting's Biography*. Framingham, MA: Old America.

NYYC (New York Yacht Club). 1901. *New York Yacht Club, 1901*. [Yearbook.] New York: Knickerbocker Press.

_____. 1906. *New York Yacht Club, 1906*. [Yearbook]. New York: Knickerbocker Press.

O'Toole, Patricia. 2006. *The Five of Hearts: An Intimate Portrait of Henry Adams and His Friends, 1880–1918*. New York: Simon & Schuster.

Platt, Charles A. 1893. *Italian Gardens*. New York: Harper & Brothers.

Porges, Max. 1933. "Reduction of Weight by Dehydration." *British Journal of Physical Medicine* 8 (9).

Portrait Gallery. 2006. "Portrait Gallery of the Larz Anderson Collection: 1913–2005." *Arnoldia* 64 (2–3): 31–55.

Proctor, Edward O., et al. 1949. *Arbitration Proceedings to Determine the Domicil of the Late Isabel Anderson at the Time of Her Death, November 3, 1948: Brief in Behalf of the Commonwealth of Massachusetts*. Boston: Addison C. Getchell & Son. Box 3, file 1, Proceedings 1949 (1 of 2). Isabel Anderson Papers. Library of Congress.

"Reconstruction of the Whereabouts of Larz and Isabel Anderson, 1897–1937." Box 2, folder 9, exhibit NH-37. Isabel Anderson Papers. Library of Congress.

"Record of Mrs. Larz Andersons' Whereabouts April 20, 1937, to November 3, 1948." Box 1, folder 3, exhibit M-32. Isabel Anderson Papers. Library of Congress.

Schneider, Dorothy, and Carl J. Schneider. 1991. *Into the Breach: American Women Overseas in World War I*. New York: Viking Penguin.

Schmidt, William. 1892. *The Flowing Bowl: When and What to Drink*. New York: Charles L. Webster.

Schulz, Emily. 2005. "In Stone and Steel: The Construction of Anderson House." *Cincinnati Fourteen* 41 (2): 18–31.

Schwartz, Abby S. 1988. *Nicholas Longworth: Art Patron of Cincinnati*. Cincinnati: Taft Museum.

Seale, William. 2013. *The Imperial Season: America's Capital in the Time of the First Ambassadors, 1893–1918*. Washington, DC: Smithsonian Books.

Shettleworth, Earle G., Jr. 2008. "Brief Biographies of American Architects Who Died between 1897 and 1947." Unpublished manuscript. Accessed 8 September 2015 on sah.org.

Smith, F. Hopkinson. 1900. *A White Umbrella in Mexico*. Boston: Houghton, Mifflin.

Smithsonian. 1903. *Annual Report of the Board of Regents of the Smithsonian Institution (For the Year Ending June 30, 1902)*. Washington, DC: Government Printing Office.

Sotheby's. 1986. *Magnificent Jewelry: Property from the Collection of Captain and Mrs. Larz Anderson [et al.]*. [Auction catalogue for sale on April 16, 1986.] New York: Sotheby's.

Stearns, Ezra S., William F. Whitcher, and Edward E. Parker, eds. 1908. *Genealogical and Family History of the State of New Hampshire*. New York: Lewis.

Stenographic Records I–XI (27–28 June 1949). [Sworn Testimony of Witnesses.] Board of Arbitration to Determine Question of Domicile of Isabel Anderson. Box 3, folders 3–6; box 4, folders 1–6. Isabel Anderson Papers. Library of Congress.

Stern, Madeline B. 1996. *Louisa May Alcott: A Biography*. New York: Random House.

Stern, Madeline B., and Daniel Shealy, eds. 1993. *The Lost Stories of Louisa May Alcott*. New York: Citadel Press.

Stetson, Richard P. 1967. "Memorial: Roger Irving Lee, M.D." *Transactions of the American Clinical and Climatological Association* 78: xlvii–xlix.

Swanberg, W. A. 1957. *First Blood: The Story of Fort Sumter*. New York: Charles Scribner's Sons.

Taliaferro, John. 2013. *All the Great Prizes: The Life of John Hay, from Lincoln to Roosevelt*. New York: Simon & Schuster.

Tharp, Louise Hall. 1965. *Mrs. Jack: A Biography of Isabella Stewart Gardner*. New York: Congdon & Weed.

Twain, Mark. 1906. *A Horse's Tale*. New York: Harper & Brothers.

Unger, Harlow G. 2007. "Langdell, Christopher Columbus." *Encyclopedia of American Education*. 3rd ed. New York: Facts On File.

US Senate. 1913. *Campaign Contributions: Testimony before a Subcommittee of the Committee on Privileges and Elections, United States Senate (62nd Congress, Third Session)*. Vol. 1. Washington, DC: Government Printing Office.

Warner, Langdon. 1911. "The Weld Bequest." *Boston Museum of Fine Arts Bulletin* 9 (52): 34–36.

Warne, Frederick. 1866. *Warne's Picture Book*. London: Frederick Warne. Box 13. Larz and Isabel Anderson Collection (1895–1948). Howard Gotlieb Archival Research Center, Boston University.

Watt, George. 1903. *Indian Art at Delhi, 1903: Being the Official Catalogue of the Delhi Exhibition, 1902–1903*. Calcutta: Superintendent of Government Printing.

Waugh, William F. 1904. *The Houseboat Book: The Log of a Cruise from Chicago to New Orleans*. Chicago: Clinic Publishing.

West, Nigel. 2010. *Historical Dictionary of Naval Intelligence*. Lanham, MD: Scarecrow Press.

Wharton, Edith. (1904) 1988. *Italian Villas and Their Gardens*. Reprint, New York: Da Capo Press.

_____. 1919. *Fighting France, from Dunkerque to Belfort.* New York: Charles
    Scribner's Sons.

Wiles, Stephanie. 1993. "The American Muralist H. Siddons Mowbray and His
    Drawings for the Larz Anderson House." *Master Drawings* 31 (10): 21–34.

Winsor School. 1910. "Register of Classes, 1893. Anderson, Mrs. L. (Isabel Weld
    Perkins)." *Winsor School Graduate Club Register.* Boston: Winsor School.

_____. n.d. *Overseas War Records of the Winsor School: 1914–1919.* Boston: Winsor
    School Graduate Club. Box 11. Larz and Isabel Anderson Collection (1895–
    1948). Howard Gotlieb Archival Research Center, Boston University.

Wyman, Donald. 1951. "The Larz Anderson Collection of Japanese Dwarf
    Trees." *Arnoldia* 11 (4): 29–35.

Ye Andersons. 1908. "Ye Andersons of Virginia and Some of Their Descendants,
    Bye One of Ye Family." *"Old Northwest" Genealogical Quarterly* (Columbus,
    OH) 11: 231–88.

Standard Reference Works

Baedeker, K. 1897. *Italy: Handbook for Travellers; Second Part, Central Italy and Rome.*
    12th ed. Leipsig: Karl Baedeker.

Beeson, Harvey C. 1908. *Beeson's Marine Directory of the Northwestern Lakes.*
    Chicago: Beeson-Payne.

Boardman, Gerald. 1987. *The Concise Oxford Companion to American Theater.* New
    York: Oxford University Press.

Burke, Arthur Meredyth. (1908) 2008. *The Prominent Families of the United States of
    America.* Reprint, Baltimore: Genealogical Publishing.

Carley, Rachel. 2001. *A Guide to the Biltmore Estate.* Ashville, NC: The Biltmore
    Company.

Curl, James Stevens. 2006. *Oxford Dictionary of Architecture and Landscape
    Architecture.* 2nd ed. Oxford: Oxford University Press.

Els, David, et al. 1994. *The National Gardening Association Dictionary of Horticulture.*
    New York: Viking Penguin.

Federal Writers' Project. 1937. *Washington City and Capital.* Washington, DC:
    Government Printing Office.

_____. (1937) 1983. *The WPA Guide to Massachusetts.* Reprint, New York:
    Pantheon Books.

Ferris, Robert G., ed. 1977. *The Presidents.* Rev. ed. Washington, DC: National
    Park Service.

Fleming, John, et al. 1999. *Penguin Dictionary of Architecture and Landscape
    Architecture.* 5th ed. London: Penguin Paperbacks.

Fleming, John, and Hugh Honour. 1977. *Dictionary of the Decorative Arts.* New
    York: Harper & Row.

Goode, James M. 2003. *Capital Losses: A Cultural History of Washington's Destroyed
    Buildings.* 2nd ed. Washington, DC: Smithsonian Books.

Harris, Cyril M., ed. 1977. *Illustrated Dictionary of Historic Architecture.* New York: Dover.

Ide, Evan P. 2004. *Larz Anderson Park.* Charleston, SC: Arcadia Publishing.

Little, Nina Fletcher. 1949. *Some Old Brookline Houses (Built in This Massachusetts Town before 1825 and Still Standing in 1948).* Brookline, MA: Brookline Historical Society.

Lucie-Smith, Edward. 1984. *The Thames and Hudson Dictionary of Art Terms.* London: Thames and Hudson.

McAlester, Virginia, and Lee McAlester. 1984. *A Field Guide to American Houses.* New York: Alfred A. Knopf.

Ochsner, Jeffrey Karl. 1984. *H.H. Richardson: Complete Architectural Works.* Cambridge, MA: MIT Press.

Rakaia.co.uk. 2013. "A History of the British India Steam Navigation Company Limited." Accessed October 9.

Rogers, Gregory Parker. 2010. *Cincinnati's Hyde Park.* Charleston, SC: History Press.

Sifakis, Stewart. 1988. *Who Was Who in the Civil War.* New York: Facts on File.

Sloan's. 2000. *Deaccessioned Property from the Society of the Cincinnati, Washington, D.C.* [Auction catalogue for sale 908 on December 5, 2000.] North Bethesda, MD: Sloan's Auctioneers & Appraisers.

Southworth, Susan, and Michael Southworth. 1992. *AIA Guide to Boston.* 2nd ed. Guilford, CT: Globe Pequot Press.

United States Army. 1989. *American Military History.* Army Historical Series. Washington, DC: Center of Military History.

Weeks, Christopher. 1994. *AIA Guide to the Architecture of Washington, D.C.* 3rd ed. Baltimore: Johns Hopkins University Press.

Wharton, Edith. (1904) 1988. *Italian Villas and Their Gardens.* New York: Century Company. Reprint with a new introduction by Arthur Ross et al., New York: Da Capo Press.

Williams. *Williams City Directory (1861–1900).* Cincinnati: C. S. Williams.

Endnotes

Many of the thirty-eight leather-bound volumes of Larz Anderson's journals, which he gathered under the collective title *Some Scraps*, include multiple pagination runs that begin with 1. Some volumes were given a unified numbering system of folio numbers handwritten in pencil by Isabel's editorial assistants. The endnotes cite the original handwritten folio number, noted with an *f*, when these are available. Otherwise, page references are to the typed page numbers, even if those numbers repeat within the same volume.

All quotations from archival materials preserve antiquated or idiosyncratic spelling, punctuation, and capitalization, including *n't* as a stand-alone contraction for *not* (e.g., "I would n't") and *an* in front of words beginning with *h* (e.g., "an hotel" or "an host").

Isabel Anderson is referenced in the notes only as *Anderson*. Other authors named Anderson are further identified with a first initial.

Prologue

1. "Medical Records of Mrs. Anderson," box 1, folder 2, exhibit M–10, Isabel Anderson Papers, Library of Congress. The quote on death comes from Anderson, "I Interview Myself," 16.

Chapter 1

1. Anderson, *Black Horse Flag*, 169; T. Anderson, *A Monograph*, 3.
2. *Ye Andersons*, 235.
3. These and other details of Dick's life come from T. Anderson, *A Monograph*, 7–10; Hume, *Captain Larz Anderson*, 3–4.
4. Anderson, *Black Horse Flag*, 177; K. Anderson, "Soldier's Retreat," 68.
5. T. Anderson, *A Monograph*, 5.
6. Levin, *Lawyers and Lawmakers of Kentucky*, 240.
7. "Cincinnati's Rich Men," *New York Times*, 10 December 1880.
8. Schwartz, *Nicholas Longworth*, 1988.
9. "Declined," *Cleveland Morning Leader*, 1 October 1860.

[10]   N. Anderson, *General Nicholas Longworth Anderson*, 7–19.

[11]   Ibid., 21.

[12]   N. Anderson, "French Missionaries in the West."

[13]   Adams, "Nicholas Longworth Anderson," 62.

[14]   N. Anderson, *General Nicholas Longworth Anderson*, 120–29.

[15]   Anderson, *Black Horse Flag*, 181–83.

[16]   N. Anderson, *General Nicholas Longworth Anderson*, 190.

[17]   Hillairet, *Dictionnaire historique des rues de Paris*, vol. 2, 96–97; Lazare, *Dictionnaire administratif et historique*, 511; Bottin, *Correspondance entre les numéros nouveaux et les anciens*, 33.

[18]   Report of Larz Anderson's birth, US consulate, Paris, 20 September 1866, copy from register H, p. 26, registration no. 16820, Anderson Collection, Society of the Cincinnati, Washington, DC.

[19]   Taliaferro, *All the Great Prizes*, 101.

[20]   Cochran, *Friendly Adventures*, 79–80; Allen, *History of the American Pro-Cathedral*, 642.

[21]   L. Anderson, *Letters and Journals of a Diplomat*, 215; E. Anderson, *Letters of Mrs. Nicholas Longworth Anderson*, 514.

[22]   Carson, *The Dentist and the Empress*.

[23]   N. Anderson, *General Nicholas Longworth Anderson*, 191.

[24]   In 1930 Larz incorrectly identified the house number as 124. L. Anderson, *Tours and Detours in 1930*, 61–62.

[25]   N. Anderson, *General Nicholas Longworth Anderson*, 192.

[26]   "The Exposition," *Cincinnati Daily Gazette*, 15 September 1874.

[27]   "The Mt. Vernon Party," *Cincinnati Daily Enquirer*, 11 February 1876.

[28]   "Religious," *Cincinnati Daily Gazette*, 10 November 1877.

[29]   "Nicholas Longworth Anderson Scrapbook," Anderson Collection, Society of the Cincinnati.

[30]   Warne, *Warne's Picture Book*.

[31]   L. Anderson, *Letters and Journals of a Diplomat*, 18–19.

[32]   Hillairet, *Dictionnaire historique des rues de Paris*, vol. 1, 555–56; Lazare, *Dictionnaire administratif et historique*, 162.

[33]   L. Anderson, *More Shreds and Patches*, 142f.

[34]   L. Anderson, *Letters and Journals of a Diplomat*, 17.

[35]   L. Anderson, *A Year of Shreds and Patches*, 152f.

[36]   Ibid., 164f.

[37]   "Our Winter Saratoga," *Washington Post*, 2 May 1880, 7.

[38]   M. Adams, *Letters of Mrs. Henry Adams*, 442.

[39]   Landon-Lane et al., "Monetary Policy and Regional Interest Rates."

[40]   "Handsome Improvements on K Street," *Washington Evening Star*, 24 October 1881.

[41]   Ibid.

[42]   N. Anderson, *General Nicholas Longworth Anderson*, 216.

[43]   Frederick Law Olmsted, drawings for Project 676, N. L. Anderson House, Frederick Law Olmsted National Historic Site Archives.

44   E. Anderson, *Letters of Mrs. Nicholas Longworth Anderson*, 38.
45   Letter dated November 5, 1882, M. Adams, *Letters of Mrs. Henry Adams*, 395.
46   E. Anderson, *Letters of Mrs. Nicholas Longworth Anderson*, 90.
47   N. Anderson, *General Nicholas Longworth Anderson*, 259.
48   M. Adams, *Letters of Mrs. Henry Adams*, 413.
49   L. Anderson, *Africa Rediscovered by North Americans—First Part*, 10.
50   L. Anderson, *Letters and Journals of a Diplomat*, 20.
51   "The Emerson Institute: An Attractive Programme and a Full List of Prizes," *Washington Post*, 21 June 1882, 4.
52   N. Anderson, *General Nicholas Longworth Anderson*, 199.
53   Ibid., 223.
54   E. Anderson, *Letters of Mrs. Nicholas Longworth Anderson*, 304.
55   Ibid., 505.
56   L. Anderson, report card, Middle Class, Fall Term, 1882, Archives of Phillips Exeter Academy; L. Anderson, Report of Scholarship, Deportment and Attendance, 24 June 1884, Archives of Phillips Exeter Academy.
57   N. Anderson, *General Nicholas Longworth Anderson*, 223.
58   L. Anderson, *A Year of Shreds and Patches*, 165f.
59   E. Anderson, *Letters of Mrs. Nicholas Longworth Anderson*, 91.
60   N. Anderson, *General Nicholas Longworth Anderson*, 232.
61   Ibid., 239.
62   Ibid., 258.
63   Ibid., 244.
64   Ibid., 255.
65   L. Anderson, English themes.

Chapter 2

1   N. Anderson, *General Nicholas Longworth Anderson*, 273.
2   L. Anderson, *A Post Graduate Course around the World*, 2f.
3   Ibid., 3f.
4   Ibid., 5f.
5   L. Anderson, *Letters and Journals of a Diplomat*, 39.
6   Ibid.
7   L. Anderson, *A Post Graduate Course around the World*, 14–15f.
8   L. Anderson, *Letters and Journals of a Diplomat*, 40.
9   L. Anderson, *A Post Graduate Course around the World*, 18f.
10   L. Anderson, *Letters and Journals of a Diplomat*, 41.
11   Ibid., 42; Coolidge, *Random Letters*, 31.
12   L. Anderson, *A Post Graduate Course around the World*, 26f.
13   Ibid., 37f.
14   Warner, "The Weld Bequest," 34–26.
15   L. Anderson, *A Post Graduate Course around the World*, 70–71f.
16   L. Anderson, *Letters and Journals of a Diplomat*, 49–50.

[17] L. Anderson, *A Post Graduate Course around the World*, 76f.

[18] Ibid., 97f.

[19] L. Anderson, *Letters and Journals of a Diplomat*, 51.

[20] L. Anderson, *A Post Graduate Course around the World*, 139f.

[21] Coolidge, *Random Letters*, 45.

[22] L. Anderson, *Letters and Journals of a Diplomat*, 58–59.

[23] Hughes, *Yale's Confederates*, 70–71.

[24] L. Anderson, *Letters and Journals of a Diplomat*, 61; L. Anderson, *A Post Graduate Course around the World*, 196.

[25] L. Anderson, *Arcs in a Circle around the World*, 11.

[26] L. Anderson, *Letters and Journals of a Diplomat*, 68.

[27] L. Anderson, *Arcs in a Circle around the World*, 28.

[28] L. Anderson, *Letters and Journals of a Diplomat*, 65.

[29] Ibid., 68.

[30] Unger, "Langdell, Christopher Columbus."

[31] Nicholas Longworth Anderson to Sevellon Alden Brown, 28 June 1891, "Anderson, Larz," box 3, RG 59 (1797–1901), National Archives and Records Administration.

[32] "Appointed by the President," *Washington Post*, 22 July 1891, 2.

[33] L. Anderson, *Letters and Journals of a Diplomat*, 70.

[34] Ibid.

[35] Ibid., 75–79.

[36] Ibid., 75.

[37] L. Anderson, *Days in & out of London*, 88–89.

[38] Ibid., 122.

[39] Ibid., 54.

[40] L. Anderson, *Letters and Journals of a Diplomat*, 83.

[41] Ibid., 77.

[42] L. Anderson, *Days in & out of London*, 43.

[43] O'Toole, *The Five of Hearts*, 90–91.

[44] Hillairet, *Dictionnaire historique des rues de Paris*, vol. 1, 207. The address is now square de l'Avenue-Foch. Lizzie Cameron's house overlooking the Bois de Boulogne is still there.

[45] Hodermarsky, "A Second Paradise," 43.

[46] H. Adams, *Letters of Henry Adams*, 555.

[47] L. Anderson, *Days in & out of London*, 46.

[48] Ibid.

[49] Ibid., 64.

[50] Ibid., 65.

[51] Henry Adams to Elizabeth Cameron, London, 11 January 1892, in *Letters of Henry Adams (1892–1918)*, 1.

[52] H. Adams, *Letters of Henry Adams (1892–1918)*, 1n2.

[53] Henry Adams to Elizabeth Cameron, London, 15 January 1892, in *Letters of Henry Adams*, vol. 3, 602.

54   Ibid., 603.
55   L. Anderson, *Days in & out of London*, 98.
56   Elizabeth Anderson to Larz Anderson, 28 January 1883, in *Letters of Mrs. Nicholas Longworth Anderson*, 24.
57   L. Anderson, *Days in & out of London*, 98.
58   Ibid., 102–3.
59   E. Anderson, *Letters of Mrs. Nicholas Longworth Anderson*, 140; L. Anderson, *Letters and Journals of a Diplomat*, 97.
60   L. Anderson, *Letters and Journals of a Diplomat*, 97–98.
61   "Anderson, Larz," box 3, RG 59 (1797–1901), National Archives and Records Administration.
62   "Not to Succeed Minister Denby," *Washington Post*, 15 September 1894, 4.
63   "Countess Laurenius Now Mrs. [George Hare] Ford," *New York Times*, 26 August 1901.
64   John L. Gardner, Travel Diaries 1895, Archives of the Isabella Stewart Gardner Museum.
65   "Triple Lynching Bee. Citizens of Louisiana Hang Three Murderers. They Were All Italians," *Allegany County Reporter* (Wellsville, NY), 11 August 1896, 1.
66   Gentile, "Larz Anderson," 463.
67   L. Anderson, *Letters and Journals of a Diplomat*, 99.

Chapter 3

1   Banks, *Planters of the Commonwealth*, 96; Anderson, *Black Horse Flag*, 6.
2   Anderson, "I Interview Myself," 9.
3   Banks, *Planters of the Commonwealth*, 97; Anderson, *Black Horse Flag*, 89.
4   Early Perkins family history is from Eliot, *Biographical History of Massachusetts*.
5   Belknap, *Letters of Capt. Geo. Hamilton Perkins*, 8–9.
6   Ibid., 215.
7   Ibid., 207.
8   Benton, *Seven Weld Brothers*, xiv. See also NEHGS, "William Fletcher Weld."
9   "Disposition of William F. Weld's Estate," *New York Times*, 17 December 1881.
10   Sargent quote from Alden, *George Hamilton Perkins*, 284.
11   Anderson, *Black Horse Flag*, 161.
12   Buxton, *History, Boscawen-Webster*, 143.
13   Elliott, *This Was My Newport*, 243.
14   "The Late William F. Weld, from the Boston Herald, Dec. 8," *New York Times*, 11 December 1881. The date of Weld's death has been erroneously recorded by several sources as December 12, 1881; e.g., Benton, *Seven Weld Brothers*, 1.
15   "Disposition of William F. Weld's Estate," *New York Times*, 17 December 1881; "The Late William F. Weld, from the Boston Herald, Dec. 8," *New York Times*, 11 December 1881; "The Estate of William F. Weld, from the Philadelphia Ledger, Dec. 23," *New York Times*, 28 December 1881; "Dividing W.F. Weld's Estate," *New York Times*, 31 December 1881; "The Late Mr. Weld's Fortune," *New York Times*, 4 January 1882.

16   Details of bequests and trusts come from William Fletcher Weld's will, written on December 3, 1873, and its six codicils written between December 23, 1873, and October 11, 1881. Box 1, folder 7, exhibit M–42, Isabel Anderson Papers, Library of Congress.

17   Winsor School, "Register of Classes, 1893."

18   "Society Events of the Week," *New York Times*, 13 June 1897.

19   Elliott, *Three Generations*, 271.

20   Grinnell, *Carrying the Torch*, 97.

21   Elliott, *Three Generations*, 272.

22   Isabel's passport is preserved in "A Book of Memories, 1895–1913," box 1, Larz and Isabel Anderson Collection, Howard Gotlieb Archival Research Center.

23   Elliott, *Three Generations*, 273.

24   Ibid.

25   Elliott, *John Elliott*, 94.

26   Elliott, *Roma Beata*, 67.

27   Elliott, *Three Generations*, 282.

Chapter 4

1   L. Anderson, *Letters and Journals of a Diplomat*, 101.

2   Elliott, *John Elliott*, 94, 118.

3   Ibid., 119. In 2012, the painting was sold, unattributed to Elliott, at auction (no. 2615B) by Skinner's in Boston for $738. The painting was subsequently sold by the online art dealer, 1stdibs.com, for an undisclosed price, this time correctly attributed to Elliott.

4   L. Anderson, *Hop, Skip and Jump—First Part*, 13f.

5   Mary Bryant Pratt (1871–1956) was twice married. Her first marriage to Charles Francis Sprague ended when he died in 1891. She then married Edward Deshon Brandegee in 1904. She was known to family and friends as May and appears in this book as May Pratt, May Sprague, and May Brandegee.

6   L. Anderson, *Hop, Skip and Jump—First Part*, 13f.

7   Elliott, *John Elliott*, 119.

8   L. Anderson, *Letters and Journals of a Diplomat*, 122.

9   Anderson, *Polly the Pagan* [endpapers].

10   Anderson, "I Interview Myself," 5.

11   Anderson, *Polly the Pagan*, 53.

12   Ibid., 107.

13   "Latest Works of Fiction," *New York Times*, 1 October 1922, 22.

14   King, *The Abolishing of Death*.

15   L. Anderson, *Letters and Journals of a Diplomat*, 128; Anderson, *Polly the Pagan*, 88.

16   L. Anderson, *Letters and Journals of a Diplomat*, 137.

17 Ibid., 175.

18 "Graced by Fine Roses," *Washington Post*, 5 December 1896, 7.

19 Anderson, *Polly the Pagan*, 141.

20 E. Anderson, *Letters of Mrs. Nicholas Longworth Anderson*, 249.

21 L. Anderson, *Letters and Journals of a Diplomat*, 149.

22 Ibid., 150; Anderson, *Polly the Pagan*, 148–49.

23 L. Anderson, *Letters and Journals of a Diplomat*, 55.

24 "Wish to Get out of Office. A Secretary of Embassy Wants to Come Home to Get Married," *New York Times*, 25 March 1897.

25 "Offices and Office-Seekers," *Washington Post*, 27 March 1897, 6.

26 Gooder, "Brief Chronology of Henry Adams' Life," iii.

27 "An Exploit in Gayety," *Washington Post*, 17 January 1897, 20.

28 Fenway Court Guest Book, Isabella Stewart Gardner Museum and Archives.

29 E. Anderson, *Letters of Mrs. Nicholas Longworth Anderson*, 249.

30 "Lawn Fete in Tents," *Washington Post*, 26 May 1897, 7; "Two Noted Families Linked," *Boston Globe*, 11 June 1897, 1; "His Bride and Heiress," *Washington Post*, 11 June 1897, 7.

31 E. Anderson, *Letters of Mrs. Nicholas Longworth Anderson*, 250.

32 "Two Noted Families Linked," *Boston Globe*, 11 June 1897, 1.

33 Clipping file, *Town Topics*, 17 June 1897, Isabella Stewart Gardner Museum and Archives.

34 L. Anderson, *Roxana Rediviva*, 100.

35 Perkins family interviews conducted by the author.

36 L. Anderson, *Our Wedding Journey*, 4–5.

37 Ibid., 13.

38 L. Anderson, *Our Wedding Journey*, 12; "Summary of Historical Eruptions, 1750–Present," US Geologic Survey, Hawaiian Volcano Observatory.

39 "A Book of Memories, 1895–1913," box 1, Larz and Isabel Anderson Collection, Howard Gotlieb Archival Research Center.

40 L. Anderson, *Our Wedding Journey*, 15.

41 E. Anderson, *Letters of Mrs. Nicholas Longworth Anderson*, 264. Osame worked for Larz at the American embassy in Tokyo in 1913.

42 L. Anderson, *Our Wedding Journey*, 18.

43 Ibid., 31.

44 Ibid., 31–32.

45 Ibid., 34–35.

46 Anderson, "I Interview Myself," 9.

47 "Social and Personal," *Washington Post*, 16 February 1898, 7.

48 "In the Social World," *Washington Post*, 15 September 1895, 16. The Italian term *piano nobile*, literally "noble floor," referred to the floor of a house one level above ground level when that floor was the main entertaining space in the home. Anderson House has a *piano nobile*. The Anderson's country estate, Weld, did not.

49 L. Anderson, *Letters and Journals of a Diplomat*, 160.

50 Ibid., 162.

51   Twain, *A Horse's Tale*, 24.

52   E. Anderson, *Letters of Mrs. Nicholas Longworth Anderson*, 256.

53   Anderson, *Presidents and Pies*, 14; E. Anderson, *Letters of Mrs. Nicholas Longworth Anderson*, 256.

54   Anderson, *Presidents and Pies*, 17.

55   L. Anderson, *Letters and Journals of a Diplomat*, 170.

56   L. Anderson, *Our Wedding Journey*, 33.

57   Ibid., 2–3.

58   L. Anderson, *Journals, 1933–1936*, 41.

59   L. Anderson, *Our Wedding Journey*, 9.

60   Ibid., 6, 9–11.

61   Bhana Rutton's biographical details are from Hunter, *History of the Missions*, 273; L. Anderson, *Hop, Skip and Jump—Second Part*, 87f; L. Anderson, *A Year of Shreds and Patches*, 48f; L. Anderson, *Letters and Journals of a Diplomat*, 172–73n.

62   L. Anderson, *Our Wedding Journey*, 18–19.

63   The character of Lady Grantham in the PBS series "Downton Abbey" (2011–2016) was based in part on Mary Leiter.

64   Gilmour, *Curzon*, 141.

65   L. Anderson, *Our Wedding Journey*, 21; Sotheby's, *Magnificent Jewelry*, 283. When Sotheby's handled the sale of the brooch, which it called the Isabel Anderson Emerald, it described the piece of jewelry as "Formerly a turban clip, now mounted as a brooch, the central emerald of hexagonal shape measuring approximately 30.8 by 26.3 by 6.3 mm., framed by 24 old-mine diamonds, and topped by a briolette emerald drop amidst foliate scroll-work accented with old-mine and rose-cut diamonds and a briolette diamond, mounted in gold, brooch attachment detachable."

66   L. Anderson, *A Year of Shreds and Patches*, 92f.

67   Watt, *Indian Art at Delhi*, 491.

68   L. Anderson, *Our Wedding Journey*, 33.

69   Ibid. Larz eventually was offered one chance for national elected office. On June 4, 1916, Arthur E. Randle of the Republican National Committee cabled Larz that he would "receive the nomination for vice president of the United States" if he agreed to put forward his name at the Republican convention in Chicago three days later. Larz turned down the offer. A. E. Randle to Larz Anderson, cable, Anderson Collection, Society of the Cincinnati.

70   "Déplacements," *Le Matin* (Paris), 12 March 1899, 2.

71   E. Anderson, *Letters of Mrs. Nicholas Longworth Anderson*, 297.

72   L. Anderson, *Hop, Skip and Jump—Second Part*, 87f.

73   "Social and Personal," *Washington Post*, 31 March 1899, 7.

Chapter 5

1   Downing, *Theory and Practice of Landscape Gardening*, 56.

2   Alden, *George Hamilton Perkins*, 282; Anderson, *Black Horse Flag*, 162.

3   Lewis, *American Country Houses*, 90.

4   Harriet Owen, *Stenographic Record VII*, 875.

5   Hopkins, "Farm Barns," 247.

6   Feree, *American Estates and Gardens*, 43–53.

7   Roger Amory, *Stenographic Record V*, 619–22.

8   "Grand Weld Estate," *Boston Sunday Herald*, 7 May 1899, 1.

9   "Social and Personal," *Washington Post*, 16 May 1899, 7.

10   L. Anderson, *Letters and Journals of a Diplomat*, 171.

11   Kenworthy, "Bringing the World to Brookline," 226.

12   Platt, *Italian Gardens*, 6–7.

13   I am grateful to John Amodeo of Boston for this insight into the artistic importance of the Anderson estate's *tapis vert*.

14   Maxwell, "Flowers from Frost to Frost"; Miller, "Full of Flowers."

15   VanDyk MacBride Color Home Movies, 1937–1938.

16   L. Anderson, *Letters and Journals of a Diplomat*, 546–47.

17   Isabel Brintnall, interview by the author, 25 September 2011.

18   Anderson, "A Japanese Garden in America," 90–91.

19   The *gorinto*'s inscriptions were transcribed and translated for the author by three scholars in Tokyo: Masahiko Kitaya, Hiroko Kitaya, and Aiko Kitaya.

20   Anderson, *Presidents and Pies*, 64.

21   "Weld Garden Scrapbook," Anderson Collection, Larz Anderson Auto Museum.

22   Platt, *Italian Gardens*, 54.

23   Details of the 1899–1900 renovations come from Little & Browne Account Books 1899–1932, "Larz Anderson, Weld Estate at Brookline, Alterations to House 1899–1900," p. 1–L.A, Vertical Files, Society of the Cincinnati Library.

24   L. Anderson, *Letters and Journals of a Diplomat*, 173–74.

25   E. Anderson, *Letters of Mrs. Nicholas Longworth Anderson*, 349.

26   Proctor, *Arbitration Proceedings*, 55.

27   Roof repairs were made in 1923, 1924, 1925–1926, 1928, and 1932. There are no records for roof repairs after 1932. Little & Browne Account Books, Vertical Files, Society of the Cincinnati Library.

28   "[Hindu] Heathenism—which is so like the Church of Rome." L. Anderson, *Our Wedding Journey*, 19.

29   Gus Anderson, *Stenographic Record I–II*, 43. In 1913, Larz commissioned another monument to his father, the Anderson Memorial Bridge (Edmund Wheelwright, architect). It connected Harvard's Cambridge campus to its stadium in Boston.

30   First Naval District, "Report on Condition and Estimate of Costs"; Proctor, *Arbitration Proceedings*, 55.

31   Details on the mansion's architecture, design, and furnishings come from Olmsted Associates, drawings for Project No. 1314, Anderson Estate Land Use Study, Frederick Law Olmsted National Historic Site Archives; Ide, *Larz Anderson Park*; and from unpublished photographs in the Anderson Collection, Larz Anderson Auto Museum.

32   Proctor, *Arbitration Proceedings*, 56.

33   Gus Anderson, *Stenographic Record I–II*, 54.

34   Ibid., 59.

35   The Little and Browne account books show the firm did $247,000 worth of
     work in Brookline between 1899 and 1917. The Italian garden, not included in
     that figure, adds an estimated $100,000 to the total.

Chapter 6

1   L. Anderson, *Hop, Skip and Jump — Second Part*, 52–53.

2   Ibid.

3   L. Anderson, *In This Year of Grace 1929 — Second Part*, 202–14f.

4   In 1948, Isabel donated Larz's collection of hats and canes to what is now the
     Boston Children's Museum, which still has the items in their collection.

5   Details of the mansion's interior furnishings come from "Appraisal of
     Personal Property Belonging to the Estate of Isabel Anderson," box 1, file 6,
     exhibit M–40, Isabel Anderson Papers, Library of Congress; Gus Anderson,
     Stenographic Record I–II, 38–88.

6   L. Anderson, *Roxana Rediviva*, 3–4.

7   L. Anderson, *Some Inside Ways*, 3f.

8   L. Anderson, *Letters and Journals of a Diplomat*, 619–20.

9   L. Anderson, *Journals, 1933–1936*, 44–45.

10   L. Anderson, *Hop, Skip and Jump — Second Part*, 45. The "salon by the entrance
     door" is a reference to the large vestibule adjacent to the Chinese ballroom.

11   L. Anderson, *Hop, Skip and Jump — Second Part*, 45.

12   "Rules and Meetings of the '95 Sewing Circle (1919–1920)," Anderson
     Collection, Larz Anderson Auto Museum. The circle's archives are housed at
     the Massachusetts Historical Society.

13   Anderson, "I Interview Myself," 14.

14   Details of the event come from "American Academy of Rome Program,"
     Anderson Collection, Larz Anderson Auto Museum.

15   Hatch, *The Lodges of Massachusetts*, 181–82.

16   "Audience of 2000 at Brilliant Persian Pageant in Brookline," *Boston Globe*, 28
     May 1913, 13.

17   Anderson, *Presidents and Pies*, 133.

18   Tharp, *Mrs. Jack*, 297.

19   "Employes [sic] to Be Her Guests," *Washington Post*, 17 December 1910, 1.

20   "Christmas Tree at Weld," *Boston Globe*, 25 December 1913, 2.

21   Anderson Financial Records and Income Tax Returns 1928–1948, box 1,
     folder 7, exhibit M–46, Isabel Anderson Papers, Library of Congress.

22   Lewis, "Rejuvenating and Reshaping the Larz Anderson Chabo-hibas"; Del
     Tredici, "From Temple to Terrace"; Wyman, "The Larz Anderson Collection
     of Japanese Dwarf Trees"; Portrait Gallery, "Portrait Gallery of the Larz
     Anderson Collection: 1913–2005."

23   L. Anderson, *In This Year of Grace 1929 — First Part*, 14, 16.

24   Hopkins, "Farm Barns," 237–48.

25   L. Anderson, *Abroad in 1906*, 22f.
26   "Automobilisme," *Le Journal* (Paris), 23 April 1906, 6.
27   L. Anderson, *More Scraps*, 50f.
28   L. Anderson, *Hop, Skip and Jump—Second Part*, 77–79.
29   L. Anderson, *In This Year of Grace 1929—Second Part*, 157f.
30   L. Anderson, *Roxana Rediviva*, 20–21.
31   L. Anderson, *Hop, Skip and Jump—Second Part*, 79.
32   Anderson, *Presidents and Pies*, 127.

Chapter 7

1   Anderson, *Presidents and Pies*, 5.
2   L. Anderson, *Hop, Skip and Jump—Second Part*, 82.
3   L. Anderson, *In This Year of Grace 1929—First Part*, 2.
4   Anderson, *Presidents and Pies*, 7.
5   Mumford, *Brown Decades*, 2.
6   Seale, *Imperial Season*, 59.
7   Gutheim and Lee, *Worthy of the Nation*, 132.
8   Ibid., 141.
9   L. Anderson, *Our Wedding Journey*, 33.
10   E. Anderson, *Letters of Mrs. Nicholas Longworth Anderson*, 268.
11   Commission of Fine Arts, *Massachusetts Avenue Architecture*, 150.
12   L. Anderson, *A Year of Shreds and Patches*, 139–40f.
13   Shettleworth, "Brief Biographies of American Architects."
14   E. Anderson, *Letters of Mrs. Nicholas Longworth Anderson*, 328.
15   "Social and Personal. Official Hospitalities of the Coming Winter," *Washington Post*, 2 November 1902, 20.
16   Larz Anderson to Elizabeth Kilgour Anderson, 9 November 1901, Anderson Collection, Society of the Cincinnati.
17   Larz Anderson to Elizabeth Kilgour Anderson, 18 November 1901, Anderson Collection, Society of the Cincinnati.
18   L. Anderson, *Letters and Journals of a Diplomat*, 5.
19   *Washington Mirror*, 4 October 1902, 3, box 6, folder 1902, Alice Pike Barney Papers.
20   Square footage calculated from the drawings in "Anderson House," Historic American Buildings Survey, Library of Congress (HABS DC, WASH, 198–11).
21   L. Anderson, *In This Year of Grace 1929—Second Part*, 135f.
22   Anderson House Inventory 1937, folios 340–54, Anderson Collection, Society of the Cincinnati.
23   Anderson, "I Interview Myself," 7.
24   L. Anderson, *In the Year of the Hejiri*, 230-31.
25   "Fire in Mansion," *Boston Daily Globe*, 4 May 1901, 6; Fire Commissioner, *Report of the Fire Commissioner of Brookline*, 185.
26   Details of the Cypress Den come from the Francis Benjamin Johnston photographs of Anderson House, May 1910, vol. 2, photographs 110 and 111, Anderson Collection, Society of the Cincinnati.

27   "Steel and Granite Stable," *Washington Post*, 24 April 1903, 12; Edward Hamilton, in conversation with the author, 7 May 2015.

28   Schulz, "Stone and Steel."

29   Hall, *Social Usages at Washington*, 132–33.

30   Anderson, "I Interview Myself," 14.

31   Isabel Anderson to Samuel H. Wolcott Jr., 4 January 1942, box 1, folder 15, exhibit M–104, Isabel Anderson Papers, Library of Congress.

32   Kerényi, *Dionysos*, 90.

33   Anderson, *Presidents and Pies*, 38.

34   Dahlgren, *Etiquette of Social Life*, 15–23.

35   Anderson, *Presidents and Pies*, 3.

36   Anderson, "I Interview Myself," 14.

37   Anderson, "Home Journal, 1909," 4.

38   Anderson, *Presidents and Pies*, 45.

39   Stearn's ownership of the Virginia is documented in the New York Yacht Club's yearbooks for 1901 and 1906; "Yacht Virginia on Long Cruise," *New York Times*, 5 April 1911, 10. The Andersons' practice of chartering yachts is documented in "Bar Harbor Horse Show a Great Success," *New York Times*, 25 August 1901, 20 (Katoomba); Anderson, *Black Horse Flag*, 226 (Virginia); Anderson, *Presidents and Pies*, 46 (Virginia); L. Anderson, *Tours and Detours in 1930*, 133f (Catania); Anderson, *A Yacht in Mediterranean Seas* (Sayonara).

40   L. Anderson, *An Embassy to Japan*, 11.

41   Some of the honors depicted in the Choir Stall Room murals were added later. For example, Isabel did not get her French Croix de Guerre until 1920. L. Anderson, *In 1920*, 37–38f.

42   Wiles, "American Muralist H. Siddons Mowbray," 24.

43   Elliott, *This Was My Newport*, 243.

44   Swanberg, *First Blood*, 35–36. Swanberg also reports that President Lincoln questioned Major Anderson's loyalty to the Union (ibid., 223–24).

45   N. Anderson, *General Nicholas Longworth Anderson*, 276.

46   "Restoring the Key Room Murals at Anderson House," n.d., Society of the Cincinnati Brochure.

47   L. Anderson, *In This Year of Grace 1929—First Part*, 33.

48   Anderson, *Presidents and Pies*, 44.

Chapter 8

1   Isabel Anderson Dinner Book, vol. 1, Anderson Collection, Society of the Cincinnati.

2   Anderson, "Home Journal, 1909," 62.

3   L. Anderson, *Letters and Journals of a Diplomat*, 551–52.

4   Maryjane Kennedy, about meeting Isabel Anderson and quote about notebooks and purses, interview by the author, 24 April 2011.

5   "Society," *Washington Post*, 31 May 1917, 7; Anderson, *Presidents and Pies*, 194.

6 Larz Anderson to Charles Evans Hughes, 12 October 1923, "Anderson, Larz," box 5, RG 59 (1901–1924), National Archives and Records Administration.

7 Charles Evans Hughes to William H. Taft, 19 October 1923, "Anderson, Larz," box 5, RG 59 (1901–1924), National Archives and Records Administration.

8 "White House Social Secretary Must Know Complex Code of Etiquette to Avoid Blunders," *Washington Post*, 7 November 1915, 17.

9 E. Anderson, *Letters of Mrs. Nicholas Longworth Anderson*, 411; Anderson, *Presidents and Pies*, 172.

10 Anderson, "Home Journal, 1909," 20.

11 Benham, *Ships of the United States Navy*.

12 "Edith Helm, Social Secretary for Three U.S. Presidents," *Washington Post*, 8 August 1962, B5.

13 L. Anderson, *More Shreds and Patches*, 31f.

14 L. Anderson, *Hop, Skip and Jump—Second Part*, 84–85.

15 Anderson, "Home Journal, 1909," 9.

16 Anderson, *Presidents and Pies*, 247.

17 Anderson, "Report of the Librarian General," 70.

18 Anderson, "Home Journal, 1909," 53. Isabel received forty-five dollars for the stories "The Moon Baby" and "Merry Jerry's Strange Visit" and one hundred dollars for three other stories published in newspapers.

19 Bachelors' Club membership, L. Anderson, *Days in & out of London*, 75; Ye Sette of Odd Volumes membership certificate, Anderson Collection, Society of the Cincinnati.

20 Androite, *Metropolitan Club*, 69.

21 L. Anderson, *Journals, 1933–1936*, 67.

22 L. Anderson, *Letters and Journals of a Diplomat*, 629–30.

23 "A Peek at Privilege: Inside the Alibi Club," *Washington Post*, 22 June 1992, B1.

24 "Fashions at the Capital," *Washington Post*, 18 May 1919, E9.

25 "Many in Smart Set," *Washington Post*, 29 November 1914, E6.

26 L. Anderson, *A Year of Shreds and Patches*, 137f.

27 Ibid.

28 Ibid., 135f.

29 Ibid., 139f.

30 Ibid., 140f.

31 "Heinrich Conried for a New Theater," *New York Times*, 22 April 1908, 8.

32 "The Playhouse and Its Controlling Spirits," *Washington Post*, 6 January 1911, 5.

33 Ibid.

34 "Playhouse Now Sure," *Washington Star*, 26 April 1910, 18.

35 "Site for New Home, Playhouse Club Purchases Property on N Street," *Washington Star*, 21 March 1910, 9.

[36] "Planning a Gigantic Stadium for Washington," *Washington Post*, 29 January 1911, MC5.

[37] "The Playhouse and Its Controlling Spirits," *Washington Post*, 6 January 1911, 5.

[38] "Playhouse Now Sure," *Washington Star*, 26 April 1910, 18.

[39] "Society in Drama," *Washington Post*, 10 February 1911, 1.

[40] "Quits the Playhouse," *Washington Post*, 6 March 1912, 2.

[41] "Hemmick Divorces Former Mrs. Barney," *New York Times*, 29 August 1920, 6.

[42] "Playhouse Now Dark," *Washington Post*, 8 June 1914, 4.

[43] "Playhouse Stage Goes," *Washington Post*, 19 September 1915, 19.

[44] Anderson Balance Sheets, 1928–1947, box 1, folder 8, exhibit M–46, Isabel Anderson Papers, Library of Congress.

[45] L. Anderson, *Tours and Detours*, 1.

Chapter 9

[1] Buxton, *History, Boscawen-Webster*, 139.

[2] Evelyn Hastings, *Stenographic Record I–II*, 104–5.

[3] Alden, *George Hamilton Perkins*, 277, 280–81.

[4] Ibid., 256–57.

[5] Buxton, *History, Boscawen-Webster*, 141–42.

[6] Ibid.

[7] Ibid., 139.

[8] Maude Howe Elliott to Isabel Anderson, Rome, 3 November 1899, box 1, item 153, George Hamilton Perkins Papers, Library of Congress; Isabella Walker Weld to Isabel Anderson, 29 March [1900], box 1, item 89, George Hamilton Perkins Papers.

[9] Mark Phillips, interview by the author, 15 August 2011.

[10] George Hamilton Perkins Will, 31 March 1897, box 2, file 10, exhibit NH–51, Isabel Anderson Papers, Library of Congress.

[11] George Hamilton Perkins Codicil, 7 November 1897, box 2, file 10, exhibit NH–51, Isabel Anderson Papers, Library of Congress.

[12] L. Anderson, *Our Wedding Journey*, 33.

[13] Morris et al., *Arbitration Proceedings*, 11.

[14] Buxton, *History, Boscawen-Webster*, 143; Morris et al., *Arbitration Proceedings*, 12.

[15] L. Anderson, *Letters and Journals of a Diplomat*, 458.

[16] Ibid., 172.

[17] Ibid., 457.

[18] Evelyn Hastings, *Stenographic Record IX*, 1265–66.

[19] Ibid.

[20] L. Anderson, *Letters and Journals of a Diplomat*, 458.

[21] Evelyn Hastings, *Stenographic Record I–II*, 139.

[22] Evelyn Hastings, *Stenographic Record IX*, 1271–80.

[23] Anderson, *Presidents and Pies*, 115–16. Butt and his friend the artist Frank Millett died on the *Titanic*.

24 Nutting, *Biography*, 13. Though five years older than Larz, they were classmates because Nutting's formal education was delayed by poor health during his childhood.

25 Evelyn Hastings, *Stenographic Record I–II*, 128.

26 L. Anderson, *In This Year of Grace 1929—Second Part*, 142f.

27 Ibid.

28 Isabel Brintnall, interview by the author, 25 August 2011.

29 Roger Amory, *Stenographic Record V*, 465; Evelyn Hastings, *Stenographic Record I–II*, 142.

30 L. Anderson, *Letters and Journals of a Diplomat*, 548.

31 L. Anderson, *A Year of Shreds and Patches*, 169f.

32 L. Anderson, *Letters and Journals of a Diplomat*, 618.

33 Ibid.

34 Gus Anderson, *Stenographic Record VII*, 1006.

35 Stearns et al., *Genealogical and Family History*, 241.

36 Green, *Proceedings to Determine the Domicile*, 6.

Chapter 10

1 L. Anderson, *Africa Rediscovered by North Americans—First Part*, 18.

2 L. Anderson, *Journals, 1933–1936*, 41.

3 Ibid., 80.

4 Ibid., 41.

5 Ibid.

6 "Reconstruction of the Whereabouts of Larz and Isabel Anderson 1897–1937," box 2, folder 9, exhibit NH–37, Isabel Anderson Papers, Library of Congress.

7 L. Anderson, *Letters and Journals of a Diplomat*, 176.

8 Ibid., 177.

9 L. Anderson, *More Scraps*, 19f.

10 In 1948, Isabel donated a collection of Native American jewelry, pottery, and ceremonial objects to what is now the Boston Children's Museum. The artifacts, representing Plains, Navajo, Hopi, Tsia, Acoma, and Santa Clara (San Ildefonso) cultures, are still in the museum's collection.

11 L. Anderson, *Yachting on Land & on Sea*, 19f.

12 Smithsonian, *Annual Report of the Board of Regents*, 55.

13 L. Anderson, *Letters and Journals of a Diplomat*, 182.

14 L. Anderson, *Knights and Dames of the Good Adventure*, 1.

15 L. Anderson, *Letters and Journals of a Diplomat*, 183.

16 G. C. Cutler to Roger Amory, 1 May 1924, tipped into L. Anderson, *Knights and Dames of the Good Adventure*.

17 Coué, *Self Mastery*, 10.

18 L. Anderson, *Knights and Dames of the Good Adventure*, 23.

19 Ibid., 16.

20 D. G. Shanke to Larz Anderson, 21 July 1924, tipped into L. Anderson, *Knights and Dames of the Good Adventure*.

[21] L. Anderson, *In the Year of the Hejiri 1343*, 9. Isabel's mother died in 1924. Gilded Age protocol required a long period of mourning.

[22] West, *Historical Dictionary of Naval Intelligence*, 271.

[23] Details of the Sayonara come from L. Anderson, *In This Year of Grace 1929—First Part*, 32.

[24] L. Anderson, *In This Year of Grace 1929—First Part*, 33–35.

[25] Ibid., 34.

[26] Ibid., 36.

[27] L. Anderson, *Letters and Journals of a Diplomat*, 562.

[28] Anderson, *A Yacht in Mediterranean Seas*, 59.

[29] Ibid.

[30] Ibid., 86.

[31] Ibid., 136.

[32] Ibid.

[33] Ibid., 145.

[34] L. Anderson, *In This Year of Grace 1929—First Part*, 49.

[35] Anderson, *A Yacht in Mediterranean Seas*, 214.

[36] L. Anderson, *In This Year of Grace 1929—First Part*, 50.

[37] Anderson, *A Yacht in Mediterranean Seas*, 217.

[38] L. Anderson, *In This Year of Grace 1929—First Part*, 59f.

[39] Anderson, *A Yacht in Mediterranean Seas*, 325–26, 332.

[40] Ibid., 324–25.

[41] L. Anderson, *Letters and Journals of a Diplomat*, 574.

[42] Gopnik, "The Back of the World."

[43] L. Anderson, *Some Inside Ways*, 4.

[44] L. Anderson, *Afloat and Ashore*, 4–5.

[45] L. Anderson, *Why Not Ireland*, 43.

[46] L. Anderson, *Abroad in 1906*, 15–16f.

[47] L. Anderson, *Roxana Rediviva*, 72.

[48] L. Anderson, *In the Year of the Hejiri 1343*, 232.

[49] L. Anderson, *A Year of Shreds and Patches*, 206f.

[50] L. Anderson, *Letters and Journals of a Diplomat*, 7.

[51] Anderson, *Presidents and Pies*, 247.

Chapter 11

[1] "Lorillard's New Houseboat," *New York Times*, 24 March 1901, 9.

[2] "Houseboat's Popularity," *New York Times*, 4 August 1901, SM6.

[3] "Mr. and Mrs. Leiter on Houseboat through Southern Waters," *Washington Post*, 24 December 1915, 7.

[4] Beebe, *Big Spenders*, 101–6.

[5] Waugh, *Houseboat Book*, 62.

[6] "John W. Gates and Party Depart for Gulf," *St. Louis Republic*, 11 November 1903, 1.

[7] "Gates's Yacht Here," *New York Times*, 11 April 1904.

[8] "Amid the Thousand Islands," *New York Times*, 30 July 1905, SM11.

9   "J.W. Gates Dead; Ill for Months in Paris," *New York Times*, 9 August 1911, 9.

10   L. Anderson, *Some Inside Ways*, 20; "Houseboat's Long Cruise," *Sedalia (MO) Weekly Democrat*, 26 October 1905, 5.

11   L. Anderson, *Some Inside Ways*, 1–2.

12   L. Anderson, *A Drift-Log of a Cruise*, 98–101.

13   L. Anderson, *Some Inside Ways*, 1.

14   Ibid., 14.

15   L. Anderson, *A Drift-Log of a Cruise*, 49.

16   L. Anderson, *Some Inside Ways*, 13.

17   L. Anderson, *A Drift-Log of a Cruise*, 9.

18   Anderson, *Odd Corners*, 26.

19   L. Anderson, *Some Side Steps*, 16–17.

20   L. Anderson, *Some Inside Ways*, 34.

21   Anderson, *Odd Corners*, 25, 27.

22   Ibid., 40.

23   L. Anderson, *A Drift-Log of a Cruise*, 21–22.

24   Ibid., 50.

25   L. Anderson, *Some Inside Ways*, 44.

26   Ibid., 26.

27   Ibid., 54.

28   L. Anderson, *A Drift-Log of a Cruise*, 60–61.

29   L. Anderson, *Letters and Journals of a Diplomat*, 227–28.

30   L. Anderson, *Odds and Ends*, 6.

31   Daniel Chester French to Isabel Anderson, 2 March 1910, box 1, item 49, George Hamilton Perkins Papers, Library of Congress.

32   Handwritten menu card, "Menu, Dejeuner, 25.6.07," Anderson Collection, Society of the Cincinnati.

33   L. Anderson, *Roxana Rediviva*, 33–34; "Crowninshield-DuPont," *New York Times*, 30 June 1900, 7.

34   Anderson, *Presidents and Pies*, 126.

35   L. Anderson, *Roxana Rediviva*, 33–34; L. Anderson, *Letters and Journals of a Diplomat*, 252.

36   Roger Amory, *Stenographic Record V*, 637.

37   L. Anderson, *Hop, Skip and Jump—Second Part*, 52.

38   L. Anderson, *In This Year of Grace 1929—Second Part*, 135f.

Chapter 12

1   Anderson, *Presidents and Pies*, 154–55 (Turkey); "Larz Anderson for Berlin?," *New York Times*, 10 May 1911, 1. Other clippings in "Belgium, 1911–1912," box 2, Larz and Isabel Anderson Collection, Howard Gotlieb Archival Research Center. The Andersons preserved all newspaper reports, complimentary or derogatory, in carefully assembled scrapbooks. These clippings provide extraordinary insight into Larz's diplomatic service under Taft.

[2]   "For Ambassador to Italy. Larz Anderson of Brookline Mentioned for Rome," 13 February 1911, "Belgium 1911–1912," box 2, Larz and Isabel Anderson Collection, Howard Gotlieb Archival Research Center.

[3]   "Statement of Larz Anderson," Rome, 13 February 1911, "Belgium 1911–1912," box 2, Larz and Isabel Anderson Collection, Howard Gotlieb Archival Research Center.

[4]   Nicholas Longworth Anderson to Sevellon Alden Brown, 28 June 1891, "Anderson, Larz," box 3, RG 59 (1797–1901), National Archives and Records Administration.

[5]   US Senate, *Campaign Contributions*, 48. In 1913, the US Senate investigated all campaign contributions made to both parties in the 1904 and 1908 elections. Larz's 1908 contribution was used as seed money to put the RNC into operation that year.

[6]   "Tangle over Potash Brings Dr. Hill Back. Others Covet His Post," *New York Times*, 10 March 1911.

[7]   L. Anderson, *Some Experiences on a Trip around the World*, 100.

[8]   J. M. Dickinson to Isabel Anderson, 27 April 1911, "A Book of Memories, 1895–1913," box 1, Larz and Isabel Anderson Collection (1895–1948), Howard Gotlieb Archival Research Center.

[9]   E. Anderson, *Letters of Mrs. Nicholas Longworth Anderson*, 455.

[10]   Roll 423, series 6, Taft Presidential Papers.

[11]   "Eight Diplomatic Posts Are Filled," *New York Times*, 9 August 1911.

[12]   "Ex-Ambassador Hill to Live in Paris. Why He Was Recalled. Berlin Post Said to Have Been Wanted by Taft for Larz Anderson, Who Was Eventually Sent to Brussels," *New York Times*, 14 November 1911, 4.

[13]   L. Anderson, *A Mission to Belgium—Volume 1*, 1.

[14]   Ibid., 2.

[15]   There is some evidence that Larz attempted to make a large contribution in person to the Republican National Committee in 1904, at the start of Theodore Roosevelt's reelection campaign, in exchange for the promise of an ambassadorship. The donation was refused. If so, this helps explain Larz's disdain for Roosevelt. See US Senate, "Testimony of George B. Cortelyou," *Campaign Contributions*, 13.

[16]   L. Anderson, *A Mission to Belgium—Volume 1*, 2–3.

[17]   L. Anderson, *Letters and Journals of a Diplomat*, 294.

[18]   Ibid.

[19]   Ibid.

[20]   Ibid.

[21]   Ibid., 295.

[22]   L. Anderson, *A Mission to Belgium—Volume 1*, 9.

[23]   Ibid., 8.

[24]   Ibid., 13.

[25]   Ibid., 5.

[26]   Ibid.

27   Ibid., 16.
28   L. Anderson, *A Mission to Belgium—Volume 1*, 15; L. Anderson, *Letters and Journals of a Diplomat*, 295–96.
29   L. Anderson, A *Mission to Belgium—Volume 1*, 20.
30   Ibid., 18.
31   E. Anderson, *Letters of Mrs. Nicholas Longworth Anderson*, 456, 459, 460.
32   L. Anderson, *A Mission to Belgium—Volume 1*, 45, 87, 94, 99, 103, 106.
33   E. Anderson, *Letters of Mrs. Nicholas Longworth Anderson*, 461.
34   L. Anderson, *A Mission to Belgium—Volume 1*, 28.
35   Ibid., 29–30.
36   Ibid., 37.
37   Ibid., 40.
38   Ibid., 41.
39   Ibid., 44.
40   Ibid., 45.
41   Anderson, *Zigzagging*, 24–25.
42   L. Anderson, *Letters and Journals of a Diplomat*, 298n.
43   Ibid., 299.
44   Ibid.
45   Ibid., 300.
46   Statutes at Large, Fortieth Congress, Session I, Res. 15, approved 27 March 1867, 23.
47   L. Anderson, *A Mission to Belgium—Volume 1*, 216–17.
48   Ibid., 84. Isabel removed Larz's complaints of homesickness from *Letters and Journals of a Diplomat*.
49   L. Anderson, *A Mission to Belgium—Volume 1*, 61–62.
50   Ibid., 76.
51   "Anderson, Larz," box 5, RG 59 (1901–1924), National Archives and Records Administration.
52   L. Anderson, *A Mission to Belgium—Volume 1*, 90.
53   The boudoir and bathroom that Larz installed for Isabel survive intact.
54   L. Anderson, *A Mission to Belgium—Volume 1*, 90. Boulanger does not appear in directories of French architects active in Europe during this era.
55   Newspaper clipping, *Boston Sunday Post*, 18 February 1912, "Belgium and Some Matters on Japan 1911–1912," box 3, Larz and Isabel Anderson Collection, Howard Gotlieb Archival Research Center.
56   L. Anderson, *A Mission to Belgium—Volume 1*, 94.
57   Ibid., 175.
58   Ibid., 102.
59   Ibid., 110.
60   Ibid.
61   Ibid., 107.
62   Ibid., 111.
63   L. Anderson, *Letters and Journals of a Diplomat*, 308–9.
64   L. Anderson, *A Mission to Belgium—Volume 1*, 142.

65 Ibid., 121.

66 Ibid., 136.

67 L. Anderson, *A Mission to Belgium—Volume 2*, 269.

68 L. Anderson, *A Mission to Belgium—Volume 1*, 125.

69 Ibid., 139.

70 Ibid., 163.

71 Letterbooks, US Legation at Brussels, vol. 061, RG 84, National Archives and Records Administration.

72 L. Anderson, *A Mission to Belgium—Volume 1*, 141.

73 Ibid., 190.

74 Ibid., 172.

75 Anderson, *The Spell of Belgium*, 55.

76 Club notice tipped into L. Anderson, *A Mission to Belgium—Volume 1*.

77 L. Anderson, *A Mission to Belgium—Volume 1*, 190.

78 Ibid., 195.

79 Ibid., 238.

80 L. Anderson, *A Mission to Belgium—Volume 2*, 267.

81 Anderson, *The Spell of Belgium*, 56.

82 Newspaper clippings, "Belgium 1911–1912," box 2, Larz and Isabel Anderson Collection, Howard Gotlieb Archival Research Center.

83 L. Anderson, *A Mission to Belgium—Volume 1*, 233.

84 Ibid., 232.

85 Ibid.

86 Undated French newspaper clipping, "Belgium 1911–1912," box 2, Larz and Isabel Anderson Collection, Howard Gotlieb Archival Research Center. [Translated by the author.]

87 L. Anderson, *Letters and Journals of a Diplomat*, 320.

88 L. Anderson, *A Mission to Belgium—Volume 1*, 239.

89 L. Anderson, *Letters and Journals of a Diplomat*, 325.

90 L. Anderson, *A Mission to Belgium—Volume 2*, 302, 309.

91 Ibid., 347.

92 L. Anderson, *A Mission to Belgium—Volume 1*, 243.

93 Ibid.

94 L. Anderson, *A Mission to Belgium—Volume 1*, 248; L. Anderson, *A Mission to Belgium—Volume 2*, 283, 326, 328.

95 L. Anderson, *A Mission to Belgium—Volume 2*, 331–32.

96 Ibid., 364–65.

97 Ibid., 377.

98 Ibid., 370. *La commedia è finite*, a famous line from Leoncavallo's opera *Pagliacci*, translates as "The farce is over."

99 L. Anderson, *A Mission to Belgium—Volume 2*, 420.

100 Undated French newspaper clipping, "Belgium 1911–1912," box 2, Larz and Isabel Anderson Collection, Howard Gotlieb Archival Research Center. [Translated by the author.]

101 L. Anderson, *A Mission to Belgium — Volume 2*, 355.
102 Ibid., 421.
103 Ibid., 423.
104 Ibid., 478.
105 Ibid., 452.
106 Ibid., 455–56.
107 Ibid., 461.
108 Roll 461, series 6, Taft Presidential Papers.
109 Ibid.
110 L. Anderson, *A Mission to Belgium — Volume 2*, 330–31.
111 "Says Campaign Fund Cost Hill His Post. American Politician Now in Berlin Tells a Story of the Ambassador's Resignation. Larz Anderson's Reward. $25,000 Contribution Resulted, It Is Asserted, in Appointment to Brussels, with Promise of Embassy," *New York Times*, 3 August 1912, 1.
112 L. Anderson, *A Mission to Belgium — Volume 2*, 518.
113 Ibid., 524.
114 Anderson, *Presidents and Pies*, 161.
115 E. Anderson, *Letters of Mrs. Nicholas Longworth Anderson*, 500; Anderson, *Presidents and Pies*, 161–64.

Chapter 13

1   E. Anderson, *Letters of Mrs. Nicholas Longworth Anderson*, 501.
2   "Anderson, Larz," box 5, RG 59 (1901–1924), National Archives and Records Administration.
3   L. Anderson, *An Embassy to Japan*, 10–12.
4   Ibid., 38.
5   Ibid., 27.
6   Ibid., 40.
7   Ibid., 39.
8   Ibid., 42.
9   "Japan's Absorption of Korea," *Washington Post*, 23 August 1911, 6.
10   L. Anderson, *An Embassy to Japan*, 57.
11   Ibid., 61. Larz's effusive praise for Japan was heavily redacted in L. Anderson, *Letters and Journals of a Diplomat*, 362.
12   "The Arrival of the New American Ambassador," *Kokumin Shimbun*, 26 December 1912. Quoted in English in L. Anderson, *An Embassy to Japan*, 92–94.
13   L. Anderson, *An Embassy to Japan*, 92–94.
14   Ibid., 79.
15   Ibid., 89.
16   Ibid., 109.
17   Ibid., 109–10.
18   Larz Anderson's drawing of the new livery is tipped into L. Anderson, *An Embassy to Japan*.
19   L. Anderson, *An Embassy to Japan*, 151.

[20] Ibid., 150.

[21] Ibid., 149.

[22] Ibid., 150.

[23] Ibid., 167.

[24] Ibid., 173–74.

[25] Larz Anderson to Charles D. Hills, cable, 15 February 1913, roll 461, series 6, Taft Presidential Papers.

[26] William Howard Taft to Isabel Anderson, 3 February 1913, roll 461, series 6, Taft Presidential Papers. The original letter is in the Manuscript File Collection (William Howard Taft), Howard Gotlieb Archival Research Center.

[27] L. Anderson, *An Embassy to Japan*, 200. The timing of these events was very close, and complicated by the fact that Washington is one calendar day behind Japan due to the international date line.

[28] Larz Anderson to Charles D. Hilles, cable, 3 March 1914, roll 423, series 6, Taft Presidential Papers.

[29] White House Memorandum Regarding Larz Anderson, Ambassador, Tokio, Japan, 3 March 1913, roll 423, series 6, Taft Presidential Papers.

[30] *Tokyo Nichi Nichi Shimbun*, 3 March 1913, "Belgium and Some Matters on Japan, 1911–1912," box 7, Larz and Isabel Anderson Collection, Howard Gotlieb Archival Research Center.

[31] L. Anderson, *An Embassy to Japan*, 187–88.

[32] L. Anderson, *Letters and Journals of a Diplomat*, 402.

[33] L. Anderson, *An Embassy to Japan*, 213.

[34] Ibid., 226.

[35] "Envoy Coming Home," *Washington Post*, 16 March 1913, 12.

[36] L. Anderson, *An Embassy to Japan*, 209–10.

[37] Leopold, "Review of Larz Anderson: Letters and Journals of a Diplomat," 731–32. In 1941, an even more scathing review pointed out Larz's "high regard for the stability of Italian fascism." See Mowry, "Review of Larz Anderson: Letters and Journals of a Diplomat," 116–17. Larz himself made clear his esteem for Italian fascism; see L. Anderson, *Letters and Journals of a Diplomat*, 518, and L. Anderson, *In the Year of the Hejiri 1343*, 223–24.

[38] *Larz Anderson in Diplomatic Uniform*, painting by DeWitt M. Lockman, 1914, Anderson House Collection; *Larz Anderson in Diplomatic Uniform*, bronze bust by Bruce Wilder Saville, 1916, Anderson Collection, Larz Anderson Auto Museum.

[39] See, e.g., Hill, *Impressions of the Kaiser*, and Gibson, *A Journal from Our Legation in Belgium*.

[40] L. Anderson, "Since Thirty Years," 76–80.

Chapter 14

[1] William Howard Taft to Florence M. Marshall, Chief, Bureau of Women's Service, the American Red Cross, Washington, DC, 27 August 1917, Manuscript File Collection (William Howard Taft), Howard Gotlieb Archival Research Center.

2   Schneider and Schneider, *Into the Breach*, 11.
3   Ibid.
4   Winsor School, *Overseas War Records of the Winsor School*.
5   Anderson, *Zigzagging*, 174.
6   Ibid., 179.
7   L. Anderson, *More Shreds and Patches*, 139f.
8   Anderson, *Zigzagging*, 180.
9   Ibid., 8–9.
10 Ibid., 22–23.
11 Ibid., viii.
12 Ibid., ix.
13 Ibid., xi.
14 Anderson, "I Interview Myself," 7.
15 Anderson, *Zigzagging*, vii.
16 Ibid., viii.
17 Anderson, "I Interview Myself," 6.

Chapter 15

1   Anderson, *Black Horse Flag*, v.
2   Ibid., 51.
3   Anderson, "I Interview Myself," 3.
4   In 1924, Larz inventoried the then-existing ten bound volumes of Isabel's diaries for 1897 to 1924. Only one volume, "Home Journal, 1909," is accounted for. The inventory appears in L. Anderson, *Frayed Ends in 1924*, 205.
5   Cheney, *Louisa May Alcott: Life, Letters, and Journals*, 121.
6   Stern, *Louisa May Alcott: A Biography*, 145.
7   Stern and Shealy, *Lost Stories of Louisa May Alcott*, xxii.
8   Cheney, *Louisa May Alcott: Life, Letters, and Journals*, 127.
9   Isabel Anderson, untitled and undated essay on Louisa May Alcott, ca. 1938, box 11, file 11–12, Larz and Isabel Anderson Collection, Howard Gotlieb Archival Research Center. See Appendix.
10 Elliott, *Three Generations*, 278.
11 Anderson, "I Interview Myself," 5.
12 Ibid., 6.
13 Eleanor Pomeroy, *Stenographic Record VI*, 803, 805.
14 Crosby, "Contemporary Writers and Their Work," 353.
15 I am grateful to Rev. Charles H. Harper for sharing his recollections of meeting Eleanor Pomeroy in 1966.
16 Eleanor Pomeroy, *Stenographic Record VI*, 804.
17 Program booklet, "Freedom," Boston Civic Theater, 6–7 August 1934, author's collection.
18 Isabel Anderson to Eleanor Pomeroy, 15 July 1938, *Stenographic Record VI*, 824.

19   "Gelett Burgess's Lady Mechante," *New York Times*, 18 December 1909, BR799.

20   L. Anderson, *Bit by Bit*, 57f.

21   "Holiday Books," *International Studio* 42, no. 165 (November 1910): L.

22   Knoedler, *John Elliott: Exhibition and Private Sale*; "Sea Horse Pictures," *Washington Post*, 9 March 1910, 7.

23   Gus Anderson, *Stenographic Record I–II*, 84; "Appraisal of Personal Property Belonging to the Estate of Isabel Anderson," box 1, file 6, exhibit M–40, p. 27, Isabel Anderson Papers, Library of Congress.

24   L. Anderson, *In 1920*, 105f.

25   Anderson, *Topsy Turvy*, 25–26.

26   Anderson, *The Kiss and the Queue*, 9.

27   Anderson, "I Interview Myself," 5.

28   Anderson, *The Kiss and the Queue*, 81.

29   "The New Books (Fiction)," *Saturday Review of Literature* 2, no. 1: 81.

30   Anderson, "I Interview Myself," 13.

31   "Anderson Palace as an Embassy. Germany Negotiating for the Purchase of the Washington Residence," *New York Times*, 7 March 1907.

32   E. Anderson, *Letters of Mrs. Nicholas Longworth Anderson*, 410–12.

33   Anderson, *Bibliography of the Works of Isabel Anderson*.

34   Anderson, "I Interview Myself," 2.

35   "All Boston Show at the Colonial," *Boston Post*, 12 January 1932; "Censor Liable to Ban 'Marina' Cast's Scanties," *Boston Traveler*, 12 January 1932.

36   The Larz Anderson Auto Museum in Brookline has in its collection several albums of publicity photographs and production stills from the Boston productions.

37   "Costumes O.K., Says Curley," *Boston Post*, 13 January 1932.

38   Newspaper clipping, "Dodge Defends Brief Attire of Dancers," "Marina Scrapbook," box 11, Larz and Isabel Anderson Collection, Howard Gotlieb Archival Research Center.

39   "Rehearsing 'Every Boy,'" *Washington Post*, 1 April 1921, 7.

40   "Renny the Fox Given," *New York Times*, 28 December 1933, 17.

41   Moses H. Gulesian, *Stenographic Record VII*, 913–14.

42   Harriet Owens, *Stenographic Record VII*, 885.

43   Ibid., 885–86.

44   "Sports and Enterprises," *Boston Breeze*, February 1931, 7–8, 56–57.

45   Isabel Anderson, "Tales from a Canteen, III: Her Strange Wanderings," *National Journal*, 52, no. 6 (November 1923).

46   Anderson, "I Interview Myself," 1.

47   "Under the Red Cross: A Record of Service, Observations and Impressions," *New York Tribune*, 21 December 1918, 8.

48   Anderson, "I Interview Myself," 9.

49   Anderson, *Presidents and Pies*, 142–43.

50 Isabel paid for the entire cost of typesetting and printing the first and only run of one thousand copies ($3,520). Memorandum of Agreement between Isabel Anderson and Fleming H. Revel Co., 30 September 1939, box 2, folder 2, Isabel Anderson Papers, Library of Congress.

51 L. Anderson, *Letters and Journals of a Diplomat*, 5–6.

52 Eleanor Pomeroy, *Stenographic Record VI*, 834.

53 Letter dated 14 November 1901, E. Anderson, *Letters of Mrs. Nicholas Longworth Anderson*, 327; Gus Anderson, *Stenographic Record I–II*, 75.

54 L. Anderson, *Letters and Journals of a Diplomat*, 7.

55 E. Anderson, *Letters of Mrs. Nicholas Longworth Anderson*, 1.

56 Anderson, *Whole World Over*, 19.

57 Anderson, *Near and Far*, 70; L. Anderson, *Letters and Journals of a Diplomat*, 660.

58 Gus Anderson, *Stenographic Record I–II*, 47.

Chapter 16

1 Lee was a congenial and popular doctor in Boston; see Lee, *The Happy Life of a Doctor*, and Stetson, "Memorial: Roger Irving Lee." Porges treated his overweight patients by having them drink sulfur water to induce dehydration; see Porges, "Reduction of Weight by Dehydration." Porges was something of a "physician to the stars." His portrait by the British painter John Lavery is in the collection of the UK Royal Academy of Arts.

2 "Larz Anderson, Diplomat and Traveler, Is Dead at 71," *Washington Evening Star*, 13 April 1931, A1–2; "Larz Anderson Funeral Friday," *Washington Evening Star*, 14 April 1937, A2; and "Deaths. Anderson, Larz," *Washington Evening Star*, 15 April 1937, A14.

3 "Anderson Rites Held Yesterday," *Washington Evening Star*, 17 April 1937, A4.

4 "Anderson Rites in Gift Chapel," *Washington Evening Star*, 16 April 1937, A3.

5 The correspondence was preserved in an Anderson scrapbook, "St. Mary Chapel, Washington Cathedral, 1927–1938," box 8, Larz and Isabel Anderson Collection, Howard Gotlieb Archival Research Center.

6 Anna Spalding Weld, *Stenographic Record III*, 254.

7 Proctor, *Arbitration Proceedings*, 65n.

8 The value of Larz's estate at the time of his death totaled $1.09 million, which included Anderson House and its art collections and furnishings, a real estate holding in Ohio, and other personal property. "In the Matter of the Estate of Larz Anderson, deceased. Order Admitting Will to Probate and Granting Letters Testamentary [plus attachments]." District Court of the United States, 13 May 1937. Archives of the District of Columbia, Washington, DC.

9 Roger Amory, *Stenographic Record IV*, 315.

10 Roger Amory, *Stenographic Record V*, 611.

11 Larz Anderson Centre, box 48, Daniel Marsh Papers, Boston University.

12 T. Lawrence Davis, *Stenographic Record VII*, 958.

13 Daniel Marsh to Isabel Anderson, 22 December 1941, file Am–AP, box 57, Daniel Marsh Papers, Boston University.

14 Isabel Anderson to Roger Amory, 5 August 1937, box 1, file 10, Isabel Anderson Papers, Library of Congress.

15 L. Anderson, *In This Year of Grace 1929—First Part*, 17–18.

16 Author's transcription.

17 L. Anderson, *Letters and Journals of a Diplomat*, 628.

18 Betts, "Patriotic Collector."

19 L. Anderson, *Letters and Journals of a Diplomat*, 628.

20 L. Anderson, *More Shreds and Patches*, 22f.

21 Green, *Proceedings*, 4.

22 Ibid.

23 Morris et al., *Arbitration Proceedings*, 51.

24 The NYC properties were at 21–29 and 31 West 4th, 13–15 Washington Place, 109–111 Spring, and 57 Leonard. The Boston properties were at 172–180 Federal, 140 Tremont, 138 Blackstone, 189–191 and 201–203 State, and a share in the Marshall Fields building on Summer Street.

25 Anderson Balance Sheets, 1928–1947, box 1, file 8, exhibit M–46, Isabel Anderson Papers, Library of Congress.

26 Anna Spalding Weld, *Stenographic Record III*, 255.

27 Isabel Anderson to Roger Amory, 11 July 1941, in Roger Amory, *Stenographic Record IV*, 467.

28 Roger Amory to Warren Motley, 17 October 1938, box 1, file 10, exhibit M–67, Isabel Anderson Papers, Library of Congress.

29 Anderson financial records include Roger Amory, *Stenographic Record IV*, 316–21; "Roxana Corporation 1948," box 1, folder 5, exhibit M–36, Isabel Anderson Papers, Library of Congress; "Roxana Corporation 1947," box 1, folder 6, exhibit M–37, Isabel Anderson Papers; and Anderson Balance Sheets, 1928–1947, box 1, folder 8, exhibit M–46, Isabel Anderson Papers.

30 Roger Amory, *Stenographic Record V*, 604.

31 N. Anderson, *General Nicholas Longworth Anderson*, 273.

32 Roger Amory to William P. Long, 18 October 1938, box 1, file 11, exhibit M–68, Isabel Anderson Papers, Library of Congress.

33 Isabel Anderson to Gus Anderson, 5 March 1942, in Roger Amory, *Stenographic Record V*, 519.

34 VanDyk MacBride Color Home Movies.

35 Gus Anderson, *Stenographic Record VII*, 1013.

36 Roger Amory, *Stenographic Record V*, 635.

37 Marion Jones, telephone interview by the author, 15 December 2010.

38 Eleanor Pomeroy, *Stenographic Record IV*, 850–51.

39 Roger Amory, *Stenographic Record V*, 635.

40 "Mrs. Anderson's Club List," box 1, folder 9, exhibit M–50, Isabel Anderson Papers, Library of Congress; "Mrs. Anderson's Club List: Membership Retained

and Resignations," box 2, folder 10, exhibit NH–39, Isabel Anderson Papers; "Resignations," box 2, folder 10, exhibit NH–40, Isabel Anderson Papers.

41 Evelyn Foster Hastings, *Stenographic Record IX*, 1261.

42 Ibid., 1255–56.

43 Ibid., 1246.

44 Proctor et al., *Arbitration Proceedings*, 74–80.

45 Gus Anderson, *Stenographic Record I–II*, 78.

46 Harriet Owen, *Stenographic Record VII*, 876–79.

47 Anna Spalding Weld, *Stenographic Record III*, 278–79.

48 L. Anderson, *In This Year of Grace 1929—Second Part*, 133f; Edmund Mettetal, *Stenographic Record VII*, 921.

49 Isabel Anderson to Roger Amory, 14 July 1942, box 1, file 15, exhibit M–118, Isabel Anderson Papers, Library of Congress.

50 Isabel Anderson to Roger Amory, 29 September 1942, box 1, file 15, exhibit M–124, Isabel Anderson Papers, Library of Congress.

51 Proctor, *Arbitration Proceedings*, 84.

52 Harold R. Whitestone, *Stenographic Record VII*, 982–83.

53 Records of the MWDC's exercises on the Anderson Estate are in box 9 of the Larz and Isabel Anderson Collection, Howard Gotlieb Archival Research Center.

Chapter 17

1 Roger Amory, *Stenographic Record V*, 569–70.

2 That the letters existed is documented in L. Anderson, *Frayed Ends in 1924*, 205. Gus Anderson testified about burning the letters in his testimony at the arbitration proceedings; *Stenographic Record I–II*, 82. Details on the bonfire came to the author from Sheldon Steele.

3 Roger Amory, *Stenographic Record V*, 639–40. Isabel's version of her epitaph was "In Time of War Member of the Red Cross French and Belgian Fronts 1917–1918. In Time of Peace Author Philanthropist. Patriotic Daughter of Patriotic Father. Doctor of Letters Doctor of Laws."

4 "Mrs. Anderson Will Benefits Many Charities. Friends, Employees to Share in Estate Totaling $7 Million," *Boston Herald*, 11 November 1948.

5 The panel's files were saved because Morris's law firm partner Allen H. Gardner donated them to the Library of Congress when their firm, Morris, Pearce, Gardner & Pratt, disbanded in 1967. Morris and his wife are famous in architectural history for having saved and moved to Washington, DC, from Danvers, Massachusetts, the historic home known as The Lindens.

6 Morris et al., *Arbitration Proceedings*, 33.

7 Ibid., 27, 32.

8 Robert Lamere, who in 1948–1949 was a young attorney in the Office of the Massachusetts Attorney General, provided the author with a firsthand account of the panel's work.

9   "Reconstruction of the Whereabouts of Larz and Isabel Anderson 1897–1937," box 2, folder 9, Isabel Anderson Papers, Library of Congress; "Record of Mrs. Larz Anderson's Whereabouts, April 20, 1937 to November 3, 1948," box 1, folder 3, Isabel Anderson Papers, Library of Congress.

10   The interior photographs of the mansion in Brookline are now at the Boston Public Library in the Leslie Jones Collection.

11   "High Cost of Being Rich Staggered Mrs. Anderson, Tax Hearing Told," *Boston Herald*, 25 August 1949.

12   Morris et al., *Arbitration Proceedings*, 32.

13   "Brookline Struggles to Solve $353,600 'Gift Horse' Problem," *Boston Sunday Herald*, 18 September 1949, 1, 34.

14   Ibid.

15   "Club Acquires Old Cars," *New York Times*, 20 August 1949, 38.

16   First Naval District, "Report on Condition and Estimate of Costs."

17   "Brookline Is Still Having Arguments about the Larz Anderson Estate," *Boston Globe*, 27 September 1953, A6; Will of Isabel Anderson, as filed with the Merrimack County (NH) Probate Court, 10 November 1948.

18   Olmsted Brothers, Job No. 1314. Harry I. Martin III used the Olmsted Brothers drawings to prepare the floor plans presented in this book.

19   Moskey, *Reinterpreting Larz Anderson Park*, 4.

Epilogue

1   With the exception of a few edits for clarity and conciseness, this is the story as Larz himself told it in *A Year of Shreds and Patches*, 185–94f. Larz's misspellings have been preserved without the notation *sic*.

Appendix

1   Isabel Anderson, essay on Louisa May Alcott and Anna Minot Weld, ca. 1938, box 11, file 11–12, Larz and Isabel Anderson Collection, Howard Gotlieb Archival Research Center. This is a complete transcript of the original essay. Original pagination is preserved.

2   Cheney, *Louisa May Alcott: Life, Letters, and Journals*.

Index

Book Group Discussion Guide

The author is available, by prior arrangement, to meet with book groups via Skype. Please contact him through his website: skipmoskey.com.

1. How did you *experience this biography of a once-famous American couple*? Were you immediately drawn into the story, or did it take you a while?
2. Which people do you particularly *admire or dislike*? What were their primary characteristics?
3. Did your opinion of anyone *grow or change* as you read the book? If so, in what way?
4. Who in this book would you most *like to meet*? What would you ask or say to him or her?
5. Does the book remind you of *your own life*? An event or situation? A time of your life? A friend, family member, boss, or coworker?
6. If you were to *talk with the author*, what would you want to know?
7. If you were to *talk with Larz or Isabel Anderson*, what would you want to know?
8. Have you read *other biographies or books about this period of American history*? How is this one similar to or different from those books?
9. What *evidence* does the author give to support the book's ideas? Does he use personal assessments? Facts? Opinions? Historical documents? Quotations from authorities?
10. What kind of *language* does the author use? Is it objective and dispassionate? Or passionate and earnest? Is it humorous or sarcastic? Does the writer's style help or undercut his premise?
11. Are the book's issues *controversial*? How so? And who is aligned on which sides of the issues? Where do you fall in that line-up?
12. Can you point to *specific passages* that struck you personally as interesting, profound, silly or shallow, incomprehensible, or illuminating?
13. Did you *learn something new* reading this book? Did it broaden your perspective about Gilded Age historical events or social issues that are still relevant today?

Larz and Isabel Anderson
Wealth and Celebrity in the Gilded Age

This book was set in Cochin Old Style
a typeface that originated
with the Peignot Foundry in Paris around 1915
based on lettering designed for Louis XV
by Charles-Nicholas Cochin II (1715-1790)
it was used for Isabel Anderson's book
A Yacht in Mediterranean Seas
published in 1930 by
Marshall Jones Company
of Boston

Printed in the United States
By Bookmasters